SELLING SEA POWER

SELLING SEA POWER

PUBLIC RELATIONS AND THE U.S. NAVY, 1917–1941

RYAN D. WADLE

UNIVERSITY OF OKLAHOMA PRESS : NORMAN

Publication of this book is made possible
through the generosity of Edith Kinney Gaylord.

Library of Congress Cataloging-in-Publication Data

Names: Wadle, Ryan, 1980– author.
Title: Selling sea power : public relations and the U.S. Navy, 1917–1941 / Ryan D. Wadle.
Description: Norman : University of Oklahoma Press, [2019] | Includes bibliographical references and index.
Identifiers: LCCN 2018039776 | ISBN 978-0-8061-6280-5 (hardcover)
ISBN 978-0-80616730-5 (paper). Subjects: LCSH: United States. Navy—Public relations—History—20th century. |United States. Navy—History—20th century.
United States—History, Naval—20th century. | Armed Forces and mass media—United States. | Sea-power—United States—History—20th century.

Classification: LCC VG503 .W33 2019 | DDC 659.2/93590097309042—dc23
LC record available at https://lccn.loc.gov/2018039776

The paper in this book meets the guidelines for permanence and durability of the Committee on Production Guidelines for Book Longevity of the Council on Library Resources, Inc. ∞

Copyright © 2019 by the University of Oklahoma Press, Norman, Publishing Division of the University. Paperback published 2020. Manufactured in the U.S.A.

All rights reserved. No part of this publication may be reproduced, stored in a retrieval system, or transmitted, in any form or by any means, electronic, mechanical, photocopying, recording, or otherwise—except as permitted under Section 107 or 108 of the United States Copyright Act—without the prior written permission of the University of Oklahoma Press. To request permission to reproduce selections from this book, write to Permissions, University of Oklahoma Press, 2800 Venture Drive, Norman, OK 73069, or email rights.oupress@ou.edu

For Jenny

CONTENTS

List of Illustrations ▸ ix

Acknowledgments ▸ xi

Introduction ▸ 3

1 The Limits of Public Relations: Disarmament, Air Power, and the Life and Death of the Navy News Bureau, 1917–1922 ▸ 20

2 Publicity and Propaganda: Navy Public Relations, 1922–1927 ▸ 41

3 A Sustained Publicity: Navy Public Relations, 1928–1932 ▸ 74

4 Compatible with Military Secrecy: Navy Public Relations, 1933–1939 ▸ 105

5 "The Finest Qualities of American Manhood": Masculinity and Manpower, 1919–1939 ▸ 135

6 Replacing the Familiar with the New: Public Perceptions of Naval Transformation, 1919–1939 ▸ 160

7 "The First Line of Defense": Public Definitions of the Interwar Navy's Mission ▸ 188

Conclusion: Evaluating the Effectiveness of Navy Public Relations on the Eve of War ▸ 214

Notes ▸ 231

Bibliography ▸ 269

Index ▸ 281

ILLUSTRATIONS

Secretary of the Navy Josephus Daniels ▶ 15
Capt. Dudley W. Knox ▶ 46
Rear Adm. William A. Moffett ▶ 63
USS *Shenandoah*, flying over New York City ▶ 66
At North Island during the filming of *Hell Divers* ▶ 92
The filming of *Hell Divers* ▶ 92
Cdr. Leland P. Lovette ▶ 131
"Navy Ships Visit Many Lands," 1921 ▶ 141
"The Navy Sees the Far East," 1920 ▶ 142
"Fellowship of the Sea," 1924 ▶ 145
Paul Cadmus, *The Fleet's In*, 1934 ▶ 154
"On the Sand at Waikiki," 1935 ▶ 156
Still frame from film trailer intended for the recruitment of African Americans, 1936 ▶ 157
"Service Afloat," 1939 ▶ 158
Honda Point disaster, 1923 ▶ 161
"Naval Vessels Sunk by Aerial Bombs," ca. 1921 ▶ 165
USS *S-4* in dry dock at Boston Navy Yard after salvage ▶ 176
USS *Saratoga* during fleet review in New York City ▶ 182
Navy Day, 1925 ▶ 193

"Navy Adopts 'Blue Eagle,'" 1933 ▶ 205

"Always Alert," 1933 ▶ 207

Acting Secretary of the Navy Charles Edison holding a press conference ▶ 220

"Enlist in the United States Navy," 1940 ▶ 221

"The United States Navy has a job to do for America," 1940 ▶ 222

ACKNOWLEDGMENTS

This book began as my doctoral dissertation at Texas A&M University in College Station. First of all, then, I want to thank my adviser, James C. Bradford, for investing much time and patience into this project. He guided me through the process, made me a better scholar along the way, and continues to offer sage advice. Brian Linn, John Lenihan, Terrence Hoagwood, and Ralph Adams also made many valuable intellectual and editorial contributions. They all have my gratitude.

I received ample support to complete the research for this project, first and foremost from the John D. Hayes Predoctoral Fellowship in Naval History I received from the Naval History and Heritage Command. Through that fellowship, I met two excellent mentors, John Sherwood and Sarandis "Randy" Papadopoulos, who have both given me friendly counsel in the years since. At Texas A&M, the Melbern G. Glasscock Center for Humanities Research, led by James Rosenheim, also provided invaluable support for this project at a critical juncture. I would also like to thank the Naval War College Foundation, particularly John Hattendorf, for awarding me the Edward S. Miller Research Fellowship to conduct additional research in the college's archives, where Evelyn Cherpak provided her exceptional service.

Elsewhere, I visited a number of archives with helpful staffs who provided much useful assistance in locating heretofore unknown materials. I thank the staffs of the Houghton Library at Harvard University, the Warner Brothers Archive at the University of Southern California, the Bancroft Library at the University of

California–Berkeley, and the Library of Congress for their research assistance. I especially want to recognize Charles Johnson and Nate Patch at the National Archives, Barbara Hall at the Margaret Herrick Library, David Chapman at Texas A&M's Cushing Library, and Mark Quigley at the UCLA Film and Television Archive for their exceptional service at their respective institutions. Also, a note of thanks to Emily Hoeflinger and especially Larry Burke for the invaluable accommodations that allowed me to conduct significant portions of my original research.

After graduation, I spent a year and a half at the U.S. Army's Combat Studies Institute as part of the Afghanistan Study Team. Under the tutelage of Col. Roderick Cox, USA (Ret.), and Don Wright, my colleagues Anthony Carlson, Michael Doidge, Scott Gaitley, Kevin Hymel, Matt Matthews, and I all quickly became experts on modern counterinsurgency operations. It took me away from naval history for a time, but it was extremely valuable in helping me to better understand the military and in giving me ample opportunities to hone my research and writing skills. It was a treasured professional experience, and I thank them all for their support.

Academic conferences were especially important in advancing this project as I worked to develop my arguments. Fellow panelists and commentators provided much beneficial feedback over the years, including Lori Bogle, John Kuehn, Charles Neimeyer, and Michael Sherry. Special thanks goes to the organizers of the Maritime Masculinities conference in Oxford in December 2016 and especially to Joanne Begiato and Mary Beth Conley for their encouragement of my research.

At the Air Command and Staff College's eSchool of Graduate Professional Military Education, Bart Kessler and Greg Teal graciously provided me with the funding and time necessary to conduct the additional research necessary to complete the project. Thanks must also go out to my colleagues who have provided encouragement over the past several years, including Karen Guttieri, Mary Hampton, Kenny Johnson, Kathleen Mahoney-Norris, Tonya Klempp, Deonna Neal, Margaret Sankey, Paul Springer, John Terino, Charles Thomas, Jacqueline Whitt, and especially to Amy Baxter for helping me to stay fit by introducing me to racquetball. Also, Rose Stoor only joined my team very late in the writing process, but her administrative acumen was absolutely essential in the waning days.

A special note of thanks must go to my colleague and "battle buddy" Heather Venable. Her arrival at ACSC in 2016 finally spurred me to complete this project that had spent too long gestating, and we spent much time editing each other's work. She provided her customary wit and tough critical eye throughout the revision process, and the final product on these pages is substantially improved because of her feedback.

Finally, completing this project took considerable time at home. Albert the Cat has been with me since the beginning of this journey, and he continued to make his nightly visits to my lap during writing and editing sessions. Most of all, my wife, Jenny Whisenhunt, has been a source of strength, and chipped in to help edit the original dissertation pages and functioned as a sounding board for ideas. Her patience has been important, but her love and understanding have been essential. She may not have written this book, but her presence is in these pages and I could not have done it without her.

I accept sole responsibility for any errors found in this text.

SELLING SEA POWER

◄ ►

INTRODUCTION

In the midst of a fraught battle for the future of naval aviation in February 1925, the chief of the U.S. Navy's Bureau of Aeronautics, Rear Adm. William Adger Moffett, made a startling confession to a friend. Moffett had become known as a tireless advocate for naval aviation and fought against the efforts of Brig. Gen. William "Billy" Mitchell to consolidate all American air assets into an independent air service. To counter Mitchell's increasingly wild stunts and rhetoric, Moffett—himself no neophyte at public relations—resorted to using his own aircraft to generate publicity for his branch. Yet, as he told his friend, "to the average Naval officer, the word 'publicity' is anathema. I was brought up to hate it myself, and I still hate it."[1] Private firms and some government agencies had embraced public relations in recent decades, seeking to inform the press and public about their activities. In spite of this growing acceptance of public relations techniques, Moffett recognized that many officers in his own service held a deep antipathy toward their use. To use an analogy drawn from the sea power theory that Moffett and his fellow officers readily understood, refusing to engage with the press and public would deny the navy any semblance of control over the sea of information accessible to the public. This could leave the navy open to attack and criticism from potential threats, and, indeed, many had materialized in the years prior to this statement. In an era of widespread mass communications, this was simply untenable.

Public relations rarely factors into the now widely accepted narrative of the interwar U.S. Navy that argues the service sought to "transform" the way it would fight future wars. In a span of twenty years, the navy worked to transition from a battleship-centric force into one that could fight on the "three planes" of war: the skies, the ocean's surface, and beneath the waves. Through experimentation, aircraft carriers took steps toward becoming independent, offensive strike weapons. Submarines built to conduct transpacific missions likewise entered service and laid the foundation for the lethal interdiction campaigns of World War II. The Marine Corps evolved from a small adjunct service into a full partner of naval warfare, tasked with seizing enemy-held islands for use as advanced naval and air bases.[2]

What is not nearly as well understood is the extremely tumultuous domestic political and cultural backdrop against which that transformation occurred. Growing dissatisfaction with high taxes and the insistence of President Woodrow Wilson and his secretary of the navy, Josephus Daniels, on a massive naval construction program led members of Congress and the American public to demand naval arms limitations by the end of 1920. This coalition insisted that further naval construction was politically, morally, and economically irresponsible. Ultimately, this pressure resulted in the naval limitation treaties signed at the Washington Naval Conference of 1921–22 and their successors. These developments denied the navy access to its traditional sources of support and funding: the president and Congress.[3]

As the arms limitation movement formed and expanded, Brigadier General Mitchell initiated his crusade to build an independent American air force. Since the navy had styled itself as the "nation's first line of defense" and received significant appropriations to execute its responsibilities, Mitchell increasingly framed the navy as obsolete in the face of modern air power. Much of his campaign was waged in the press, but he received a grand forum to test his propositions in the summer of 1921. In a series of highly publicized bombing tests off the Virginia Capes, army and navy aircraft sank several former German warships capped by Mitchell himself leading a flight of aircraft that sank the battleship *Ostfriesland*. Even if this act proved mostly symbolic because the battleship was stationary and of an older design, it helped establish air power as a political threat to the fleet by threatening to cut into naval appropriations.[4]

This technological challenge to naval supremacy combined with arms limitations and postwar parsimony all threatened to stagnate the navy's budget throughout the 1920s. The onset of the Great Depression only further compounded these problems since it left many convinced that the navy was an unaffordable luxury for the nation. These fiscal issues complicated the navy's gradual transition from a surface fleet centered on the battleship to a balanced fleet that incorporated aircraft carriers and submarines. The cost of developing new weapons systems, particularly aircraft and submarines, threatened to overwhelm the navy's increasingly limited budgets.

How Americans learned about and understood these issues changed dramatically throughout the interwar period as the methods by which they consumed news and entertainment underwent a dramatic shift. The various forms of print media, including newspapers, periodicals, and literature, continued to thrive, and they were joined by the rapidly growing film and radio industries during the 1920s. Movies had ceased being a mere novelty and had become a serious business by the 1910s, and the industry grew at such a pace throughout the 1920s that ninety million people were attending films weekly by 1929. Broadcast radio only started in 1921 with the first commercial radio stations, but more than a third of Americans owned radios by the end of the decade with even more dramatic increases in the years that followed.

This expansion of the sources for information and entertainment required a significant adaptation for the navy because the service traditionally eschewed direct involvement in public relations. The navy, at least officially, embodied a "silent service" culture that disdained releasing information to the public regardless of whether the news would attract adulation or condemnation. Officers who sought publicity represented outliers rather than the norm of the officer corps, and even those like Moffett only did so with great reluctance.

To counter the threats posed by arms limitations, by Mitchell, and by others, the navy built its own publicity apparatus within the Office of Naval Intelligence (ONI). A previous public relations office, the Navy News Bureau, had been established in 1917 but disbanded in September 1921 due to lack of funds. Months later, in February 1922, Secretary of the Navy Edwin Denby established the Information Section of the ONI. Tasked with collecting naval information and disseminating that information to the press, this new office of three officers, a civilian aide, and a marine orderly constituted the core of navy public relations. Upon this small cadre fell the immense task of repairing the navy's wounded public image at a critical juncture. This office did not have the resources to completely change the navy's institutional aversion to publicity, but its staff would be forced to overcome those cultural limitations and develop ties with the mass media.

Several studies have examined the development of navy public relations, including a master's thesis and dissertation that originated with a 1960s-era graduate program at the University of Wisconsin, where public relations historian Scott M. Cutlip taught public affairs (public relations in military parlance since World War II) officers the history of their craft. Two of these studies, F. Donald Scovel's "Helm's a Lee" (1968) and R. Dale Klinkerman's "From Blackout at Pearl Harbor to Spotlight on Tokyo Bay" (1972), examine some of the navy's interwar public relations efforts. Both projects benefited greatly from personal interviews of key individuals who worked within the navy's public relations offices that provided information not found in documentary sources. Yet both argue that the navy took a conservative approach to public relations, at least in part because they focus almost exclusively on the activities of the Information Section/Public Relations Branch and also do little to examine how the public saw the service. Other studies, including Frederick Harrod's *Manning the New Navy* (1978), William F. Trimble's *Admiral William A. Moffett* (1994), and Lawrence Suid's *Sailing on the Silver Screen* (1996), tackle aspects or key individuals of navy public relations underserved by Cutlip and Klinkerman, but none of these addresses the entirety of the topic.[5]

Finally, Peter Karsten's *The Naval Aristocracy* (1972) examines a critical issue—organizational culture—largely ignored in other studies. He argues that by the 1880s the naval officer corps had consciously embraced publicity as a means of expanding the fleet.[6] Certainly, figures like Alfred Thayer Mahan, Stephen Luce, and others helped evangelize sea power to the American public, but this was an undirected public relations campaign aimed at elite Americans coming from officers in what many viewed as a profoundly conservative organizational culture. They broke free of their cultural confines, but this was not part of a professional public relations office.

The subjects left unexamined by these previous studies raise several critical questions. First, and most critically, how did the navy and the Information Section respond to the myriad public threats to the service's organizational prestige? Second, how did naval officers adapt to the rise of new media outlets? Third, what themes dominated the publicity disseminated by the Information Section? Lastly, did the navy devise successful public relations strategies and techniques?

Answering these questions would reveal much about a hitherto hidden side of the navy, but tracing these early public relations activities is difficult. The personnel of the Information Section received and acted on directives from their superiors in the ONI and the Office of the Chief of Naval Operations (OpNav). Owing to its small size, the office generated limited amounts of intraoffice paperwork, meaning that much of the record for how the section interpreted and executed policy comes from the products it disseminated. These include press releases, speeches, transcripts of radio broadcasts, and Hollywood films that received the navy's cooperation. In fact, Hollywood film productions constitute one of the best sources for understanding navy public relations because these movies were an industrial form of cultural expression. The factory-like nature of the Hollywood studio system combined with the need for dozens, if not hundreds, of cast and crew to produce a film meant that the process was rigorously documented. The amount of paperwork then multiplied when a studio sought the navy's assistance on a project. In a sense, it is ironic that the most fluid visual form of publicity left the longest paper trail.

These disparate sources paint a complex picture of navy public relations between the world wars. First, it lacked an identifiable pool of personnel from which to recruit into public relations billets. Second, the small size of the Information Section limited its reach, and only intermittently could its personnel officially rely on officers at the various naval districts scattered around the country to aid them. Third, it did not always have the ability to control or even coordinate its activities with other parts of the naval bureaucracy, such as Rear Admiral Moffett at the Bureau of Aeronautics and Capt. Dudley W. Knox, USN (Ret.), at the Office of Naval Records and Library. Fourth, even though the Information Section operated semiautonomously within the ONI, the boundaries between public relations work and counterintelligence activities frequently blurred. Finally, the conservatism of the officer corps and its concerns over security—the latter of which only deepened in the 1930s—often led to self-limiting public relations strategies.

In spite of these difficulties, the interwar navy gradually learned how, in the desperate words of one of the fathers of navy public relations, to "sell the Navy to the people."[7] It developed an increasingly professionalized public relations establishment in spite of the predominant "silent service" culture that dominated the officer corps and thus projected a multifaceted view of the service to the American public. In many respects, the "silent service" culture worked to the navy's benefit because, while it meant that the Information Section's own work would hew strictly to factual information and mostly avoid "human interest" stories, it created space for outsiders to "endorse" the navy. In essence, the navy masked its desire to promote itself by encouraging its allies to sponsor the service by generating their own pro-navy publicity. To do this, for example, the navy's leaders leveraged their relationships with the Navy League to establish Navy Day, which sought to overcome the physical and cultural isolation of the service from the public. Furthermore, the navy also collaborated with film producers, journalists such as Hanson Baldwin, authors, and others—many of whom had naval backgrounds—to help overcome the cultural conservatism of the officer corps. In addition, the centralized means of control and production for the new forms of media, especially motion pictures, inadvertently compensated for the lack of naval personnel assigned to public relations duty. The Information Section and its supporters did not overcome or change the culture of the officer corps, but they did successfully maneuver around it and insert the navy into civilian culture. In doing so, publicity overwhelmingly emphasized three themes: the benefits of naval service for young men, the ability of the navy to safely incorporate new technologies into the force structure, and the navy's value to the nation's security and economic well-being.

Before proceeding further, a few terms require clear definitions. Publicity is the content or notice generated to attract attention to a specific product or organization, whereas public relations is the overall strategy of communicating to the media and the public.[8] Even though Congress had "banned" government agencies from conducting publicity under the 1913 Gillett Amendment, the navy during the interwar period used the term public relations to describe its activities.[9] Only after World War II did the navy and the other services begin to use the term public affairs to describe their public relations activities, but there is no substantive difference between the two terms. In more recent years, the Defense Department has also used the term "strategic communications," which connotes a link between defense strategy and public information that also incorporates, according to defense expert Rosa Brooks, elements of public relations and advertising. This term has had a controversial life, yet the blend of information and marketing has applicability in the interwar era.[10]

By the interwar period, the term public relations was still relatively new. In 1906, Ivy Lee articulated both the legitimate need for public relations and its ultimate purpose in his *Declaration of Principles*: "In brief, our plan is, frankly and openly, on behalf of business concerns and public institutions, to supply to the press and public of the United States prompt and accurate information concerning subjects which it is of value and interest to the public to know about."[11] Within this manifesto, Lee also sought to differentiate public relations from advertising. The navy's Information Section, at least in its early years, focused its efforts on the press in a manner similar to that described by Lee. Its portfolio expanded, however, as its officers found themselves supporting the advertising campaigns that constituted the navy's recruiting efforts, working with motion picture studios to shape the navy's image in commercial films, and even occasionally overlapping with counterintelligence work. In effect, circumstances and the needs of the service forced the Information Section to move beyond the traditional bounds of public relations work.

The process through which the Information Section assumed these responsibilities occurred organically as the navy developed nearly all of its public relations capability from scratch. Learning how to do so was no easy feat because, prior to World War I, the navy as a corporate body had only intermittently paid official attention to using public relations to its benefit. During the Civil War, the Union Navy struggled to create an effective working relationship with the press. Gideon Welles, who had worked in newspapers prior to his appointment as secretary of the navy, often released information to the press faster than his counterparts in the War Department, but his timeliness was balanced by frequent self-censorship of information. Unlike the Union Army, the navy had no comparable class of "political generals" whose background and connections could help generate positive publicity.[12] This stemmed from a long-running cultural problem because the navy was only well known in major port cities, and much of the small peacetime fleet spent time on squadron duty overseeing American interests around the globe. The antebellum navy saw little need to directly engage with the American public, and the rapid onset of the war left little need to develop any official publicity apparatus.[13]

The rise of the "new navy" and the accompanying navalist movement by the 1880s has been well chronicled by Peter Karsten, Mark Russell Shulman, and other historians and will not be recounted in full here, but public relations constituted a significant component of this era of expansion and reform. To be clear, this publicity often originated with the navy's officer corps, but it had no official sanction behind it. Historians and budding navalists such as Theodore Roosevelt sought to redefine the history of the U.S. Navy to criticize the *guerre de course* strategy of commerce raiding and protection that had long defined American naval strategy. Rear Adm. Stephen Luce and Capt. Alfred Thayer Mahan became evangelists for sea power, using magazines such as *North American Review*. Mahan, in particular, produced a series of books that started with his epochal *The Influence of Sea Power upon History, 1660–1783*, published in 1890.[14] As one Mahan scholar noted, his "primary concern was the indoctrination of his fellow countrymen."[15]

In the 1890s, navalism evolved from a niche issue into a social and cultural phenomenon linked to America's increasingly outward-looking worldview. For instance, separate groups of naval veterans based in Boston and New York combined their respective organizations in 1893 as the Naval Order of the United States dedicated to the preservation of naval history. Meanwhile, the so-called "yellow" journalism of Joseph Pulitzer's *New York World* and William Randolph Hearst's *New York Journal* used the newspaper page to point out the shortcomings of the U.S. Navy relative to the European powers and to press for more construction. These papers also helped draw Americans' attention to the rebellion in Spanish Cuba that eventually led to the Spanish-American War. The navy's role in securing victory in the Philippines and Cuba only led to further acclaim and support for expansion.

Changing the public perception of the value of sea power was vital, but the navy still relied on what historian Vincent Davis calls *direct action*, or direct lobbying to members of Congress.[16] Through this lobbying in the 1880s and into the 1890s, a bipartisan consensus emerged supporting naval expansion. Every president and

Congress supported naval expansion to some degree, and debate increasingly focused on the size of the new building program rather than whether there should be one at all. The Panic of 1893 barely slowed the pace of expansion, but naval construction temporarily halted during the first two years of William McKinley's presidency. During the brief conflict with Spain, however, Congress authorized eight battleships, six armored cruisers, and a host of smaller vessels.[17]

The success of this lobbying may have led some officers to underestimate the value of publicity, but the navy's relationship with the public only continued to deepen in the decade and a half after the war. Theodore Roosevelt's wartime exploits had increased the political stock of the former assistant secretary of the navy, allowing him to secure the nomination for vice president in 1900 and, following the assassination of McKinley, the presidency in 1901. With one of the most prominent navalists in the White House, the navy's political and cultural cachet continued to rise. Roosevelt supported further naval construction and used the fleet as a tool to expand American control over the Western Hemisphere. Although he briefly advocated a moratorium on battleship construction in his second term and called for a disarmament conference at The Hague, the commissioning of HMS *Dreadnought* in 1906 and the renewal of the naval arms race recommitted him to construction. The cruise of the Great White Fleet from 1907 to 1909 served as a capstone to Roosevelt's publicity of the fleet and his use of it as a tool of diplomacy. What began as a public demonstration of the navy's commitment to defending the Pacific Coast instead attempted to signal America's naval strength to the other established and rising global powers.[18]

During the Roosevelt years, advocates of naval expansion sought to generate even more public goodwill for their cause. Many members of groups such as the Naval Order, which drew some of its members from the active-duty officer corps, felt uncomfortable with expanding their activities into direct public lobbying on the service's behalf. This reluctance materialized in spite of fears that the tradition of postwar American military and naval retrenchment would sacrifice many of the gains in naval strength that had made victory possible. Models for organizations devoted to naval lobbying, known as Navy Leagues, existed in both Great Britain and Germany by the turn of the century, each possessing more than a quarter of a million members. Although the events surrounding the formation of the two foreign navy leagues differed, both organizations intended to raise public awareness of the importance of a strong navy in maintaining the national interest.[19]

The Navy League of the United States, formed in December 1902, included a number of members of the Naval Order in its articles of incorporation. The league limited its membership to civilians and retired officers to avoid any appearance of being a mere mouthpiece for the navy existing outside the normal chain of command, although members of Congress and active-duty officers could become nonvoting members. Despite quickly receiving public support from President Roosevelt, the league had little appreciable effect on public opinion for several years after its inception. Too few members and a minuscule operating budget devoted almost entirely to the publication of the *Navy League Journal* hampered the league's ability to promote the navy, and the organization's exact goals appeared muddled to both Congress and the public.[20]

Even as Roosevelt and the Navy League focused their attention on issues of expanding naval appropriations and increasing construction, the growth of the fleet drove far-reaching changes to the navy's recruiting practices. Although the growth of the fleet greatly benefited officers whose careers stagnated prior to the mid-1880s, finding enough high-quality men to operate the new ships proved a mammoth challenge. The authorized strength of enlisted personnel more than quadrupled from 10,000 in 1897 to 44,500 in 1909. As a result, the navy stepped up its recruiting efforts from inland states, expanded its infrastructure of recruiting stations and manpower, and adopted more modern methods of recruiting.

Recruiting inland, where the navy was a relatively unknown institution, required new ways of reaching the public. To accomplish this, the Recruiting Service expanded its physical reach while adapting to changes in media consumption to attract recruits. In 1903, the Recruiting Service possessed only seven permanent recruiting stations, but it doubled this number by 1907. Concurrently, it abandoned the nineteenth-century practice of relying on bounties to entice sailors and instead experimented with a number of new recruiting practices, some more successful than others. The Post Office began distributing navy pamphlets and brochures in 1902, greatly increasing the recruiters' reach. The Recruiting Service attempted to advertise in newspapers and magazines, but the high cost of ad placements limited the number used. Instead, recruiters often focused their efforts on friendly newspapers willing to print articles extolling the benefits of the service free of charge. These innovations proved so successful that roughly three-quarters of the men recruited by the navy in 1907 came from inland states, an almost complete reversal of previous recruiting trends.[21]

As the navy improved its method for disseminating recruiting publicity, the Navy League finally worked through its early growing pains and reached perhaps its peak period of influence between 1909 and 1914. By 1909, the league became much more effective in promoting the navy for several reasons. The formulation of

"Patriotic Reasons for the Navy League of the United States" gave it a clear platform that formed the basis of its activities for the next decade: promoting a strong navy, a vibrant merchant marine, an effective naval militia, and a consistent construction program that hoped to prevent the constant political wrangling in Congress that accompanied the introduction of new naval construction bills. Critically, the league adopted a nonpartisan approach in advocating new naval construction, which allowed its base of support to continue growing. Money now flowed in from numerous small donations and a membership base of more than 7,000, allowing the league to issue regular press releases to publicize specific issues of naval policy. Pamphlets, many of them produced by the league's secretary, Henry M. Ward, and the organization of speaking tours led to further expansion of the league. At times, the league drew criticism from pacifist groups that raised harsh questions about the depth of its relationship with the Navy Department, which sometimes had the effect of turning debates about naval policy into arguments over the league and its methods. In spite of these attacks, the league continued to grow, and by 1914 it had even attracted members from the usually disinterested or hostile Midwestern states. This allowed the league to assume an important position as a distributor of naval publicity.[22]

Likewise, the Recruiting Service received an unofficial boost from a new media outlet: youth-oriented literature. Magazines such as *Youth Companion* and ghost-written adventure books published by Edward Stratemeyer's eponymous Syndicate and other firms had become quite popular by the turn of the century. With its increasingly global reach and influence, the navy became a natural setting for youth books. In 1908, Lt. Cdr. Yates Stirling published the first of a series of youth novels titled *A United States Midshipman Afloat*. Authored while Stirling served at the Naval Academy, the book tells the story of a recent Annapolis graduate who becomes embroiled in a mission to prevent the overthrow of a Latin American leader. Within a few years of Stirling's publication, the first books of both Irving Hancock's *Dave Darrin* series and Frank Gee Patchin's *Battleship Boys* series appeared. Although neither of the latter authors had a connection to the service, their books met with success as new entries in both series continued to appear for the remainder of the decade. These books focused on young men with good moral compasses and patriotic vigor in positions where their character or even their manhood is challenged as they square off against rivals or confront foreign foes. These books kept abreast of current events, taking their protagonists to places where the navy operated, such as the Philippines, Latin America, and, of course, the European theater during World War I.[23]

The development of a nascent motion picture industry also created new opportunities for naval publicity. As early as the Spanish-American War, filmed reenactments of wartime battles attracted audiences throughout the country, with depictions of the Battle of Manila Bay and of Admiral Dewey making frequent appearances. In the following years, the navy began to experiment with film and use it to enhance recruiting, eventually screening a series of films produced by the Biograph Company about life in the service at the 1904 World's Fair in St. Louis, Missouri, and the following year at the Lewis and Clark Exposition in Portland, Oregon. As these early experiments continued, the production of commercial films quickly became the predominant means by which the service utilized the new medium as filmmakers attempted to broaden the settings for their films.[24]

During these early days of the medium, the navy issued only limited instructions that sought to regulate cooperation with the commercial film industry. Given the shift toward recruiting a better class of sailor, the service often eschewed formal cooperation with a medium then associated with working-class audiences in cheap nickelodeons. Furthermore, the Motion Picture Patents Company—a consortium formed by American film producers to standardize production, informally known as "The Trust"—had mired early film producers in a series of legal battles over control of film patents, which complicated attempts at cooperation. Even still, the quality of films continued to improve, causing a significant spike in film attendance from twenty-six million weekly viewers in 1908 to forty-nine million by 1914. Although the navy had worked with the producers of *The Peril* in 1912 and authorized a navy torpedo boat to sink a yacht for the film, the rapidly growing medium remained underexploited as a vehicle for pro-navy sentiments.[25]

Through this expansion of the mass media and the increasing opportunities for publicity, the navy lacked a clear public relations policy and any kind of structure to manage it. This was not for lack of trying; in 1905, Admiral Dewey proposed to both the secretary of war and the secretary of the navy that Congress allow the military to restrict the publication of potentially sensitive information such as the movement of ships during times of war or national emergency. As F. Donald Scovel argues, Dewey's proposal grasped the value of public information, but his proposal suggested more a change of policy than advocating for the establishment of a censorship office. Dewey's proposal also crucially failed to address the management of peacetime public relations, which accounts for the decision by Secretary of the Navy Charles Joseph Bonaparte to set aside the proposal until a situation arose necessitating its reconsideration.[26]

Ironically, the navy's sister service, the United States Marine Corps, entered into public relations at this time using a unique model. In 1912, the Marine Corps established the Publicity Bureau to nominally oversee its own burgeoning recruiting efforts, but, in practice, it built on long-standing efforts to remake the image of the entire corps. In many respects, the corps had combined the recruiting and public relations functions in a single office in a manner unlike either the army or the navy. Through the publication of pamphlets and recruiting posters, and the forging of closer ties with the press corps to ensure favorable coverage of the Marine Corps and its activities, the bureau sought to bring attention to the corps and clearly differentiate it from the navy. Given the fears the corps' leaders held about its own long-term ability to survive, a clear impetus to formalize its public relations activities existed.[27]

The same year the Corps established its Publicity Bureau, Secretary of the Navy George von Lengerke Meyer circulated a letter within the navy's bureaucracy asking for suggestions to improve the service's overall efficiency and effectiveness. In response, an officer attached to the General Board, Lt. Cdr. Walter S. Crosley, suggested the creation of a formal public relations bureau capable of managing the navy's public image. Crosley received a reply indicating that his plan would receive careful consideration by the Navy Department, but nothing ever came of it and the matter quietly disappeared.[28] To date, the navy had expanded its public relations activities only as a reactive measure, indicating the continued prevalence of the "silent service" culture. Still, the navy continued to grow in spite of this inhibiting culture and thus lacked a clear organizational incentive to modernize.

The appointment of Josephus Daniels as secretary of the navy in 1913 finally saw this calculus begin to change. Daniels came to his post after spending three decades in the newspaper business in North Carolina, most prominently as the owner of the *Raleigh News and Observer*, and gradually set out to better engage the mass media. One of his first actions after taking office was to define firmly the relationship between the navy and the film industry. In 1913, the navy issued its new set of *Naval Instructions* that allowed filmmakers access to naval facilities, ships, and personnel only after its producers obtained written consent from naval officials to do so. The General Board issued Order No. 78 the following year to refine the previous year's policy. The new order demanded that filmmakers submit to the navy any film produced with service cooperation prior to its public release, a requirement it would impose on filmmakers for decades to come. Newsreels enjoyed access to ships and installations so long as they did not film sensitive material. Most importantly, the new guidelines gave greater definition to the types of assistance the navy would provide filmmakers. For instance, the navy allowed the filmmakers of *Via Wireless* (1915) to shoot scenes aboard the battleship *New York*. Conversely, the

Secretary of the Navy Josephus Daniels, n.d.
Naval History and Heritage Command, Photo NH 2336, Photographic Section.

navy denied requests for cooperation on other films, such as an adaptation of the Puccini opera *Madame Butterfly* (1915), which it deemed detrimental to the service's image.[29] These early instructions and orders constituted the first attempts by the navy's leadership to shape the service's publicity.

Daniels's appointment also led to further evolution of the Recruiting Service's practices. The number of stations nationwide continued to grow, and its new methods attracted a flow of quality recruits. Daniels, however, sought to improve the lives of enlisted men and then in turn publicize those improvements to boost recruiting. These included overseas travel, educational opportunities that included the possibility of entering the Naval Academy, and physical improvement through athletics. Despite all of these changes, the navy took care not to convey overly optimistic impressions of navy life in recruiting materials. Secretary Daniels even ordered increased movements of ships just so that the service could live up to the famous slogan "Join the Navy and See the World."[30]

Surprisingly, given Daniels's background, changes to traditional public relations activities occurred more slowly. Some executive branch agencies, such as the Panama Canal Commission and the United States Forest Service during Gifford

Pinchot's tenure, had pioneered government use of public relations techniques. Congress, viewing such work as wasteful and a symbol of executive overreach, "banned" government public relations activities in 1913. This was not a hard ban by any means, and the Marine Corps Publicity Bureau continued to operate as before. Still, Daniels pressed forward slowly in this arena in the following years. He and his aides began to issue press releases in 1914, oftentimes providing notice of directives issued by the navy secretary's office. The frequency of these news releases increased dramatically in 1915. In addition to these written releases, Daniels also began holding press conferences twice a day for correspondents. In a sense, he had assumed responsibility for navy public relations without formally assigning personnel to the task or reorganizing the department.[31]

The maelstrom in Europe, however, prompted Daniels to reevaluate a number of positions that he and President Wilson had held. Both had been skeptics of naval expansion, and Daniels had included statements in support of international naval arms limitations in each of his annual reports. Pressure, however, forced Wilson and Daniels to support further naval construction. In 1914, Wilson acquiesced to Congress and endorsed the construction of two new battleships. Fears that the conflict could spread to the Western Hemisphere ignited a preparedness campaign by several private societies, including the Navy League. This forced Wilson and Daniels to support even larger appropriations to uphold American neutral rights. As a result, they both championed the monumental Naval Act of 1916, which included provisions for ten battleships, six battle cruisers (the first of their kind authorized for the U.S. Navy), and 127 smaller warships.[32]

By the end of 1916, the navy had ridden the navalist wave to a status as a potentially dominant maritime power driven by domestic political support and the need to bolster national security. The navy had become more of a public quantity during this time period, but the Navy Department had done little to provide official support for public relations. Only briefly and intermittently did anyone raise the possibility of coordinating publicity across the service, but, in spite of the seeming success enjoyed by the Marine Corps in its own outreach efforts, these suggestions never came to fruition. So long as the navy continued to enjoy bipartisan political support, there existed no compelling need to devote personnel and resources to such a task. Secretary Daniels had made some halting moves toward centralizing publicity under his civilian leadership prior to 1917, but these fell well short of the publicity work conducted by other government agencies. As will be seen, the calculus behind navy public relations changed markedly in the years ahead as individuals began to recognize that public attitudes and pressure could drastically affect naval policy.

INTRODUCTION 17

This book tells the story of how navy public relations evolved by examining the organizational and policy growth of navy public relations while analyzing what the public could actually see of the service through the variety of media available to them. As such, the first four chapters discuss the organizational evolution of navy public relations from 1917 to 1939. Chapter 1 discusses the birth, life, and death of the navy's first public relations office, the Navy News Bureau. Established by Navy Secretary Daniels just before America's entry into World War I, this civilian-led office constituted a significant break in practice for the Navy Department. Even though the bureau signified an awareness of how institutions could adapt in an era of mass politics and media, it also demonstrated the limits of effective public relations. Policy decisions, including many made by Secretary Daniels himself, invited public skepticism and controversy. These included the decision to press for completion of the 1916 Naval Act ships, which sparked an international naval arms race. A virulent public backlash helped stop this race in its tracks and led to the Washington Naval Conference.

Chapter 2 analyzes the birth of the navy's second public relations office, the Information Section of the Office of Naval Intelligence. Naval officers perceived the naval arms limitation movement as a grave threat to national security and to the navy's prestige, and thus sought to utilize public relations to respond to the challenge. Navy Day, possibly the most important public relations effort of the interwar period, emerged from these same anxieties. Yet, the arms limitation movement constituted only part of the public relations problem confronting the navy as Rear Admiral Moffett sought to use his fledgling air assets in a public relations campaign to stave off General Mitchell's independent air service. The work of Moffett, Knox, and others, while sometimes successful, revealed just how unprepared the navy was to curry public favor on a mass scale.

In the later 1920s, renewed attention to public relations finally yielded experienced personnel and, perhaps more importantly, better policies to govern the relationship with the increasingly popular mass media of radio and film. Chapter 3 shows how the navy successfully forged a relationship with film producers and established its own Motion Picture Board, which gave the navy significant control over its on-screen image. Even amidst this amazing technological advance, the service struggled with several major challenges. The Great Depression and internal discord nearly incapacitated the Navy League, making the navy even more reliant on contacts within the mass media. Furthermore, the placement of the Information Section within the ONI led to instances where public relations and intelligence work overlapped in uncomfortable ways.

Chapter 4 shows how, during the mid- to late 1930s, the newly renamed Public Relations Branch continued to exert influence over the Motion Picture Board as its members grew increasingly savvy about how best to maximize the cooperation granted the film industry. In fact, with the resurgence of the Navy League and the support provided to filmmakers, authors, and academics, the branch had developed a number of external allies through which the navy could burnish its image. This occurred, however, as the international political situation grew increasingly chaotic, which put more pressure on naval officers to restrict the amount and types of information released to the public.

Equally important as the organizational development of public relations is how the themes and messages of the publicity the American people were exposed to also evolved. Chapter 5 analyzes the literature, recruiting posters, and Hollywood films used to entice young men into joining the navy or enter the Naval Academy. These materials varied in the level of official sanction, yet consistently promoted how naval service could help young men acquire physical strength and enjoy an adventurous career. The navy believed that potential officers and men should develop strong morals and sound judgment, but leaders often found themselves battling images that advanced the idea that sailors had progressed little from the rough, seedy men of previous generations.

Chapter 6 analyzes the publicity of transformation, specifically how the navy sought to promote aviation and submarines. This chapter provides greater nuance to Admiral Moffett's role in selling transformation while highlighting the contributions made by other individuals in these campaigns. The promotion of these new weapons systems and technologies had two requirements: to demonstrate their effectiveness in potential future conflicts and to show that they posed little risk to their operators. In fact, the navy would be forced to develop effective public relations crisis-management techniques as a result of numerous high-profile accidents that occurred during the interwar period.

Finally, chapter 7 describes how navy leaders and public relations practitioners advocated for a strong fleet in an era of naval arms limitations. Doing so often required emphasizing the service's role in protecting America's overseas commercial interests and merchant marine as well as promoting humanitarian relief and scientific missions. The onset of the Depression also brought about a shift in messaging to stress the importance of naval construction in easing the country's employment woes. Only the worsening of the international situation in the mid-1930s and the breakdown of the Washington Treaty system finally allowed naval advocates to fully embrace a national security message to support naval construction.

By the end of the interwar period, the navy had developed a series of mutually beneficial relationships with many sectors of the mass media; in addition, it cultivated contacts with key individuals within those industries. Significant flaws remained in the navy's approach to public relations, but by 1939 the service could credibly claim to have established an enduring, systematic presence in the public arena for the first time in its history.

◄ 1 ►
THE LIMITS OF PUBLIC RELATIONS

DISARMAMENT, AIR POWER, AND THE LIFE AND DEATH OF THE NAVY NEWS BUREAU, 1917–1922

In early 1917, Secretary Daniels made a small but significant change to the Navy Department. Throughout his first four years as secretary of the navy, Daniels had gradually assumed responsibility for the navy's public relations activities. He had issued press releases, held press conferences, and established policies to govern cooperation with commercial filmmakers. More so than any previous secretary of the navy, Daniels ensured that the peacetime navy could develop and maintain access to the mass media. This meant, however, that in addition to his own executive responsibilities of overseeing one of the world's largest fleets, Daniels operated as his own PR agent. By early 1917, he recognized that he could no longer assume the burden himself and must delegate someone whose sole responsibility was press relations. Thus, Daniels assigned Lt. Charles Belknap Jr. to review releases of public information and to respond to press inquiries. As F. Donald Scovel notes, "In deed, if not in name, the Navy had appointed its first public affairs officer."[1]

This small but noteworthy assignment would soon be overshadowed by America's entry into World War I. The war was one of the most momentous events in human history, claiming the lives of more than sixteen million people and resulting in the destruction of four powerful empires. It became a total war with industry providing a staggering amount of matériel to each belligerent's vast war machine while giving rise to new weapons systems, including tanks, submarines, and aircraft. These same combatants also applied the principle of mass in the realm of information, using techniques of propaganda and persuasion on a hitherto unseen scale. The

United States proved no different as the war finally forced the navy to take public relations seriously, even if only to coordinate with the larger domestic propaganda campaign. The incredible havoc that the war wreaked upon the world created a confused aftermath as the remaining powers sought to make sense of the new global order. As with virtually every other aspect of politics and policy, the navy underwent its own dramatic upheavals as the prewar consensus supporting naval construction suddenly collapsed in the face of political and public fears of a news arms race and the possibility that aircraft would supplant naval vessels as the first line of national defense. When combined with a number of additional distractions and complications for naval leaders, these factors created a problem too large for the navy's first nascent public relations office to solve. By the end of 1921, it seemed as if the public had turned its back on the navy.

Just days after the declaration of war against Germany in April 1917, President Wilson issued an executive order establishing the Committee for Public Information (CPI), headed by George Creel. This organization intended to promote the war effort throughout the country and used a variety of propaganda techniques for doing so. The CPI distributed films, many of them using footage shot by the Army Signal Corps, as well as posters and other materials. The CPI also employed public speakers known as "Four Minute Men" to extol the virtue of the American war effort against Germany. Individuals prominent in the fields of advertising and public relations worked for the CPI in some capacity, most notably public relations pioneer Edward Bernays.[2]

The establishment of the CPI forced Secretary Daniels to further organize the navy's own public relations activities. On 17 April 1917, Daniels invited his friend and fellow newspaperman John Wilbur Jenkins to assume the post of civilian director of information and to manage the new Navy News Bureau, which Daniels placed directly under his own office. Daniels soon asked Marvin Hunter McIntyre to join the new public relations office as Jenkins's assistant. The Navy News Bureau filled out its staff positions with other men from the newspaper trade, but, at Jenkins's insistence, the office operated with as few employees as possible. Jenkins believed that a larger organization would cause unnecessary delays in the release of information to the public and could potentially harm the navy's image.

Given the predominance of civilians from the newspaper profession in the Navy News Bureau, its members had to work with naval officers to execute their duties effectively. The assistant chief of naval operations, Capt. William Veazie Pratt, and the aide to the secretary of the navy—a rotating position assigned to officers with the rank of commander—served as the naval advisers to the bureau and often helped shape the material released to the public. The Navy News Bureau issued press releases regarding the navy's activities during the war and also prepared transcripts of Daniels's press conferences. The releases and feature articles prepared for syndication by the bureau, and sometimes by Jenkins himself, typically concerned the fleet's antisubmarine and convoy missions.[3]

Daniels's official purpose behind creating the Navy News Bureau had been to liaise with the CPI, and, in fact, the CPI paid the salaries of the bureau's civilian staffers.[4] In practice, however, the two organizations may not have always cooperated well with each other. The inner workings of the Navy News Bureau remain somewhat obscure to this day, but a rare article about its work, written by Albert Fox, appeared in the *Washington Post* on 14 October 1917. Just weeks earlier, the bureau began releasing a series of feature articles to run in Sunday newspapers around the country. The first few entries in the series drew praise from editors who clamored for more content, but the CPI—believing it had primacy in releasing news to the public—blocked the bureau from continuing the feature articles. Newspaper editors, not surprisingly, disdained the CPI's decision to supplant the bureau's articles with its own inferior work that one of Fox's sources labeled as reminiscent of "unsuccessful efforts which often attend attempts of amateur fiction writers to break into the magazines."[5] The article's appearance and tone suggests his sources likely worked in the bureau and sought to promote their work at the expense of the CPI, but it is not clear whether their attempt to shame the CPI succeeded in resolving the boundary dispute. In any case, the squabble showed that Jenkins, McIntyre, and others had felt secure enough in the bureau's position that they could take on the bureaucratic behemoth that was the CPI.

Daniels certainly empowered the Navy News Bureau and took many critical steps forward for navy public relations, but he made two additional crucial decisions during the war that led to significant problems after the war's end. First, Daniels prohibited filming aboard navy ships and at shore installations in most circumstances, arguing that wartime security prevented the navy from cooperating in the production of feature films. Given that the navy's primary mission of convoy protection during the war lacked the glamour of major surface engagements and lessened the attractiveness of navy-themed films, Daniels's decision did not result in much immediate harm.[6]

Daniels's second important wartime decision involved the banning of the Navy League from official ties with the service from 1917 until the end of his tenure as secretary of the navy. Dating back to Daniels's initial appointment, the Navy League had disagreed with some of his policy recommendations, such as the scaling back of the 1914 ship authorizations, but American entry into the war created new tensions between the two parties. At first, Daniels blocked the Navy League from engaging in some types of relief work for sailors and their families and turned over such duties to the government and the Red Cross. The final break between Daniels and the Navy League, though, occurred after the July 1917 explosion at Mare Island that killed five individuals. The Navy League believed saboteurs aided by labor unions caused the explosion and that Daniels hid evidence to this effect. Daniels and the head of the Navy League, Col. Robert Thompson, both issued calls for the other to resign due to their handling of the crisis. In response, Daniels issued an order in August 1917 banning the league and its representatives from all navy ships and installations. The report of the initial inquiry released a week after the ban supported the claim of a deliberate explosion but disproved the other allegations, and the Navy League attempted to apologize to Daniels. Unfortunately for the league, the damage had been done and Daniels left the ban in place. This order would remain in effect until Edwin Denby became the secretary of the navy in Warren G. Harding's administration. The league remained active in efforts to support naval personnel for the duration of the conflict, but the organization faced several serious problems when it lacked any official recognition by the navy. The navy itself suffered few immediate consequences from the ban, but it devastated the league's finances and status.[7]

The conduct of the war itself also proved problematic for the navy because the large and expensive battleships that constituted the core of the fleet did not see any meaningful action during the war. In fact, the Mahanian fleet engagement that most participants anticipated occurred at Jutland in 1916, nearly a year prior to American entry into the conflict. The inconclusive battle between the German High Seas Fleet and the Royal Navy's Grand Fleet may have confirmed British strategic supremacy in the North Sea, but it did not prove the climactic naval duel that contemporary naval doctrine promised. Even worse, perhaps, a lack of fuel oil in the British Isles forced the U.S. Navy to send its older, coal-fired battleships to serve alongside the British Grand Fleet, relegating America's most modern battleships to patrolling or lying in reserve in coastal waters. Given the devastating impact of German submarines on the Allied war effort, modern capital ships appeared superfluous.[8]

The severity of the U-boat threat to Allied shipping brought capital ship construction to a halt as demands for escort vessels took priority. A majority of the larger vessels authorized in the 1916 Naval Act sat unfinished on the ways at war's end when the inevitable public demand for demobilization endangered plans for their completion. Naval leaders, oblivious to the possibility that the public might reject further naval construction, continued to press for an ever larger expansion of the fleet. In 1918, the General Board called for the construction of twenty-eight capital ships in addition to the sixteen previously authorized in 1916. Although Secretary Daniels and President Wilson eventually pared the board's new request down to sixteen additional ships, the newly proposed construction program would give the United States a navy superior to all others in both quality and quantity.[9]

These complications were momentarily forgotten in the immediate wake of the armistice. Just six weeks after the Germans sued for peace, the U.S. Fleet entered New York Harbor for public review in a seeming moment of triumph. The war's end brought a sense of elation that the Navy News Bureau quickly capitalized on. Reverting to peacetime tendencies when major movements of the fleet became fodder for public relations, the bureau worked in the weeks leading up to the fleet's arrival to issue press releases, coordinate visits to vessels of the fleet, and make other arrangements to facilitate reportage of the event. Reporters added their own flourishes to coverage, with one editorial labeling the review a "spectacle of sea power." A one-day postponement caused by bad weather did little to tamp down the enthusiasm over the fleet's arrival. Even Secretary Daniels participated in the festivities by helping to drum up press coverage and reviewing the incoming ships from the presidential yacht *Mayflower*. Ten thousand sailors soon paraded through the streets of New York, attracting tens of thousands of local spectators. In the days that followed, the press chronicled the fleet's commander, Adm. Hugh Rodman, and the activities of the sailors as they took full advantage of their time in the city.[10]

By spring, the CPI had wound down its domestic operations, leaving the Navy News Bureau to operate on its own. Soon afterward, Director of Information Jenkins left his position and was replaced by his deputy, Marvin McIntyre. These changes both internal and external to the Navy News Bureau seemingly did little to hinder its ability to generate publicity for the service. That April, another publicity opportunity presented itself when the navy launched the battleship *Tennessee* from the New York Navy Yard in Brooklyn. As it had done during the fleet review five months earlier, the bureau encouraged press coverage and public attendance at the event. The navy issued more than 75,000 tickets for what was billed as the launching of the "largest battle unit in the world." A newspaper reporter described the crowd of at least fifty thousand as a varied lot in which "the banker and the merchant rubbed elbows with the mechanic and the carpenter." A dozen bands hired specifically for the occasion played "The Star-Spangled Banner" as the ship slid down the ways in perfect weather; the scene prompted siren calls from the battleship *New Mexico* and other vessels in the harbor. Assistant Secretary of the Navy Franklin Delano

Roosevelt watched as Helen Roberts, the daughter of the governor of Tennessee and the sponsor of the new ship, christened the vessel.[11]

These highly effective public spectacles masked the difficulties Daniels encountered in convincing Congress to fund the proposed construction program. Congress had passed the Naval Act of 1916 with great enthusiasm, but the request for an additional $2.46 billion for construction in the fiscal year 1919 proved a much tougher sell. In testimony before the House Naval Affairs Committee in December 1918, Daniels not only pressed resuming construction on the 1916 program ships but argued that American naval expansion could also serve as a hedge against the possible breakdown of the postwar peace process. If the League of Nations failed to materialize, Daniels argued, the enlarged fleet could ensure hemispheric security and enforce the Monroe Doctrine; if the peace process succeeded, however, the navy could help enforce League policy and act as a deterrent against aggressive states. In this manner, the United States Navy and those of its fellow League members could serve as a naval policeman for the world. Several newspapers accepted this reasoning and printed favorable editorials on the matter well into 1919 arguing that an enlarged navy would strengthen the role of the United States within the League of Nations. The bill eventually passed through the House at the reduced but still staggering sum of $1.1 billion.[12]

When members of Congress questioned the wisdom of passing such a bill while peace negotiations were under way, Wilson assured them that the new construction would be terminated if any potential disarmament conference came about. While Daniels's motives remained somewhat less clear, Wilson viewed the fleet as potential leverage in negotiations involving any number of issues between the United States and the remaining Great Powers. Still, the bill stood little chance of passage in the Senate, and, in a harbinger of the coming naval arms limitation movement, newspapers in the Midwest ran editorials against the program's cost. In the end, though, the 1919 program served Wilson's intended purpose. In April, British diplomats agreed to support the League Covenant in exchange for American cancellation of the building program contained in the bill. Thus the proposed building plan played a crucial role in securing Wilson's League of Nations.[13]

The end of the 1919 program did not deter Daniels from continuing to press for completion of the 1916 program in the months that followed, but constructing a convincing messaging strategy that he and the bureau could propagate proved difficult. In his own statements, Daniels argued that the failure of either the peace negotiations in Paris or the League of Nations would force the United States to uphold the Monroe Doctrine and defend the Western Hemisphere from outside aggression. Only by constructing a fleet capable of deterring or repelling any potential aggressor could the United States guarantee the safety and sovereignty of neighboring nations. Therefore, Daniels reasoned, the United States needed to choose between accepting membership and participation in the League of Nations or building up its fleet to unprecedented strength. Some prominent newspapers accepted Daniels's view, while others remained unconvinced by his logic and opposed it. Perhaps more troubling for Daniels, editorials in the *Baltimore Sun* and other newspapers questioned whether American foreign and naval policy could be boiled down in such stark terms.[14]

To continue the construction program, Secretary Daniels and the rest of the Wilson Administration would need to buck more than a century of American tradition. Dating back to the American Revolution, distrust of a standing military establishment stemming from Radical Whig ideology and the nation's geographic isolation had led to dramatic postwar demobilizations after each significant conflict. After the Revolution, Congress rapidly reduced the size of the Continental Army and sold off the meager remnants of the Continental Navy. The expansions of American military and naval strength during the next three major American conflicts—the War of 1812, the Mexican-American War, and the Civil War—similarly came to abrupt ends at the conclusion of those conflicts. The acceptance of imperial commitments after the Spanish-American War allowed the army and naval establishments to maintain their strength in the years afterward, but this recent experience did not necessarily mean that the trend had been broken.[15]

To some, a reading of American history combined with the lack of congressional enthusiasm for the 1919 program had raised the possibility that disillusionment and pacifism could imperil the navy and also the nation's position in the postwar world. Capt. Dudley W. Knox, then instructing at the Naval War College and a former staff officer for Adm. William S. Sims, published an article entitled "Our Post War Mission" in the August 1919 issue of the Naval Institute's *Proceedings*. Knox claimed that only a change in "human nature" could successfully eliminate war, yet he concluded that the tide against the service ran strongly and predicted that the navy would need to weather a storm of low budgets and limited public support in the coming years. Such changes in the political and public mood threatened to re-create "former conditions of hostility" toward "adequate naval preparation," suggesting a return to the prenavalist era of a smaller fleet. Knox's prosaic prescriptions for the service and his fellow naval officers to stave off trouble included maintaining high standards of training and readiness to ensure the navy's continued effectiveness during hard times. Knox also believed that a "certain amount of publicity be given the Navy constantly." He acknowledged the possibility that overt public lobbying on behalf of the service could be detrimental both to the service and to individual officers engaged in such work but believed the "importance of the matter" required taking such a risk.[16] Knox's work proved prescient in outlining the navy's pending problems and also signaled his interest in the navy's public relations practices in the years ahead.

In late 1919, as the fate of the 1916 naval construction program hung in the balance, a new challenge to the navy's status emerged in the form of Brig. Gen. William "Billy" Mitchell, who proposed an effective and economical solution to national defense: the airplane. Mitchell, born into a wealthy Wisconsin family in 1879, began his career in the Army Signal Corps but became interested in the military potential of aircraft. While a major, Mitchell took private flying lessons in late 1916 and, upon completing his training, was sent to Europe as an aviation attaché. He later served as the head of the air component of the American Expeditionary Force under the command of Gen. John J. Pershing. A contentious personality, Mitchell created enemies within the army, but he served with such distinction in Europe that he emerged from the war as America's most prominent, but by no means only, air power advocate.[17]

As the war raged, Mitchell grew convinced of the necessity of creating a separate air service. In 1918, raids by German Gotha bombers against British cities compelled David Lloyd George's government to consolidate its disparate aviation branches, including aircraft aboard Royal Navy ships, into a new Royal Air Force to combat the aerial menace. Mitchell closely monitored this development and believed that the consolidation enacted by the British should be duplicated in the United States. Proposals for an independent air service that would include naval aviation assets first circulated in Congress in late 1918, but this initial effort quickly failed to gain the support necessary for passage and rapidly disappeared.[18]

Mitchell's return to the United States, however, promised to breathe new life into the cause he championed, and he spent much of 1919 working to further the cause of an independent air service. At one point in spring 1919, Mitchell even testified before the navy's General Board, offering advice on a number of aeronautical topics, although his primary purpose was to describe how the transfer of naval aviation assets to a unified air service might occur. A new opportunity presented itself in late July with the introduction of bills in both the House and the Senate that proposed to create a Department of Aeronautics and an independent air force. These bills led to the creation of an army board to investigate aviation, which sparked months of public debate. Mitchell himself garnered coverage on 20 August for openly criticizing the state of army and navy aviation, even claiming that the latter "does not exist as an air arm." In October, Mitchell gave a statement to the press claiming that air power could defend the United States from any European or Asian foe. The debates over the bills continued for months afterward, but neither bill ever survived to a full floor vote.[19]

In the midst of Mitchell's campaign and the debates over the fate of the navy's construction programs, Daniels himself came under public scrutiny. In his zeal for reform, such as the 1914 ban on alcohol aboard ships and in naval stations, he had made many enemies within the officer corps that not even his growing support for naval expansion could mollify.[20] Most notably, disagreements with Admiral Sims on multiple issues led to congressional hearings and unflattering press coverage for Daniels and the rest of the service.

The first such incident came in 1919 when Daniels overrode Sims's recommendations for wartime commendations by omitting staff officers and including officers who had lost their ships in combat. Sims and Adm. Henry T. Mayo wrote letters to Daniels protesting the list, and Sims went further and refused to accept his Distinguished Service Medal. Other senior officers soon followed suit and gave up their own medals as well, but the protest failed to spread among junior officers as Sims had hoped. Congressional hearings held in January 1920 revealed the haphazard and less than systematic methods by which Daniels arrived at his list but also the fundamental disagreements between the officer corps and Daniels regarding the definition of meritorious service. Secretary Daniels rejected the views of Sims and others, arguing that officers who lost their ships could still be worthy of decoration if their ships sank due to no fault or negligence of their own. Ultimately, the hearings into the medals controversy resulted in no policy changes, thus allowing Daniels's list to stand unaltered.[21]

In the midst of the medals hearings, another letter written by Sims to Daniels indicting the navy's wartime administration became public. The letter, titled "Certain Naval Lessons of the Great War," attacked the navy's overall war effort as ill-planned, undersupplied, and too meager to fight a war the United States had been observing for nearly three years prior to entry. As Sims wrote, these problems affected his administration of the naval war effort from London and combined to cost the Allies time, money, and manpower in the early months of 1917. Additional hearings into these new charges lasted from early March until late May 1920 and revealed a split among the senior ranks of the navy. Sims received support from retired admiral Bradley Fiske—who resented Daniels for not appointing him the first chief of naval operations—and a recently retired former aide to Secretary

Daniels, Rear Adm. William Fullam. However, the Chief of Naval Operations, Adm. William Benson, and most other senior officers opposed Sims. Although Sims apparently hoped to gain public support for administrative reforms, the hearings devolved into a messy affair centered on the prominent individuals at the core of the dispute. Fiske, who had retired and become a noted public advocate for naval aviation by early 1920, testified before the committee in late March but spent much time attempting to support Sims's case by lobbying for support from prominent newspaper editorial staffs. However damming the accusations Sims made against the Navy Department and Daniels were, he never provided enough evidence in support of the claims to move the dispute beyond the level of clashing personalities or partisan politics. The committee eventually faded from public view, and its final report, issued in 1921, failed to recommend any of the substantive changes in naval administration that Sims hoped might result from his criticisms. The hearings also undermined the case being made for naval construction: if the navy could not manage itself competently during wartime, why provide an enlarged fleet for the service to mismanage in peace? From the navy's perspective, the hearings provided an unnecessary public distraction from the case for construction and conjured up memories of a war Americans seemed eager to move beyond.[22]

As if these two fractious debates were not enough, a third scandal that reflected poorly on Daniels and Assistant Secretary Roosevelt came to light in early 1920. The scandal began in February 1919 when Daniels ordered the commandant of the Newport Training Station to investigate allegations of homosexuality, drug use, and prostitution at the station. Incredibly, the commandant allowed a chief machinist's mate with only some prior investigative experience to oversee the probe, and the investigator's team of amateur sleuths even went so far as to participate in hetero- and homosexual acts with suspects. The April 1919 arrest and subsequent punishment of several enlisted men seemingly brought the matter to a close, but Assistant Secretary Roosevelt, responding to requests from local and state officials, allowed the team to continue investigating local citizens. This second probe eventually ensnared a local Episcopal preacher, whose trial brought the investigations and the methods of evidence collection into public view. At this point, the inquiry caught the attention of John R. Rathom, the editor of *Providence Journal*, who began printing stories about the investigation. Rathom's interest in the case may have been sparked by his acquaintance with Admiral Sims, who was then serving as the president of the Naval War College. Regardless of Rathom's motivation in the case, unflattering articles on the scandal appeared on the *Journal*'s front page beginning in January 1920 and sparked more media interest in the affair.[23]

The shocking nature of the Newport scandal led to a pair of investigations: a navy committee of inquiry ordered by Secretary Daniels and also a separate Senate investigation. Both investigations began in January 1920 and proceeded for months thereafter. As the inquiries began, Rathom wrote telegrams to other leading newspapers in an effort to increase attention. He also testified twice before the inquiry, both times providing information on the nature of the *Journal*'s coverage. The reporting of the affair strongly criticized Roosevelt, especially after he became the Democratic nominee for vice president in the 1920 election. Roosevelt initially attempted to counter Rathom's coverage but eventually chose to ignore it lest he draw more attention to the investigations. The Newport scandal rarely hit the front pages of newspapers, but stories about the investigations appeared over several months. The Committee of Inquiry did not release its final report until March 1921. Meanwhile, the final report issued by the Republican majority committee on 19 July 1921 severely criticized Daniels and Roosevelt for their management of the affair but also damningly cited the lack of good morals among navy recruits and the general atmosphere around naval stations as preconditions for the scandal. The release of the report finally brought the affair to a close but resulted in a rather unique headline in the *New York Times*: "Lay Navy Scandal to F. D. Roosevelt. Senate Naval Sub-Committee Accuses Him and Daniels in Newport Inquiry. Details are Unprintable."[24]

As these myriad embarrassing investigations wore on, concerns about naval construction continued to grow. By late 1920, the U.S. Navy's budget stood at a peacetime-high of $768 million as construction of nine of the ten battleships and three of the six battle cruisers from the 1916 program was under way. While the British had announced their One-Power Standard in March, no new construction was forthcoming to match the Americans.[25] The Japanese, on the other hand, sought to keep pace with the new American ships. In the fall of 1920, the Diet authorized the Imperial Japanese Navy (IJN) to begin work on what became known as the "8:8" program. Eight battleships and battle cruisers each would constitute the core of a Japanese fleet roughly 70 percent as strong as the U.S. Fleet, a level the Japanese believed sufficient to counter the American presence in the region.[26]

Senator William Borah, an Idaho Republican, looked upon the international situation with alarm and took action. Borah believed that the naval race between Germany and Great Britain prior to 1914 prevented the two nations from settling their disputes, and he feared that the United States might be headed toward a similar path with its recent British and Japanese allies. On 14 December 1920, Borah proposed a resolution calling for a "building holiday" that would suspend further naval construction for five years. He also urged the leaders of the United States, Great Britain, and Japan to hold a summit to settle their disputes and thus try to put the brakes on any looming naval arms race. Learning of the proposal, Daniels quickly made an appearance before the House Naval Affairs Committee to denounce the move due to the imbalance of completed construction between the United States, Britain, and Japan. Two days later, Daniels spoke before the committee again and threw his support behind a conference that would discuss the reduction of all armaments among all nations, not just the three principal naval powers.[27]

Borah's amendment tapped directly into the public's contemporary misgivings about the construction programs and into the recurring idea of arms limitation. Within days, his measure received strong statements of support from many of the nation's newspapers, with only a few, such as the *Cincinnati Enquirer* and *Los Angeles Times*, clearly opposing the idea of arms limitation. Concurrent with the Borah resolution, the editors at the *New York World*—Joseph Pulitzer having died in 1911, leaving the paper in the hands of his three sons—reversed their earlier support for naval construction and instead published editorials in favor of disarmament. Within a matter of weeks, thousands of letters poured into Capitol Hill from citizens all across the nation expressing support for the building holiday and disarmament in general.[28]

Soon after Borah's announcement, Mitchell's criticism of the navy reached a new crescendo. Mitchell had renewed his public campaign for an air service in September 1920 in the pages of the *American Review of Reviews* in a way that signaled a critical shift in his thinking. By this time, Mitchell had come to view defense budgeting as a zero-sum game; no new money was likely forthcoming during a period of demobilization, so any funds for an air service would need to be carved out from the existing appropriations for the War and Navy Departments. The navy had traditionally formed the "first line of defense" for the nation, but Mitchell believed his proposed independent air service could better accomplish that mission. To wrest this position of status from the navy, Mitchell began to frame the navy as an expensive, hidebound service that, in addition to hampering the development of air power in the United States, was growing increasingly obsolete as the technological capabilities of aircraft matured.[29]

On 4 January 1921, Mitchell appeared before the House Committee on Appropriations ostensibly to discuss the next fiscal year's appropriations. During his testimony, he boldly proclaimed, "We can tell you definitely now that we can either destroy or sink any ship in existence today." Secretary Daniels attempted to rebut Mitchell's claims at a later hearing, but on 23 January the *New York Tribune* published a series of photos taken of the battleship *Indiana*. The aged warship had recently undergone a series of secret experiments designed to test the effects of aerial attack on naval vessels. The photos had originally appeared in a British newspaper in December, but it is unclear if Mitchell had had anything to do with either leak. In any case, the release of the photos touched off a firestorm of criticism against the navy for not having released any information about the tests. This led Mitchell and others to call for more tests. While Daniels had engaged in official discussions for nearly a year about using the German warships given to the United States as war reparations in aerial bombing tests, he only made a public announcement of the tests in February 1921 just before leaving office. The timing furthered the impression that Mitchell's crusade had directly led to the tests scheduled for that summer.[30]

Emboldened by his successes, Mitchell continued to spread the gospel of air power to the American public. A series of articles appeared in the *American Review of Reviews* and *Sea Power* (the Navy League's magazine), culminating in an April 1921 piece in *World's Work* titled "Has the Airplane Made the Battleship Obsolete?" In it, Mitchell claimed that the thin deck armor of modern battleships combined with the accuracy of high-explosive ordnance from aircraft rendered even the most advanced warships defenseless against the new technology. The comments in the issue clearly showed that the *World's Work* editors agreed with the conclusions of Lt. Cdr. Lee P. Warren's companion piece, "The Battleship Still Supreme," which dismissed the threat posed by air power to modern battleships. Still, while the editors dismissed Mitchell's claims, they gave him a high-profile venue through which he could promote air power as the usurper of the traditional surface fleet.[31]

Our Air Force, Mitchell's book-length argument in favor of a united air service, also appeared in the late spring of 1921. Mitchell's book ironically owed an intellectual debt to both Col. Emory Upton and Capt. Alfred Thayer Mahan, the latter especially when Mitchell framed the United States as geographically and culturally suited to become an air power.[32] Much of the book, however, elaborated on many of Mitchell's assertions made in various public settings over the previous two years. He argued that "neither the Army nor the Navy nor both combined" could adequately manage an air service capable of providing all the nation's defensive needs. Only by cultivating officers trained solely in the ways of air power and placing them in their own executive department could the United States wrest the lead in the military development of air power from European nations. If the United States did not do so, Mitchell warned, the nation would become vulnerable to forms of air attack not seen during World War I and unable to exploit the military and commercial possibilities that aviation offered. The new threat posed by air power meant that the navy could not maintain its predominant national security role as the "first line of defense."³³

The peak of Mitchell's crusade for an independent air service came during the summer of 1921. The long-awaited bombing trials began on 20 June with three U-boats being targeted. On 29 June, the decommissioned battleship *Iowa* served as a radio-controlled target for navy aircraft engaged in mock search operations that culminated in the dropping of dummy bombs on the ship. Mitchell participated in the tests on 13 July, leading an attack on the German destroyer *G-102* that sent the ship to the bottom in twenty minutes. A combined force of army and navy aircraft next attacked and sank the German cruiser *Frankfurt* on 18 July.³⁴

Members of the media observed these tests from the naval vessels monitoring the proceedings and described in detail the levels of damage inflicted by the aircraft on the various vessels. Their reports also highlighted the activities in which Mitchell engaged during the various tests, such as leading the attacks or conducting low-altitude flights to inspect the damage inflicted on the *Frankfurt*. The climactic test against the German dreadnaught *Ostfriesland* received the most press attention because it was the first significant public test of air power against a capital ship. The first day of bombing on 21 July left the ship largely intact. Bad weather and an inordinate number of duds among the bombs dropped on the ship prevented Mitchell's airmen from achieving success, prompting observers to label the vitals of the *Ostfriesland* "practically safe" from air attack.³⁵

Mitchell, however, remained undeterred and returned the next day with six Martin bombers each armed with a single 2,000-pound bomb. To maximize the public relations value of the bombing, Mitchell's aircraft attacked the *Ostfriesland* in rapid succession in violation of rules that called for an inspection of the battleship's hull and internal spaces after each strike. The *Ostfriesland* lacked the modern hull subdivisions and watertight protections of ships designed during the war years and sank after only twenty-five minutes. An apocryphal anecdote relates that senior naval officers observing the tests began to weep at the sight of the sinking battleship, but contemporary press accounts display a more mixed reaction to the tests. Certainly, Mitchell's luster remained bright as the tests "vindicated" his rhetoric, but some press accounts made important distinctions in interpreting the tests' results. Whereas Mitchell claimed that air power had rendered battleships obsolete, these more nuanced analyses recognized that aircraft were now one among many credible threats, including submarines, to surface ships.³⁶

The tests contained a number of flaws, on which some commentators quickly seized. First, the *Ostfriesland*, unlike during the previous tests against the *Iowa*, remained stationary throughout the entire process. The *Ostfriesland* also lacked any air-defense capability, so the bombers could fly over the craft unmolested. These factors cast doubt on some of Mitchell's claims, but his exploits added to an already noteworthy public profile. For several months after the tests, Mitchell fielded interview requests from media outlets throughout the country and used these events to further his case for aviation development in the United States.[37]

The 1921 bombing trials may have given Mitchell a great public victory in his quest for an independent air service, but his tactics of ridiculing the navy to further his cause cost Mitchell whatever chance he may have had at gaining the support of naval aviators. Even outspoken critics of the Navy Department such as Sims and Fullam who strongly supported the development of aviation could not support Mitchell's cause. Ultimately, Mitchell's tactics drove away support from moderates. In addition, as Charles Melhorn argues, the navy legitimately feared that Mitchell's quest for a separate force that controlled all air power assets might succeed, prompting the service to better support its own aviation branch. Amid the bombing tests in June 1921, the navy created the Bureau of Aeronautics to oversee the development of naval aviation and installed Rear Adm. William A. Moffett as its head. Moffett would prove a superb choice, but he faced a significant challenge in Mitchell while needing to mollify the concerns of officers and naval aviators alike who believed the general to be a legitimate threat to their organizational existence.[38]

The months-long affair concerning Mitchell and the bombing tests took place as the movement for naval arms limitation gained momentum. Borah's announcement had aroused and greatly expanded on previous public sentiments in favor of limitations. As a result, public support in favor of naval limitations mushroomed in the spring of 1921 following the release of a Bureau of Standards report that claimed a staggering 93 percent of current government expenditures went to either to current defense spending or to pay for previous wars. A new wave of denunciations of naval construction appeared in newspapers and magazines throughout the country. The editorial opposition included nationally-prominent periodicals and newspapers, including *World's Work*, the *New York Times*, and the *Atlantic Monthly*. Even the editors of the *Saturday Evening Post*, typically one of the most reliable supporters of naval expansion in the mass media, wrote in favor of disarmament because they desired a reduced tax burden more than an enlarged navy.[39]

By mid-1921, the push for disarmament had transformed from a cause driven by elected leaders and the mass media into a true social movement that drew from every corner of American life. Women's groups, farmers' associations, organized labor, and interdenominational religious organizations all pressured Congress and

President Warren G. Harding to support disarmament, but the president proved more difficult to persuade than Congress. Harding's previous record in the Senate indicated his general support for naval construction bills. While on the campaign trail, moreover, he only agreed to the principle of disarmament if the United States could negotiate from a position of strength and dictate the terms. Harding worried about the nation's ability to defend its overseas interests as well as the potential loss of prestige should the United States relinquish naval superiority to its rivals. In addition to Harding's sentiments, his secretary of the navy, Edwin Denby, as well as the assistant secretary of the navy, Theodore Roosevelt Jr., also frequently spoke out in favor of continuing naval construction.[40]

The first, and largest, of the groups that formed to support disarmament grew out of the women's movement. The nascent peace movement that first appeared in the years following the Spanish-American War amidst the American effort to consolidate colonial rule in its new possessions frequently ignored the desires of women to contribute to the movement. After several years of continued slights, the female supporters formed the Women's Peace Party, later the Women's International League for Peace and Freedom, in 1915. During the spring and summer of 1921, several additional women's organizations rapidly coalesced and began to place pressure on Congress to support the cause of naval disarmament. The most effective of these new organizations, the Women's Committee on World Disarmament, formed in March 1921 following a split in the National Woman's Party over the issue of disarmament. Emma Wold served as the head of the new organization, which established very close ties to Senator Borah himself during its early months. Other prominent women's political organizations, including the National League of Women Voters and the Women's Non-Partisan League, also expressed their support for disarmament.[41]

The disarmament movement attracted support from across the ideological spectrum. The head of United States Steel, Elbert Gary, spoke in favor of disarmament as early as December 1920, and several leading business journals followed suit the following year, desiring a reduction of taxes and government expenditures. At a time when labor and industry remained largely at odds with one another, the leading industrial union, the American Federation of Labor, also favored the cause of disarmament. Its leader, Samuel Gompers, attempted to distinguish between disarmament, which he regarded as a legitimate and noteworthy issue, and pacifism, which he detested and strove to avoid. During a meeting with President Harding in June 1921, Gompers pressed the president on the issue of disarmament and later called on foreign labor unions to make similar demands of their own governments.

Gompers would later help form the General Committee on the Limitation of Armaments in October 1921 and molded the new organization's beliefs to match his own.[42]

The growing public support for disarmament began to overwhelm the Harding administration. During his first few months in office, Harding continued to oppose disarmament but felt pressured to alter his stance on the issue. Secretary of the Treasury Andrew Mellon and Secretary of Commerce Herbert Hoover argued against further naval construction so that government expenditures could be reduced. Secretary of State Charles Evans Hughes also opposed a naval buildup, and his dominance within the foreign-policy establishment gave his views enhanced visibility. The combination of the social movement, Hughes's influence, and diplomatic overtures from the British finally compelled Harding to formally announce on 11 July 1921 that a naval conference would be held in Washington in November. Secretary Hughes sent out formal invitations to foreign nations ten days later.[43]

In the months after Harding's announcement, the tide in favor of disarmament continued to swell. Nondenominational religious bodies as well as nationally organized student groups became strong public advocates for disarmament. The Federal Council of Churches and the Church Peace Union had openly supported the *New York World*'s campaign in December 1920, but several new organizations rapidly appeared in the following year all supporting disarmament. The Quakers as well as the Women's Christian Temperance Union collected more than thirteen million letters and signatures on petitions to Congress from the public all desiring "divine intervention" to make disarmament possible. The Eastern College Committee for the Limitation of Armaments formed in 1921 and quickly organized a meeting of representatives from forty-nine colleges and universities in order to coordinate student support for disarmament. As with the religious organizations, the student organization grew rapidly and the National Student Committee formed in November to incorporate the Eastern College Committee with groups in the Midwest.[44]

The Harding administration gave further credence to the disarmament movement in the months between its announcement and the beginning of the conference. Harding created the American Advisory Committee and appointed former Utah senator George Sutherland to head the new organization. The committee would monitor newspaper editorials and letters sent in by citizens and provide the American delegation to the conference with "sound and well-informed public opinion." Curiously, Secretary Hughes feared that the data provided by the committee would overwhelm the delegation and make it overly dependent on the whims of the public. Instead, the committee solely collected information about the burgeoning movement favoring disarmament. In all, it received more than fourteen million letters, eleven million of which favored disarmament, during its short time in operation.[45]

Harding's election had naturally led to a shift in the navy's civilian leadership. Within days of President Harding's inauguration, the new assistant secretary of the navy, Theodore Roosevelt Jr., proposed a plan titled "Intelligent Publicity" to invigorate the navy's flagging public relations establishment. At a time when the press clearly favored naval arms limitation, Roosevelt believed that the navy's public standing had suffered because journalists lacked basic knowledge of the navy and sea power. To remedy the situation, Roosevelt proposed a two-pronged solution: First, he recommended that a summer course be established at the Naval War College in Newport, Rhode Island, designed specifically for journalists. The course would not be exceptionally rigorous but would provide reporters with enough information to enable them to write more frequently and with greater accuracy about the navy. Second, Roosevelt proposed that the navy encourage major daily newspapers throughout the country to publish a weekly column covering naval affairs. Information for the column would be supplied by a high-ranking naval officer capable of exercising "discretion" when choosing which news items to release. The plan received enthusiastic endorsements from the General Board and also from Admiral Sims, then serving as the president of the Naval War College, but the funds required to maintain the program at the college could not be carved out of the navy's appropriation and the idea died stillborn.[46]

This development reflected the cost-conscious culture that reigned over the Navy Department. To be clear, it is highly unlikely that any concerted public relations effort mounted by the navy against arms limitation could have succeeded, but budget cutbacks had left the small staff of the Navy News Bureau increasingly beleaguered. Director of Information McIntyre had taken a temporary leave of absence to manage Franklin Roosevelt's 1920 vice presidential campaign, but, by the summer of 1921, the navy no longer had the funds for the director's salary. In September 1921, cutbacks forced the Navy News Bureau to cease operations and consolidate remaining press operations into the new Navy Press Room. The Navy Press Room consisted of a "staff" of one: Res. Lt. Wells Hawks, who held the title of information officer. In fairness to Hawks, he had a proven record of public relations success over the preceding years, having worked to promote Broadway plays. He also had helped oversee a 1919 Mississippi River recruiting tour that included an antisubmarine warfare flotilla, navy baseball team, several navy bands, and even a glee club. This success had attracted official attention to Hawks, and he also occupied a leadership position within the American Legion and had lured other former officers into publicity work. But despite his talents, Hawks was severely handicapped by the lack of a staff to support his endeavors.[47]

Hawks also could not count on the support of the mass media. During its years of operation, the Navy News Bureau had received little positive assistance from the film industry in promoting the service. Secretary Daniels's ban on cooperation with film studios ended when he left office in 1921, but they did not rush to produce naval films in the succeeding years. The navy's World War I service failed to inspire riveting plot lines, and so it lacked a consistent presence in American cinemas until the mid-1920s. The temporary divide over film content between Hollywood and the navy meant that the service had absolutely no control over films with a naval setting released during the period. A few films released immediately after World War I drew the ire of naval officials who believed them to be detrimental to the service and to recruiting. A 1919 film entitled *Broken Blossoms* contained several scenes of drunken sailors and prompted the navy to demand, unsuccessfully, that the offending scenes be cut prior to its export overseas. Another 1919 film, a Keystone Cops comedy called *Bright Lights*, also featured scenes of inebriated sailors riotously destroying a waterfront dive. Such portrayals of enlisted men created "unfavorable advertising" for recruiters, who argued that the films demeaned the naval service as a whole. Unfortunately for the navy, little could be done to prevent the representation of negative images so long as the film's producers did not request any assistance from the Navy Department.[48]

A rare example of a film in which the navy figured prominently was Fred C. Newmeyer's *A Sailor-Made Man*, released in December 1921. The film's producers requested and received limited production assistance from the Navy Department, which facilitated the filming of scenes aboard the USS *Frederick* and the use of sailors as extras. Its subject matter, however, did not involve any contemporary issues. The film's primary purpose was to showcase rising comedic film star Harold Lloyd, a task at which the film succeeded. Naval officers displayed a decidedly mixed reaction to the film. One recruiting officer argued that it represented "the best picture he [had] ever seen" for recruiting purposes. By contrast, the head of the Navy Recruiting Bureau refused to endorse purchasing copies of the film for the Motion Picture Exchange, citing the film's "harmful influence" because it "ridicule[d] the sailor's profession, cast aspersion on the quality of our discipline, and [held] the navy generally in disrespect." Opinion on films' relative merits for publicity and recruiting would remain a point of contention throughout the interwar period.[49]

The Navy League of the United States represented another possible source of such support, but its feud with Secretary Daniels during World War I had nearly crippled the organization. Navy League elections held after the feud with Daniels in 1918 kept the current leadership in place, thus precluding any possibility of Daniels lifting the ban on contact between the navy and the league. The league's Comforts Committee and other relief work performed on the behalf of sailors serving in the war demonstrated the organization's willingness to not lose sight of its mission, but these activities severely drained league finances. The publication of the journal *Sea Power* also burdened the league, and the organization struggled on more than one occasion to pay for printing. Several fund-raising drives barely affected its balance sheet. The confluence of these factors caused a spike in the league's debts, from $39,000 in April 1918 to $138,000 a year later. Funds provided by Col. Robert Thompson, a former league president, saved the organization from bankruptcy.[50]

The postwar turn toward disarmament helped bring about the Navy League's increasingly enfeebled position and caused members concern about the organization's future. Reflecting the public's disenchantment with the navy, the league's membership rolls declined precipitously. It lost two-thirds of the 9,300 members it had in 1918. As early as 1916, members began to debate openly the organization's continued usefulness given the passage of the Naval Act of 1916, but the league's desire to aid the naval war effort temporarily halted such talk. Between 1918 and 1920, further efforts at cost cutting and fund-raising came to naught, and even the restoration of ties between the league and the Navy Department in March 1921 following Daniels's departure failed to have an appreciable effect on the group's fortunes.[51]

In June 1921, the same month that President Warren G. Harding formally announced the Washington Conference, the Navy League's president, Henry S. Breckinridge, recommended that the organization disband. Secretary of the Navy Edwin Denby supported this initiative, believing that the league had achieved its goal of lobbying for an enlarged navy, and he and Breckinridge both agreed that the financial future of the organization looked bleak. When the league's directors committed to continuing operations at least temporarily, Breckinridge elected to resign. Robert Kelley assumed the presidency and kept the league solvent by shedding staffers and suspending the publication of *Sea Power*. While these moves allowed the league to survive, it rendered the organization prostrate just as public support for disarmament was rapidly growing. Recognizing this state of affairs, Kelley and league declined to mount a campaign in opposition to the Washington Conference.[52]

Amidst largely impotent public relations in the navy, the Washington Conference convened on 12 November 1921 and met for nearly three months. Secretary Hughes served as its chair and proposed in his momentous opening address that the participants suspend all naval construction, accept existing ratios of strength relative to the other powers, scrap older and obsolete vessels in their inventories, and accept capital ship tonnage as the basis of comparison between nations. Hughes's proposal received immediate public acclaim, and these ideas served as the basis for negotiations in the weeks that followed. Other issues remained the subject of contentious debate, including the upper limit of battleship tonnage, whether to abolish submarines as a legitimate weapon of naval warfare, the exact ratio of Japanese construction relative to that of the United States, and the status of naval aviation developments in the respective countries. Over time, however, the nations involved reached a series of compromises and eventually signed nine treaties and twelve resolutions.[53]

Two of the treaties agreed on at the conference had lasting impact on American naval policy. The Four-Power Treaty between the United States, Japan, Britain, and France terminated the controversial Anglo-Japanese Alliance and created a nonaggression pact in the Pacific built on the recognition of the territorial claims of each party. In addition, the treaty called on its signatories to not fortify their possessions. The Five-Power Treaty codified building ratios for capital ships and aircraft carriers at 5:5:3:1.75:1.75 between the United States, Britain, Japan, Italy, and France, respectively. This latter treaty established naval parity between the United States and Britain and also included the ten-year building holiday for battleships first proposed by Hughes during the conference's opening session.[54]

The Washington Conference was the culmination of one of multiple seemingly existential threats to the U.S. Navy. The modern navy had known mostly uninterrupted growth and increasing global power and reach for nearly four decades. Still, both Mitchell and the arms limitation movement had completely overwhelmed the increasingly beleaguered Navy News Bureau and, more critically, threatened the political and financial support necessary to continue the U.S. Navy's expansion and surpass the Royal Navy for naval mastery. These twin shocks rocked the American naval establishment to the core, and many officers and influential observers recognized that the model that had permitted the navy to garner that support must be scrapped and begun anew.

◄ 2 ►

PUBLICITY AND PROPAGANDA

NAVY PUBLIC RELATIONS, 1922–1927

From a naval officer's perspective, the year 1921 was a disaster of epic proportions as the political and public support for the navy collapsed in favor of naval arms limitation. Yet, in that dark year were sowed the seeds for the birth of a more lasting and permanent public relations organization as naval officers and public advocates regrouped and organized to more forcefully shape naval policy. Officers in the Office of the Chief of Naval Operations (OpNav) concluded that the navy had found itself in a war of information, with some even believing the naval arms limitation movement was part of a dastardly foreign plot designed to weaken America abroad and prevent the U.S. Navy from achieving supremacy over its rivals. Furthermore, these officers held that the service had voluntarily disarmed itself by not maintaining a public relations office to manage the myriad threats to the navy's reputation.

The Office of Naval Intelligence, then, served as a hub for the rebirth of navy public relations, and its officers forged ties with outsiders to further the policy goals of maintaining a "treaty" navy. These ambitions, however, quickly ran afoul of a naval culture that hesitated to promote itself and often sought to hide the extent of its PR activities. The naval bureaucracy also proved resistant to information sharing, meaning that best practices pioneered by other parts of the Navy Department remained underutilized. In addition, it had to contend with the personality-driven publicity practiced by Dudley W. Knox and William Moffett, both of whom skirted the attempts to fully centralize public relations under the Information Section.

The arms limitation movement and General Mitchell had exposed a cultural shortcoming in the navy's officer corps: its isolation from the public had led it to become a "silent service" that shunned publicity. William O. Stevens, a civilian English faculty member at the Naval Academy, had asserted that this remained the prevailing culture in his November 1921 Naval Institute *Proceedings* article, "The Naval Officer and the Civilian." To Stevens, civilians disdained the officer corps for three reasons: First, they believed that officers were snobs who looked down on civilian life. Second, they believed that all officers were inherently militaristic and embraced war. Finally, Stevens argued that civilians' ignorance of the navy and officer corps had led them to hold these mistaken beliefs. To be clear, Stevens did not assert this was a one-way problem because some officers had thought only universal conscription could cure the looseness that afflicted civilian culture. As a solution, Stevens proposed that the officer corps "educate" their fellow citizens about their service and culture to bridge that divide. Doing so, however, would require a fundamental change in mind-set for many naval officers because, according to Stevens's view of the officer corps, it was "bad form, not to say improper" for them to engage the press and the public.[1] Through this process of education, the officer corps would then gain greater understanding of the civilian world while building allies in the Midwest and among the new mass of women voters.

Stevens's outsider status made it easier for him to diagnose what ailed the naval officer corps, but the Washington Conference had clearly forced officers to take a harsh look at their own flaws in engaging the public. Lt. C. K. Blackburn's January 1922 *Proceedings* article "Mistaken Publicity" argued that press coverage of the service in recent years created a false impression of the navy in the public mind. Blackburn echoed the mutual mistrust of naval and civilian society noted by Stevens and argued that the public viewed the navy as an institution rife with needless ceremony that allowed its officers and men a "joy ride" as a career. To overcome this mistrust, he advocated publicizing foreign visits by American naval vessels to highlight the role the navy played in facilitating trade and diplomatic relations with other nations. He also believed that an untapped source of publicity existed in the fleet's annual training exercises, such as the winter cruises in the waters of the Caribbean and eastern Pacific. Press releases describing the results of target practices, Blackburn argued, could not only highlight the hard work the officers and men aboard ship put into their profession but also illustrate the navy's commitment to defending the nation.[2]

However modest Blackburn's and Stevens's solutions to the navy's crisis may have been, the articles illustrated frustration and worry about naval policy brought on by isolation from the public. This concern stretched through the navy's hierarchy, including Assistant Secretary of the Navy Theodore Roosevelt Jr., who, like his father, maintained an active interest in promoting the service. Deeper within the Navy Department, several key individuals within OpNav also shared these concerns by early 1922. These officers included Rear Adm. Clarence Williams, the head of the navy's War Plans Division; Capt. Luke McNamee, the head of the Office of Naval Intelligence; and McNamee's subordinate, Capt. (Ret.) Dudley W. Knox, who headed the Office of Naval Records and Library. All three were late-nineteenth-century graduates of the Naval Academy—Williams in '84, McNamee in '92, and Knox in '96—an era when, to use Peter Karsten's phrase, "Annapolites" developed a distinct corporate culture that formulated strong and swift responses to periods of status anxiety.³ Perhaps not coincidentally, all three men had recently served on Admiral Sims's staff either during or immediately after the end of World War I. These officers all saw the danger that the navy's abandonment of public relations posed to the health of the service, and each would soon play a critical role in the development of navy public relations.

Much like Lieutenant Blackburn, Rear Admiral Williams had grown concerned over the press coverage of the navy, believing it rife with misinformation. In January, he recommended to the chief of naval operations, Adm. Robert E. Coontz, that the navy create an office of "Press Relations" within the ONI. Without identifying specific culprits, Williams thought that an increasing number of articles contained errors of fact. The Press Relations office he envisioned would provide accurate information and respond to inaccurate information about the navy that appeared in the public sphere. More broadly, the office could also work to promote "general interest" in the service and to facilitate greater understanding by the public of the service and its mission.⁴

Captain McNamee eagerly endorsed Williams's proposal. McNamee had already voiced his doubts about the navy's current predicament to his peers, especially the shortfalls in funding and personnel. Unlike Williams's vaguer concerns about misinformation, McNamee's support directly stemmed from the outcome of the Washington Conference. He accepted the principle of parity set out in the Five-Power Treaty, but he darkly lamented that congressional indifference would never allow building to those limits and thus the 5:5:3 ratio would instead become 5:2:3. In this context, the proposed Press Relations office could serve as an ideal vehicle to secure more of the resources the navy needed. In his endorsement, he suggested that "an officer of special talent" be assigned to run the proposed office and remain in close contact with the chief of naval operations, the secretary of the navy, and other high-ranking officials within the Navy Department.⁵

On 21 February 1922, Secretary of the Navy Edwin Denby approved Williams's plan and ordered the creation of the Information Section of the Office of Naval

Intelligence with Cdr. Ralph A. Koch as its head. This new public relations office, however, would be far less powerful and ambitious than that envisioned by either the War Plans Division or Captain McNamee. Reflective of the cost-consciousness of the time, Denby directed that the responsibilities of the new office be spread across other offices and bureaus to save on personnel. The Information Section itself would handle daily press contacts, the Photographic Section of the Bureau of Aeronautics (BuAer) would fill photographic needs, and the Morale Division of the Bureau of Navigation would manage the collection and dissemination of general service information. Denby ordered the Information Section and the Recruiting Bureau in New York to cooperate closely, although they were not formally linked. For most of the interwar period, the Information Section numbered five personnel: the director of information, two junior officers, a marine orderly, and a civilian aide. Helene Philbert served as the section's civilian aide, while the other postings changed at varying intervals through the years.[6]

The creation of a new office, even a small one, during a time of personnel cuts demonstrates the concerns held by a number of the navy's leaders about its public image. Unfortunately, the navy lacked an identifiable pool of men from which to draw to man the Information Section. Officers such as Wells Hawks, who left the navy following his tour with the Navy Press Room and returned to a civilian career as a publicist, were rare commodities in naval circles. In time, the navy could hope to build up a small cadre of officers with PR experience and build a distinct career field within the officer corps. Until then, the navy relied on officers such as Koch to perform public relations activities. Koch had begun his career in submarines, but during World War I he served as the executive officer of the battleship *Vermont* and later the battleship *Texas*. He also had two separate stints serving in the Bureau of Navigation; during the second posting he played a critical role in building up the Naval Reserve.[7] His administrative acumen, not any identifiable skill in handling the public, led him to the Information Section.

Despite lacking a background in publicity, Koch became a quick study on the responsibilities of his position. Helene Philbert worked closely with her uniformed counterparts and had ample opportunity to study their methods as well. In a 1946 speech, she recounted several lessons learned by Koch in his time as head of the Information Section:

> "Straight naval information is our function."
> "Make every effort to obtain news items. If you help the press, they will help you."

"It is important to give out unfavorable news. If you give out the news, you put a bad case in its most favorable form. If you don't give out the news, it will be put in its worst form."

"Meet people, but keep yourself in the background publicly. Don't do anything that would give sound reason for you being classed as a propagandist. You supply information, that is a duty. You answer requests of constituents of Congressmen, or them or anyone else."

"Give data to your enemies, if they ask for it, as well as your friends. Your enemies will get the data anyway. A good case is not hurt by discussion. Frequently your enemies help you. They give something to hang a story on."[8]

From these lessons, Koch set out a path to establish legitimacy and credibility for the Information Section both within the navy and externally among the reporters assigned to cover naval affairs for the various newspapers. Doing so required Koch to account for a number of disparate factors including the political and public sensitivities to "propaganda" and the navy's own cultural reluctance to engage in public relations. In addition, the immense public support for naval arms limitation meant that the navy must be careful not to directly attack the legitimacy of the Washington treaties. Generating goodwill for the navy under these constraints proved a daunting task.

Koch also recognized the absurd organizational limitations his office labored under. He later advised his successor, Cdr. Halsey Powell, "Your office is young, you will get plenty of moral support, not to be underestimated in its value, but you will get little material help easily. You will spend considerable time to get mimeographing done, to beg paper, etc."[9] If, as Rear Admiral Williams surmised, the navy was waging an information war, Koch's warning showed that his superiors had not provided the section with many weapons.

Dudley Knox, a retired navy captain who headed the Office of Naval Records and Library, assumed, like McNamee and Williams, that the public's failure to support a strong navy after the war stemmed from ignorance much more than outright hostility.[10] Even after decades of informal publicity, Knox believed that the public still lacked basic information about the navy's value and purpose to the nation. The reason for this poor state of affairs lay not with the press but with Knox's fellow naval officers. Writing to Capt. Thomas T. Craven in January 1922, Knox remarked, "The navy has always been reluctant to use the press in a manner which, in my opinion, is perfectly proper and which can result in a great deal of good to it. The value of publicity is a closed book to the average naval officer if

Capt. Dudley W. Knox, n.d.
Naval History and Heritage Command, NH 48462, Photographic Section.

their attitude in the past is any criterion."[11] To Knox, a failure of organizational culture had led to the Washington Conference; the naval officer corps refused to break free of the "silent service" ethos that had defined its relationship to the press and to the public for decades.

As an interested head of an affiliated organization, Knox worked to facilitate contact between Koch and interested parties, including the head of Emergency Fleet Cooperation responsible for managing the United States Merchant Marine.[12] Developing these ties was important, but Knox's position, deep reservoir of knowledge, and writing acumen afforded him the opportunity to publicly challenge naval policy in a way that the Information Section—with its emphasis on building connections and flows of correct information to the press—could not. Since Knox viewed the Washington Conference as the ultimate symbol of the navy's failure to establish an effective public relations policy, he logically set his sights on changing public perceptions of the conference and its implications.

In the months after the conference concluded, Knox set about penning a book-length analysis of the conference and its effects on American naval policy.

The finished product, *The Eclipse of American Sea Power*, appeared in May 1922. Throughout his book, Knox argued that the general public remained profoundly ignorant of the true state of naval affairs in the aftermath of the Washington Conference. Knox argued that naval officers shared in the blame for the outcome of the conference: "But American naval officers have long since formed the habit of ultraconservatism in regard to publicity, partly on account of many years of officially imposed repression, and partly because of seeming belief in many quarters that American naval officers differ from other Americans, and from officers of other nationality, in that they place selfish interests above their patriotism."[13] This statement reinforced similar claims made by Knox in public and private for three years, albeit with the added wrinkle that public disdain for their profession had caused the officer corps to become more insular. Frustratingly, Knox failed to elaborate further on this charge, and it remained unexplored in this and future writings.

In addition to the officer corps, Knox identified another culprit for naval arms limitation: the American press. In what was to become a recurring theme of Knox's writings and public relations work, Knox argued that many American newspapers had ceded their reporting obligations and instead became mere stenographers to the pacifist groups that had been among the earliest voices in favor of arms limitation. Furthermore, the newspapers exacerbated this troubling trend by soliciting so much information from the foreign delegations during the conference itself. Knox failed to provide any concrete examples to support either of these assertions, but his later writings would help clarify his position.

While Knox included his diagnosis for the emergence of the arms limitation movement, he focused much of the text of *The Eclipse of American Sea Power* on the geopolitical and naval implications for the United States of the Washington Conference. Knox claimed to support disarmament in principle but believed that the specific provisions of the treaties profoundly weakened America's position in the international system. In essence, a misguided idealism had led the United States to surrender its potentially dominant naval power while the realists in Britain and Japan jealously guarded their own power. In Knox's words: "with noteworthy generosity *America offered to give up a certain first place* (with no close second) *in sea power and a positive ability to safeguard American interests the world over—and furthermore offered to do so at stupendous financial loss to herself.*"[14] Even though the treaties had promised to make a more peaceful world, Knox argued they only left the navy unable to defend all of America's possessions and interests around the globe. Moreover, by leaving some issues such as cruiser tonnage unresolved, Knox felt that Hughes had made additional future conferences likely—to redress the grievances left or created at Washington.[15] To fix these problems, he asserted that the nation should maintain a fleet within treaty limits but large enough to give the United States leverage at future conferences.[16]

Knox hoped that *The Eclipse of American Sea Power* might spark a political or public reaction to naval arms limitation, but this was not to be. The American-born but English-bred writer Hector Bywater had released his analysis of the emerging arms race between the three maritime powers, *Sea Power in the Pacific*, just before the Washington Conference, and the book had received much acclaim, including a favorable review in the September 1921 edition of the ONI's *Monthly Information Bulletin*. Knox's book, however, was seen by many as "a dud" and failed to gain any traction in the marketplace.[17] By publishing *The Eclipse of American Sea Power*, Knox had set out to criticize the foundation of naval policy in a way that the Information Section could not, but the book ultimately had little effect on the public debates over naval arms limitation.

Still, the spring of 1922 saw other signs of life for naval advocacy. After several months of hiatus, the Navy League returned to the public arena in support of the naval personnel bill then under debate in Congress. A proposed bill threatened to cut the navy's authorized personnel strength to 67,000 officers and men—a figure too small to maintain readiness in the fleet even once the Five-Power Treaty's tonnage limits took effect. League president Robert W. Kelley and others published bulletins and actively lobbied Congress to support Secretary Denby's call for 86,000 officers and men. In the end, Denby's figure won out in Congress, and the league claimed some of the credit for staving off a potential manpower crisis.[18] This lobbying effort represented a return to the Navy League's core mission, but this reappearance served only to limit the impact of cuts to the navy's funding.

The springtime debate over the navy's authorized personnel strength buoyed McNamee and others worried about the long-term health of the fleet, but they continued to believe that public support for pacifism continued to harm the navy's public standing. To rectify this, he sought to enhance the ties between the service and the Navy League and encourage their outreach efforts to the general public. In June, McNamee wrote Kelley proposing that the Navy League initiate a word-of-mouth campaign to educate the public on the navy's value. The United States, wrote McNamee, needed "a navy, second to none" to deter the nation's enemies, but, more importantly, the navy as the nation's instrument of sea power guaranteed that the United States could serve as "one of the great custodians of civilization."[19] The grandiosity of McNamee's rhetoric aside, a word-of-mouth campaign from an organization as small as the league likely would have had little impact. Furthermore, both McNamee and Kelley recognized the dangers that could result from the discovery of such close contact between the navy and the league, meaning that the campaign had to rely solely on the league's meager resources.[20]

Kelley ably served as the league's president, but by 1922 William Howard Gardiner emerged as perhaps its most influential member. Gardiner had retired from a career in public utilities, but he parlayed his long-standing interests in sea power and world affairs into a second career with the league. The previous year, Gardiner had been a driving force behind Kelley's tough but financially wise decision to suspend publication of *Sea Power*, leading some members to advocate that Gardiner become president over Kelley. For the time being, however, Gardiner served as a member of the league's executive committee and helped shape the group's policies.[21]

Gardiner had already taken an interest in the navy's public relations policies and parlayed the thaw in relations with the Navy Department to gain an audience for his ideas. In September 1921, concurrent with the dissolution of the Navy News Bureau, Gardiner sent a lengthy memorandum to the new assistant secretary of the navy, Theodore Roosevelt Jr., outlining a plan for navy public relations. Gardiner argued that the public would only fully support the navy if it possessed the prerequisite knowledge of national policy and the navy's place within it. Gardiner suggested framing broad themes of such a message around the navy's ability to protect the nation's "social evolution" by defending the country and its overseas possessions. To better understand the value of sea power beyond simply counting battleship hulls or measuring the size of their guns, the public should be targeted by an information campaign.

To accomplish this task, Gardiner proposed that the service create an Office of Public Information headed by a senior captain who could articulate naval policy and other critical information for public audiences. He also suggested the secretary of the navy should issue regular statements to the public and the press either directly or through this new office. Furthermore, officers should be encouraged to publish professional discussions in books and periodicals to hone their messages and writing skills to prepare them for engaging with the public. Perhaps more importantly, Gardiner argued that the navy must foster the growth of a class of civilian naval experts capable of bridging any gaps that remained between naval officers and the public at large. Ever mindful of the damage caused by the break in relations between the Navy Department and the Navy League during Secretary Daniels's tenure, Gardiner also called on the navy to rely more on external organizations such as the league and the Naval Institute to help increase awareness of naval affairs, believing them to be reliable partners for the navy and champions of navalism.

Finally, Gardiner also believed that the navy should sponsor an initiative to have a memorial erected in honor of Capt. Alfred Thayer Mahan and his contributions to the naval art, an idea he had first concocted two years earlier. Assistant Secretary Roosevelt did not directly act on Gardiner's proposals, but it is worth noting that the navy created the Information Section of the ONI just months after Gardiner submitted this memo.[22]

Always an active presence, Gardiner also played a central role in the Navy League's most significant public relations success—Navy Day—which became the primary means by which the organization cultivated pro-navy sentiments among the general public. Until now, Gardiner's exact role in its creation has eluded historians. The Navy Day established during the interwar period had a precedent in the onetime event staged in October 1906 by the Navy League's Philadelphia section in Atlantic City, dubbed Navy Day, the commemoration drew more than two thousand people to hear Secretary of the Navy Charles Bonaparte and other speakers celebrate the navy. The traditional narrative of Navy Day—propagated by the Navy League itself and through Armin Rappaport's history of the league—describes how league president Kelley proposed the creation of "Navy Day" to the Navy Department in August 1922, suggesting October 27, Theodore Roosevelt's birthday, as the date in honor of the former president's contributions to naval expansion. Secretary Denby signed off on the proposal, and the endorsement of Assistant Secretary Roosevelt gave the endeavor added legitimacy. As the accepted narrative goes, Navy Day was a masterstroke that finally allowed the league to capture public attention and move beyond its typical role as a direct lobbying organization.[23]

This version of events, however, omits mention of the original source of the Navy Day idea. Assistant Secretary Roosevelt had spent considerable time lobbying Congress in the spring of 1922 during the debates for the funding and personnel bills, and the immense difficulty of this task weighed on him for months. Fortunately for him, a possible solution to congressional intransigence and public apathy soon appeared. On 6 July 1922, Mrs. William Hamilton visited Roosevelt in his office to request assistance for the New York Navy Club, which her deceased husband had helped establish. Her appeal for Roosevelt to aid the club failed, but the conversation inspired Roosevelt to think of "a naval day for all the land" to promote the service.[24] Days later, Roosevelt met with the commander in chief of the U.S. Fleet, Adm. Hillary P. Jones; the commander of the Pacific Fleet, Adm. Edward W. Eberle; the commandant of the Marine Corps, Maj. Gen. John A. Lejeune; and Rear Adm. William Veazie Pratt of the General Board. All agreed with the idea of a "naval day," but not what form it should take.[25]

Roosevelt trusted Pratt's advice in particular, asking him to review notes of both conversations and draw up a plan. Pratt subsequently recommended that any celebration should be linked to a historical event or person, but that the date should occur in the fall due to weather and to avoid conflicts with fleet training. Pratt settled on 27 October, President Theodore Roosevelt's birthday, a suggestion to which his son reluctantly agreed. Pratt also envisioned a series of events that could display many different aspects of the service to appeal to communities all across the nation. To accomplish those goals, he suggested a variety of actions: partnering with the Chamber of Commerce and other groups; declaring Navy Day a servicewide holiday; distributing the fleet along the Atlantic and Pacific coasts; covering inland areas by sending ships up the Mississippi River, dispatching airplanes to local communities, and even staging a football game between Atlantic Fleet and Pacific Fleet sailors somewhere in the Midwest. Most importantly, he recognized that the navy could not claim Navy Day as its own. The navy needed the league to propose the event as cover because he believed that neither Congress nor the public would accept such a brazen act of self-promotion.[26] Left unstated by Pratt was that the idea of Navy Day ran counter to the "silent service" mantra, but that outside sponsorship made it culturally acceptable to the navy's leadership.

Roosevelt accepted Pratt's outline, but the next step was finding an outlet to communicate this information to the league. McNamee, because of his correspondence with Gardiner, offered the perfect conduit to the league's hierarchy. McNamee wrote Gardiner on 28 July, just weeks after Roosevelt's meeting with Mrs. Hamilton and a month after McNamee's exchange with Kelley. In his letter, McNamee argued that making "the whole country pause for an hour and give serious thought to its Navy" could significantly enhance the public perception of the service. He predicted dire circumstances should the navy not improve its image: "If we cannot sell the Navy to the people, it will not take long to start bankruptcy proceedings in Congress."[27]

Recognizing the potential controversy that his proposal could create, McNamee instructed Gardiner to keep this correspondence secret to all but Kelley and a few other high-ranking and trustworthy league officials. The plan must appear to have originated with the Navy League, McNamee reasoned, or the scheme would be denounced by Congress and dismissed by the public as blatantly self-serving. He continued, "The plan would come as a complete surprise to the Navy Department, but being put up to us would of course gracefully assist and then we would go to the limit—'get me'?"[28] McNamee then reprinted almost verbatim Pratt's suggested list of Navy Day events.

Gardiner responded enthusiastically to McNamee's proposal, saying it contained "FIRST RATE ideas." McNamee provided Gardiner with detailed instructions on how Kelley should write to Secretary Denby to ask for permission to hold Navy Day, but Gardiner suggested that McNamee ghostwrite Kelley's letter of proposal as well as a response letter to be signed by Assistant Secretary Roosevelt. The available records do not indicate whether McNamee followed through on Gardiner's suggestion to ghostwrite the letters, but, in any case, McNamee and Gardiner's relationship proved vital in helping to create Navy Day and shaped the way it would be celebrated in succeeding years.[29]

In later correspondence, Gardiner informed McNamee of the poor state of league finances at the time, saying this shortage of funds would likely inhibit the league's ability to promote Navy Day. Gardiner continued to work despite this handicap and wrote Secretary Denby to request a clear statement of naval policy that he could use to better design a promotional campaign for Navy Day. Denby responded with a five-page document that outlined the historical context for the navy's development, its current missions, and the navy's value to the nation. The navy, Denby argued, provided for the nation's defense, assisted in humanitarian operations, and served as a "training school for the youth of the country." The navy promoted international peace and stability because its power and potential dominance after World War I made possible the disarmament agreements reached at Washington.[30]

The navy itself also worked to ensure the success of Navy Day to the extent that McNamee proclaimed the service did "most of the work."[31] Secretary Denby ordered ships to return to port and to prepare to receive visitors. While most of the fleet gathered at New York City for the first Navy Day, Denby dispatched ships along the Atlantic seaboard from Bath, Maine, to Miami, Florida, and at various West Coast ports. The navy also sought to highlight its past successes and traditions for Navy Day and exhorted officers to evoke the exploits of John Paul Jones, John Barry, and Stephen Decatur, among others. Rather conspicuously, this same list omitted David Farragut, David Dixon Porter, Raphael Semmes, and other prominent Union and Confederate naval heroes from the Civil War, likely in an attempt to avoid any association of the navy with sectional discord.[32]

Organizers also secured assistance from several media outlets. Theater owners from across the country pledged to show naval films. Radio stations devoted blocks of time in their programming schedules to Navy Day material. The navy also received assistance from newspapers and several periodicals, most prominently *McClure's* magazine. *McClure's* had previously published some of Mahan's work in addition to articles supporting naval expansion prior to World War I, so the two articles published in the November 1922 issue in support of Navy Day represented a return to form for the magazine. The first, a glowing tribute to Adm. William S.

Sims authored by S. S. McClure, the magazine's founder, credited Sims with several reforms, including the development of long-range gunnery and his involvement in the post–World War I hearings into the Navy Department's management of the war effort. Sims himself wrote the second article in the issue. Titled "Roosevelt and the Navy: Recollections, Reminiscences, and Reflections," it described the support Theodore Roosevelt provided to the navy throughout his life. *McClure's* ran parts 2 and 3 of Sims's article on Roosevelt in succeeding months.[33]

The Midwest remained a key target for Navy Day proponents because they believed that, in spite of more than two decades' worth of naval publicity, the people of the region remained indifferent and even hostile to the navy due to a lack of information. As McNamee had initially proposed, naval aviation units flew to inland cities and towns on Navy Day. A group of seaplanes flew from Pensacola, Florida, to Hannibal, Missouri, stopping several places en route to demonstrate the capability of naval aviation. Another aircraft traveled from Washington, D.C., to Indianapolis, making similar landings along its path. The *Chicago Tribune* editorialized that the public's "unthinking optimism" had led to the degradation of the navy and implored all "clear-headed Americans" to recognize the value of the service to the nation's physical security and economic well-being. Hopefully, the *Tribune* added, the holiday would help citizens realize that the Washington treaties did not eliminate war or the need to maintain an adequate national defense.[34]

Officers based in the Nashville area proved especially industrious in support of Navy Day. These officers submitted articles to papers throughout Tennessee that prominently displayed the date of Navy Day and emphasized the peacetime duties of the service, including the education of enlisted men and humanitarian work. The advance publicity they arranged for Navy Day included references to Navy Day by ministers in their weekly church sermons, the use of specially made rubber stamps for mail that included the date of Navy Day, and notices placed into menu cards in restaurants. Local officials were called on to promote Navy Day, the governor of Tennessee led a parade of the local ROTC organization through the streets of Nashville, and many schools held special outdoor exercises and events for students. This combination of activities proved so successful that the Information Section, when drawing up plans for Navy Day in 1923, circulated a description of the advance publicity and events held in Tennessee to other areas to serve as a model.[35]

Prominent naval officers also promoted Navy Day. General Board member Rear Adm. Ledyard Rogers granted an interview with the *Chicago Tribune,* in which he carefully avoided criticizing the Five-Power Treaty while warning of the price paid for "unpreparedness" brought on by the desire for reduced government expenditures and a lower tax burden. Prominent naval officers visited inland areas, most notably Adm. Hugh Rodman, the commander of the American battleships attached to the British Grand Fleet during World War I, who spoke at a public gathering in Des Moines, Iowa. In his speech, Rodman highlighted the growth of the navy over the last forty years, stressed the importance of Theodore Roosevelt in fostering the growth of the service, and argued for the benefits of a strong navy.[36]

Navy Day was a noteworthy success in most areas, but considerable room for improvement existed. The late start in planning such a large and complex event limited the effect that it could have in mobilizing public opinion. For instance, the solicitation of media support failed to prevent the editors of the *Christian Science Monitor* from condemning Navy Day as the "obtrusive advertising of war."[37] To some, Navy Day failed in its purpose to improve the service's public standing, particularly in the inland areas that McNamee believed vital to the ultimate success of the venture. A naval reservist in Worcester, Massachusetts, wrote Secretary Denby to complain that the Navy Day celebration in his town relied too much on the rehashing of war stories rather than providing more information about a "sailor's life." If the navy included more of this type of information, the reservist reasoned, the public would gravitate more toward the service because they presently "know little or nothing" about the service and have yet to find an acceptable means of satisfying their curiosity.[38]

Emboldened by the relative success of Navy Day, Gardiner continued to use his access to Roosevelt to recommend new public relations policies on the premise that the public remained ignorant of the benefits of a navy. Following a conversation with Admiral Sims at the Naval War College in the summer of 1922, Gardiner revisited an element of his 1921 naval publicity plan. In January 1923, Gardiner proposed to Roosevelt to create a civilian writers' course at the Naval War College. Gardiner believed that many members of the press corps lacked a basic understanding of naval affairs and required instruction so that they could "correctly" write on the subject for their readers. A four-month course, he reasoned, would be sufficient to familiarize newspaper correspondents, authors, and editors with the value of sea power as a tool of statecraft. Rather than serve all four months consecutively, those taking the course would attend for one month at a time and then break for many months while working through a reading list of important works on naval affairs supplied by their War College instructors. By breaking up the course in this fashion, Gardiner hoped that the effect of "indoctrination" would be more pronounced than if the course were taken in a single four-month period.[39]

Though the idea bore many similarities to Roosevelt's own "Intelligent Publicity" plan, Gardiner elaborated much further than Roosevelt had on what he hoped the course could accomplish for the navy. Gardiner admitted that he and Sims agreed on the necessity of creating such a program but differed considerably on its desired results. Sims hoped that graduates would write as many articles as possible describing the navy and its activities and appeal to the general public. Gardiner, on the other hand, assumed that appealing to the public was too inefficient. As the product of a well-connected Boston family, Gardiner adopted an extremely patrician view: the common man was, in his view, "inadequately informed, his intellectual reasoning faculties are not developed, and his willful control over his emotions is slight." Instead, Gardiner, who believed that Mahan's works had mostly attracted an influential audience of "thinkers and doers," advocated appealing to elite decision makers and those whose faculties were controlled "somewhat more by reason." Gardiner never assumed his program could result in the discovery of a new Mahan, but rather that it could achieve success by appealing to the influential segment of the public.[40] Gardiner's views befitted a man of his background, one whose experience lay in lobbying and not public relations, but his naval counterparts viewed their service as a national, public institution and thus could ill afford to write off the masses on whom they relied for manpower.

Concurrent with the writers' course, Gardiner also proposed to Roosevelt a narrower scheme designed to use retired officers in public relations work. Retired officers represented a source of publicity as yet untapped by the navy's official public relations apparatus and offered a means of circumventing the reticence that naval officers in uniform sometimes possessed about such work. Gardiner suggested that the navy initiate regular communiqués, perhaps on a bimonthly schedule, for circulation to retired officers to include recent information about the service and its activities. Gardiner outlined three significant advantages of this scheme to Roosevelt: retired officers could remain up-to-date with the latest news of the fleet, external organizations such as the Navy League or the media would gain new sources of information to draw on, and the retired officers could prove a more reliable and accurate conduit to release information to the general public. This scheme proved far more attractive to Roosevelt given the minuscule costs required to initiate the plan, unlike Gardiner's more expensive Naval War College plan, and he quickly approved its implementation.[41]

Soon after Gardiner developed these plans, he and the league returned their attention to Navy Day. Even though many in the league believed that Navy Day had tapped into a latent pro-navy sentiment that had previously gone unnoticed, continued concern about the group's financial condition led some members to question the wisdom of holding a second Navy Day in 1923. Only with the pledge of funds from Kelley and several other donors did the league's leadership feel secure enough to press for a repeat of Navy Day. League officials began by contacting the Navy Department seeking assurances that it would support the undertaking, to which Assistant Secretary Roosevelt heartily agreed.[42]

Despite worries about the league's financial health, the group never scaled back its ambitions for the second Navy Day. The league reached out to automaker Henry Ford, who had spoken in favor of an expanded navy in recent months, to seek his endorsement for the celebration. Samuel Gompers, who had previously supported the Washington Conference, also pledged the American Federation of Labor's support for Navy Day, saying the navy was the institution most responsible for the defense of "the lives and the heritage of our citizenship." The media became a focal point for cooperation again as the Navy League concentrated its efforts on newspapers, radio stations, and the film industry to publicize various scheduled events. The latter proved even more helpful in 1923 as the head of the new Motion Picture Producers and Distributors Association (MPPDA), Will Hays, pledged his support in securing publicity for Navy Day.[43]

The combined efforts of the Navy League and the Navy Department made the second celebration of Navy Day much larger than the first. The navy dispersed the fleet far more widely than in 1922, and CNO Adm. E. W. Eberle sought greater participation on the West Coast by dispatching an entire battleship division to San Francisco Harbor. In all, more than 2,100 local celebrations were planned and announced in advance. The governors of thirty-six states and more than a thousand city mayors issued statements or proclamations regarding Navy Day, and businesses, women's groups, and other organizations all pledged their participation in 1923. Small ceremonies were held in foreign countries wherever the service had a presence, spanning from Constantinople to Chunking. Naval aircraft overflew inland areas, with the navy's new airship *Shenandoah* a featured participant. The *New York World*, whose reportage helped give credence to the disarmament movement in late 1920, even issued an editorial on Navy Day advocating construction of enough warships to bring the navy up to treaty limits.[44]

In the days following Navy Day, accounts reached Washington of celebrations held across the country. Two junior naval officers who visited Fresno, California, reported receiving a warm welcome from the mayor of the city and that more than five thousand people attended a local luncheon to celebrate the event. The reserve unit in Cincinnati, Ohio, opened its new reserve center on Navy Day and also arranged for flag displays throughout the city. The sole naval reservist in Sandusky, Ohio, took it upon himself to perform a considerable number of tasks to promote

Navy Day. This reservist persuaded the local chapter of the American Legion to lobby the local press to print several articles in support of Navy Day, some of which were contributed by the reservist himself. He also secured the cooperation of local ministers and the Boy Scouts to make public announcements in the days and weeks leading up to Navy Day. Additionally, he coordinated the visit of a lieutenant commander to Sandusky including a speaking engagement at the local Kiwanis Club, a service club whose membership base often comprised local businessmen.[45]

The successes of the first two Navy Days created enough momentum for it to become an annual event that provided a regular and consistent source of publicity for the navy. The celebrations in the mid-1920s followed the same basic pattern established by the 1922 and 1923 iterations. Vessels visited ports along both coasts and were opened to the public for tours, and prominent officers and individuals gave public addresses celebrating naval history and imploring the public to support the maintenance of the fleet. As the radio industry matured, the number of radio stations airing Navy Day broadcasts increased and allowed audiences to listen to speeches and other naval-themed programming. In 1926, the motion picture industry increased its support for the celebration after the navy requested films for production and distribution to theaters. This proved somewhat of a challenge as each of the primary newsreel makers wanted footage that differed from that of their counterparts, but the navy ultimately secured this support by granting the companies permission to film a variety of activities, including a mock air attack by aircraft from the Scouting Fleet on a group of destroyers. The support from the film industry also resulted in a film produced by Adolph Zukor's Paramount Pictures with the assistance of the MPPDA titled *Don't Give Up the Ship* (1926), which highlighted the importance of the nation's merchant marine and its impact on the national economy. Secretary of the Navy Curtis D. Wilbur screened the film on 1 October 1926 and quickly endorsed it, giving the MPPDA time to produce two hundred copies of the film for exhibition on Navy Day.[46]

Navy Day certainly counted as a major publicity triumph, but the subterfuge at its origins demonstrated that the navy would continue to mask its involvement in public relations, a move that undercut the Information Section's attempts to establish legitimacy. Even as Navy Day took off, basic decisions remained unsettled for how the section should acquire and disseminate information. In May 1922, Secretary Denby ordered each major command to assign one or more officers to collect information and photographs and then to prepare a newsletter. These officers would then forward all this material to the Information Section for recruiting or publicity purposes. That fall, Koch embarked on a series of visits to the fifteen separate naval district headquarters around the country in order to discuss the dissemination of press information at the district level. To reinforce this process, Denby issued a memo in February 1923 that reminded the officer corps that "it is the right of the Congress and the people of the United States to be fully informed concerning the ships, men, and operation of the Navy." To live up to this mandate, Denby ordered the entire officer corps to cooperate fully with the press and ensure the release of all nonclassified information for public consumption. The order also tasked the director of naval intelligence (DNI) with coordinating the work of other bureaus, offices, and commands to ensure compliance with these policies.[47]

Beginning in 1924, the Information Section—now led by Cdr. Halsey Powell, an officer with meritorious service aboard a Queenstown, Ireland–based destroyer during World War I and during the evacuation of Smyrna in the Greco-Turkish War—received a significant boost with the assignment of officers for publicity work in each naval district. Since 1903, the navy had divided the United States and its overseas possessions into naval districts each headed by a flag officer. Mimicking the placement of the Information Section within the ONI, each district intelligence office would task one of its officers—typically a reservist—to liaise with local press outlets to disseminate information. Given that local and regional newspapers still dominated the mass media of the 1920s, this represented a significant effort at decentralization with the promise of allowing the districts to forge their own valuable ties to the press.[48]

The spate of orders certainly provided more definition to the operations of the Information Section, but the duties of its personnel remained enough of a work-in-progress that the May 1923 edition of the ONI manual *Instructions for Intelligence Officers* included no provisions for public relations work. In this somewhat unsettled atmosphere, Commander Koch and his successors at the Information Section took a conservative approach to public relations during the early years of operation. In 1924, the chief of naval operations, Adm. E. W. Eberle, described the Information Section as having not been "organized for purposes of propaganda, but to furnish the public with correct information regarding the Navy, its mission, and its use in peace and war." The press releases issued by the navy during much of the interwar period reflected this conservative but professional approach to public relations. The section's releases dealt with a wide range of service activities, including the announcement of fleet maneuvers, anniversaries of historic events, and accidents to both men and machines.

Yet for much of the interwar period, the mandate to avoid propaganda reigned supreme when issuing press releases. Henry H. Douglas, an officer attached to the Office of Public Relations in 1941, asserted that the 1913 Gillett Amendment "banning" government public relations had prevented the navy from overtly shaping information prior to its release. The navy's policy to train line officers for public relations work rather than using trained public relations specialists to perform such tasks may also have played a role in the decision to avoid propagandizing in press releases.[49] The navy's "silent service" culture also played a role and resulted in publicity that was certainly less bombastic than that propagated by its ever-eager and aggressive sister service, the Marine Corps.[50] For these reasons, Information Section press releases often consisted of perfunctory statements of information that consciously avoided "spinning" the news.

The navy intended the Information Section to function as a centralized clearinghouse for naval information, but the short staffing of the office had forced it to rely on the submission of information from the ships and stations of the fleet. Yet, from the top of the naval hierarchy down, information was not always forthcoming. Continuing a practice started by Josephus Daniels, successive secretaries of the navy held twice-daily press conferences for purposes of releasing information, but, as Admiral Eberle admitted, "he frequently ha[d] no news to give" the press. The Information Section created reference files so that requests for information from the press or other sources could be responded to in a timely manner, but sometimes the office would forward these requests to officers with the appropriate expertise for response. Occasionally, the navy secretary's office periodically reminded various commands and offices to forward press inquiries to the proper authorities.[51] In this manpower-strained environment, the Information Section needed, but did not always get, the cooperation of the rest of the naval bureaucracy to function properly.

Security concerns also presented a significant challenge for the Information Section. Even though part of the ONI, the section operated with relative autonomy within its parent organization and thus remained at some remove from the classified environment that characterized the intelligence world.[52] Still, this presented problems for the section in attempting to publicize certain naval activities, among them the U.S. Navy's annual exercises known as Fleet Problems. In 1923, the navy's Atlantic-based Scouting Fleet and Pacific-based Battle Fleet used the annual concentration of the fleet in warmer waters to inaugurate a series of annual exercises intended to test elements of the navy's campaign plans by pitting a friendly force, usually labeled Blue, against an enemy Black force. While the specifics of the campaign plans remained classified, the concentration of the fleet presented opportunities for publicity. No correspondents traveled with the fleet to Panama for Fleet Problem I, but Secretary Denby granted the press access to witness Fleet Problems II, III, and IV, all held in Panama in early 1924. The insistence on security, however, prevented correspondents with the fleet from sending off their reports on the exercises until after they reached port, thus slowing the release of information to the public and limiting the value of the reportage. In the competitive newspaper business of the day, this delay in publishing meant the news could be several days old by the time it reached newsstands. Only in 1927 did the navy begin allowing the press to use shipboard communications equipment to file reports.[53]

As the Information Section established itself during the tenures of Koch (1922–23) and Powell (1923–25), there was little sign of cooperation with the other offices performing public relations duties.[54] Knox, for instance, insisted that his office had little contact with the Information Section despite their shared status as subsidiaries of the ONI.[55] This lack of contact, however, provided cover for Knox to continue using his position to engage in his own publicity campaigns as a self-described "naval propagandist."[56] Within the context of navy public relations, Knox's ideas and methods made him an exceptional figure, and his individual, personality-driven brand of publicity made him a throwback to the days of Mahan and Luce.

Knox returned to a theme briefly mentioned in his diagnosis of the naval arms limitation movement at the opening of *The Eclipse of American Sea Power*: the threat posed by overt British propaganda within the United States directed against the navy. Even prior to the closing of the Washington Conference in early 1922, Knox began to assert that British success at the negotiating table stemmed from the ability to infiltrate American newspapers with pro-British sentiments. He further argued that this propaganda caused the public to question the need for a large navy and left American possessions in the western Pacific virtually undefended. Knox's strong belief in this conspiracy not only kept him vigilant to any press articles that might confirm his suspicions of foreign propaganda, but also led him to allege that British interests controlled the content of the *New York Times*.[57]

One of Knox's most frequent targets was the periodical *Scientific American*. By 1925, he became convinced that the magazine propagandized the public against a pro-American naval policy, and over the next several years, Knox engaged in a bitter feud with its editor, Orson Munn, as well as its British-born contributor Bernard Walker. Knox argued that a biased article authored by Walker had led to the defeat of a bill in Congress authorizing the modernization of older American battleships, thus leaving the navy's battle line inferior to that of the British. In October 1926, Knox wrote Munn to complain that a recent article by Walker disparaging the American "treaty cruiser" design would harm American interests. Knox deepened the criticism by accusing the magazine of deliberately publishing the article to coincide with Navy Day in the United States. Munn denied publishing propaganda and cited praise received by the magazine from past and present secretaries of the navy. The letter had little effect on Knox, who wrote Munn the following month that "technical inaccuracies" printed in the *Scientific American* and other publications constituted a primary cause of American naval weakness because they consistently overstated America's present naval strength relative to its peers. The feud only ended when Munn left the magazine and Walker died in 1928. Succeeding editors soon invited Knox to contribute again to the magazine.[58]

Occasionally, Knox's screeds against the *Scientific American* targeted Hector C. Bywater, a British-born naval affairs writer who occasionally contributed to the magazine but who also wrote for American newspapers after World War I. Initially, Bywater's articles appeared in the *New York Herald*, but in 1921, the *Baltimore Sun* hired Bywater to cover the Washington Conference for the paper. The *Sun* article that announced his hiring to readers described Bywater as a "neutral but friendly" analyst, and Bywater remained employed as a *Sun* correspondent for a decade. Over the course of his career, Bywater authored several influential books, including the aforementioned *Sea Power in the Pacific* and also *Navies and Nations* (1927), but his most famous work was his speculative fiction of a future war between the United States and Japan entitled *The Great Pacific War* (1925).[59]

Bywater and Knox came into contact through their work with the *Baltimore Sun*. Beginning in 1924, the paper periodically enlisted Knox to comment on naval affairs, first assigning him to work alongside Bywater to cover the navy's Fleet Problems held in Panama that January. Later, the paper pitted the two authors in a pair of lively debates in the summer of 1926 and early 1927 over American and British naval strength. In these debates, Bywater questioned the purpose of any enlarged American fleet and reminded readers that American construction programs had led to the entire arms-limitation system. Knox, naturally, argued that America remained the inferior naval power and that British propaganda had left the navy weaker than its rival. While the debates between the two men often appeared acrimonious, Knox's favorable reviews of Bywater's *The Great Pacific War* and *Navies and Nations* indicates that he held his British counterpart in some esteem. Knox eventually resigned in protest from the *Sun* in 1929 following the paper's publication of a political cartoon alleging that the United States and Great Britain had colluded over the years to prevent true disarmament.[60] Knox had been a forceful public advocate for American sea power, but his Anglophobia ultimately won out and led him to sacrifice his position with a leading newspaper.

Knox's contributions to naval public relations went beyond his direct attacks against naval arms limitation and foreign influence. His most lasting and influential support came in his recognition of the public relations value of American naval history upon the present fleet. Knox wrote an article that appeared in the January 1926 issue of the Naval Institute's *Proceedings* entitled "Our Vanishing History and Traditions," in which he described with alarm the disappearance of documentary sources on naval history in Europe. Desiring to prevent a similar occurrence in the United States, Knox pleaded with the officer corps to preserve their own papers for future research. Knox's call to action led to the creation of the Naval Historical Foundation in 1926. The Naval Institute and Naval Historical Society supported the new organization, and many of their members become members of the foundation. Rear Adm. Austin M. Knight served as the foundation's first president, but Knox became a fixture within the organization and served as its secretary for the next two decades.[61] The Naval Historical Foundation could help cover critical gaps in naval history and serve as a resource for public relations activities in the years ahead.

The Information Section could not easily manage Knox even though they shared the same corner of the naval bureaucracy. Rear Admiral Moffett, who ran his own bureau, proved even more difficult to control. Like Knox, Moffett practiced a much more personal public relations campaign, albeit one with a specific technical and organizational focus. A Medal of Honor recipient with a distinguished record, Moffett possessed a talent for public relations work developed during his tenure as head of the Great Lakes Naval Training Station beginning in 1914. The station's existence stemmed from the navy's long-standing desire to forge a stronger connection with the Midwest as a way of building political support for the service and of tapping new reservoirs of manpower. As he commanded the station during the mobilization before and during World War I, Moffett became keenly aware of the value of public relations and inaugurated a variety of practices designed to raise the station's regional stature. He built a close relationship with William Wrigley and the editors of the *Chicago Tribune* that resulted in the creation of a base newspaper and long-term support for his policies. In addition, Moffett's wife, Jeanette, was the subject of an article printed in the *Ladies' Home Journal* in 1918 highlighting the contributions of women to the war effort. Moffett also persuaded the retired bandleader and composer John Philip Sousa to head the Battalion Band and play concerts throughout the Midwest and eastern states.[62] These activities helped link the station to the community and the region while also setting up Moffett for success in his future endeavors.

As his biographer William Trimble notes, Moffett confronted three significant challenges upon taking charge of the Bureau of Aeronautics in 1921. First, he needed to improve the standing of the aviation branch within the service as a whole by

Rear Adm. William A. Moffett, ca. April 1933.
Naval History and Heritage Command, NH 1208, Photographic Section.

convincing skeptical senior officers of the value of aviation in naval warfare. Second, Moffett had to maintain control of aviators resentful that many in their service did not embrace the promise that naval aviation offered. Moffett lacked total control over aviation operations and had to deal with officers who had disagreed with past superiors over the proper course of aviation policy. Finally, Moffett also faced the external threat posed by Brig. Gen. William Mitchell's campaign to create a unified air service. Fortunately for Moffett, few, if any, officers in the navy accepted the proposition that naval aviation could blossom in a unified air service, presenting Moffett with a clear opportunity to unite the officer corps.[63]

Improving the public image of naval aviation could help meet each of the three challenges, so Moffett launched public relations campaigns. Convincing Congress and the general public of the effectiveness of naval aviation could also strengthen the organizational support for naval aviation and potentially increase the appropriation of funds to expand its operational capabilities. Moffett consistently emphasized the benefits of naval aviation to the fleet as a whole in prosecuting naval campaigns. Moffett also directly courted prominent political and financial allies, but PR activities became a defining aspect of his management of naval aviation.[64]

In his work, Moffett personally embodied the fundamental contradiction of the navy's attitudes toward public relations. At times, Moffett behaved as one of Peter Karsten's "Annapolites" who displayed an eagerness to engage the public and openly chafed at the conservatism of naval officers toward PR. For instance, following Cdr. Eugene E. Wilson's assignment to the Bureau of Aeronautics in 1923, Moffett told him that the "old fogeys" in the Office of the Chief of Naval Operations had prevented him from publicly responding to Brig. Gen. William Mitchell's claims about the navy and aviation during the 1921 bombing trials. Recognizing his own aptitude for public relations, Moffett also boasted to Wilson that "if they had let me handle the publicity on the bombing off the Virginia Capes, I could have made a monkey out of [Mitchell]."[65] Still, as evidenced by his 1926 letter mentioned in the introduction, he continued to express reservations about his involvement in public relations.[66]

Moffett's position at the Bureau of Aeronautics made him the public face of naval aviation, and he often accepted requests for appearances and speaking engagements. Perhaps more importantly, it allowed him to wage his own public relations campaigns with little to no assistance from the Information Section. In late 1923, Moffett represented the navy at the celebration of the twentieth anniversary of the first flight by the Wright Brothers in Dayton, Ohio, and at a gathering of the Navy League in Little Rock, Arkansas, in honor of Navy Day. Moffett also sought to capitalize on the fame of well-known naval aviators. In June 1923, he ordered Cdr. A. C. Read, the pilot of the transatlantic flight of the flying boat NC-4, to represent the bureau at a celebration commemorating a new airline route between New York and Newport, Rhode Island. Moffett took advantage of such engagements to build goodwill from the American public's fascination with aviation feats.[67]

Moffett used a variety of means to publicize naval aviation. In June 1923, he arranged for the USS *Langley*, the navy's first aircraft carrier, to visit Washington, D.C. Commissioned from the conversion of the collier *Jupiter* in 1922, the *Langley* would spend the next several years as the navy's sole testbed for carrier flight operations and thus became a valuable asset despite the ship's numerous technical limitations. Its commanding officer, Capt. S. H. R. Doyle, desired a year's worth of uninterrupted time to experiment with flight operations at Pensacola before proceeding on a scheduled cruise up the Atlantic coast in July 1924. Moffett, however, recommended to the CNO Adm. Robert E. Coontz that the carrier steam northward earlier so that it could reach Washington in time for the Shriner's Convention in early June 1924. Even at this juncture when much remained unproven regarding the management of flight operations from a carrier deck, Moffett reasoned that the ship's display would put "the accomplishments of the Navy and Naval Aviation before the people throughout the country" and as such outweighed the extra month of training and experimentation. Ultimately, Moffett's view prevailed, and he even joined the *Langley* for some of its port visits along the Atlantic coast in the summer of 1924.[68]

Moffett also strongly supported the navy's entry into competitive air racing and often attended the races himself. He argued the research and development that went into constructing the navy's racing craft improved the quality of the navy's air arm, but such comments glossed over the fact that air racing and combat operations required very different levels of performance from their respective aircraft. In actuality, entering aircraft in competitions such as the Schneider Cup allowed naval aviation to demonstrate its capabilities in a public setting against the United States Army Air Corps, which had entered into air racing largely at the insistence of Brigadier General Mitchell. The bureau took these races so seriously that one of its pilots, Lt. Alford Williams, spent much of his time in the service preparing for and participating in the races.[69]

Outside of air races, Moffett frequently staged flights designed to demonstrate the capability of naval aircraft, especially the navy's dirigible program. Moffett himself flew aboard some of the first flights of the *ZR-1*, later named the *Shenandoah*, in September 1923, which attracted an estimated fifteen thousand onlookers and set the stage for a series of promotional flights prior to the airship's formal commissioning ceremony the following month. Over the next two years, the airship became a centerpiece of Moffett's publicity efforts. In 1925, Moffett used film footage of the *Shenandoah* and other significant naval aviation events to liven up a presentation delivered to professional engineering societies in an attempt to turn interested groups away from supporting Mitchell's unified air service concept.[70]

In 1924, Moffett proposed one of the more ambitious plans of his tenure. It would have involved a series of flights from the Pacific coast of the United States to Hawaii and then to Australia. Moffett planned the flights to occur in spring 1925 to coincide with naval exercises held in Hawaiian waters and a subsequent goodwill visit by the fleet to Australia and New Zealand, but Adm. Robert E. Coontz, the commander in chief of the U.S. Fleet, objected to the lengthy flight owing to the considerable logistic support the aircraft would require, thus indicating that at least some in the Navy Department disagreed with Moffett's desire to constantly promote naval aviation. Coontz's letter to the chief of naval operations noted that although Moffett "favors the advancement of Navy aviation in every possible line, he does not consider that flights of this character which bring no commensurate

USS *Shenandoah,* flying over New York City, ca. 1923.
Naval History and Heritage Command, NH 51492, Photographic Section.

Naval advance, and which are exceedingly costly, should be undertaken at the expense of approved Departmental Joint problems, approved Departmental overseas expeditions, or even of Fleet training of a routine nature."[71] The flight's cancellation did not dampen Moffett's ardor for such events, but it showed that other senior leaders found his methods of dubious practical benefit to the service.

But the use of the latest and most advanced aircraft in the navy's arsenal won Moffett and the Bureau of Aeronautics public acclaim and, when combined with Moffett's keen political maneuverings, tempered threats to establish an independent air service. Using naval aircraft and the unproven airships for public relations, however, always posed risks, and these manifested in September 1925. In the previous months, the bureau had planned a long-distance "hop" from California to Hawaii using a pair of PN-9 flying boats. Moffett initially had proposed to employ navy aircraft for an around-the-world flight similar to the Army Air Corps' circumnavigational flight, but the army's mission had involved a significant logistic effort and eventually required navy ships and personnel to maintain the flight. The press estimated that the flight cost the army $200,000 but that the navy spent $300,000 to support the venture. Admiral Coontz rejected Moffett's proposal for an around-the-world flight and instead scaled back the flight to traverse the California–Hawaii route. The Pan-Pacific Union, a group dedicated to fostering ties between nations along the Pacific Rim, had already broached the subject of such a flight to Moffett, arguing that proving the feasibility of the California–Hawaii route would garner interest from airlines interested in establishing a regular route.[72] With the backing of the Pan-Pacific Union, Moffett could curry favor with civic associations while continuing to draw attention to naval aviation.

In September 1925, the bureau also planned a flight of the *Shenandoah* to several sites in the Midwest to visit state fairs and other public gatherings from Ohio to Minnesota. The airship's commanding officer, Cdr. Zachary Lansdowne, attempted to postpone the trip from the first week of September to the following week to avoid predicted thunderstorms. Lansdowne's experience with the 1923 transcontinental flight of the *Shenandoah* allowed him to recognize the potential dangers of extended overland flights, but the CNO, Adm. E. W. Eberle, denied his request for postponement because the states' fairs would conclude by Lansdowne's proposed starting date. Lansdowne raised no further objection to the flight plan, although he privately expressed some reservations to his wife prior to the *Shenandoah*'s departure from Lakehurst Naval Air Station, New Jersey, on 2 September. The next day, the *Shenandoah* encountered a violent updraft while flying through a storm and broke apart over Ava, Ohio. The crash killed fourteen of the forty-three men aboard the airship, including Lansdowne. It was one of the deadliest accidents the navy suffered during the interwar period.[73]

On that same day, news reports began announcing that one of the PN-9 flying boats making the California–Hawaii flight had disappeared somewhere over the Pacific Ocean. The plane, piloted by Cdr. John Rodgers and crewed by four men, exhausted its fuel supply before reaching its destination and failed to appear over the guardships positioned to provide essential navigational aid and fuel. Using ships and aircraft, the navy searched the seas east of Hawaii but found no trace of the PN-9. The navy gave up hope of finding the flying boat, but, on 11 September, the craft appeared off the coast of Kauai with all its crew members alive and in good spirits. After having run out of fuel, Rodgers and his crew fashioned a makeshift sail in the hope that the wind currents would carry them to the Hawaiian Islands and allow them to be seen before drifting to their seemingly unavoidable deaths in the central Pacific. The furor over the crash eventually led to General Mitchell's strong criticism of the War and Navy Departments, which in turn led to his court-martial and also to creation of the Morrow Board, which overhauled American aviation policy. While these incidents did not mark the end of Moffett's efforts to publicize naval aviation, they resulted in a significant shift in how he promoted the burgeoning air arm in the years ahead.[74]

Moffett had effectively consigned the Information Section to a spectator role to his publicity efforts, but the orders establishing the section had called on it to collaborate closely with other elements of the naval bureaucracy. In particular, the orders specifically tasked the new section to assist the long-established Recruiting Bureau. In practice, the Information Section and Recruiting Bureau infrequently coordinated their activities; the remarkably uniform "Annapolite" culture ensured a consistency of messaging regarding the recruiting of enlisted personnel. The navy clearly viewed public relations and recruiting as distinct operations in spite of the numerous areas of overlap between the two fields, a marked difference from the Marine Corps, whose Publicity Bureau handled both organizational public relations responsibilities as well as recruiting.[75] Given that the Information Section was formed in response to what was as much a political crisis as a social phenomenon, the navy likely viewed the use of the latest marketing and advertising knowledge as inappropriate for activities that were originally conducted through the lobbying of Congress. As a result of this divide, the Recruiting Bureau as a corporate body possessed decades of experience in reaching out to the American public that the new Information Section lacked.

Furthermore, the immediate postwar period forced the officers of the Recruiting Bureau to adapt and update their approaches to recruiting to account for shifts in public tastes and the postwar funding cuts. Traveling recruiting parties, such as those used to recruit men for the *Tennessee*, proved to be an increasingly ineffective method of finding new recruits. Shortages in publicity materials compounded the problem for a time, leading the bureau to try even more-elaborate schemes such as the Mississippi River recruiting trip organized by Lieutenant Hawks in 1919. While successful, this too proved a temporary solution to a growing problem.[76]

These issues forced the bureau to modify its approach using best practices pioneered by other organizations. In 1919, the army signed contracts with advertising firms to modernize its recruiting methods, causing navy recruiters to press the Bureau of Navigation to copy the army's campaign. The idea quickly received official approval, and within three months, the navy entered into a $300,000 contract with the Advertising Agencies Corporation. Although the contract stipulated that money be spent on newspapers in traditional recruiting areas, the firm also allocated considerable sums to papers in small farming communities and daily and weekly newspapers in larger towns not currently serviced by naval recruiters. Disagreements soon appeared between recruiters in the field and their superiors in Washington and New York over who should control the funds for the campaign. Recruiters believed their knowledge of local newspapers could allow them to use the funds in targeted campaigns, but their leaders objected, arguing that many recruiting officers simply lacked the knowledge or ability to design and manage recruiting campaigns on their own. One commenter on the subject argued that "the Navy is not a local affair" and that all publicity should be managed by the Recruiting Bureau and not individual recruiters. It is not clear exactly when the navy's foray into paid advertising ceased, but the contract ended sometime in the early 1920s.[77]

In addition to the direct employment of professional advertisers, the Recruiting Bureau also attempted to glean methods from the private sector to aid recruiting. In 1920, Capt. C. E. Courtney, the recruiting inspector for the Eastern Division, pushed for the Recruiting Bureau to adopt standard "sales talks," such as those given by salesmen at the Marshall Field's department stores, in order to increase the effectiveness of bureau posters and advertisements. During a period of lagging enlistments in 1922, the Bureau of Navigation directed each recruiting station to initiate competitions among its various substations in an effort to drive up the number of enlistments, arguing that "competition is an important principle of salesmanship" and that such a program would lead recruiters to become more aggressive. The scheme was immediately effective, but it was abandoned once the bureau achieved its recruiting goal.[78]

Most importantly, although the Recruiting Bureau continued to produce posters and handbills to attract recruits, it increasingly shifted attention and resources to the production and display of recruiting films. The navy, which had first experimented with the production of recruiting films in the early 1900s, increased its production dramatically during World War I. The Recruiting Bureau typically assembled finished films from footage collected by camera crews sent out among the fleet. In 1919, the bureau departed from this pattern when it authorized the recruiting station in St. Louis, Missouri, to enter into a six-month contract with the National Film Publicity Corporation to produce a series of short animated films for recruiting purposes. Although the pace of production on recruiting films slowed in the immediate aftermath of the war, more than a dozen films remained in circulation by 1921.[79]

The Recruiting Bureau began to phase out older titles by 1922 while retaining films with "live news interest" or those that were "of an artistic or unique educational value." For a humorous take on naval service, the Recruiting Bureau produced *Crossing the Line* (1920), a comedy about the bizarre rituals staged for officers and enlistees who crossed the equator for the first time and which showed men singing, dancing, and having their heads shaved by the "Royal Barbers." This contrasted with more sober fare, such as *Our Navy in the Near East* (1923), which dealt with the navy's post–World War I intervention in Turkey and interspersed footage of sailors aiding the transport of refugees with that of seamen visiting such landmarks as the Giza pyramids and St. Peter's Basilica. These films proved increasingly vital tools for recruiters who believed the public reacted more enthusiastically to the films than to posters or still photographs.[80]

The Recruiting Bureau found multiple ways of presenting its films to the general public. Movie theaters were the most obvious venue of display, and the recruiting officers frequently solicited the cooperation of theater owners and managers to arrange screenings. For a time just after World War I, the bureau entered into an agreement with the Fox Film Corporation that provided for the screening of recruiting films free of charge in the theaters owned by the company. Recruiting officers did not focus their efforts solely on theaters, though; in 1922, the Recruiting Bureau recommended to the Bureau of Navigation that it be allowed to loan out films to boys' clubs and patriotic organizations such as the American Legion for screenings. Some enterprising recruiters found yet more ways to exhibit films, and by the early 1920s recruiting stations began to mount film projectors and other equipment on the back of trucks that would then be sent out to different locations for screenings. This last method proved unworkable in some areas as high fuel consumption and the dilapidated condition of many roads drove up the ancillary costs considerably. One officer who confronted this latter problem turned instead to local schools to screen films.[81]

During the interwar period, the Recruiting Bureau recognized that among the best sources of publicity were the recruiting officers themselves. By 1931, the bureau managed forty-one recruiting stations scattered throughout the country, and each of these stations, in turn, oversaw several substations. The authorized complement of enlisted personnel for the navy remained stable at roughly 86,000 men from 1923 until 1936. The Recruiting Bureau continued its attempts to attract high-quality recruits by improving the service's public image. The Bureau released occasional directives on policies, but usually left officers free to use their own discretion in trying to drum up public support for the navy and for recruiting. Typically, recruiters designed campaigns around local individuals who had previously entered the navy. Showing the advantages that a life in the navy conferred on a fellow citizen, recruiters argued, would lead individuals to consider joining the service themselves. The Bureau of Navigation supported this effort by instructing fleet commands to submit photographs of its men for distribution to the recruiting stations closest to each man's hometown. The recruiting officers would then add brief stories and submit these and the photos to local newspapers for publication. Recruiting officers also contacted local radio stations seeking air time for the officers to give brief recruiting speeches. Since recruiting officers often served in their hometown areas, these efforts created networks of local media and business contacts to draw on to improve the navy's image.[82] In many respects, these policies and their implementation demonstrated that the Recruiting Bureau was breaking free of the "silent service" culture that held sway with more traditional forms of publicity.

In the drive to reach the public, some recruiters took their inventiveness too far. In 1925, a recruiter in Cincinnati distributed a fabricated story to local newspapers about a woman who attempted to enlist in the navy so that she could be reunited with her lover already in the service. The editor of the *Cincinnati Commercial Tribune* apparently believed the story to be true initially, but, upon discovering it was not, printed a story stating that the "Recruiting Office Descends to Faking" and wrote an angry letter to Secretary of the Navy Curtis Wilbur about the incident. The chief of the Bureau of Navigation reprimanded the recruiting officer for his failure to "stimulate recruiting or reflect honorable credit to the service" and admonished him not to repeat the scheme. More importantly, the chief recognized that such incidents would hurt relations with local media that recruiters relied on to convey their message.[83]

Perhaps the most important advantage enjoyed by the Recruiting Bureau was its ability to develop ties at the local and regional levels. The establishment of press liaisons at the district level in 1924 demonstrates that the Information Section and its civilian and uniformed superiors understood the value of the Recruiting Bureau's decentralized structure, but Powell and his replacement, Cdr. John T. G. Stapler, lacked the personnel to fully manage the flow of information into and out of the Information Section. Thus, in 1927, the press liaison system with the districts came to an end, leaving the Information Section dependent on the ties that its staff—still numbering five personnel—could generate themselves.[84]

A September 1927 incident offered a stark reminder of the difficulties caused by the shortage of manpower for the Information Section. On 24 September, the *Saturday Evening Post* published an article entitled "The Navy and Economy" authored by Rear Adm. Thomas P. Magruder that created controversy. Magruder claimed that the navy was anything but an efficiently run bureaucracy and pointed out instances of rampant waste, including the maintenance of seven navy yards when three could likely perform all of the necessary work. The *Nation* echoed Magruder's charges and argued that the lackluster quality of many recent secretaries of the navy had contributed to the problem. While this was neither the first nor the last article of Magruder's published by the *Post*, Navy Secretary Wilbur sent a ten-page letter to Magruder rebutting his comments, correcting factual errors (for instance, fixing the number of typewriters for the *Saratoga* at forty-four, not sixty-six), and demanding to know how he arrived at his conclusions. Among the more egregious errors cited in the secretary's letter to Magruder was the admiral's claim that the fleet reviewed by President Calvin Coolidge in 1927 was "inferior" in strength to the fleet reviewed by President Theodore Roosevelt two decades earlier even though the modern fleet possessed far more powerful weaponry. Secretary Wilbur also asserted that Magruder had incorrectly reported the navy's personnel strength and the costs incurred for both repairs and the construction of the naval base at Alameda, California. Given that the navy's press policies listed the inaccurate spread of information as a primary menace, an article authored by an admiral that contained factual mistakes could not be tolerated. A few months after the article's publication, the navy transferred Magruder from his post as commandant of the Philadelphia Navy Yard for supposedly unconnected reasons, causing Hearst's usually pro-navy paper, the *New York American*, to label it as yet "another example of a high-handed dictatorship in Washington."[85]

Magruder's article dealt with a critical issue, at least to naval officers: the state of the fleet in an era of arms limitation. The Washington Conference had certainly inspired the creation of the Information Section, and the treaties cast a shadow over naval policy for many years thereafter, but directly countering the arms limitation movement was not part of the section's mandate. The stunning success of the Washington Conference had satisfied many of the disparate social groups that had thrown their support behind the transnational cause, but the diminished disarmament movement continued to be a political factor for many years after. The persistence of this movement in addition to the lingering political questions left unsettled at Washington—namely, the inability to extend the tonnage restrictions to cruisers and other small naval vessels—built enough momentum for President Coolidge in early 1927 to call for a new arms limitation conference to be held in Geneva, Switzerland, that summer. The Geneva Conference proved a very different affair than that held in Washington in 1921–22 because only the three maritime powers—the United States, Great Britain, and Japan—attended. Furthermore, whereas the delegations at Washington had been led by diplomats with naval officers left only to debate technical questions, officers had much more influence within their delegations at Geneva. The narrower focus of the conference combined with the wrangling over ever smaller details largely divorced from the larger security concerns addressed at Washington led to the failure of the Geneva negotiations. Whether this was a success for naval policy is a different debate, but the Information Section's efforts clearly played little or no role in the conference's outcome.[86]

By the end of 1927, the Information Section had been operational for nearly six years. In that time, it had received institutional backing from the highest levels of the Navy Department and, for a brief period, had grown into a nationwide concern with connections to local and regional media outlets. In addition, its leaders had rebuilt ties with the Navy League and had brought this ally back into the fold by covertly creating Navy Day. The small size of the Information Section, however, had limited its ability to coordinate with the Recruiting Bureau and exert influence over the public relations campaigns waged by Moffett and Knox from the Bureau of Aeronautics and the Office of Naval Records and Library, respectively. In fact, while the Information Section worked to develop ties with the media, Knox waged a one-man war against publications that he believed had willingly allowed themselves to serve as dupes for British propaganda. The inconsistency with which the Navy Department applied its policies on publications by its personnel, especially an officer as senior as Magruder, only added to the confusion. This combination of successes and setbacks limited the Information Section's ability to shape naval policy during this period of fiscal retrenchment and left its personnel unable to achieve the lofty goals set for the office.

◄ 3 ►
A SUSTAINED PUBLICITY

NAVY PUBLIC RELATIONS, 1928–1932

By the latter 1920s, the Information Section had seemingly made little headway in repairing the damage caused to the service surrounding the Washington Conference. The question was, why? Dudley Knox attempted to answer this question in his June 1929 *Proceedings* article, "The Navy and Public Indoctrination." Knox, using Great Britain as a historical example, astutely argued that the navy possessed the right to promote itself in the public sphere and that publicly linking the navy to national interests could be done without resorting to warmongering. But, rather than continue this forceful defense of the navy's use of PR, Knox returned to a familiar, and tired, theme: propaganda spread by foreign (British) agents had kept the navy underfunded. Only by identifying and counteracting these sources of propaganda could an "education and indoctrination in maritime matters" lead to a "national awakening."[1] Within the Navy Department, Knox was relatively unique in his forceful public warnings of the efficacy of foreign propaganda, but his arguments echoed those made by Arthur Sears Henning, a Washington-based correspondent for the *Chicago Tribune*, in his 1927 book, *Government by Propaganda*.[2] Still, Knox's essay attracted enough support from the Naval Institute to garner an "Honorable Mention" in the year's prize essay contest, indicating at least some extant hidden support for his views.

Eighteen months after Knox's broadside, *Proceedings* published Hanson Baldwin's "Newspapers and the Navy." Baldwin was a relatively fresh-faced military and naval affairs reporter for the *New York Times* with an earlier stint at the *Baltimore Sun* under his belt. Most importantly, Baldwin brought credibility to the discussion of public relations policies because he was a 1924 Naval Academy graduate who had entered journalism after resigning his commission in 1927. Whereas Knox blamed the state of navy public relations on an external problem, Baldwin insisted that the navy need only to look within for its predicament. By not doing enough to encourage "effective and sustained publicity," the service had failed to properly explain its importance to the public. The reason for this failure, according to Baldwin: an insular officer corps incapable of recognizing the faults of its own publicity apparatus and mistrustful of the press. Baldwin argued that officers, rather than considering journalists as an avenue for gaining popular support for the navy, tended to view them as incompetents, drunks, or, as in the case of Knox, tools of foreign propaganda desiring to squelch any positive news about the service. Baldwin criticized the navy for the poor treatment he received from the service as a member of the press corps. He acknowledged the Navy Recruiting Bureau performed "noble work" but believed that its effort was confined solely to garnering enlistments. To address the service's public relations problem, he advocated for each ship or command to designate a media liaison to foster better ties with local media. Beyond this structural improvement, Baldwin believed the navy needed to reassess its attitude toward the media and respect press representatives. Only by understanding how publicity could aid the service, he reasoned, could these changes truly take hold among naval officers.[3]

The two articles reveal the fundamental difference between an insider's perspective—in this case Knox, one of the most influential officers in building the navy's public relations capacity—and Baldwin's outsider perspective. Frustratingly, Knox provided only scant details on how to encourage the "national awakening" he sought, but Baldwin's assessment suggested that the navy's own misplaced priorities and cultural shortcomings were the primary culprits behind its meager public relations capacities. Even as Baldwin's analysis rings true, his career in the printed press likely limited his critique to the navy's interaction with his own medium. By the time he wrote his article, the navy had finally laid the foundation for improving its image by deepening its ties to other media.

Navy public relations found itself at a crossroads by the latter 1920s. In its early years, the Information Section had been populated by personnel with no public relations background who had to train on the job. It did not routinely collaborate with the Recruiting Bureau or the navy's two PR savants, Knox and Rear Admiral Moffett. The section also remained confined to the Navy Department headquarters, having had a promising effort of using reservists for public relations duties in each naval district cancelled in the name of fiscal prudence. Yet, for all these problems, some noticeable signs of improvement began to appear by the end of the decade. The regular rotation of personnel into the Information Section finally yielded an experienced hand with prior expertise in different facets of publicity. The expansion of radio and, far more importantly for the navy, film under the control of a small number of Hollywood-based studios afforded the navy new means of promoting itself and its capabilities. Amid these successes, however, the onset of the Great Depression and the near collapse of the Navy League threatened a partnership that had defined one of the more successful aspects of navy public relations in the 1920s. Furthermore, the placement of the public relations function within the Office of Naval Intelligence created cases where the lines blurred between public relations and counterintelligence work. In essence, as the Information Section slowly professionalized, members of its staff found themselves confronting numerous situations outside the traditional bounds of the public relations profession.

A problem that plagued the early years of the Information Section was the lack of a pool of officers with public relations experience to staff the office. The early heads of the section had no identifiable public relations skills, and there appears to have been little consideration given to what might make a good public relations officer beyond basic administrative skill. This forced officers such as Commander Koch, the first head of the Information Section, to learn on the job. This trend continued with Cdr. Allan Farquhar, the head of the Information Section from early 1928 through mid-1929. This pattern changed, though, with Farquhar's replacement, Cdr. Charles C. Gill. He possessed critical skills in writing and publishing, having edited the Naval Institute's *Proceedings* for several years and also authored two books: *Naval Power in the War* (1918) and *What Happened at Jutland* (1921). Furthermore, Gill also had the administrative acumen that the position required. One of his peers described Gill as possessing "a flare [sic] for pen pushing and volumes of information at his elbow."[4] As the Information Section remained woefully understaffed, it needed officers willing and able to move large amounts of paperwork to keep the office operational.

Gill entered the Information Section during Capt. Alfred W. Johnson's tenure as director of naval intelligence (1928–30). Johnson was likewise an active administrator for the ONI and displayed a greater interest in the Information Section than did his predecessors. He understood that a public relations program directed from Washington may lack the necessary nuance to reach effectively the disparate cultural and geographic segments of the public. Even though syndicates such as William Randolph Hearst's controlled papers in many different cities, the editors and reporters at each newspaper still wielded considerable influence in shaping the news within their markets. Devising a practicable and effective solution, however, proved a difficult task for Johnson.

In July 1929, Johnson's office sent a letter to each of the naval district commanders requesting information on articles that had appeared in newspapers within their districts that had printed incorrect information about the navy. Crucially, Johnson was on leave when his staff sent the letter. They misinterpreted his guidance and sent a letter stating that the ONI and the Information Section would then seek redress from the offending papers. Commandant of the First Naval District—ComOne, in navy shorthand—Rear Adm. Philip Andrews wrote directly to the CNO, Adm. Charles F. Hughes, stating that the order was a "mistake," that newspaper editors would resent being "dictated to" from Washington, and that press relations must be handled at the "immediate and local" level within the districts themselves.[5] Hughes concurred with Andrews's response and rescinded the order before the ONI attempted to contact any of the newspapers. Johnson, for his part, admitted that both his staff and Andrews had misconstrued his order, interpreting it as a potentially disastrous framework for retribution against unfriendly outlets. The organizational element of his plan had merit because it reinforced the ONI and the Information Section serving as a hub of official, factually correct information that personnel in the districts could then disseminate to the news outlets in their district.[6] The policy itself, however, was more problematic because Johnson's scheme of retroactively checking the accuracy of news stories was a very cautious and conservative policy. That his staff erred on the side of retaliation when disseminating the order certainly did not reflect well on its own instincts in handling the media.

The botched rollout of this new initiative did not deter Johnson from continuing to find ways of improving both the quality of information and its methods of dissemination. In March 1930, Johnson again wrote the district commandants to solicit suggestions for a public relations policy to be drafted for inclusion in the Monthly Information Bulletin—the ONI's internal newsletter—and in the *Intelligence Manual*. Johnson believed the navy had successfully mastered the ability to craft press releases but concluded the service was "not so well informed" on how to disseminate information via other media. "All points of contact with the public" should be considered in crafting public relations policy, but, Johnson reasoned, "press relations are of primary importance." Johnson's memo advocated a policy of transparency and equality in public relations so that officers showed no favoritism toward particular media outlets, that individual press releases "should be confined to a concise, clear statement of facts and attending circumstances," and that "care should be exercised to eliminate expression of opinion." Officers could speak publicly on policy matters if granted prior clearance to do so, but Johnson implored officers to display good judgment and to not attempt to withhold information from the public. Johnson specifically directed that officers attempt to correct any mistaken facts about the service that made it into the public realm.[7] Yet again, Johnson had given serious thought to the organizational and structural factors in disseminating publicity, but he still insisted on the most conservative framing of the information to be released.

Johnson's promised statement of policy via the Monthly Bulletin never materialized, but this did not bring an end to his continued emphasis on factual correctness, transparency, and effective dissemination. In November, Secretary of the Navy Charles F. Adams directed that the Information Section release any and all information "not incompatible with military secrecy." Adams also ordered the service to cooperate with the Office of Information and to direct all inquiries related to the media to the office for review. The memo attached to his directive, "The Supply of Naval Information to the Public—Discussion of Press Relations," reasoned that constant and cordial contact must be maintained with the press to ensure that unexpected crises would not result in negative portrayals of the service. The prompt and accurate release of information would counter the natural tendencies of curiosity and suspicion of most reporters. The memo also encouraged the development, apart from the basic factual press releases, of feature stories that could arouse "human interest" in a part of the navy's operations that typically remained unknown to the public.[8]

In combination, Captain Johnson and Secretary Adams had diagnosed several critical issues with navy public relations. Johnson understood how best to funnel information from the Navy Department out among the press, but he never quite grasped that the information itself needed to be compelling for it to have an effect. Secretary Adams's orders sought to overcome that deficit of interest in the navy's press strategies. Both of their orders demonstrated that the naval officer corps remained a conservative collective. So long as much of the publicity work remained confined to the small staff of the Information Section, Knox, and a few other select individuals and groups, it remained easy for the overwhelming bulk of the officer corps to maintain an insular attitude regarding publicity. Thus, the navy remained dependent on the Information Section to professionalize and continue to seek out new methods of reaching the public.

These efforts were especially important because the officer corps, as evidenced by Lt. Cdr. F. E. M. Whiting's September 1931 *Proceedings* article, "A Further

Application of Our Publicity Policy," remained shackled by conservative attitudes toward PR. Whiting, as did Knox, blamed many of the navy's problems on the proliferation of pacifist organizations, although Whiting did not ascribe the supposed prevalence of these groups to foreign influence. In fact, much of the piece defended the navy's need to operate and train in peacetime as a prudent measure of security rather than as a symbol of an offensive national security policy. Yet, within his article, Whiting recognized the recent and vast growth of mass communications and the power of the increasing number of radio broadcasts, advertisements, and newspapers to permeate the public consciousness. Furthermore, as Whiting argued, "to the average American, the only purpose of a navy is to permit him to proceed in the even tenor of his way without interference or molestation from an outside source."[9] In his estimation, naval officers must individually counter the "careful what you say"[10] culture of the "silent service" and recognized that, no matter how much they value secrecy, no information could stay hidden for long once a ship or aircraft enters service. Publicity that presumably took full advantage of the new mass communications was vital to build a navy capable of national defense.

By the time Whiting's article appeared in *Proceedings*, the navy had moved more aggressively to establish a presence in new forms of mass communications. The phenomenon cited by Whiting had caused a profound shift in Americans' news and entertainment consumption habits that led to substantial changes in the Information Section's practices and also its influence over public relations policy.

One of these changes was the growth of radio in the post–World War I era, which provided another medium through which the navy could reach the public. Compared to its relationship with the print media, the navy's interactions with the radio industry were much more haphazard and inconsistent. This is ironic given the navy's direct involvement in the development of the American radio industry prior to the 1920s. During the Wilson administration, Secretary of the Navy Josephus Daniels had encouraged a government monopoly over the radio industry, but the vision of civilian control advocated by the Naval Communication Service eventually won out. To advance private development, the service encouraged General Electric to establish the Radio Corporation of America (RCA) in 1919, and commercial radio broadcasting began the following year with the establishment of the radio stations KDKA in Pittsburgh and WWJ in Detroit. After 1923, the navy played no role in managing radio broadcasting, but the number of commercial stations continued to grow, with many of them either attached directly to manufacturing interests or owned by local newspapers. The National Broadcasting Company formed in 1926 and the Columbia Broadcasting System the following year, providing the industry with two national networks. Yet while the radio industry underwent a significant expansion in the 1920s, its biggest growth did not occur until the following decade. In 1924, only a fraction of American households owned a radio, but this number jumped to nearly half the country by the early 1930s. This rising number of households owning radios coincided with the growing number of broadcast stations, which allowed audiences to pick up radio signals in much of the country, as radio truly became a national medium.[11]

Due to its closeness to the development of the technology, the navy established an early presence on America's commercial radio airwaves. The Navy League proved especially helpful in securing time on radio networks for Navy Day, particularly by 1925 when it secured airtime on more than one hundred radio stations nationwide. In 1927, the Navy League renewed its radio contacts when NBC agreed to support broadcasts for that year's Navy Day.[12]

Radio also provided the means for the Navy Band to become nationally known by the latter 1920s. The navy had supported various bands attached to its ships and stations throughout the years, including the Battalion Band headed by John Philip Sousa during World War I, and maintained a musicians' school at Norfolk, Virginia. In 1919, Charles Benter became the bandmaster at the Washington Navy Yard and set about rebuilding a band that had lost many performers due to the postwar demobilization of manpower. In this endeavor, Benter received the backing of the Navy Department, which desired the band to "superbly represent the United States Navy, both in the Nation's Capital and throughout the country."[13]

Once reconstituted, the Washington Navy Yard Band played live shows in Virginia and the Washington, D.C., area but lacked a following outside of the region. The growing network of commercial radio stations that developed after World War I gave the band an opportunity to broaden its audience. When the band began its concerts in 1923, only radio stations in and around the Washington area broadcast the shows, but soon other stations, one of which received backing from RCA, began rebroadcasting the concerts across the nation. As a sign of the band's growing popularity, the Navy Department received thousands of laudatory letters and telegrams praising it. The navy rewarded Benter's efforts with increased funding, by allowing the band to accompany President Harding on his cruise to Alaska in the summer of 1923, and by increasing its size to seventy-five after January 1924.[14]

The navy began referring to the Washington Navy Yard Band as "The Navy Band" as early as 1922, but this title lacked any official standing. President Calvin Coolidge rectified this situation when he signed a law on 4 March 1925 designating the Washington Navy Yard Band as the official United States Navy Band. This new status enhanced the profile of the band and enabled it to mount lengthy tours and play at several key events during the next several years. The band's first tour in late 1925 took it to seven states over an eight-week period in which the band played fifty-one shows. The band played numerous shows with the president in attendance and also performed at a benefit concert for the restoration of the USS *Constitution* in June 1926 as well as the reception ball for Charles Lindbergh following his return from his transatlantic solo flight in 1927. Its radio profile increased as the band played four weekly concerts for CBS and NBC. In 1929 and 1930, the band also became the subject of three newsreel shorts produced for Fox Movietone News and the Hearst Metrotone newsreel services.[15]

Even with the common use of radio for special events and for broadcasting Navy Band concerts, the navy only first attempted to develop a policy for cooperating with radio broadcasters in 1930. That year, the commander of the Fleet Base Force, Rear Adm. Thomas P. Magruder, and the commander of the Battle Fleet, Vice Adm. L. M. Nulton, submitted suggestions for a department-wide radio policy: it would require that broadcasts receive prior approval, that no navy communications equipment be used for such a purpose, that the navy could incur no expenses for such activities, and that broadcasts be restricted during maneuvers or other sensitive activities. The plan's authors argued that when broadcasts originated from naval personnel, the navy should grant access to all broadcasting companies. Programs intended to entertain naval personnel would require prior approval, but such events would not require equal access for all broadcasters. These suggestions were sent to the CNO, but do not appear to have been formally implemented.[16] As a result, the navy's use of radio continued absent any clear statement of policy.

If radio offered a useful, if haphazardly managed, medium for the navy to use, the dramatic growth in the power and influence of the film industry in the latter part of the 1920s proved far more influential for the service. This expansion coincided with a renewal and strengthening of ties between the navy and major film producers. This was a long and slow healing process whose roots lay during World War I. Although lifted in 1918, Secretary Daniels's order severely restricting cooperation with commercial filmmakers as the war raged had stifled the creative relationship with filmmakers, leading to only a small number of films produced depicting the navy, with few of these receiving any kind of official support. For a number of years, the studios also had little appetite for producing naval films, thus depriving the navy of an increasingly influential media outlet well into the 1920s.

Three factors helped heal the breach between the navy and the film industry during the 1920s. First and foremost, the navy and the industry maintained a business relationship even as their creative relationship lay dormant. Soon after the armistice, the navy entered into a series of agreements with emerging film studios to create the Navy Motion Picture Exchange to ensure that sailors aboard ship or in distant stations could, for morale purposes, view movies. In September 1919, the navy contracted to buy films from the motion picture studios at a discounted rate for exhibition aboard ships and at naval stations. From the beginning of the enterprise, studios supplied two copies of each film to the exchange simultaneously with its release in theaters so that ships in both the Atlantic and the Pacific could view them in a timely fashion. To house the films, the navy converted a warehouse in New York into the headquarters for the Motion Picture Exchange. It took time for the exchange to build up its film library, with a 1920 estimate stating that the navy would need to spend more than $200,000 to fully meet the demands of the service. Over the next several years, the exchange expanded its operations, and by 1925 it possessed more than 2,200 complete eight-reel films and purchased new films at a rate of twenty-five per month. The exchange also developed a system of distribution during these years, first sending new films to the navy's principal commands—after 1922, the San Pedro–based Battle Fleet and the Hampton Roads–based Scouting Fleet—and then out to the lesser commands, such as the Special Service Squadron in the Caribbean and the Asiatic Fleet in the Philippines.[17]

This relationship between the navy and the studios benefited all involved. Officers and men aboard ships and at naval stations enjoyed almost nightly screenings of films, thereby reducing the amount of cultural isolation that previously marked life in the naval service. The navy as an organization benefited as it believed that film screenings prevented its sailors from engaging in potentially destructive behaviors by frequenting disreputable establishments ashore. The studios profited from the arrangement as the films granted them access to a market that oftentimes remained out of the reach of typical centers of film exhibition. The agreements between the navy and the film studios stipulated that movies could only be shown to naval personnel and must not compete with any local screenings of the respective titles. The navy argued that the system had ancillary benefits, such as sailors providing positive word-of-mouth "advertising" or their taking wives or girlfriends to local commercial screenings of the same films. The navy always ensured adherence to the terms of the contract with the film studios and even went so far as to rebuke the San Diego Naval Air Station for purchasing films through commercial means rather than procuring them through the exchange.[18]

As this relationship matured, the film industry itself went through a dramatic economic restructuring. The Trust that controlled the nascent film industry in the

1910s had broken down, creating new opportunities for entrepreneurs. Through a number of shrewd business decisions, Hungarian-born Adolph Zukor created the first major vertically integrated film studio, Paramount Pictures, which controlled all three phases of the motion picture business: production, distribution, and exhibition. By 1921, Paramount controlled more than one-fourth of the film business within the United States, and Zukor began to create distribution systems for his films in several other countries. Paramount quickly became the largest Hollywood studio, but soon Marcus Loew's Metro Goldwyn Mayer, the Fox Film Corporation, and Warner Brothers all rose to prominence through vertical integration.[19]

As these studios grew, they collectively established the Motion Picture Producers and Distributors Association (MPPDA) in 1922 to act as a lobbying organization to work on behalf of the entire industry; later, it would most famously devote itself to warding off campaigns of censorship initiated by state and local governments. With the growth and consolidation of the studios and the existence of a professional lobbying organization on its behalf, the film industry rapidly transformed into a powerful and mature industry. The introduction of sound pictures in the late 1920s only served to increase further the popularity of the medium, as the average weekly attendance in theaters reached 80 million in 1929. The onset of the Depression led to a decline in attendance to between 60 and 70 million by 1933, but half the nation's population still attended films on a regular basis. These large audiences indicated the degree to which movie attendance had become a social ritual and, when combined with the content of the films themselves, allowed movies to become a dominant socializing influence for Americans.[20]

Within this atmosphere, the studios began to show an interest in producing films depicting war and military life. The first of these, King Vidor's *The Big Parade* (1925), depicted World War I combat for American film audiences on an epic scale. The film was followed by *What Price Glory* (1926) and *Wings* (1927), which also focused on the war from the perspective of marines and fighter pilots, respectively. Each of the productions attracted large audiences, turned sizable profits, and set standards for later films to follow. As a result, the studios continued to develop military-themed films in the years ahead.[21]

While not on the same scale of success or prestige, the 1924 film *Classmates* provided filmgoers with a positive portrayal of cadet life at the United States Military Academy. The film's financial success led to other studios exploring similar projects. Metro-Goldwyn-Mayer (MGM) soon started producing their own movie set at the Naval Academy in Annapolis, Maryland, to capitalize on the previous film's success. Naval officials matched the studio's enthusiasm and heartily cooperated with the production. The navy hoped *The Midshipman* (1925) would feature a well-known actor and received its wish when the studio cast rising film star Ramon Navarro as the lead. To improve upon the template provided by *Classmates*, the service granted the filmmakers liberal access to the academy and took the extraordinary step of allowing a uniformed Navarro to participate in the academy's graduation ceremony.[22]

The film sparked a sustained interest in Naval Academy films for the next dozen years but, more broadly, helped renew the creative relationship between the service and Hollywood. As the number of collaborations increased over the next decade and a half, the relationship between the navy and the film industry grew from a commercial one to a political one as well. In the all-important quest for profits, the motion picture industry developed a propensity to distort perceptions of the nation's past and present and shy away from entirely realistic treatments of controversial subjects. To that end, the medium created "a semblance of reality" in which a heavily manufactured representation of everyday life appeared on movie screens and created heightened expectations among viewers. Religious and government authorities fretted that movies could bypass the usual methods of social control and profoundly influence the public, but, as Garth Jowett and James M. Linton argue, film content during the interwar period tended to reinforce prevailing social attitudes and beliefs.[23]

These tendencies of the film industry positively affected its relationship with the navy as each institution sought to exploit the other for its own benefit. In the case of films in which the motion picture industry and the navy cooperated, neither party wished to depict any of the negatives that might accompany either a brief stint or a lengthy career in the service. Films did not necessarily shy away from showing the potential for injury or death while in naval service, but they did not dwell on the possibility of long separations from families during cruises of the fleet or on the low pay of servicemen. Because of this, film became an ideal medium through which the navy could improve its public standing.[24]

The Recruiting Bureau eventually came to view these films as recruiting opportunities and coordinated activities with theater owners, though not at first. For example, it rejected an offer in 1926 from the producer of the film *Shore Leave* to coordinate recruiting activities with local premieres of the film because it "had no special publicity value for the Navy," although the film had been partially shot aboard the battleship *Arkansas*. Yet, with the release of *Annapolis* in 1928, the navy began to look more favorably on such requests. For *Annapolis*, the Recruiting Bureau requested that recruiting stations across the country coordinate with local theaters so that recruiters could help publicize the film. The bureau hoped that filmgoers would be so enthralled with a positive depiction of life at the Naval Academy that they might entertain the notion of joining. Recruiters in San Diego even prepared elaborate navy-themed displays in theater lobbies. The recruiting officer in Baltimore reported that local theater owners profited handsomely from *Annapolis* and hoped that the navy might assist with the production of similar pictures each year.[25]

Not everyone shared this level of enthusiasm about cooperating with the promotion of commercial films in such an overt fashion. The commander of the Battle Fleet, Vice Admiral Pratt, objected to anyone under his command cooperating with local theaters for the promotion of the film and described such activities as "ill-advised, undignified, and cheap." Pratt clearly supported the principle of cooperation between the navy and Hollywood but believed that the job of promoting the finished films fell on the studios' shoulders rather than the service's. Recruiting officers deemed *Annapolis* beneficial overall for the navy's image, but they found that the public displayed no extraordinary enthusiasm for the film and that it possessed little value in recruiting. A recruiting officer in St. Louis suggested the film might only succeed in areas of the country where the public already held positive views of the Naval Academy.[26]

The mixed reaction among naval officials regarding screenings of *Annapolis* did not prevent the navy from continuing the practice with other films. In 1929, a new opportunity to cooperate with local theater owners came with the release of the film *Salute*. Like *Annapolis*, *Salute* was set at the Naval Academy, but the newer film combined the setting with a story centered on the academy's football team. Yet again, recruiters remained divided on the film's ability to affect short-term recruiting needs. Two officers questioned the value of attempting to drum up recruits at events designed to showcase the appeal of becoming a naval officer. Others, however, believed the film improved the navy's image, with one reporting that ticket sales for the film ran 50 percent higher than typical film releases at local theaters.[27]

Annapolis and *Salute* both appeared as the Navy Department received an increasing number of screenplays from the studios; the navy assisted some, but not all. One especially difficult case arose in 1928 when Lt. D. L. McCarthy wrote the Navy Department regarding his film screenplay entitled "The Big Gun" that he intended to pitch to the major film studios in Hollywood. He argued to the head of the Bureau of Navigation that the navy should emulate the army, which had recently been the subject of the successful film *The Big Parade*. McCarthy reported that his unfinished screenplay supported expansion of the merchant marine to bolster national prosperity, which would in turn require a larger navy for support and protection. The ONI labeled the scenario submitted by McCarthy as "propaganda" and called one scene in which a corporation used its own submarines to attack a foreign navy "ludicrous." Ultimately the navy refused to provide any cooperation on the grounds that it could not approve a story that "constitutes propaganda for a bigger Navy and Merchant Marine," a decision that ultimately led to the cancellation of the project.[28] McCarthy's screenplay, if produced, would have put the navy in a difficult position of sanctioning criticism of contemporary naval policy by one of its own officers, which certainly violated the "silent service" ethos.

Given the increasing numbers of screenplays and the lack of a recent, clear statement of policy regarding cooperation with film productions, action was needed to bring clarity to the navy's relationship with the studios. In December 1928, the head of the Bureau of Navigation, Rear Adm. Richard H. Leigh, suggested to the Chief of Naval Operations that a permanent board be created to review motion picture scenarios and determine the appropriate level of cooperation. Secretary of the Navy Curtis Wilbur approved the proposal, creating a standing Motion Picture Board in January 1929. The Navy Department Motion Picture Board consisted of four permanent members: the Bureau of Navigation's morale officer; the head of the Navy Recruiting Bureau; the officer in charge of censorship and domestic intelligence within the ONI, who monitored attempts at foreign subversion within the United States; and the head of the Information Section.[29]

Assistant Secretary of the Navy David S. Ingalls reformed the Motion Picture Board in 1931 by adding three provisional members from the Office of Ship Movements, the Bureau of Aeronautics, and the Marine Corps. The new orders directed that film studios send all requests for cooperation to the board, but the original orders from 1929 remained largely unchanged.[30]

Between 1929 and 1939, the studios submitted approximately sixty requests for cooperation. The board's members would review the submitted scripts and then make the appropriate recommendation to the Chief of Naval Operations. After accepting a script and cooperating with the subsequent production, the board viewed the completed film prior to its release to ensure compliance with the navy's wishes. The CNO again revised the orders in 1937, but the system outlined in 1929 and 1931 remained in place for the remainder of the interwar period.[31]

If the board objected to a film in any way, it conveyed its objections to the studio and advised how it should attempt to fix the flaws for resubmission at a later date. The recommended changes specified by the board ranged from rewriting specific lines of dialogue to altering significant portions of the film's plot or characters. After accepting a script, the board would advise the CNO, whose responsibilities included notifying any affected ships, stations, or personnel of the decision reached.

Following the conclusion of filming, board members viewed the completed film prior to granting approval for release. The navy also typically received two complimentary prints of each completed film to include in the rotation of the Motion Picture Exchange, which was no small financial consideration as complete copies normally sold for approximately $1,000 apiece.[32]

The establishment of the Motion Picture Board was a significant step forward for a number of reasons. First, it bestowed upon the Information Section and other groups vast authority in dictating public relations policy. The board's members could not issue orders to cooperate on a film production themselves, but the CNOs all invariably followed the board's guidance. Furthermore, the board placed the Information Section in regular contact with the Recruiting Bureau, thus finally coordinating the actions of these two independent offices. Finally, it was a remarkably efficient method of reaching a national audience. Certainly, wire services and radio networks allowed for national dissemination of news through those media, but identical prints of films would screen across the nation as they moved from theater to theater. Through strategic insertions into the production process, the navy could realize substantial public relations benefits for a small investment of time.

Ultimately, the Navy Department Motion Picture Board accepted a majority of the requests for cooperation because the film studios desired assistance so strongly that they accepted the navy's stringent conditions. Scripts that failed to meet these standards, however, usually did so for one of three reasons. First, the board refused to assist when screenplays called for U.S. Navy vessels to stand in for those of a foreign country, as was the case with Warner Brothers' "Night Watch" (1931) and Paramount's "The Devil and the Deep" (1932).[33] This refusal to depict foreign vessels made it virtually impossible to depict any naval combat during World War I. Some films set during the war, such as *The Seas Beneath* (1931), received cooperation, but the navy rejected a request from Samuel Goldwyn to assist in the production of his proposed film "U-Boat" because it believed that the film might be upsetting to the now-friendly German navy.[34]

Second, the board occasionally argued that concerns about security prevented the navy from offering any assistance in film production. For obvious reasons, the navy preferred not to publicize doctrine or equipment of a sensitive technical nature and rejected screenplays that delved too deeply into such matters. Should such information reach the screen, it might prove invaluable to a foreign navy seeking to advance its own naval technology. For instance, in 1931, the Motion Picture Board denied a request for cooperation on the film "Anchors Aweigh" because it would have displayed images of navy catapults and directoscopes.[35]

Third, the Navy Department Motion Picture Board demonstrated intense concern that inaccurate portrayals of the life and customs of servicemen might reach theatergoers. The aforementioned "Anchors Aweigh" drew criticism for depicting a brawl between a lieutenant and an enlisted man, which, according to one member, "strikes a blow at discipline and self-control in the Navy itself."[36] Surprisingly, the board managed to reach a compromise with the studio that was producing "Anchors Aweigh" and approved cooperation on the film, eventually released under the title *Shipmates*.[37]

The establishment of the Motion Picture Board represented a major step forward for navy public relations, but the board possessed one significant flaw from its conception. The attempt at uniformity in policy could not totally compensate for changes to personnel who composed the board. Scenarios approved for cooperation in one instance sometimes failed to receive the same consideration in others. For instance, the navy approved two films, *Submarine* (1928) and *Men without Women* (1930), that included submarine accidents as major plot elements. Yet, in 1933, the board refused to approve the proposed film "The Goldfish Bowl" for no other reason than it was "unwise to feature submarine disasters" so prominently in motion pictures. In his study of the navy and Hollywood's decades of collaboration, Lawrence Suid notes that "inconsistency became the hallmark" of the Motion Picture Board's decisions.[38]

Several of the screenplays submitted to the board between 1929 and 1932 came from one writer: former naval aviator Frank "Spig" Wead, whose prolific career made him an influential figure in navy public relations. A 1916 graduate of the Naval Academy, Wead first achieved fame in the early 1920s as part of the navy's teams that participated in the Schneider Cup seaplane races, but a freak accident at home in 1926 left him paralyzed and brought his promising flying career to a premature end. While still in the service, Wead had written several insightful articles about naval aviation, and, following his rehabilitation, he capitalized on his skill as an author for a new career. He initially devoted himself to writing fiction for print outlets but soon turned his attention to screenplays. In 1928, Wead served—at the suggestion of future Chief of Naval Operations Arthur Radford—as the technical adviser for the MGM film *The Flying Fleet* (1929) and contributed enough to the writing of the film that he received his first screenplay credit. *The Flying Fleet* became the first film of the interwar period to focus primarily on the development of naval aviation, thus serving as the foundation for Wead's new career.[39]

Between 1929 and 1941, Wead worked on more than two dozen feature films, nearly all of which centered on the navy, aviation, or some combination thereof. He drew on his experiences in the navy to create scenarios and sold his work to several studios, including MGM, Columbia Pictures, and Warner Brothers. Wead's work in Hollywood was a microcosm of the larger relationship that developed between the navy and the film studios. All three parties in this particular relationship benefited: the navy benefited from the positive depictions in Wead's scenarios; Wead profited handsomely from his screenwriting work, which allowed him to pay off his considerable debts; and the studios employed a prolific screenwriter who could facilitate the production of exciting feature films.[40]

To understand Wead's influence and how the Navy Department Motion Picture Board executed its duties, MGM's 1931 film *Hell Divers* provides a useful example for two reasons. First, it was one of the highest-profile films produced in cooperation with Hollywood in these early years of the board and thus carried special significance. In addition, its production process illustrates how the board and its Hollywood studio counterparts negotiated their relationship, especially because the film overcame significant problems that had led to the cancellation of previous projects. The film's genesis dates to 1930 when Wead, fresh off of writing the screenplay for Frank Capra's successful 1930 film, *Dirigible*, began work on a screenplay for MGM initially titled "Sea Eagles." Even in the early days of the project, MGM's representative on the East Coast, William A. Orr, promised the board that "Sea Eagles" would be "an epic of the naval air service" that would require the studio to access the Naval Air Station in San Diego and the San Pedro–based Battle Fleet, which included the *Lexington* and the *Saratoga*.[41] Orr later added, "We believe that this production could not fail to further a tremendous good will from the public to naval aviation" as well as "a clean and wholesome projection of life in the Navy's aviation division."[42] The board preliminarily approved cooperation in January 1931, but it recommended that a technical adviser be assigned to assist the production in order to avoid filming any sensitive equipment or procedures.[43] The navy typically avoided assigning technical advisers to film productions in an effort to avoid favoritism—believing that assigning an adviser would show a preference for some films and studios over others—and adhered to that policy in the case of "Sea Eagles"; however, this decision would cause significant problems in the months and years ahead.

Typically, the film production process called for studios to send in complete screenplays for the board to review and then recommend to the CNO whether cooperation should be extended. The board approved cooperation with "Sea Eagles" based only on a short description of the plot and the projected filming locations in order to allow for MGM to send Wead and a camera crew aboard the *Saratoga* to film the fleet during spring exercises. This was highly unusual as it placed the navy in the possible position of granting MGM permission to film—thus causing MGM to spend considerable money on the project—only to later potentially revoke that cooperation.[44]

MGM finally submitted the complete screenplay for review in June 1931. The plot centers around Windy, an effective but troublesome chief machinist's mate serving as the gunner on a navy dive-bomber aboard the carrier *Saratoga*. His discipline problems and advancing age cause Windy to feel upstaged by a younger gunner, Steve Nelson. The two men's growing professional and romantic rivalry is set against the backdrop of their squadron preparing for and then participating in exercises off the coast of Panama. Both men are shown as heroic and selfless, but Windy ultimately saves his pilot and Steve after the latter's aircraft crashes on a rocky islet. Windy, who is not a trained pilot, ultimately flies Steve and his own pilot back to the *Saratoga*, saving their lives but dying as he crash-lands the aircraft on the deck. Wead's story highlights many of the critical components of contemporary naval aviation, such as the new carriers and a demonstration of their enhanced offensive capabilities, as the air group attacks remote-controlled target vessels during the exercises. The story also includes brief references to the navy's airship program just as its new dirigible *Akron* entered service.[45]

Despite these benefits to naval publicity, the board found many objectionable elements in the film's plot. As relayed to MGM by the board via the CNO, Admiral Pratt, "Our chief petty officers are of a very high type and they would have just cause for resentment should this picture be released in its present form." Specifically, board members believed that scenes depicting Windy borrowing money from his commanding officer, bribing Panamanian officials, and brawling with Steve and other characters in the film would adversely affect naval recruiting. For decades, naval recruiting and publicity had sought to distance the image of sailors from the hard-living days of the past associated with drunkenness, tattoos, and prostitution. Windy's heroism aside, his personality seemed a throwback to that bygone era.[46]

The board proposed a solution: tame, but not eliminate, some of these objectionable scenes and depict Windy as a unique case who pays consequences for his actions. Doing so required changing a scene of Steve and Windy openly fighting to make it appear that the fight started by accident and then escalated in the heat of the moment, and altering dialogue so that Windy's exceptional nature was made explicit to the audiences. The studio, however, kept the scene showing Windy borrowing money from his superior officer, leading to some open difference of opinion among members of the board. The senior member, Cdr. Henry C. Gearing of the Recruiting Bureau, reluctantly accepted this decision and refrained from further commentary until he saw how the scene would be filmed. Meanwhile, Gill's successor as the head of the Information Section, Cdr. Mark L. Hersey, relayed to Orr that the disagreement over the scene was only a minor matter.[47] Ultimately, the board decided that the changes to the screenplay had not fully addressed their issues, but presumably the publicity opportunity for naval aviation outweighed these objections and led them to recommend that the film proceed.

Production on the film continued through the fall with a completed copy of the film finally making it to the board for final review in December 1931 just days before its premiere at New York's famed Astor Theater. Over the summer, Orr had expressed MGM's belief that "Sea Eagles" was not a strong enough title for the film. As such, the completed print bore the film's final name: *Hell Divers*, after the first purpose-built dive-bomber that entered navy service, the Curtiss F8C, in 1925. The board never revived any of the objections raised during production about the portrayal of Windy, and, unlike with some other films, no one ever lodged a formal complaint with the Navy Department about the character's effect on the image of the enlisted force. The review of *Hell Divers*, however, revealed a new problem: the surprising amount of information that could be discerned about U.S. Navy carrier operations from such a film.[48]

As early as the first submission of the film synopsis to the board, *Hell Divers* had required a balancing act between showcasing as much of contemporary naval aviation as possible to an intrigued public while keeping vital matériel and procedures secret. Save for a few dramatized sequences in the film, the visually stunning aerial scenes shot for the film depicted the *Saratoga* and her air group conducting only routine operations, but these scenes still generated considerable alarm. Soon after viewing the completed print of *Hell Divers*, Commander Hersey wrote to Wead, "I am surprised that Comairons [Rear Admiral Joseph Mason Reeves, Commander Aircraft Squadrons, Battle Fleet] let you shoot that stuff for according to Bureau of Aeronautics that is just the stuff the British have been trying to learn from us."[49] The board focused its attention on footage showing aircraft landing aboard the *Saratoga* by utilizing a hook to catch a series of arresting wires laid across the carrier's deck. Even though the United States, Britain, and Japan all had a working understanding of carrier operations and arresting gear, the board feared that one of these competitors could gain an edge with this knowledge.[50]

In response, the Bureau of Aeronautics representative, Lt. Cdr. Frank D. Wagner, proposed cutting several scenes from the film's final print. To Orr and other MGM executives, however, this would create significant continuity issues with the film's

At North Island during the filming of *Hell Divers*, 16 September 1931. (*From left to right*) actor Cliff Edwards; Lt. (jg) John S. Thach, USN; actor Clark Gable; actor (and USNR Officer) Wallace Beery; Lt. (jg) H. S. Duckworth, USN; and Lt. (jg) E. P. Southwick, USN.
Naval History and Heritage Command, NH 80-G-450865, Photographic Section.

The Filming of *Hell Divers*, ca. 1931.
Naval History and Heritage Command, NH 2014.30005, Photographic Section.

plot and potentially harm its box office take. Agreeing on a solution was difficult, and the board and MGM conducted five separate reviews of *Hell Divers* in an attempt to ameliorate all of their concerns, with one of these personally attended by Assistant Secretary of the Navy Ernest Jahncke and Rear Admiral Moffett. In fact, the navy completed its review of the film only after some of the first public screenings of *Hell Divers* had already occurred, including its premiere at the Astor Theater in New York. Only on 26 December did the board and MGM agree to a solution that allowed MGM to substitute the final reel of the film. To address BuAer's concerns, MGM inserted into this reel a very noticeable black bar at the bottom of the screen during all the landing sequences. While the extent of the bar's coverage varied from one landing to another, it obscured much of the carrier deck and the arresting wires from view, thus limiting the film's intelligence value to foreign powers.[51]

While the review process cleared up the matter of the final print, the navy worked for many months to determine the status of the unused footage shot by MGM's camera crew aboard the *Saratoga*. On 22 December 1931, the board wrote MGM requesting that all footage not used for the film be turned over to the navy for inspection. MGM failed to honor this request immediately, prompting Commander Hersey to write Orr again on 1 March 1932 to ask the studio again to comply. Orr later replied that the studio had "junked" all the relevant footage, but the DNI, Capt. Hayne Ellis, remained unconvinced and launched his own inquiry. That summer, Ellis discovered that MGM had shot 136 reels of film for *Hell Divers*. ComEleven, Rear Adm. Thomas J. Senn, secured the studio's cooperation to have this film sent to Washington for censoring. This review lasted for months, and only in early 1933 did the navy conclude that 48 reels of film required censorship and allow the remaining footage to be returned to MGM. As Hersey noted in an unprecedented review of the production process for Captain Ellis, tighter control of the film crew by the ComAirRons could have prevented many of these problems from occurring.[52]

The review and the final disposition of the film failed to quell all the concerns about the film. Some of these came from members of the public who could not, as one man put it, "see the need of the navy or the army lending itself out as a prop, a location for Hollywooders."[53] Other worries stemmed from fears of divulging too much information about carrier operations. In discussing the possible release of sensitive information in two magazine articles in April 1932, Rear Adm. Harry Yarnell, who had succeeded Reeves as the ComAirRons, stated his belief that *Hell Divers* had released far more information about carrier operations into the public sphere than either of the two articles.⁵⁴ Months later, in October 1932, the navy learned via a *New York Times* article that theatergoers in Tokyo had caused traffic jams to see *Hell Divers*, which had been billed as "The Bombing Corps of the Pacific." The film's aerial sequences had also impressed Japanese audiences, but the *Times* reported that *Hell Divers* served as a kind of backdoor propaganda to encourage the further development of the IJN's carrier force.⁵⁵

The production of *Hell Divers* had raised numerous concerns within the Navy Department, but it was not the first time that questions had been raised about the service's relationship with Hollywood. The navy quickly understood the benefit of assisting in film production to boost its image, but, as with the case of Navy Day, the service still sometimes clung to the "silent service" mantra, believing that the less the public knew or understood about its public relations practices, the better. In 1930, a woman named Maud C. Stockwell complained to President Herbert Hoover that the nation's defense establishment should uphold the spirit of the Kellogg-Briand Pact of 1928, which had committed several dozen nations, including the United States, to renouncing war as an instrument of national policy. Stockwell accused the War and Navy Departments of the "use of the screen for purposes of advertising" and called for such practices that encouraged militarism and the glorification of war to be brought to a halt. Admiral Leigh, the chief of the Bureau of Navigation, responded that the navy "does not and, to my knowledge, has not at any time in the past used the motion picture screen for purposes of propaganda" and that films depicting the navy are produced "solely for entertainment purposes."⁵⁶

The board may have presented a unified front to the film studios seeking assistance, but, within the navy, some senior officers objected to the accommodations made to produce these movies. In July 1931, the Navy Motion Picture Board approved a request for cooperation on a film entitled *Mystery Ship*, but the commander of the Battle Force, Rear Adm. Frank Schofield, lodged a complaint about the proposal. Schofield, who three years later would help film director John Ford join the Naval Reserve, cited no specific problem with the film at hand; rather, he objected to the entire scheme of cooperating with Hollywood film studios in any way. Schofield complained that recent support for the filming of *The Seas Beneath* had disrupted the fleet's normal operating routines. In addition, he stated that while the navy cooperated on films in an effort to improve its image, the studios continued to produce such movies as *Shipmates* that Schofield believed to be "injurious" to the service because they conveyed numerous misconceptions to the public about life in the navy. Schofield offered no remedy for this state of affairs except the complete elimination of all future cooperation on commercial films. His proposal still allowed for the filming of events for newsreels, which, ironically, were owned by the same studios whose cooperation he otherwise deemed nonbeneficial for the navy. Schofield renewed his protest the following month when he recommended the navy not participate in the production of a screenplay entitled "Summerville Number Four," arguing that the film would "cheapen the Naval Service in the eyes of the public."[57]

Schofield's protest prompted a reply from the CNO, Admiral Pratt, who saw merit in the work that Schofield detested and provided a clear rationale for the service to collaborate with the film studios. Working alongside the film studios meant that the navy could control its on-screen image, whereas a film produced entirely within the studio remained outside such control. The films generated goodwill among the studios and made it more likely that films released that depicted the navy would provide the service with good publicity and generate recruits. This goodwill also extended to the financial realm as, in addition to the two free prints the navy received, the Motion Picture Exchange could keep its film library current for $250,000 a year, or roughly half of what it might cost to buy films at market rates. The studios absorbed any cost beyond those normally incurred by the navy's normal operating routines, and the rules for cooperation also stated that the filming could not significantly disrupt normal operations. Thus, in Pratt's view, the navy was "well repaid" for the relatively low cost of minor interruptions to its training routines.[58]

Occasionally, the film studios released films that cast the navy in a negative light, which prompted the navy to lobby for edits before and after the films' release in order to exert control over the service's image. The Paramount Pictures film *A Lawyer's Secret* (1931) aroused attention because it showed a sailor gambling away significant sums of money, losing a service automatic in a gambling parlor, and stealing a car while attempting to make it back to his ship before the end of liberty. The navy could attempt to eliminate objectionable film content, as when it persuaded RKO to delete scenes from the film *Sailor Be Good* (1933) after its commercial release, but this was not always guaranteed to succeed. The navy could certainly control content on films that it assisted, but any attempt to compel edits to other films ran the risk of angering the studios. Fortunately for the navy, such films proved exceptions to the rule of a functional and mutually beneficial relationship between the service and the film industry.[59]

Still, the Motion Picture Board did not control every facet of the relationship with Hollywood. By the 1920s, several motion picture studios began producing their own newsreels for distribution alongside their fiction film releases, providing yet another medium for the public to get a glimpse of the navy. While filming of newsworthy events began occurring at the same time as the advent of the medium, the regular production of newsreels began with the creation of the *Pathé Journal* in 1909. The Pathé company distributed this first newsreel in Europe for two years before it began producing the *Pathé Gazette* for American audiences in 1911. The first release of the *Gazette* showed images of European armies marching on maneuvers as well as American warships steaming at sea. During World War I, newsreels became a leading source of news for the public, even though they included much staged footage. Even in these early years, newsreel producers favored visually exciting and easily obtainable material—a practical consideration given the size and clumsiness of many early film cameras—and these two factors continued to determine much of the content that went into newsreels until their demise in the 1950s and 1960s.[60]

By the late 1920s, the transition to sound led to a period of consolidation in the production of newsreels, and thereafter five companies affiliated with the largest film studios dominated the format: Fox Movietone, Hearst Metrotone (MGM), Universal, Warner-Pathé, and Paramount. Most newsreels consisted of roughly ten minutes of total footage, beginning with the primary story and followed by stories of progressively shorter length. The navy required newsreel crews to request permission from the service to film specific events, but the service typically approved these requests. Newsreels benefited from the cooperative relationships established between the studios proper and the service, and the activities of the navy constituted a ready source of footage from which the newsreels could draw when compiling their releases. Ship launchings, commencement ceremonies at the Naval Academy, and the movements of ships and formations of aircraft fit the criteria of easy access, visually exciting, and nonpolitical that typically dominated newsreel content. For the navy, newsreels containing footage of any service activities constituted perhaps the most widely disseminated of all sources of naval publicity. The public may not always have read newspapers with stories about the navy or attended feature films in the production of which the service cooperated, but a filmgoer would almost certainly view newsreels that accompanied feature films.[61]

Even as the Information Section worked to modernize and develop a relationship with an emerging form of media, its officers sometimes contended with a very different set of public relations challenges. During its early formative years, the Information Section operated with some autonomy within the ONI, but this independence did not mean that public relations and traditional intelligence work never overlapped. In the months after the Geneva Conference of 1927, a raconteur named William Shearer came into the public spotlight. Shearer had briefly served as an enlisted man during the Spanish-American War and later, during World War I, successfully sold a plan to the navy to build one-man midget submarines for use in Europe, only to have the contract quickly cancelled due to lack of interest. A suspected larcenist, fraudster, and gambler, Shearer styled himself a "naval expert" and sought connections with the shipping industry, William Howard Gardiner of the Navy League, and the Hearst newspaper syndicate by sometimes writing on naval affairs for the chain. Despite Shearer's connections, the navy's leadership and political allies did not take his expertise seriously. Summing up a private 1924 inquiry into Shearer, Representative Burton French, the head of the House Naval Affairs Committee, concluded "that there is no evidence in the Department that Mr. Shearer has any greater expert knowledge of Naval affairs than is to be expected of an electrician, second class, the rating in which he served as an enlisted man in the Navy, and it is clear that he is unworthy of confidence and ought not to be entrusted with any information concerning the Navy."[62]

After the Geneva Conference, Shearer insisted that his campaign in favor of preparedness had been correct and that the navy had attempted to discredit him by denying his past connections to the service. The following year he published a book, *The Cloak of Benedict Arnold*, that promised a revelation: "A true story of idealism, intrigue, and treachery to destroy the United States as a Sea Power. A lawyer-bound, slave-thinking people, under the lash of internationalism. Both parties are sacrificing America's welfare under the dictates of the Invisible Power."[63] Like Dudley Knox, Shearer believed that subversive pro-British interests had created the arms limitation movement, but he broadened his claim to state, "There is little difference between the British, Japanese, Pacifist, and Bolshevik objective. It is to weaken America."[64] Shearer's screed concluded on a note of optimism, a promise: "The Hope: The crucible that once produced red blood and sturdy hearts will surely give us a leader, a Paul Revere, sounding the alarm and riding the hell over these Babylonian architects who would take from us the sea, and who are spreading the *Cloak of Benedict Arnold* over the younger generation and driving seditious nails into the cross of national crucifixion."[65] Through all of the grandiose claims and the not-so-veiled view of himself as the heroic savior of Americanism, Shearer failed to provide any clear evidence for the allegations contained within *The Cloak of Benedict Arnold*.

Shearer presented a public relations problem for the navy because his pretensions to credibility undermined efforts by the service to portray itself as a reliable defender of the nation's interests and not some rogue bureaucratic entity undermining national policy. Shearer's persistence, however, helped transform his case into a counterintelligence issue. In 1928, he began touting the existence of a letter written by Sir William Wiseman to David Lloyd George in 1919 wherein Wiseman claimed that a British espionage campaign had fomented pro-British sentiments in the United States to facilitate a return of the country to the British Empire. This wild claim led Captain Johnson to interview Shearer via telephone about the provenance of the letter in January 1929. Even though the ONI had begun investigating the matter, Shearer wrote President Hoover in February contending that a lawyer could provide additional documentation to verify the letter's contents.[66] The ONI continued to seek more information and suggested to the officer investigating Shearer that "if you have an opportunity I should say by all means ransack the gentleman's office with the object of finding out just what his game is. Though he appears rabidly pro-navy and an exaggerated form of Anglophobe, yet his activities usually react to our discredit. I have a feeling that a careful perusal of his confidential files would disclose something of a great deal of interest."[67]

The matter came to public attention in August 1929 when Shearer sued shipbuilding firms for failure to pay him more than $250,000 in lobbying work conducted at Geneva. Shearer claimed that while in the employ of the shipbuilding companies, he sought to sabotage the negotiations to ensure the resumption of construction in private yards. The navy's involvement stemmed from claims that Shearer acquired information and encouragement from several senior naval officers while in Geneva. Adm. Hillary P. Jones, the navy's member of the delegation at the conference, was believed to be beyond reproach, but Shearer's allegations led to a Senate investigation into the links between the navy, shipbuilders, and private lobbying concerns. The charges, if true, threatened to destroy the credibility of the Navy Department with respect to national defense and preparedness. It was one thing for naval officials to speak their minds, even if their opinions ran counter to present policy, but quite another if the Navy Department actively had been undermining the policies set by its civilian leadership.[68]

Shearer's efforts had no real discernible effect on the outcome of the Geneva Conference, but the allegations continued to swirl. Congress at first focused its attention on the shipping magnates who hired Shearer, but, on 26 September, *Baltimore Sun* columnist Drew Pearson alleged that several naval officers had aided Shearer's lobbying efforts, including Rear Adm. Joseph Reeves and Rear Adm. Frank Schofield in addition to naval historian Cdr. Holloway H. Frost. Appearing before the committee, Reeves denied the allegations and reiterated that the navy supported an "equitable" system of arms limitation as a means of guaranteeing certainty in the size of navies at home and abroad. Speculation about the navy's involvement in the affair receded after Reeves's defense, but the entire imbroglio did not end until June 1930 when the Senate declined to file an official report on its investigation.[69]

Shearer's zeal had attracted William Howard Gardiner's attention at a time when the latter's own increasingly suspect judgment created rifts within the upper echelons of the Navy League. Navy Day remained unaffected, although circumstances often prompted some year-to-year variations in the conduct of the celebration. The 1928 celebration was a muted affair because the league chose not to distract attention away from the heated presidential campaign between Hebert Hoover and Alfred Smith. The league returned to its former levels of activity in succeeding years, but the navy itself ultimately subsidized a greater portion of Navy Day activities for both 1929 and 1930.[70] So long as the celebration still enjoyed the league's official sponsorship, the navy's leaders felt increasingly emboldened to divert its own resources into Navy Day.

In 1930, the ascension of Admiral Pratt to CNO and the onset of the Great Depression presented two new challenges to the league's commitment to Navy Day. The Depression had a significant impact on economic activity during the first months of 1930, and the escalating crisis brought into question the expenditures incurred by the service to conduct the promotion. Pratt initially questioned the value and utility of many of the key components of Navy Day celebrations, especially the financially costly dispatch of ships to port cities all along the coasts. When the Navy League presented Pratt data regarding the past successes of Navy Day in drawing visitors and public attention to the fleet, the CNO ultimately agreed to participate in the celebration that year and made a public speech to mark the occasion. In the end, the level of press coverage and attendance continued to remain high. By this point, the regularity of the event allowed the league to reduce its Navy Day expenditures because sufficient momentum had been created to allow for regular coverage of the event absent the prompting and requests that had marked previous Navy Days.[71]

Although Navy Day became popular, self-sustaining, and inextricably linked to the Navy League, the organization remained a target for criticism. In February 1931, Representative Burton French, an ardent opponent of naval expansion, alleged on the floor of the House that the Navy League served as a front for arms manufacturers and other industries with a vested interest in naval expansion. The chairman of the Navy League's board, Walter Bruce Howe, drafted a strong reply to French in which he itemized the league's sources of income, denied the remaining charges, and reaffirmed the league's support for naval construction within the confines of the treaty limits. While French overstated possible ties with industry, he remained unaware of the deep connection between the league and the Navy Department. His allegations created a more cautious atmosphere within the league, some of whose members feared an eventual investigation into its activities. When the organization circulated a draft of the minutes of an executive committee meeting held in June 1931, member James W. Wadsworth was appalled at the level of detail regarding the league's present and future activities included in the transcription. He wrote Howe that future examples of meeting minutes should be written more vaguely so as to avoid "embarrassment" for the league and any of its supporters should any outsider ever view them. Howe recognized the value in Wadsworth's warning and pledged that the group would not produce such detailed records of future meetings.[72]

By the fall of 1931, Gardiner had been at the forefront of Navy League policymaking for nearly a decade, but his presence and personality started to become liabilities for the league and its desire to promote naval expansion. Gardiner provoked a public feud with President Hoover when he issued a press release on 28 October 1931 entitled "The President and the Navy." The communiqué attacked Hoover's proposed cuts in naval spending as rooted in "abysmal ignorance," believing belt-tightening would force the United States to fight "bigger and bloodier wars" and subordinate American naval policy to foreign powers.

Gardiner had shown some restraint in the past in his criticisms, but the press release brought forth a wave of denunciations from the nation's newspapers, eventually leading to the resignation of some Navy League members in protest, most prominently the wife of Rear Admiral Yarnell. The attacks also angered the Naval Order of the United States, whose commander general, Rear Adm. Albert Gleaves, exhorted his organization and its companions to support Hoover in this matter. Hoover even organized a committee stocked with political allies to investigate the league's accusations, but the committee's final report issued in late 1931 noted only some factual errors in Gardiner's release but otherwise ignored the opportunity to discredit the league further or to defend the president.[73]

Gardiner's attacks on President Hoover's naval policy created a deep schism within the Navy League itself. Other members of the league, particularly Howe, disapproved of Gardiner's decision to criticize the president, and the disagreement between the two men ended their long-term friendship. In May 1932, Howe informed Gardiner that he would not continue serving as the league's chairman unless he was allowed to approve all Gardiner's writings prior to their public release. Given that Gardiner had written nearly everything released under the league's auspices since 1921, such loss of control represented an affront to Gardiner's authority, but he ultimately consented to the restriction. This arrangement did not last long because, in 1932, disputes over the Navy League's fund-raising efforts again led Howe and Gardiner into open conflict. Gardiner enlisted other league members' support by arguing that Howe's inattentiveness toward fund-raising in recent years had limited the organization's ability to operate, although Gardiner's controversial attacks likely complicated fund-raising efforts. At a pivotal meeting in January 1933, Gardiner maintained his hold on the league's presidency, thus precipitating Howe's withdrawal from the organization and that of several other long-standing and prominent members.[74]

In addition to coordinating with other elements of the Office of Naval Intelligence and the Navy League, the Information Section also facilitated coverage for one of the traditional forms of publicity: covering major movements of the fleet. Doing so presented the navy with a delicate balancing act of guaranteeing access to all media outlets that wished to cover the events while maintaining operational security. The navy's annual Fleet Problems offered excellent opportunities for news coverage, but the exercises of the latter 1920s were limited affairs. Fleet Problem IX in 1929, however, represented a public relations opportunity because the new carriers, the large converted battle cruisers *Lexington* and *Saratoga*, participated for the first time. For the exercise, the *New York Times* employed a retired Royal Navy officer, Lewis Freeman, to serve as a correspondent and sail with the Battle Fleet as it steamed toward the Pacific coast of Panama. This access afforded the paper excellent coverage of the mock mass aerial attack on the locks of the Panama Canal by the carrier *Saratoga*'s air group, and even Secretary of the Navy Wilbur noted in his annual report that the coverage of Fleet Problem IX earlier that year was "unusually accurate."[75] Still, the public relations value of the Fleet Problems remained secondary to their importance for training, and, in spring 1930, the navy blocked all media access from Fleet Problems X and XI in the Caribbean to keep the proceedings secret.

Following the Fleet Problems, the Information Section worked that spring to coordinate press coverage for a fleet review off the Virginia Capes in late April with President Herbert Hoover and numerous other political figures and luminaries in attendance. Although the navy initially considered granting open access to the media, the large numbers of guests attending and the desire to manage visitors aboard the ships caused the service to limit more strictly the number of media invitations granted. In all, the navy approved access to representatives from four major wire services, three photographic services, three silent newsreel producers, and two sound newsreel makers. All were assigned to either the carrier *Lexington* or the transport *Aroostook*.

The navy also took great care to maximize the publicity value of the event by staggering the release dates of the news depending on the medium. They dictated that newswire services could release their stories first, but that sound newsreels went last. The only stipulation given by the navy to the various correspondents was that they not use navy communications equipment to file their reports and that any photographs or films taken aboard ship could be subjected to possible censorship. The navy ultimately proved so accommodating to the press that it granted a request by Paramount Pictures to have a blimp overfly the fleet during the review for the sole purpose of providing different camera angles for the event.[76]

In 1932, the navy attempted an entirely new method for covering Grand Joint Exercise 4—a massive exercise held in conjunction with the army and similar in size and scope to a Fleet Problem—and Fleet Problem XIII. These exercises, held in Hawaiian waters and between Hawaii and California, respectively, posed significant challenges for the navy. Race relations on the islands were on edge because, in September 1931, five local men allegedly raped the wife of a sailor, Thalia Massie. Inconsistencies in Massie's story led to a mistrial. In January 1932, just weeks before the fleet's scheduled arrival, Massie's husband, Tommie; her mother; and other accomplices kidnapped and executed one of the five defendants. The social tensions prompted ComFourteen, Rear Adm. Yates Stirling, to prohibit sailors from going ashore after the completion of Grand Joint Exercise 4 and complicated attempts to coordinate press coverage of the maneuver.[77]

Both exercises had regular press correspondents, but, rather than send a journalist, the Associated Press employed Capt. Charles M. Austin, the assistant chief of staff to the commander, Battle Force, to cover the exercise on its behalf. The regulations permitted Austin to serve in this capacity, and he began issuing releases even prior to the start of the exercises. Austin's permission to work for the AP did not include any provision to clear his articles prior to release, presumably because, as a senior officer, he would know what material should and should not be publicized. In fact, the navy allowed Austin's releases to go out immediately rather than holding them until the maneuver's conclusion. This confluence of factors quickly became a problem because, on 3 February, the *Washington Star* and other papers published Austin's release that divulged information about the fleet's communications equipment and cryptography capabilities.[78] Nothing Austin printed was classified, but this was still sensitive information. The director of naval communications asked that Austin not release any additional information on the subject because the recent release of Herbert Yardley's *The American Black Chamber* had given the public the impression that the navy lacked a cryptology unit and he did not want Austin's releases to alter that perception.[79]

More difficulties occurred in Fleet Problem XIII. For the second exercise, Austin wrote his eight releases in advance and submitted them for inspection and transmission on specific dates. Even these precautions failed to prevent yet another complication. The exercise featured the airship *Akron*, which served in its designed role as a long-range scout in advance of the fleet. In a release dated 14 March, Austin stated that the Blue Fleet advancing on the West Coast relied on secrecy to evade the defending Black Fleet, but that the latter would rely on submarine and airship patrols to locate Blue. This portion of the release was acceptable, but Austin also claimed that the *Akron* possessed limited capability to be an effective scouting craft. Making matters worse, the *Washington Post* and many other prominent newspapers published Austin's release. The DNI argued that Austin violated Article 114 of the U.S. Navy Regulations, 1920, which allowed officers to report on activities of the fleet so long as the information was of public interest, did not violate security, and, most importantly for Austin, did not contain the author's personal opinions.[80] The release profoundly displeased Rear Admiral Moffett, who said that Austin's article "[justified] the belief that the author [had] little if any knowledge of the capabilities of airships or of the fundamental principles entering into their operations."[81] Of added concern to Moffett was that Austin's status as an officer gave the article additional credibility that Moffett felt was undeserved because it threatened his continued efforts to support airship development.

Other than an unofficial written rebuke, Austin escaped punishment for both of his publishing problems, but the episodes highlighted the lingering issues with the navy's execution of public relations policy. On the one hand, by centralizing public relations into a single headquarters office, the navy's leadership made it easier for the service to communicate with the public with a unified voice and ensured that the navy's image would not need to rely on the fortuitous appearance of gifted messengers as in the days of Luce and Mahan. On the other hand, the demands on the small Information Section stretched its manpower to the limit, and the creation of the Navy Department Motion Picture Board only added to its responsibilities. Thus, while it did not necessarily need a Luce or a Mahan, the section still needed officers like Austin to help disseminate publicity and compensate for its own understaffing. In addition, Austin's work meant that the navy could avoid bringing correspondents aboard ship when senior leaders decided that security concerns outweighed regular press coverage. Even though the navy had some justification to complain about Austin's performance as a correspondent, the episode demonstrated the relative ease with which officers who engaged the public could run afoul of official policy and the navy's "silent service" culture.

Surprisingly, in the midst of such a chaotic period, the navy made a minor but symbolically important change to its public relations office in 1931. The Information

Section was so named in 1922 because of its mandate to collect and disseminate appropriate naval information to the public, but also so as to not attract attention from Congress or the public about its purpose. Even as some of the section's practices and methods remained conservative, the navy finally embraced its mission by bestowing upon the office a new name: the Public Relations Branch.[82] Fittingly, this change occurred with no formal announcement or fanfare. Furthermore, the branch remained a part of the ONI and did not receive any additional manpower to execute its duties, but its new name reflected the added importance the office had assumed after ten years in operation.

By the end of 1932, the Public Relations Branch had dealt with a number of significant challenges. The Shearer episode revealed that the boundary between intelligence and public relations could blur easily, though the case's resolution offered little guidance for how to handle similar challenges in the future. The Navy League, whose influence had historically waxed and waned, hit a trough due to internal disagreements and ill-considered criticism of President Hoover. Captain Johnson and Commander Gill brought organizational legitimacy and professionalism to the branch, but the former found it difficult to dramatically improve relationships with the press. Despite these challenges, the success of the navy in forging virtual partnerships with the Hollywood studios provided a vastly important new tool for the service to reach the public. This notable achievement would help set the stage for continued development of navy public relations in the following years even as onetime foes and erstwhile allies sought to upset the international system.

◄ 4 ►

COMPATIBLE WITH MILITARY SECRECY

NAVY PUBLIC RELATIONS, 1933–1939

In late 1935, Warner Brothers sought to secure the cooperation of the Navy Department in a prospective submarine picture. The Navy Department Motion Picture Board found nothing objectionable in the proposal, having previously cooperated in the production of *Men without Women*, *Submarine*, and *Pigboats* earlier in the decade. The CNO, Adm. William H. Standley, accepted the recommendation, but, in a rare twist of events, the commander in chief of the U.S. Fleet, Adm. Joseph Mason Reeves, later pleaded with Standley to rescind the cooperation. His argument ran against the grain of more than a decade of official policy and practice: "a fertile field for the activities of foreign agents has been and is, either directly or indirectly, the news reel, motion picture, and news agencies." Reeves, a naval aviation pioneer who had risen to command the entire fleet, thought that exposing submarine operations to the public could be dangerous because "the filming of the aerial picture 'Hell Divers,' despite the fact that it was censored and supervised, gave to foreign naval air forces the benefits of at least five years advantage in this field which the United States at that time held. A repetition of this should by no means be permitted for our submarine service."[1] Reeves's strident opposition, based on his interpretation of production of *Hell Divers*, led to the project's cancellation. Ultimately, Reeves won the battle and lost the war; Warner Brothers and Columbia would both soon receive cooperation on separate submarine films, *Submarine D-1* (1937) and a remake of Capra's *Submarine* retitled *The Devil's Playground* (1937), respectively.[2]

The episode revealed two significant trends that defined navy public relations in the latter 1930s. First, it provided yet another reminder that the navy's seemingly clear policies on the types of films that could receive official sanction were subject to wide interpretation. Second, and more importantly, Reeves's complaint highlighted the growing difficulty of reconciling the needs of publicizing the service with the requirement to maintain secrecy. This was especially important now that the navy had developed fertile relationships with every form of mass media by the mid-1930s. As the international situation worsened in the latter part of the decade, this dilemma only became more pronounced. Yet, the fact that Reeves's strident criticism of the Warner Brothers submarine film only temporarily abated production demonstrates that the navy had finally understood the value of publicity. If the navy closed ranks and denied all contact with the mass media, it risked sacrificing the gains it had made since the dark days of 1921. The officers of the Public Relations Branch, however, would find ways of executing their mission in spite of pronounced security restrictions.

The election of Franklin Delano Roosevelt to the presidency in 1932 heralded a shift in the navy's political fortunes that reinforced the efforts of the Public Relations Branch. While Roosevelt continued to support the naval arms limitation agreements, he and the Democratic majorities in Congress—especially Representative Carl Vinson of Georgia and Senator Park Trammell of New York—displayed far greater interest in ensuring that the fleet be built up to the limits of the Five-Power Treaty. The bipartisan support for naval construction leading up to World War I had disincentivized and hindered the development of public relations policy within the navy, but this was not to be the case in the latter 1930s.

The Roosevelt administration also encouraged government agencies to engage openly in public relations work, a marked change from previous administrations. FDR's administration issued frequent press releases, particularly during his first two years in office, and often tailored news for rural newspapers with low circulation. New Deal agencies eagerly embraced radio as a means of spreading news and information to a wide audience efficiently, and the president famously used the medium to great advantage via his "fireside chats." These new agencies also realized that while maintaining a steady flow of information to the public certainly helped promote their activities, the withholding of information from the public could often be just as effective in shaping agendas. Interestingly, the favorable relationship between the press and the administration soured somewhat after 1935, but Roosevelt still managed to use this to his advantage as his personal attacks on the media could arouse the public's mistrust of the media.[3]

Thus, the Navy Department benefited from newfound political support and found itself in a more welcoming environment toward government public relations. The historical waxing and waning of navy public relations suggests that the increased political support for naval expansion might have curtailed the work of the Public Relations Branch. Instead, the leaders of the Navy Department had seemingly learned the lessons of their predecessors who had reduced their publicity once the immediate threat had passed. Thus, at no point did the navy's senior leaders give serious thought toward undoing the organizational development accomplished by the Information Section over the previous decade.

Events occurred in the months just before and after Roosevelt's inauguration that showed just how much the navy's public relations practices had evolved. The Navy League had occupied a key role in publicity efforts for decades, but feuds had torn apart its leadership. In January 1933, during the lengthy "lame duck" period between Roosevelt's election and inauguration, the Navy League held a critical meeting to discuss issues raised over the previous three years of controversy caused by William Howard Gardiner's unprecedented criticism of President Hoover. The discord instigated by Gardiner and his allies had led to significant fund-raising issues that threatened to drain the league's reserves and put the organization in a state of financial limbo not experienced since immediately after World War I. Gardiner, however, remained resolute and maintained his hold on the league's presidency, forcing other prominent individuals such as Walter Bruce Howe to resign their positions in protest. The victory proved Pyrrhic, however, as Gardiner finally stepped down as president later that year, replaced by Nathaniel Hubbard. He continued to play a role in shaping news releases, however, and these releases remained sharply critical of Great Britain as well as the continued reluctance in the United States to build up the fleet. As a result, the league finally stripped Gardiner of editorial power and established a public relations subcommittee to clear all future news releases. Still, the continued problems complicated Hubbard's efforts to attract new funding sources, thus limiting the league's ability to assist the navy's own public relations activities save for Navy Day.[4]

But the league's internecine conflict opened up space for the Public Relations Branch to take more control over the navy's public image. In October 1933, the ONI finally released an update to its 1923 *Intelligence Manual* to govern all the organization's assigned duties. For the first time, the manual included a list of policies and best practices for public relations. The earlier manual had made no mention of PR despite having been issued more than a year after the creation of the Information Section, but the decade's worth of experience acquired since its publication provided plenty of lessons to include in the updated version. Additionally, while many policy directives governing public relations practices had been issued by both the secretaries of the navy and the service's uniformed leaders, the 1933 *Intelligence Manual* constituted the first practical guide for how to interpret and execute those duties. This is especially important as there is no evidence that the navy's public relations officers ever read any of the nascent theory of their profession, such as Walter Lippmann's *Public Opinion* (1922) or Edward Bernays's *Crystallizing Public Opinion* (1923) and *Propaganda* (1928). Doctrine not based on a clear knowledge of the underlying theory of the profession was perhaps an imperfect solution, but its issuance ensured a greater degree of continuity for the Public Relations Branch and guidance for officers with less knowledge of PR practices.

The 1933 *Manual* offers key insights into the state of navy public relations at the time while reinforcing the primacy of the Public Relations Branch. First and foremost, it named the ONI as the collector, analyzer, and disseminator of all types of naval information, a broad mandate that included public relations. To fulfill those responsibilities, the manual stated the ONI should "provide for and maintain cordial relations with the public, the press, and other new agencies, with a view to proper dissemination of naval matter and pertinent information."[5] It also collected into a single volume the many policy directives governing photography, motion pictures, and press access issued over the past several years. These included the now-common reminders to prevent the leakage of confidential information to the public and to ensure, except perhaps in cases of movie production, that all press outlets be granted equal access to stories and events.

The manual spelled out the clearest advances in public relations policy in the guidance for district intelligence officers (DIOs). From 1924 to 1927, the navy set aside billets for reservists to serve as public relations officers in the naval districts, but the end of this program had forced the undermanned Public Relations Branch to coordinate all such activities. The 1933 *Intelligence Manual*, however, directed that the DIOs conduct public relations duties when necessary, such as liaising with local and regional press outlets and veterans groups. Given that this was a new policy, the amount and specificity of guidance was much more extensive than that provided to the officers of the ONI. For instance, the guidelines forcefully directed that the Public Relations Branch could assist the DIOs in coordinating special events and the like, "but the Press Officer himself must make earnest efforts to find *news*. Every effort must be made to stick to *facts*. Official statements should be quoted, and opinions and controversial matters avoided."[6] This guidance codified the practices that had been in place with navy press releases since the inception of the Information Section.

Furthermore, the *Intelligence Manual* decreed, "Successful press relations are based, first, upon securing, classifying, and preparing interesting releases for the press, which may include illustrations; second, upon the release of such news to the proper sources in such a way that it will be presented in the proper light, and be given its due importance in the press." DIOs should make it known that they are available to the press at all times and that all information released must be "*authentic*."⁷ Finally, the manual extolled the virtues of networking by reminding the DIOs that "friendly contacts are of inestimable value from a service standpoint. The value received will be proportionate to the ability of the contact officer to sell the navy and to win support. Courtesy in dealing with civilians is an excellent investment. The relations between officers and newspapermen should be sincere and cordial and should reflect a high standard of mutual confidence and respect. Goodwill should be the keynote. The Press should not have to beg for news and the Navy should never beg for space."⁸

Interestingly, the *Intelligence Manual* only accounted for the official *peacetime* duties of the ONI and DIOs but contained a number of radical assumptions about a hypothetical wartime public relations policy. According to the manual, the onset of war would lead to the creation of a large, civilian public relations agency that would oversee all activities in a manner reminiscent of George Creel's Committee on Public Information during World War I. With no wartime need for a navy Public Relations Branch, the service would instead fully decentralize the public relations function by adding considerable manpower to each District Intelligence Office and creating a subordinate District Press Branch.⁹ These plans show that, even after ten years of peacetime operations and while serving in a PR-friendly political and social climate, the ONI viewed its control over PR as temporary. Still, these wartime hypotheticals only occupied a small part of the text devoted to public relations and did not detract from the otherwise considerable policy and organizational advances contained in the 1933 manual.

The *Intelligence Manual* had codified a decade's worth of orders and practice even though fiscal shortfalls had curtailed the use of the Navy Band. This occurred even though during the first year of Roosevelt's term, Congress passed the Vinson-Trammell Act, which, along with a portion of the preceding National Industrial Recovery Act, sought to use funding of public works projects such as shipbuilding to stimulate the economy. This did not immediately trickle down to the Navy Band, which had lacked the funds to tour since 1932. Nevertheless, the public continued to adore the band as evidenced by the continued popularity of its radio shows and the existence of a strong market for the dozens of phonograph recordings of the band's concerts. In early 1933, however, the Navy Department attempted to cancel the radio broadcasts of Navy Band concerts. It eventually relented when listeners sent a deluge of complaint letters to Secretary of the Navy Claude Swanson. Despite its small size and limited budget, the Navy Band achieved a national reach during the interwar period and added to the navy's prestige by showing that "poets" served in the navy. Eventually, in 1936, the Navy Band had its funding restored, finally allowing it to go back on the road.[10]

Still, the main effort of navy public relations remained focused on disseminating publicity through the mass media. As the number of consumers of movies, radio, and print media only continued to grow in the 1930s, the policies outlined in the 1933 *Intelligence Manual* became even more necessary. One factor not fully accounted for, however, was how to deal with the growing multimedia conglomerates of the day, especially one as influential and controversial as William Randolph Hearst's. By this time, the Hearst empire included a large newspaper chain, a movie production company, and a prominent newsreel outlet. Hearst columnists could even be heard by millions of Americans over their radio sets. As a professed advocate of a vigorous national defense with a strong battle fleet at its core, Hearst had a well-developed political and military philosophy and the means to attract millions of Americans to his causes. Thus, for the navy's leaders and its undersized Public Relations Branch, devising a consistent policy for managing interactions with Hearst's various and vast holdings proved a daunting challenge. In fact, for all of Hearst's vaunted support for navalism, he and his employees often created more problems than they solved.

Even before Roosevelt's first inauguration, Hearst sought to filter the American people's hopes and dreams for the incoming administration through the film *Gabriel over the White House*, released in January 1933. Produced under Hearst's own Cosmopolitan Pictures imprint through a distribution deal with MGM Studios and starring Walter Huston, *Gabriel over the White House* tells the story of President Judson Hammond, an ineffectual and corrupt leader wholly incapable of confronting the Great Depression. A car accident puts Hammond into a coma, but the archangel Gabriel—represented in the film by a breeze blowing through a White House window—transforms the president into an activist leader who stops at nothing to solve the nation's "problems." Hearst toned down the revolutionary politics of its source novel of the same name and instead inserted his own political views, particularly concerns over lingering European debts from World War I, Prohibition, and national defense. To accomplish the tasks before him, Hammond declares martial law, dissolves Congress after it attempts to impeach him, and, in a nod to another long-running concern of Hearst's, dramatically solves the naval arms limitation problem. In the film, Hammond demonstrates to foreign leaders the power of American military might and thus compels them to accept true disarmament. As fictional President Hammond gives a speech aboard an American battleship to foreign dignitaries, in which he derides previous attempts at naval limitations as inequitable to the United States, a horde of naval aircraft attacks several battleships moored in the distance and sinks them. The scene reflected Hearst's growing interest in the destructive capabilities of air power, but also his own beliefs on naval disarmament: the Five-Power Treaty and the London Naval Treaty of 1930 were products of European subterfuge and thus fatally flawed agreements. To Hearst, only disarmament backed by American might and benevolence could bring about a lasting peace. Hearst resisted interference on the project from Louis B. Mayer, the production head of MGM, who, after receiving a request from Roosevelt himself, insisted to Hearst that the speech's setting be changed from the deck of a battleship to the presidential yacht. Hearst only agreed to the change so long as he felt the scene retained its power to persuade audiences.[11] The *Motion Picture Herald*'s review cited the scene as Hammond's "last grand gesture," but audiences did not regard the film highly and it made only a small profit for the studio.[12]

By the date of *Gabriel over the White House*'s release, Hearst had been advocating for a strong fleet for nearly four decades using the media empire he had built starting with the *San Francisco Examiner* in the 1880s. By adopting methods pioneered by Joseph Pulitzer's *New York World* that incorporated a mix of salacious content and hard journalism at a low price, Hearst's media reach grew substantially in the decades that followed. Hearst described his business strategy in 1922: "Try to get scoops in pictures. They are frequently as important as news. . . . PAY LIBERALLY for big exclusive stuff and encourage tipsters. . . . Make a paper for the NICEST KIND OF PEOPLE—for the great middle class. Don't print a lot of stuff that they are supposed to like and don't. . . . Be Fair and Accurate."[13]

Hearst's media outlets voiced some of the fiercest opposition to the Washington Conference, yet this outlier stance had not affected his company's bottom line. Indeed, Hearst embarked on a major expansion of his print media holdings during the early 1920s, and this segment of his empire reached its peak size in the mid-1930s. In 1937, Hearst owned papers in nearly every major market in the country and boasted a circulation of 6.9 million papers for weekday editions and 7.3 million for Sundays. Total daily readership of the papers in the Hearst chain totaled approximately 30 million people or just shy of one-quarter of the entire population of the United States at that time.[14]

During this period of rapid growth, Hearst maintained close editorial control of the newspapers in his chain via wire services and through a series of editors with whom he maintained contact. This gave Hearst the ability to affect the size, content, and even the placement of stories within his newspapers. When revenues declined during the early years of the Depression, Hearst began placing editorial pieces in prominent positions on the front of his papers. Hearst wrote some of these, but other writers, such as James T. Williams, also contributed. In this vein, the Hearst-owned *New York Daily Mirror*, a nationally syndicated tabloid, helped popularize the columnist and naval reservist Walter Winchell. Hearst personally approved all editorials that were published across the Hearst line, a system that allowed him to conduct sustained personal campaigns in favor of issues close to his heart.[15]

With these vast holdings at his disposal, Hearst could propagate his view of the United States and its place within the international system, of which the navy occupied a key place. In his writings, Hearst zealously advocated maintaining American sovereignty and freedom of action within an international system that he viewed as predatory and covetous of American success. He believed American diplomats lacked the guile necessary to stand up to their European counterparts, which prevented the United States from receiving repayment on war debts incurred during World War I. He generally distrusted disarmament as practiced in the 1920s and 1930s and viewed the various naval arms limitation treaties as a British conspiracy to limit American power. Hearst also frequently warned his readers about the rise of Japanese power in his writings. In fact, Hearst often alleged that Japan and Britain secretly maintained the naval alliance formally abandoned at the Washington Conference, putting the U.S. Navy at a distinct disadvantage in a potential war. As a result, Hearst's America sat isolated and surrounded by potential threats, and only a strong navy—backed by a strong land-based air arm—could guarantee American security.[16]

Hearst's jingoist view of sea power could also be propagated by his burgeoning film business. Throughout his professional life, Hearst maintained a strong interest in the film industry, and his power granted him considerable influence among industry leaders. Louis Pizzitola argues that Hearst understood the ability of images—particularly moving images—to transfix the public mind. Even prior to the turn of the twentieth century, Hearst experimented with early film technology and assisted in the production and promotion of films shot during the Spanish-American War. He later used the medium during his unsuccessful campaign for the governorship of New York in 1906, and over the next several years he experimented with films using a mix of real and staged footage designed to sensationalize contemporary events. In 1914, Hearst financed his first feature film and five years later formed Cosmopolitan Pictures to focus on feature film production. Between 1919 and 1924,

Cosmopolitan distributed its films though Paramount Pictures, but afterward Hearst shifted affiliations to Metro-Goldwyn-Mayer.[17]

Hearst's most direct interactions with the navy came after the commercial failure of *Gabriel over the White House* helped end the Cosmopolitan-MGM partnership, leading Hearst to sign a new distribution deal with Warner Brothers Pictures the following year. Hearst's contract with Warner Brothers called for the two companies to collaborate on twelve films over two years, and for Cosmopolitan to receive 30 percent of the net receipts for each of the films produced. Four of these films were showcases for Hearst's longtime companion Marion Davies, but Warner Brothers retained the right to select which eight films on its production schedule would receive the Cosmopolitan label. For Warner Brothers, Hearst's media holdings became the primary consideration as the studio sought to choose films that would receive the biggest benefit from coverage in Hearst's newspapers. Naturally, Warner Brothers selected films that reflected Hearst's political viewpoints, and four of these—*Shipmates Forever*, *Devil Dogs of the Air*, *Submarine D-1*, and *Wings of the Navy*, all directed by Lloyd Bacon—had naval themes.[18] It should be noted that since these films were all selected during or after their approval by the Navy Department Motion Picture Board, production proceeded smoothly under the friendly auspices of Warner Brothers.

Hearst's support for the navy was also reflected in the various newsreels his company produced during the interwar period. He first began producing newsreels in 1913 when he partnered with William Selig to distribute newsreels nationwide under the banner of Hearst's International News Service. In 1920, Hearst began distributing his *International Newsreel* through Universal, and in 1927, he began producing a second newsreel, this time for MGM. Two years later, Hearst became affiliated exclusively with MGM and produced a silent newsreel and a new sound reel entitled *Hearst Metrotone News*. From its inception, the *Hearst Metrotone* newsreel quickly gained a reputation for controversy reflective of the style often associated with Hearst's newspapers. The newsreel also displayed a definite pro-navy stance, giving politicians such as Representative Fred Britten and Senator Frederick Hale a national forum to attack the London Naval Treaty and other arms limitations agreements. It is unclear how audiences reacted to these particular scenes, but the dislike of Hearst and his politics expressed in some segments of the public led to negative reactions toward the screening of his newsreel. After the chorus of boos grew with each screening and picketers threatened to block entrances to theaters that played Hearst's newsreel, *Hearst Metrotone News* became *News of the Day* in 1936.[19]

Even though the navy's leaders never went out of their way to court Hearst, any public dissatisfaction with Hearst threatened to taint the service. Hearst remained a divisive figure throughout his life and held many views that contradicted his navalist sentiments, such as supporting a strong air force or sympathizing with fascism as when he invited Adolf Hitler and Benito Mussolini to produce articles for his newspaper syndicate. Some of Hearst's causes, such as isolationism and anticommunism, did not necessarily conflict with the navy's interests, but the service had to contend with the possibility that the public would see the service as tainted as long as it received Hearst's endorsement. As it was, naval officials maintained their distance from Hearst and avoided any direct prodding for support of naval policy. Through it all, Hearst's advocacy of a strong navy gained the service increased visibility, but the navy had little control over Hearst or his mercurial views.[20]

The case of columnist and radio host Boake Carter helps illustrate the promise and frustration of the navy in working with Hearst's empire and also the continued overlap of public relations with traditional intelligence work. Carter, the son of an Englishman born in Azerbaijan, first rose to fame as a newspaper columnist, but by the 1930s he was a nationally syndicated radio host and the narrator of *Hearst Metrotone News*. His broadcasts proved incredibly popular, but he never shied away from discussing controversial topics in his show. Like Hearst, Carter supported a vigorous national defense undergirded by a strong navy, but, in late 1933, he grew increasingly critical of naval aviation and argued in favor of a strengthened Army Air Corps and an enlarged bomber fleet. The sudden change so alarmed Cdr. Jonas Ingram, the head of the Public Relations Branch (1932–34), that he wrote Cdr. William D. Kilduff, the Fourth Naval District's intelligence officer, to ask that Carter be investigated for having fallen under the spell of a "disgruntled manufacturing concern that is not getting government contracts." The ultimate goal for Carter, according to Ingram, should be to "convert him" to the cause of a strengthened naval air arm.[21] To hedge his bets against any failure to persuade Carter to support naval aviation, Ingram also requested assistance from Cdr. Sidney M. Krause at Philadelphia's Naval Aircraft Factory, writing that "the time is nearly ripe for us to unload a load of bricks on him" because of rumors that the Army Air Corps had endorsed his tirades.[22]

Once again, jealously guarding the service's image had led the ONI to investigate potential public relations threats, but initial inquiries apparently bore no fruit. In fact, Carter soon broadened his criticisms of the navy from aviation matters to include seemingly minor slights such as the perceived failure to invite a relative of Civil War–era Adm. John L. Worden to the launching of his namesake destroyer in October 1934. ComNine, Rear Adm. Wat T. Cluverius, thought Carter's remarks tended dangerously close to "seditious thought" and recommended pressuring Carter's sponsor—the radio manufacturer Philco—by threatening a product boycott.[23] The director of naval intelligence, Capt. William Puleston, instead approached Walter Winchell, a prominent radio host and columnist for Hearst's holdings—in a semiofficial capacity—due to the latter's Naval Reserve commission—to look into Carter's status, observing, "It is possible that [Carter] is a plant to interfere with the up-building of the Navy—by bringing general discredit to the Navy Department. On the other hand, he may be one of those misguided fanatics who believe everything that Billy Mitchell says."[24] Winchell's examination also seemed to yield nothing substantial, but, for the next two years, the ONI asked CBS radio to forward transcripts of Carter's broadcast for review, and the cancellation of these reviews in 1936 was contingent on Carter never "again break[ing] out with such unwarranted, misleading attacks as he formerly did."[25] Much of the tracking and proposed retaliation against Carter occurred behind the scenes, and the willingness to resort to subterfuge indicated that the "silent service" culture remained in place even in the mid-1930s. Furthermore, even if much of the posturing never led to concrete action, it again highlighted the dangers of associating public relations with counterintelligence.

Whether because of Hearst's ability to court unwanted controversy or the desire to grant equal access to media outlets, the navy never showed any favoritism toward Hearst. This, however, did not mean that the service would not court allies who could generate favorable publicity outside the bounds of traditional news. By the 1930s, comic strips had become entrenched as a popular feature of most major American newspapers, and, while their creators typically avoided controversial subjects such as religion and politics, they did attempt to infuse contemporary trends into their strips. Within this context, a navy-themed comic strip entitled *Don Winslow of the Navy* entered syndication in 1934. Its author, Frank Martinek, served in the Office of Naval Intelligence during World War I as the fleet intelligence officer for the Asiatic Fleet. He became an early proponent of scientific investigation techniques, including fingerprinting. Martinek shared his expertise with other members of the ONI and helped organize its Physical, Chemical, and Photographic Laboratory. He continued this work after the end of the war as an agent for the Bureau of Investigation—the forerunner of the modern Federal Bureau of Investigation—but left public service for a career with Standard Oil.[26]

Despite his transition to civilian life, Martinek remained in close contact with some officers still serving with the fleet, including Rear Admiral Cluverius. In 1934, Cluverius, whose Ninth Naval District included the Great Lakes Naval Training

Station outside Chicago, remarked to Martinek that the navy still had difficulties in appealing to recruits from the Midwest. That same year, Martinek published a juvenile fiction book entitled *Don Winslow of the Navy*, which he loosely based on his own career with the ONI and as an investigator. Cluverius's suggestion about recruiting inspired Martinek to transform Winslow into a comic strip character. Martinek and Leon Beroth, the strip's artist, quickly found a publisher with the *Chicago Daily News*, then headed by Frank Knox, the future navy secretary. Knox helped sell the strip to the Bell Syndicates, and Martinek's creation soon graced the pages of more than 150 papers across the country. Martinek's series and the character became so popular over time that they crossed into other forms of media: a weekly *Don Winslow of the Navy* radio show began in 1937 that eventually led to film serials in 1942. Not until the 1950s did production cease on the *Don Winslow of the Navy* books and comic strip.[27]

Since Martinek based Don Winslow partly on his own experience, the character engaged in intelligence and counterintelligence work rather than shipboard service. The books and strip depicted Commander Winslow, along with his band of sidekicks—including a disabled admiral who was his superior officer; the admiral's daughter; and his loyal subordinate, Lt. Red Pennington—constantly battling the forces of the Scorpion. The Scorpion had no national affiliation but, from his "secret" base in the South China Sea, plotted to bring the United States and other peace-loving countries into a state of general war. Martinek claimed to infuse the stories with as much "authentic Navy" material as possible and assured readers that, "since Don Winslow is approved by the Navy Department, I cannot allow him to do anything that is contrary to the ideals, traditions, or motives of the Navy." Interestingly, in 1937, when a listener of the *Don Winslow* radio show complained that it propagated "insidious militarism" to young American boys, the navy stated that the program was "in no respect sanctioned, supported, or inspired by the Navy."[28] As with "Spig" Wead's screenwriting career, Martinek had been encouraged by friendly naval officers, but his independence provided useful cover for the service to distance itself when circumstances required.

Martinek had found an ideal vehicle through which to reach America's youth, but the navy continued to rely on Hollywood to publicize its work to the majority of the public and broaden its influence. The continued presence of former naval officers within the film studios also worked to bring an extra level of familiarity to the increasingly close relationship between the navy and Hollywood. Wead continued to produce a profligate number of naval- and aviation-themed screenplays into the latter 1930s, and other officers attempted to break into the business alongside him, including Lt. Daniel A. Frost, who wrote several "Navy stories" with an eye toward selling a script to the studios. His efforts failed, but, perhaps not coincidentally, Frost eventually joined the Public Relations Branch in late 1937.[29]

The relationship with Hollywood deepened in the 1930s to include not just the studio heads and Wead but also several film directors. Producers employed by the studios held the most power in the movie industry at the time, but directors occupied a prominent creative position within the studio system. By the mid-1930s, multiple directors with naval experience were working in Hollywood and often found themselves directing naval-themed productions. These included Christy Cabanne and Lloyd Bacon, both of whom sometimes relied on their knowledge of the service when making naval-themed films. A third director, John Ford, helmed a quartet of films set in the service and entered the Naval Reserve in 1934. With the backing of Rear Adm. Frank Schofield, Ford taught courses on the uses of photography, and some of these emphasized the use of film for propaganda. Cabanne, Bacon, and Ford combined to direct more than one hundred films during the latter 1920s and 1930s. Their navy films made up only a small percentage of their total output, yet the three accounted for one-third of the film collaborations between the navy and the motion picture industry. The studios also drew on their naval experience to aid in the production process or the promotion of these films upon their release.[30]

These allies certainly facilitated the navy's close relationship with Hollywood, but, by the mid-1930s, the stability created by the Motion Picture Board had become the primary reason for the growing number of navy films at a time that historian Laurence Suid labels "the golden age of navy movies."[31] The seemingly constant string of film releases that had received cooperation did not go unnoticed by members of Congress. Multiple inquiries with the Navy Department seemed intent on gathering information about how the system of cooperation worked, but the navy's responses fell short of full disclosure. In 1934, Senator Elbert Thomas wrote the Navy Department after reading a column by Arthur Brisbane in the Hearst-owned *Washington Herald* praising the recent film *Devil Dogs of the Air*, which mentioned the assistance the navy provided in producing the film. Secretary of the Navy Claude Swanson replied, disingenuously, that the navy only cooperated in "rare cases" with the production of commercial films and that "it is believed that the benefits derived by the Navy in having appropriate scenes of Naval life presented to the public in good pictures, more than compensates for the amount of work involved." In 1936, Representatives Arthur Lemneck and Thomas Amlie—the former an Ohio Democrat, the latter a Wisconsin progressive and frequent collaborator of Senator Gerald Nye, whose committee was then investigating the so-called "merchants of death" thought to be responsible for luring the United States into World War I—requested information on every instance of collaboration between the navy and Hollywood in the last two years. CNO Adm. William H. Standley responded that the navy only cooperated on films that "acquaint our citizens with their Navy" and that these films were not intended to give the general public "a view of propaganda or a glamorous presentation of the Navy."[32] While the navy rejected assisting with the production of blatant propaganda pieces and sought to dispel notions of using the film industry for such a purpose, naval officials nevertheless perpetuated the "silent service" culture by evading any direct examination from outside sources, including from sitting members of Congress, that had guessed at the depth and scope of its cooperation with the motion picture industry.

As an organization responsible for national defense, the navy needed to strike a balance between transparency and security as it sought to develop a publicity apparatus. In fact, it is this tension that drives much of F. Donald Scovel's earlier analysis of navy public relations.[33] During the early years of the Roosevelt administration, the enthusiasm for publicity waxed thanks to experience and also the many formal and informal relationships to external media and organizations. This dynamic stood in contrast to the 1920s when cautiousness and a lack of organizational familiarity defined the early work of the Information Section. However, things slowly began to change, and, by the middle of the decade, security concerns began to play a larger role in shaping policy and decisions on publicity efforts.

The increasingly uncertain international situation certainly helped force a reevaluation of this balance. German rearmament had only just begun to alter the balance of power in Europe by 1935, but, in any case, the navy's leaders paid little to no attention to that development. As had been the case earlier in the interwar period, Japan remained the navy's primary concern. Japanese leaders willingly had participated in the arms limitations process at Washington and agreed to the collective security pacts that mostly stabilized the western Pacific and capped the Imperial Japanese Navy's capital ships at 60 percent of American and British tonnage. The London Naval Treaty of 1930 had granted the Japanese 70 percent of U.S. cruiser tonnage, but the domestic politics of arms limitation in Japan had changed considerably since 1922. Japan's military leaders pressed for expansion in China and chafed at the restrictions placed on their country by the Western powers under the previous agreements. Thus, on 29 December 1934, the Japanese government announced its intention to withdraw from the Washington and London agreements. The second London Naval Conference began in late 1935, but Japan formally exited the proceedings in January 1936 before the signing of the new treaty. Japanese intransigence did not immediately start a new arms race, but it raised tensions to a level not seen in many years.

As might be expected, this more security-conscious environment led to some aspects of navy public relations drawing increased scrutiny. Rear Admiral Cluverius and other officers tolerated, if not encouraged, Frank Martinek for his relatively light, adventurous take on naval intelligence and spycraft, but this acceptance did not extend to a pair of potential film projects. In early February 1935, MGM sought cooperation for *Murder in the Fleet*, a film depicting the attempted espionage of naval fire-control equipment aboard an American vessel. In addition to showing foreign agents aboard ship, the film also implied disloyalty of Filipino messmen.[34] These objections were significant, but the board also expressed discomfort with depicting the navy's involvement in espionage or counterespionage activities. Given the intelligence backgrounds of some of the board's members, they disliked the idea of their work gaining any public notoriety and thus discouraged the production of films that featured the service's involvement with clandestine operations. As a result, the navy denied MGM's request for cooperation but, curiously, later allowed the studio to film a few exterior shots aboard the cruiser *Louisville* so long as the navy's assistance remained unacknowledged.[35] As *Murder in the Fleet* was in production, the board rejected a screenplay, "Soldiers of the Sea" (1935), because of the inclusion of "communistic sequences" and the potential release of information about aircraft operations and the use of shipboard antiaircraft guns.[36] Both of these projects clearly ran afoul of the board's unofficial rules against certain types of film content and demonstrated how much more seriously the navy looked at the security implications of films over some other media.

As even slight projects such as *Murder in the Fleet* tested the navy's new emphasis on security, maintaining personnel strength would be vital. In April 1935, the Marine Corps attempted to reclaim its enlisted billet assigned to the Public Relations Branch. This enlisted marine served as an orderly, with duties including stenography and delivering navy press releases to the headquarters of patriotic organizations and "administrative and publicity centers" in Washington. A marine had been performing these duties since 1923, but Maj. Gen. John H. Russell, the commandant of the Corps, explained that the shortage of enlisted men in the Corps necessitated the elimination of a position that was initially intended only as an expedient. The acting chief of naval operations, Adm. J. K. Taussig, vetoed the removal because it would force the department to either employ a civilian messenger or rely wholly on commercial messenger services to distribute its material; oddly enough, Taussig never broached the idea of assigning an enlisted sailor to the branch. According to Taussig, removing the marine would disrupt the office at a time when "its activities have expanded and its responsibilities increased."[37]

Keeping even a lowly orderly within the branch proved especially important as the following month Secretary Swanson issued a series of policies that increased the amount of oversight on matters of publicity. These new directives defined in greater detail how the navy would interact with outside groups, and all showed that, at least in some respects, the service would not automatically shy away from publicity in spite of the international situation. General Order No. 32 regulating naval equipment allowed the navy to turn over obsolete equipment to museums and other public entities for display in public settings. Should a modern piece of equipment or technology be exhibited, the order required that it be escorted by naval personnel who were to monitor it at all times. General Order No. 36 allowed commercial advertisers to specify in their ads that the navy used their product, subject to review by officers of the naval district in which the ad was produced and released. Perhaps most importantly, General Order No. 9 granted naval officers permission to publicly express their opinions but warned that the release of any information the Navy Department found objectionable would be deemed an "offense against military discipline."[38]

Even as Swanson's general orders signaled the navy's continued engagement with the public despite international tensions, the Public Relations Branch sought to maximize the benefits of the relationship with Hollywood on presumably less controversial projects. By 1935, the head of the branch, Cdr. Paul H. Bastedo, desired to link the navy's prestige and cachet to high-profile film releases, and, as with the earlier example of *Hell Divers*, the service had to overcome some significant obstacles to do so. The on-screen dance pairing of Fred Astaire and Ginger Rogers that began with RKO Pictures' film *Flying Down to Rio* (1933) had yielded hits with *The Gay Divorcee* (1934) and *Top Hat* (1935). For the couple's next on-screen outing, RKO sought the navy's cooperation to produce *Follow the Fleet*, a partial adaptation of the play *Shore Leave* that RKO had previously adapted into a successful 1930 musical *Hit the Deck*. RKO had requested and received minimal navy assistance in producing the earlier film, but filming amidst the fleet offered an air of authenticity for a dance film that required extensive soundstages. In addition, RKO attempted to build goodwill by reminding the Motion Picture Board that Rogers had served as "Navy Girl" during a previous Navy Day celebration, leading Lt. A. D. Blackledge of the Public Relations Branch to state that "the Navy likes to feel she is one of its own."[39]

Yet, the navy's cooperation with *Follow the Fleet* was by no means assured. RKO's producers felt some concern that their request might fall on deaf ears, so they approached the MPPDA—whose leaders had remained on very favorable terms with the navy since the group's inception—to make first contact. Their request also stressed that filming could be completed in five days and would only require access to the deck of a battleship and perhaps one or two smaller vessels. One early reviewer of the script labeled it "innocuous" and believed it warranted cooperation, but the board found numerous faults with the script's depiction of enlisted men and shipboard customs.[40]

Recognizing that the incredible publicity opportunity outweighed any concerns he or others may have with the script, Commander Bastedo vigorously argued in favor of cooperation with RKO. First and foremost, Bastedo pointed to the success of the previous Astaire-Rogers pairings: "*Follow the Fleet* is a medium with a naval background for what is probably the most attractive and popular combination now on the movie stage—the Fred Astaire, Ginger Rogers, Irving Berlin combination. . . . There are no heroics. The final production, if it follows the last two productions by this combination, will be clean, amusing, attractive, and distinctly popular. This combination has just completed a five-week run at the Keith's Theater here in Washington." Furthermore, he reasoned that "the benefit to the Navy lies in the above and in the fact that Fred Astaire will certainly popularize sailor men throughout the country." Bastedo believed that the board's refusal to cooperate with the production *Murder in the Fleet*—with its depictions of lax security and shipboard espionage—had led to an unnecessary public relations headache that should not be repeated. By extending the limited cooperation requested by RKO, as Bastedo advocated, the navy could exert some control over the production by forcing changes to the script and thus ensuring that the public saw its sailors in a more wholesome light.[41] Factoring in the popularity of the previous Astaire-Rogers films did not require any great insight into the movie industry on Bastedo's part, but his advocacy on behalf of the project demonstrated a savvy not usually displayed by his predecessors in understanding the benefits of attaching the navy's prestige to a production so popular and attractive.

Bastedo's plea persuaded the board to accept the script, but it required numerous adjustments prior to filming. These included minor alterations such as requesting that RKO change the setting of a sequence from Gibraltar to a new location, but more significant objections included the staging of an entire dance sequence aboard a battleship deck, showing officers drinking wine aboard ship—a practice outlawed in 1914—and enlisted men striking an officer during a melee on deck.

This latter scene represented an especially serious breach of naval discipline. RKO studio representatives ultimately agreed to the changes requested in order to retain navy cooperation with the production.[42] Bastedo's battle on the film's behalf was ultimately vindicated when the film became a hit at the box office.

Shaping *Follow the Fleet* constituted a victory for Bastedo and again signaled the navy's continued intent to engage the public, but security concerns remained at the forefront for the Public Relations Branch. In April 1936, just months after the film's release, the ONI issued an updated *Intelligence Manual* that superseded the 1933 version. Even as many of the specific guidelines remained unchanged, the tone of the new *Intelligence Manual* regarding public relations notably differed. In explaining the navy's information policy, the manual guided officers to "keep the public informed of the activities of the Navy, compatible with military secrecy."[43] This statement symbolically redefined the information environment in stark terms intended to influence how intelligence officers interpreted their responsibilities in this realm.

The new policies also strengthened the position of the Public Relations Branch as it directed all Navy Department bureaus to coordinate with and forward all requests for information to the branch for dispensation.[44] The manual also included an entirely new section titled "Emergencies" that offered guidance on PR crisis management; it encouraged openness and promptness stating, "Withholding information at once breeds suspicion and curiosity. Where carelessness or blame is involved, to attempt to hide it may easily be the surest way to have it paraded and exaggerated."[45] On balance, the 1936 *Intelligence Manual* built on the clear directives released in 1933, but it embraced the need for heightened information security while continuing to encourage a vigorous public relations establishment. In many respects, the manual's seemingly contradictory tone would be reflected in the execution of policy over the next few years.

Most of the renewed emphasis on security occurred away from public view, but, at times, outsiders noticed the change. Reporter Oliver Pilat of the *Brooklyn Eagle* claimed that the navy was at the highest level of security since the end of World War I. The navy prevented all photography and even written descriptions of the ships under construction at the New York Navy Yard. Navy Day had remained, as ever, an annual publicity bonanza marked by public access to ships and stations all across the country, but, as Pilat lamented, "Even on Navy Day, when shops in the Navy Yard used to be thrown open to visitors, the shops are now represented by posters in the streets and each building is guarded like a walled town."[46] To the navy's credit, Admiral Standley took Pilat's criticisms so seriously that he forwarded the article to all naval districts so that the commandants could raise awareness among the press outlets in their districts and obtain their "cordial and intelligent cooperation" in helping to maintain fleet security.[47]

In this heightened state of concern, even a recruiting film became subject to investigation. In October 1936, a recruiting inspector in New York discovered that a private individual held more than 3,000 feet of film originally filmed by Paramount Pictures aboard the heavy cruiser *Tuscaloosa* for use in a newsreel. Paramount eventually declined to use the film, so the Recruiting Bureau acquired and edited the film for a recruiting short, *Let's Join the Navy*. It was standard procedure for newsreel producers to request permission from the Navy Department to film and then send their reels to ComThree for censorship.[48] Cdr. F. E. M. Whiting of the Recruiting Bureau had observed Paramount's crew aboard the cruiser and helped to censor the film on the spot, but not all of the duplicate material had been accounted for. Whiting darkly lamented of the duplicate reels that, "probably earmarked 'Confidential,' they are undoubtedly in the 'morgue' of this company under the care of a $20-a-week clerk."[49] Left unaddressed was how the film had ended up in the hands of a private citizen in the first place, but Whiting's proposed solution that the navy develop all newsreel film at the producer's expense would help prevent further spillage of classified material.

This incident indicated the navy's desire to control information released to the public, yet it also showed both confusion and sloppiness, which appeared on other occasions too. Aviation and submarines existed at the leading edge of naval technology during the mid-1930s and also constituted significant parts of the navy's publicity efforts, but these innovations were just the tip of the spear for a force structure designed to wage a transpacific campaign against "Orange": Japan. As early as 1935, the ONI sought to keep the logistical underpinnings of that transpacific fleet hidden from public view. To facilitate significant repairs in the western Pacific and to limit the number of transits from theoretical battlegrounds to the major shipyards on the West Coast, the navy built a series of floating dry docks, capable of accommodating a battleship, that could be towed to forward harbors and lagoons for ready use.

Keeping the docks secret proved absurdly difficult and laid bare much confusion about which equipment and capabilities should remain classified. In spring 1935, Captain Puleston refused a request from Republic Steel to use photos of the Auxiliary Reserve Dock (ARD-1) in a series of advertisements, stating that the navy "desires a minimum of publicity" for ARD-1 and all future floating dry docks.[50] This refusal to release information ultimately had little effect as the existence of the docks themselves was not a secret, just some of their capabilities. *Popular Science* eventually published an article by Alden Packard Armagnac titled "Monster Dry Docks Keep Our Navy in Fighting Shape" about ARD-3 in its February 1937 issue that included sketches of its design. The publication prompted the new CNO, Adm. William Leahy, to launch a "discrete investigation" about the possible leak of classified information, but the chief of the Bureau of Yards and Docks, Rear Adm. Norman M. Smith, correctly noted that it was likely very easy for Armagnac to cobble together all of the necessary information from disparate sources—in this case, via an 18 November 1936 press release, a *New York Herald Tribune* article, and inquiries by the reporter to a shipyard—to construct an accurate portrait of the dock.[51] Admiral Smith followed up his response with a note that two officers had been rebuked from publishing articles about ARD-1 out of security concerns even though the navy's new docks differed little in design from private-sector floating dry docks. The attempt to keep the docks out of public view finally ended the following month when an AP dispatch with an unknown source prompted the *San Diego Union-Tribune* to report that ARD-3 would participate in upcoming fleet maneuvers. At this point, the ONI saw that further investigation seemed fruitless and let the matter rest.[52] Clearly, some in the navy had thought the docks should remain a secret, but this decision was never coordinated across the Navy Department or even with the Public Relations Branch.

Within this security-conscious environment, people not previously identified as possible threats to the navy became much more suspect. In 1934, Commander Ingram wished to offer information to a freelance writer and artist, L. U. Reavis, who had been attempting to work with the Navy Department for several years. Ingram ultimately decided that the worsening international situation prevented him from releasing publicly information about ships under construction. Reavis continued to make inquiries in the years that followed, causing the ONI to increasingly view him as a possible security threat. In summer 1937, he attempted to inspect and photograph the submarine *Cuttlefish*, intending to produce cross-sectional drawings for magazines. When the navy denied requests, he persisted by asking specific questions about the submarine's capabilities, which then prompted the ONI to interview him for counterintelligence purposes. Reavis told his interviewers that he desired to become the navy's "semiofficial artist" to publicize new ships. His interviewer, Lt. Cdr. Courtney E. Taylor, reported, "I informed him that the Navy Department did not want to attempt to educate the American public in the details of ship construction, that the Navy Department would not object to his drawings as long as they were wrong—the more incorrect, the better." Taylor strongly recommended that the navy not disclose any information to Reavis in the future because he "could be used by foreign interests, innocently or otherwise, as an unlimited source of information on new developments."[53] The matter did not end here, however; in February 1938, CNO Admiral Leahy directed that any additional requests for information from Reavis be immediately reported to the ONI.[54]

Despite the appearance of these myriad security issues, the Public Relations Branch continued to seek out new publicity opportunities. As the navy's public relations officers learned, the renewed focus on security would not squelch their work or invalidate the years of accumulated lessons they had learned about their craft. The close relationship with Hollywood that allowed naval officers to acquire considerable organizational knowledge about the film business eventually developed into business savvy. With this knowledge, some officers advocated that the navy should cooperate on more prestigious projects. This would require the service to begin focusing on the quality of the product and not just the quantity.

By the mid-1930s, a typical show at an American theater involved newsreels, animated shorts, a lesser movie typically referred to as either a "B-movie" or a "programmer," and finally the feature film. Feature films received the largest budgets, had the biggest-named stars, and stood a much better chance of enjoying a long life in circulation as prints of these films moved from theater to theater. B-movies, naturally, enjoyed none of these advantages, but allowed the studios to develop on- and off-screen talent and fill the need for more films. While the quality of B-movies varied and sometimes resulted in favorable publicity, feature films offered the best opportunity to showcase the navy to the American public.

The Motion Picture Board began to express some doubts about the value of B-movies during the production of Columbia's *The Devil's Playground* in 1936. The film was a sound remake of the 1930 Frank Capra film *Submarine*, a silent film that had depicted a love triangle between two enlisted men and a woman and, as its climactic sequence, portrayed a submarine accident and the heroic rescue of the crew. In fact, *The Devil's Playground* changed little about the overall plot of the first film. One of the members of the board recognized that Columbia intended the film to be a B-movie and argued against cooperation, believing that the public would recognize the "cheapness" of such a remake. Curiously, the board collectively rejected the screenplay of the remake citing its demeaning characterization of enlisted men and the "unnecessary worry" the film might cause for the families of submariners by depicting a submarine accident. Still, the CNO, Adm. William H. Standley, desired that Columbia Pictures be given the opportunity to revise the script. The studio eventually chose to cooperate with the navy only because the service could otherwise block the reuse of stock footage from *Submarine* for inclusion in *The Devil's Playground*.[55]

The concerns expressed during the production process of *The Devil's Playground* and the success of *Follow the Fleet* seemingly demonstrated the value of supporting popular feature films. Commander Bastedo may have been the first to press for an emphasis on feature films, but a concern over film quality began to spread to other officers in the ONI, Public Relations Branch, and Recruiting Bureau. In September 1937, Lt. Cdr. Courtney Taylor of the ONI wrote the board that the low cost of producing films that received navy cooperation had inadvertently led to these pictures being released not as feature films but as B-movies. This relegation of navy films to the lesser half of a double-bill, Taylor argued, "result[ed] in a saturation of public interest in Navy pictures."[56] As an example, he argued that MGM had recently explored producing a feature set at the Naval Academy but had eventually switched the setting to West Point. This project, released later that year and titled *Rosalie*, bore some similarities to *Follow the Fleet* because its martial setting served as a vehicle to showcase the dance talents of a rising studio star, Eleanor Powell. Taylor estimated that *Rosalie* cost MGM $1.5 million to produce, a hefty sum for the day and well above the typical $200,000 cost for a B-movie, but that two of the most recent films that received navy cooperation, *Wings over Honolulu* and *Annapolis Salute*, cost approximately $100,000. To remedy the situation, Taylor recommended that the board flatly refuse to approve any future scripts that would not result in a feature production. Taylor's memo made a compelling case for the Public Relations Branch to further emphasize the quality of publicity over quantity and to make the navy appear more extraordinary, but this would come at a cost. Rebuffing requests from the studios likely would dampen their enthusiasm to continue working with the navy, so the possible "saturation" that concerned Taylor seemed worth the cost.

Although the Motion Picture Board never formally adopted Taylor's advice, other members shared his concerns about low-quality B-movies. A few lesser studios collectively known as "Poverty Row" only produced B-movies, and one of these companies, Monogram Pictures, submitted a script titled "The Marines Are Here" to the board in May 1938. One board member, Lt. Cdr. S. H. Hurt, found nothing overly objectionable in the film but felt it had "so little entertainment value that it is regretted that the naval service is presented."[57] The studio had not requested cooperation, but Hurt recommended that the board's disapproval be lodged with the company. Admiral Leahy, however, took Hurt's criticism even further in his letter to Monogram, warning, "The Navy Department desires that picturization of naval subjects maintain a higher standard than shown in the subject picture. Future photoplays of the type similar to 'The Marines Are Here' will be considered as not maintaining the desired standard."[58]

Debates over these projects focused on quality, not security, but both issues came to a head in 1936 as Warner Brothers sought to make a new submarine film. Reeves's objections to the studio's submarine film the previous year effectively killed the project, but this did not prevent Warner Brothers from trying again the following year with a Wead-penned script titled "Submarine Story." Wead worked with members of the Motion Picture Board through the summer of 1936 to craft a story that would pass muster, but, again in a nod to the shortcomings of the production process with *Hell Divers*, he also requested that a technical adviser be assigned to the picture to limit security concerns on the spot rather than deal with the years of investigations after the fact. Wead also leveraged his naval background in drafting the letter that studio liaison Hal Wallis sent to the Motion Picture Board formally requesting assistance. Still, even with Wead's background and insider guidance from the Board, a review of the early script noted eighteen possible security issues. Despite this, the board thought Wead's story so strong that it recommended cooperating on the project.[59]

Because of the navy's reluctance to reveal current technical or operational details about submarines, the production process proved a challenge for both the navy and the studio. The navy desired to assign a technical adviser to the project to ensure that the camera crews did not shoot any sensitive equipment aboard the submarine, but it balked at the studio's request for the adviser to follow all their movements, not just their time aboard ships and at stations, as unnecessary. Eventually, Lt. Cdr. (Ret.) G. W. Dashiell, who had joined Warner's payroll, served as the adviser.[60] Even with his assignment, the navy took many steps to ensure that no confidential material ended up on-screen. Well before filming began, the head of the Public Relations Branch, Cdr. Frederick G. Reinicke, wrote the commander of Submarine Squadron Two, Capt. Ralph Edwards, with constructive advice: "We have found that it is much better to limit and restrict photographers on the spot than it is to depend on censoring a picture afterwards."[61] Edwards took the guidance seriously, but he later noted that this task proved difficult because of the "vagueness as to what is confidential." For instance, the navy allowed exterior shooting aboard older boats that included the firing of a deck gun. Even though the scene was to be staged so as to block out any confidential material, Edwards thought "there [was] nothing particularly confidential about it."[62] The new regulations prevented the filming of submarine launchings, so the navy furnished the studio with stock footage from an old recruiting film. The navy heartily approved of the finished film, retitled *Submarine D-1*, but even such a hands-on process required last-minute adjustments to the prints prior to release in late 1937.[63]

Follow the Fleet and *Submarine D-1* both had technical advisers, indicating that the navy had finally overcome its long-standing objections to assigning advisers to oversee both screenwriting and production. Initially, the navy frowned on the practice and believed that providing advisers would become a burden on the service as every studio would request one. In addition, the "silent service" ethos played a role as the navy also harbored fears that the public would disapprove if it discovered just how closely the service and film industry worked together. Because of these concerns, the navy had shown considerable reluctance in assigning active-duty personnel to advise the studios. As this aversion decreased, some active-duty officers served in this capacity, but it also represented an important outlet for retired officers, such as Dashiell and Cdr. Harvey Haislip, who worked as an adviser for several MGM projects and eventually received a screenwriting credit for *Flight Command* (1940).

No clear policies existed governing the work of technical advisers, but these officers could address many issues, including security, during the production process. They fulfilled three basic functions, all of which ultimately benefited the service and the film studios; first, they increased the level of accuracy and, by extension, the "navy" atmosphere of the films. Given the importance the navy attached to films favorably depicting the service and its customs, the assignment of advisers meant that the films they worked on could better ensure a positive portrayal of the service. The second benefit accrued by both the navy and the studios was the assistance rendered by technical advisers in eliminating potentially objectionable material in the screenplays even prior to their review by the Navy Department Motion Picture Board. This reduced the amount of time the board needed to review film scripts and saved the studios money, both of which were valuable commodities within the factory-like nature of the studio system. Finally, as seen with Captain Edwards's involvement with *Submarine D-1*, they could ward off any potential security problems in advance.[64]

The lack of clear policies for technical advisers and continued inconsistencies in the board's approval process became evident in 1938 due to a pair of competing naval aviation projects. In January, Warner Brothers submitted a script titled "Pensacola" for review. In an especially unusual circumstance, the board and the Bureau of Aeronautics had each assigned an active-duty officer—Capt. Arthur L. Bristol and Lt. Aurelius Vosseller, respectively—to work as script advisers prior to submission, indicating a high level of interest in the project. The studio, however, initially ignored their advice and submitted a screenplay that emphasized a love story the studio's representative described as "a little more honest, and a little more adult than the type of thing that we, or any other company, have attempted before." This greatly displeased the board, which had assumed it would receive a heroic picture.[65] Lieutenant Commander Taylor wrote a devastating review of the script, stating that it "will make the lousiest motion picture in years—does not portray, even remotely, the Navy service." He added, "If this picture is allowed to be made, it will kill all chances of a good picture based on Pensacola training being produced" and that "the Story of Pensacola training is incidental to a muggy love story. It is nauseating."[66]

In nearly all other circumstances, the reviews—all of which shared Taylor's strong displeasure with the project, albeit not articulated in such harsh teams—would have been enough to stop the project from proceeding further.[67] The subject matter, however, appealed enough to the board and, more importantly, to the Bureau of Aeronautics, that the studio was granted an opportunity to refashion the script. After a month of strenuous effort, the board approved a heavily revised script that BuAer deemed "excellent publicity."[68] The finished film, retitled *Wings of the Navy* and directed by Lloyd Bacon, eventually reached theaters in February 1939 but not before an advance screening for members of Congress, Roosevelt's cabinet, and naval officers in the D.C. area.[69] The *Motion Picture Herald* praised the film while declaring that its subject matter "fits the national and international situation, the newspaper headlines of the world and the box office needs of the American exhibitor like a glove fits a fist."[70]

As Warner Brothers' Pensacola project got under way, Columbia Pictures submitted its own naval aviation training script to the board titled "Heroes Come High." As with the earlier project, the board strongly disliked the original script. One board member found it so problematic he informed his colleagues that it "does not deserve an official critique" due to numerous problems, including an overemphasis on a "chief instructor" who had no real-life counterpart at Pensacola, the weakness of the training staff in handling ill-behaved cadets, and several inaccuracies in its depiction of training procedures.[71] Perhaps because the board deemed the script unsalvageable or because of the considerable investment in a competing project, "Heroes Come High" never received the necessary endorsement, thus ending the project.

As always, the vagaries of the movie production process made it easy for the navy to carve out an oversight role to manage content and security, but this level of control and coordination still did not extend to the radio networks. In fall 1937, WNYC radio agreed to broadcast a series of talks by a naval reservist, but ComThree, Rear Adm. Harris Laning, noted in a letter to the ONI that regulations did not require him to submit the scripts in advance. The ONI certainly recognized the reach of radio and its publicity value, but its officers noted that they still had yet to develop a clear and consistent policy for that medium.[72] Capt. Frank Leighton thought that transcripts of broadcasts should be kept on file for security reasons, but also argued that "the requirement that radio address script be submitted would impose an additional expense and burden on the Department for which no provision has been made. Before this burden is accepted the need for acceptance should be real and clearly evident. This is not at the present time the case."[73] Leighton's point rang true because radio, even with the existence of national broadcasting companies, was far more decentralized than the film industry; the latter could be easily monitored by a small number of personnel, but the former could not. Absent a dramatic increase in manpower for the ONI, radio would continue to be a frequently used but haphazardly monitored medium for naval publicity.

The growth of the Public Relations Branch and the cooperation of new mass media such as film and radio had lessened the navy's dependence on the Navy League to promote the service. Yet, by the latter part of the 1930s, the league had finally recovered from the internal disputes that had previously plagued the organization. The league's upward trajectory had begun when Nelson Macy replaced Nathaniel Hubbard as league president in July 1934 and helped attract trained personnel to oversee the group's public strategies. Macy also sought to reinvigorate the league's fund-raising and recruiting methods. In 1935, he undertook a long tour of the Midwest to replenish the organization's coffers and membership rolls. Newspapers in the Los Angeles area aided Macy's campaign by printing Navy League applications in their pages. In this new, more professional environment, Gardiner finally stepped away from the league after having been its driving force for fifteen years. Macy's fund-raising efforts were so successful at revitalizing the league that it revived the periodical *Sea Power* that same year. In addition, several prominent league members returned to the organization after having left it in disgust during Gardiner's tenure, including Howe, who rejoined the league board of directors. While the league remained a relatively small organization and its importance to the navy had certainly diminished, by the latter 1930s it again became a reliable ally for the navy to call on when necessary.[74]

The league's resurgence coincided with a period of growth for the Public Relations Branch, which finally received more manpower to execute its manifold mission. The navy's authorized personnel strength also grew in the latter 1930s, partially because of the need to man the ships authorized by the Vinson-Trammell Act and succeeding construction authorizations. This expansion trickled down to the Public Relations Branch in 1938 when the Navy Department added billets for five

Cdr. Leland P. Lovette, ca. 1937–38.
Naval History and Heritage Command, NH 50224, Photographic Section.

officers, two enlisted men, and six civilian aides, thereby more than tripling the number of personnel assigned to the office.[75] As these new personnel arrived, Helene Philbert, the branch's first civilian aide, assumed greater importance. In this period of expansion, she kept the organizational memory and continuity since her tenure had begun with the birth of the Information Section under Commander Koch in 1922. Thus, while some heads of the Information Section and Public Relations Branch proved more natural fits for the position than others, her presence kept the organization functioning smoothly.

Not only did the branch receive more men, but those that joined possessed more experience as the navy's personnel system finally validated the value of the branch's work. In 1937, the navy assigned Cdr. Leland P. Lovette to head the branch, replacing Commander Reinicke. Lovette had publishing experience prior to the appointment, having authored several editions of *Naval Customs, Traditions, and Usage* with the Naval Institute Press since 1933.[76] His deputy and press relations officer, Lt. Bernard L. Austin, described Lovette as a "raconteur" and an "extrovert" who had become renowned for his ability to author excellent speeches for senior officers to deliver to public audiences.⁷⁷ While Lovette's skills certainly qualified him for the position in advance, public relations work proved such an excellent match for his skills that he continued in PR work during World War II, eventually heading the wartime Office of Public Relations and becoming the first officer to reach flag rank largely through a public relations career track.

Lovette benefited from a favorable organizational climate because Secretary Swanson had worked to ensure that the branch maintained tight control over the release of information. Swanson reinforced instructions dating back to 1935 directing officers to refer all press inquiries to the Public Relations Branch. This had been standard procedure for several years, but Swanson felt that it bore repeating because sensitive information sometimes appeared in the press when officers failed to follow this policy and dealt with the media themselves. In fact, Lieutenant Austin's first assignment as press relations officer was to determine who had leaked information regarding the navy's legislative agenda to the press. Such incidents prompted Swanson to remind the officer corps again in November 1938 to follow established procedures regarding press inquiries.⁷⁸

Security concerns proved no obstacle to Lovette as he maintained good relationships with the film producers and also developed a network of contacts in other forms of media. In 1938, Kendall Banning, an army reserve lieutenant colonel who worked as an author and editor for *Cosmopolitan* magazine and other Hearst publications, published a friendly examination of the Naval Academy, *Annapolis Today*, for Funk and Wagnall's. The publisher requested that Banning write a new volume, which at the suggestion of Cdr. Walter S. De Lany, the commander of Destroyer Division 7, would focus on the navy as a whole. As Banning pitched the idea to Lovette, "the main purpose of the book will be to interest the American public in the work of the Navy today, to give the public a sense of pride in the naval service and to tell the reader what is going on and what he is getting for his money paid in taxes." Banning argued that his outside opinion might give the book added credibility in the market because his third-party status could mute any "charges which would be made by pacifists, communists, internationalists, and other radicals that the book is merely inspired propaganda."⁷⁹

Banning's proposed book certainly appealed to Lovette because of its content but also because, once again, Banning's claim to be a neutral observer allowed the navy to benefit from publicity it helped shape but did not claim as its own. As a result, Lovette, DNI Capt. Ralston S. Holmes, and even Admiral Leahy enthusiastically endorsed the proposal. In spite of the endorsement, Lovette admitted to Banning that the Public Relations Branch did not approve and reject book projects as it did films. Instead, Lovette offered to assist Banning as if he were writing an exclusive feature story for a magazine by arranging interviews with senior personnel, granting him access to the submarine base at New London, and even granting him passage on a training cruise aboard the reserve battleship *Wyoming*.[80] Such access proved necessary because, as Lovette stated, "this is the old story for this office—authors want to write pieces but do not know just where to begin."[81] Funk and Wagnall's released the book in 1940, and Banning thanked Lovette for his "indefatigable cooperation."[82]

Lovette also worked to develop a greater number of knowledgeable and sympathetic correspondents among major American newspapers and magazines. First and foremost, Lovette and his deputy, Austin, maintained a friendly correspondence with Hanson Baldwin and furnished him information for his articles and columns in the *New York Times*. Baldwin's depth of knowledge about naval affairs meant that his writing continued to receive praise for its accuracy, and Lovette even saw to it that his work caught the attention of the navy's senior leadership. Still, Lovette recognized that more correspondents and columnists would be needed to disseminate vast quantities of information to the public in case of a heightened emergency. To that end, he attempted to cultivate a list of influential media figures, including Roy Larsen of *Time* magazine, who would be willing to join the naval reserves.[83] This ambitious scheme did not result in a spate of reserve commissions as Lovette had hoped; still, the fact that Lovette believed the scheme to be feasible revealed how much the social and media climate for the navy had improved.

The organizational and policy state of navy public relations by the beginning of 1939 was strong. In spite of the increased concerns over secrecy, the Public Relations Branch had, by this point, developed a number of contacts, including some with navy backgrounds, in nearly every major form of media consumed by the public; enjoyed a healthy relationship with the leaders of the Hollywood film studios who continued to produce naval-themed films and newsreels at a high rate; and received the additional backing of groups like the Navy League, whose membership remained small but whose reach extended to members of Congress and other influential people. Certainly, some gaps remained, such as the navy's constant inability to develop a clear policy for radio broadcasts, but the number of successes easily outweighed the failures. These accomplishments occurred despite the navy's continued tendency to mask its involvement in its own publicity even to the point of obfuscating its relationship with Hollywood when questioned by members of

Congress. The Public Relations Branch also had to contend with the imposition of more-stringent security measures due to the international crises in Europe and the Pacific. Remarkably, the branch never retreated from the public sphere. In fact, in this more challenging operating environment, it had only continued to expand its reach and manpower while continuing to professionalize. These advances would help set the stage for several stunning public relations successes before the outbreak of the war in Europe.

Yet, as the Public Relations Branch contended with organizational growing pains, its staff also had to learn both what themes of publicity to project to the American public and also how best to do that. As the next chapters will make clear, the development of the core themes of interwar publicity proved just as fraught.

◄ 5 ►

"THE FINEST QUALITIES OF AMERICAN MANHOOD"

MASCULINITY AND MANPOWER, 1919–1939

Soon after the end of World War I, the United States Public Health Service launched a multistate publicity campaign announcing the "War on Venereal Disease to Continue" and "The Country Must Be Kept Clean." The Public Health Service had coordinated anti-VD efforts with both the army and the navy during the war, and all three agencies publicly committed to continue this work even past the armistice by supporting programs of education and "wholesome recreation" to ensure that the "profiteers of vice" cannot "take advantage of the days of festivity to dishonor" America's returning servicemen. The Wilson administration had embraced many aspects of the social reform movement, with Secretary of the Navy Josephus Daniels becoming one of its most forceful adherents. His predecessors dating to the turn of the century had sought to attract a better class of recruit, but Daniels had built on this work to portray the navy and its men as a bastion of morality. The advertisement for the anti-VD campaign included a quote from Daniels stating, "One of the compensations for the tragedy of war is the fact that an enlightened opinion is behind the organized campaign to protect the youth against venereal disease. The campaign begun in war to insure the military fitness of men for fighting is quite as necessary to save men for civil efficiency."[1]

Daniels's open commitment to this public health campaign reflected the fear that the rapid demobilization of so many men could create social chaos, but also dovetailed with the public's continued association—even after nearly twenty years of publicity to the contrary—of sailors with vice and licentiousness. Over the next two years, Daniels along with the Recruiting Bureau and the Navy News Bureau projected traits of what gender theorist R. W. Connell has described as "hegemonic masculinity."[2] These characteristics included an implicit and explicit belief in the superiority of the white race, selflessness of service to the nation, and superior physical and moral fitness, the latter especially prompting Daniels's specific involvement in the public health campaign. The outlets through which these traits were propagated varied widely and included officially produced recruiting films and posters, juvenile fiction, newsreels, and Hollywood feature films. Remarkably, even as the Republican administrations of the 1920s repudiated Wilson's policies, the naval bureaucracy continued to promote many of Daniels's ideas. The new Information Section created by Daniels's successor, Edwin Denby, unofficially took on the task of publicizing the positive actions of sailors while countering negative press even as the Recruiting Bureau continued to propagate a positive image of the benefits of naval service. The image of sailors evolved over time and through different media, but the larger message remained constant: to show how the navy could make men out of American boys and bring forth the "finest qualities of American manhood."[3]

Even after twenty years of recruiting campaigns, naval officers believed the public perceived the navy as, in the words of historian Frederick Harrod, "the last refuge of the drunken or incompetent."[4] There was some truth to this because where one found a naval base, areas of vice could be found nearby. Drinking, gambling, and prostitution were rampant in the vicinity of Mare Island Navy Yard near Vallejo, California, and nearby San Francisco had its infamous Barbary Coast district that was a popular liberty port destination for naval personnel. San Diego's Stingaree district housed numerous saloons and brothels into the twentieth century, and sailors were among the most frequent customers. Likewise, Adams Street near the New York Navy Yard became known as the Brooklyn Tenderloin, a takeoff on the much larger Tenderloin district in Manhattan.[5]

While such areas clearly had been concerns in the first decade of the century, Secretary Daniels enacted measures to solve this and other problems and then sought to publicize those reforms during his tenure. Reforms aimed at living conditions and at the morals of both officers and enlisted men included banning alcohol aboard ships and campaigns to clean up areas around naval bases to limit the temptations presented to sailors. Daniels believed that enacting these reforms would lead to an increase in operational efficiency by reducing the number of man-hours lost to drunkenness or venereal disease. In a speech entitled "Men Must Live Straight If They Would Shoot Straight," delivered during World War I, Daniels outlined his efforts to straighten the moral compass of enlisted men. He appointed a Naval Commission on Training Camp Activities that created alternative forms of recreation, namely athletic events, for the servicemen on or near naval stations. The navy also worked alongside the army to persuade individual communities to eliminate red-light districts that catered to soldiers and sailors.

However well-intentioned these efforts may have been, Daniels's zeal in reforming service culture and stamping out vice sometimes created new problems. For a time, Daniels banned the distribution of prophylactics to sailors going on liberty, believing that the restriction would discourage men from seeking illicit sex. Unsurprisingly, this policy proved completely ineffective, forcing Daniels to eventually relax his stance on only issuing condoms after exposure to venereal disease. Still, Daniels's paternalistic and heavy-handed approach to improving the lot and the morals of men in the navy continued throughout his tenure and peaked with the disastrous Newport scandal in 1919.[6]

As Daniels's crusade against licentiousness continued, the postwar drawdown of the navy put the fleet's manpower into a state of flux. Rapid wartime mobilization had swelled the service's authorized personnel strength to nearly 450,000 officers and men, an eightfold increase from 1916. In 1919, the authorized strength fell to 272,000, but even this decrease masked the discharge of 80 percent of wartime enlistees that summer. The authorized strength then fell even further in 1920 and 1921. Attempting to recruit even as the status of so many personnel remained unsettled was a difficult proposition, but the themes and imagery used to attract recruits during this period would echo throughout the interwar period.[7]

At the forefront of Daniels's concerns was that demobilization could harm the public's views of sailors. As Daniels's aforementioned work with the Public Health Service illustrates, he and other officials feared that demobilization might lead to tens of thousands of aimless discharged men passing through American cities. In such an unsettled environment, Daniels and the navy continued to promote the linkage of physical and moral fitness. Part of the navy's emphasis on living "correct" lifestyles focused on the officers and men maintaining not only their moral well-being but sustaining or improving their physical condition. Reflective of the growing interest and participation in organized sports in the civilian world, the navy encouraged enlisted men to take up such sports as football or boxing. Daniels intended for athletics and physical activity to instill discipline and order into the lives of sailors while distracting men from lascivious pursuits. As with Daniels's campaign to rid the navy of vice and improve sailors' moral fiber, the navy's support for athletics continued into succeeding administrations and sporting events became fixtures in the lives of navy men.[8]

Fortuitously, Daniels had allies among children's literature authors who emphasized the value of physical fitness for sailors and created a standard for young men to live up to. By showcasing the physicality of everyday duties, these outlets linked the physical strength of the men to the figurative strength of the service and the nation. Remarkably, this occurred even with books that had no ties to the navy, such as Halsey Davidson's *Navy Boys behind the Big Guns; or, Sinking the German U-Boats* (1919). The frontispiece for the novel showed the men aboard the fictional battleship *Kennebunk* as it steamed into battle against the German High Seas Fleet in a sequel to the Battle of Jutland. Whereas the titular *Navy Boys* often relied on their quick thinking and selflessness to succeed in combat situations aboard the destroyer *Colodia*, service aboard the *Kennebunk* required more muscle than the boys were accustomed to displaying as they handled the shells fired by the battleship's larger guns. The image of the boys "stripped for action" highlighted the ability of men to develop their bodies in the service.[9] In a series of books with few illustrations, the rendering of the boys' physiques stands out as an overt representation of physicality. Even though the book's setting had been overtaken by events, the scene explicitly linked the need for physical strength in the pitched naval battles that everyone anticipated.

As the nation transitioned to peacetime, such narratives of the war as *Navy Boys behind the Big Guns* receded, forcing the navy to promote the physical and moral benefits of athletic competition among sailors. The participation of a team of naval officers in the 1920 Olympic Games in Antwerp afforded an excellent opportunity to connect physical prowess and naval service. The Bureau of Navigation invested much time and resources in identifying athletes and training them prior to the Games, even releasing them from their regular duties for several months. The navy's wrestling team, which included midshipman Daniel V. Gallery, failed to medal, but other sailors found success in shooting and rowing. The eight-oared crew described as "husky giants" became the "great favorites" of the crowd as they broke the world record at the 2,000-meter distance by more than five seconds. The navy's shooting team, including Lt. Cdr. Willis A. Lee Jr., won more medals in the sport than the Marine Corps and army teams combined. In all, the navy's team won nine of the twenty-six American gold medals and thirteen of the forty-two total medals earned during the competition.[10]

Daniels's stressing of physical and moral fitness was critical to recruiting, but foreign travel had long proven a successful draw because prospective sailors saw it as an immediate, tangible benefit of service. The navy's popular recruiting slogan "Join the Navy and see the world!" appealed to the curiosity-wonder instinct described by public relations pioneer Edward Bernays, with its implication that sailors could travel to exotic and remote locations for free simply by joining the naval service. After World War I, the navy retired the slogan, but travel remained a core theme of recruiting publicity. This remained an arena where the navy enjoyed an advantage over other careers because, even though the cost of international travel fell in the 1920s as steamship companies sought to replace the declining numbers of immigrant passengers with travelers and tourists, international travel remained a luxury for most Americans throughout the interwar period.[11]

Some popular media, such as juvenile fiction, made the explicit linkage between service, travel, and American imperialism that depicted young, fit sailors using their abilities to eliminate injustice abroad. Attempting to find a new postwar setting for his children's literature, H. Irving Hancock, who also did not collaborate with the Navy Department in his books, continued his long-running Dave Darrin series with *Dave Darrin's South American Cruise* (1919). The plot took the eponymous character and his trusty sidekick, Dan Dalzell, to the fictional Latin American country of Vengara, where they became embroiled in a coup plot. Throughout the novel, Hancock contrasts the savage ways of the tyrannical Benedito and his men, which include the execution of unarmed prisoners, with Darrin's "civilized" American masculinity. In an encounter with one of Benedito's men, Darrin says, "Manhood includes truth, justice, honor, mercy, and all attributes of whatever is divine in man." As the book's plot unfolds, only the actions of the righteous Americans save the Vengarans from disaster as Darrin and Dalzell repel Benedito's coup attempt.[12] The drive for adventure had combined with American hemispheric hegemony to imply that sailors could continue to seek action in the navy even in a time of peace.

Likewise, Halsey Davidson's *Navy Boys* series transitioned its characters, a group of teenaged enlisted men hailing from an idyllic New England town, from World War I convoy duty to a peacetime setting in which foreign naval threats remained on, or under, the seas. *The Navy Boys on Special Service; or, Guarding the Floating Treasury* (1920), which appeared in the midst of the Red Scare, saw the sailors encounter a highly advanced Soviet submarine while escorting a shipment of gold bullion across the Atlantic. The boys, awestruck and concerned by the submarine's advanced technology, contrasted the "fanatical" nature of the communist crew with their own sense of righteousness and justice as they worked to remove this new threat from the seas.[13]

These books, while aimed at America's youth, echoed the messages of American benevolence abroad that originated with official media, primarily recruiting posters. During the postwar drawdown, the Recruiting Bureau experimented with different methods of recruiting, including briefly contracting with an advertising firm, using soon-to-be discharged enlisted men to attract new recruits in their hometowns, and even sponsoring recruiting competitions using private-sector methods of salesmanship.[14] These experiments notwithstanding, the bureau still attempted to draw recruits using a series of posters first devised during the war. Titled "What the Navy Is Doing," these posters, of which several dozen were put into print, continued to appear through 1921 and offered a widely varied approach to naval service. The standard format was a picture or a series of pictures with descriptive text beneath. At times, these posters depicted naval activities that seemed to have little to do with recruiting, such as the navy's participation in the 1921 Virginia Capes bombing tests (see chapter 6). Most often, however, they depicted sailors benefiting from their decision to join the navy.

Many of the recruiting posters that emphasized foreign travel contrasted the navy's "representative Americans" with strange, yet interesting foreign peoples and cultures. Since the service desired that recruits and entrants to the Naval Academy come from all regions of the country, travel still held the power to entice individuals from inland states who otherwise had little opportunity to venture from their hometowns. At times, the navy even highlighted the possibilities of men from small towns or inland states visiting domestic locations they had never seen before. A recruiting poster issued in 1921 claimed men could visit "strange lands" all around the world or large, cosmopolitan cities closer to home such as New York and San Francisco.[15]

The Far East, especially China, where the U.S. maintained an imperial presence, factored heavily into official and unofficial depictions of sailors abroad. Media outlets portrayed the navy's far-flung China Station, where the navy maintained a fleet of river gunboats to patrol and protect American interests, as one of the last frontiers available to American men. This portion of the service stood a world apart from the bulk of the fleet, both literally and figuratively. The China Station, along with the Caribbean-based Special Service Squadron, represented the last vestiges of the navy's old squadron system of organization that protected U.S. interests abroad. The officers and men who served on Yangtze River gunboats engaged pirates and rebels, visited polyglot cities like Shanghai and Nanking, and, sometimes, engaged in acts of debauchery unavailable to their counterparts in the American-based Battle and Scouting Fleets. To entice men to potentially serve in such remote locales, the Recruiting Bureau emphasized the exoticism and novelty of cultures very different from that which the men were familiar with. The recruiting poster "The Navy Sees the Far East" displayed Shinto monuments in Nagasaki and the ubiquitous rickshaws in Chinese cities as attractions available to men who committed themselves to naval service.[16]

"Navy Ships Visit Many Lands," 1921.
Naval History and Heritage Command, NH 76765-KN, Photographic Section.

That same year also marked the release of *A Sailor-Made Man* (1921), one of the first naval films released after the war. Naval officials held a decidedly mixed view of the movie's value as a recruiting tool, but the film uses sailors to demonstrate the moral superiority of American values. Harold Lloyd's character, the Boy, is an arrogant dilettante who mistakenly enlists in the navy and embarks on a naval vessel bound for the fictional south Asian country of Khairpura-Bhandanna. The Boy is a less-than-ideal sailor during his time aboard ship, until he coincidentally happens upon a former flame, the Girl, and has to rescue her from the clutches of evil foreigners. The distinction between American and foreign values is made apparent as the Boy's actions stand in sharp contrast to the opulence and barbarism of the local Raja, who covets the Girl for his harem. The Boy reacts instantly and rescues her after several madcap chase sequences through the Raja's palace and

"The Navy Sees the Far East," 1920.
Naval History and Heritage Command, NH 76751-KN, Photographic Section.

the surrounding city. The Boy ends the film newly transformed into a defender of womanly virtue and a resourceful young sailor.[17]

Fitness and travel may have provided immediate tangible benefits, but, since only a small number of enlisted men remained in the navy for a career, the navy was forced to translate these benefits into improving a sailor's appeal in the civilian job market. Peter Karsten argues that the navy had long been suspicious of businessmen and the private sector—ironic given that the service's raison d'être had long been to protect American commerce abroad—but the navy sought to downplay this wariness in recruiting and publicity. For instance, in 1919, when recruiters in West Virginia denigrated civilian jobs as inferior to a naval career, their superiors rebuked them.[18]

Just after he left office, in an April 1921 article in the *Saturday Evening Post* titled "Training Men for the Navy and the Nation," Secretary Daniels explicitly argued that learning a trade in the navy could lead to a successful civilian job. Daniels described a fictional everyman turned naval recruit named George Dewey Jones, a "tall, clear-eyed, boyish chap." Jones decided to enlist in the service to break free of his "land-born and land-bred" background and to see the "wide, wide world." Once in the navy, Jones took advantage of the service's perks, including "manly sports" and educational opportunities designed to have a "democratizing" effect on both the service and the nation, and, most importantly, to develop technical skills that earned the praise of potential employers. Thus, the navy served as a means for enlisted men, especially those who had no desire for a lengthy naval career, to forge ahead in their own lives. For years thereafter, recruiters and naval officials described the navy as the "largest trade school in the nation," one capable of taking relatively raw and unskilled men from across the nation and teaching them not just morals and discipline but practical skills valued in the civilian job market.[19]

The number of billets available for aspiring young men to join the "largest trade school in the nation," however, would decline significantly after the signing of the Five-Power Treaty in 1922. The passage of the personnel bill in spring 1922 capped manpower at 95,000 officers and men, a figure that remained constant for the next fourteen years.[20] The navy still required recruits to man ships and stations, albeit at a reduced rate. Still, as was the case during demobilization in previous years, senior leaders, the new Information Section, and the Recruiting Bureau continued to project the image of sailors as self-actualized men who could thrive in both a naval and a civilian environment.

The transition from the progressive Wilson administration to the more conservative Harding administration and the onset of the era of naval arms limitation had led to many breaks in policy, but the core ideas that Daniels used to discuss and attract the navy's manpower remained in effect. One area where his legacy can be seen is in the use of travel to attract recruits. The Harding administration remained committed to interventionism and imperialism just as his predecessor had, although the language used to justify these policies shifted somewhat. The early 1920s gave birth to the notion of "Americanism" espoused by such men as publisher William Randolph Hearst and political figure and administrator Herbert Hoover. This creed maintained that Americans now represented a distinct and superior people free of the political and social baggage that continued to plague Europe. Within the new administration, Assistant Secretary of the Navy Theodore Roosevelt Jr. sought to mimic his father's career path and used the spirit of Americanism to describe the navy's purpose. In an address to the Naval Academy's graduating class of 1922, Roosevelt argued that America stood ascendant among the relatively small number of "great high-thinking countries." The navy, he continued, served as one of the guarantors of power and status in the world, and, along with other seafarers, it had upheld a centuries-old tradition of broadening both cultural contact and commerce. Thus, officers and men who served in the navy embodied these values as they served their nation and visited foreign lands.[21]

The Recruiting Bureau relied on some of the rhetorical overtones of Americanism in their recruiting films. The 1923 film *Our Navy in the Near East* focuses on the humanitarian relief provided by the navy during the Greco-Turkish War. In particular, the film shows some of the more than 200,000 Greeks and Armenians transported to safety aboard American naval vessels. The effort was described as the navy "bringing credit to itself and the country of which it is a part," but the film strongly emphasizes the contribution of American sailors in bringing about such a positive result. Only the intervention of this "this country's best manhood"—the quoted text in this case laid over the image of a smiling American enlisted man—could save the disadvantaged from their fate.[22] Even though the United States had refused to join the League of Nations and seemingly remained aloof from international affairs, the film argued for America's continued presence as an impartial force for good made possible by the efforts of its upstanding sailors.

Our Navy in the Near East may have supported the idea of a masculine American exceptionalism while other recruiting materials continued to espouse the opportunity for travel overseas as a navy-provided educational journey. Released by the Recruiting Bureau in late 1924, the recruiting poster "Fellowship of the Sea" showed a jovial group of American sailors posing for the camera in front of a nondescript building in a European city. Rather than promoting mere sightseeing, the poster invited men to seek an "education and experience through travel."[23]

In building up this exceptional, masculine image, the bureau produced posters and films designed to attract men into service, but the Information Section served a different role. During the mid-1920s as it endured growing pains, the section's role in shaping the image of sailors mostly consisted of issuing press releases and encouraging favorable accounts in the press recounting the heroic deeds of servicemen. One such instance occurred in the wake of the deadly Honda Point disaster that occurred on 8 September 1923 when an entire destroyer squadron ran aground off the California coast. While the aftermath of the accident brought about recriminations and the assignment of blame, the actions of the men involved in the rescue efforts received significant press coverage that conveyed to the public the willingness of navy men to risk their own lives for those of their shipmates. A feature story in the *St. Louis Post-Dispatch* about the accident described the "coolness and courage" that

"Fellowship of the Sea," 1924.
Naval History and Heritage Command, NH 76783-KN, Photographic Section.

led to the rescue of hundreds of men on the trapped destroyers despite the terrible conditions at the scene. The destroyer *Young* suffered the worst in the accident when it struck the rocks and began to sink. The article notes how men from the *Chauncey*, a destroyer that had itself run aground when it moved in to provide assistance to its stricken sisters, engaged in daring rescue operations to remove many of the men from the *Young* before the latter ship capsized. The article also recounted the efforts of the crewmen aboard the *Delphy* who failed to reach a shipmate covered in fuel oil, helplessly watching as he drowned in the surf. Perhaps the most selfless act occurred in the aftermath of the accident when the squadron commander, Capt. Edward Watson, accepted all blame for the accident in an effort to spare the other senior officers involved. Watson's actions earned him praise and likely helped all but one of the other officers tried by court-martial to escape punishment.[24]

The tragedy at Honda Point represented a onetime occurrence where goodwill was salvaged from a disaster, but the navy needed more consistent sources of publicity in its effort to reform the image of sailors. As with the rhetoric of travel and imperialism, Secretary Daniels's departure had done little to abate the promotion of athletics and its benefits for sailors. The growing popularity of football in the 1920s provided one such source. This type of publicity often occurred at the local level where naval stations and ships formed teams to compete with one another when possible or, occasionally, against teams from nearby cities and towns. These teams accomplished the basic goal of maintaining the physical health of naval personnel and strengthening ties with local communities.[25]

The success of the Naval Academy's football team in the 1920s put the midshipmen at Annapolis in the national spotlight and created many publicity opportunities. The amount of attention only grew each year in anticipation of the rivalry game against the cadets of the United States Military Academy. The Army–Navy game provided officials with reason to praise the "high morale and unconquerable Navy spirit which honors the Navy alike in battle and on the gridiron." The 1926 game between the two academies broke from tradition as the game, typically held at Franklin Field in Philadelphia, was moved to Chicago in honor of the opening of Soldier Field. A virtual frenzy occurred when officials opened the stadium's box seats for bidding, eventually netting more than $100,000, or nearly forty dollars per seat. The game itself took on extra importance after Navy beat Michigan to remain undefeated and prompted speculation that the annual rivalry game with Army could decide the national championship. Before a crowd of 110,000 and a radio audience that spanned the globe as the navy broadcast the game over its network of radio stations, the two teams fought to a 21–21 tie in a contest hailed as "one of the greatest football games ever played." The midshipmen's successful season earned the Naval Academy a shared national championship, a feat their cadet counterparts would be unable to match until 1944. The pro-navy *Chicago Tribune* editorialized that the game would hopefully provide Midwesterners with a "new understanding, a new upholding of the national defense" and lead to greater scrutiny of the present diminished state of the armed forces.[26]

Even with the success of Annapolis football, it remained at some remove from the concerns of the fleet and the men needed to man the ships. Generating a consistently appealing narrative of naval service required regular engagement with the press. The Information Section, however, lacked contacts with the press and other media outside of a few major cities, especially after the demise of the program utilizing reservists as district press officers in 1927. Instead, the Recruiting Bureau with its extensive network of stations filled a need by supplying regional and local media outlets with information. For instance, in the late 1920s the station in Boston began tracking more than seven hundred men who had been recruited there. As these men progressed through their tours, they supplied information back to the recruiting station for collection and dissemination as articles for local newspapers. These included letters extolling the benefits of travel and learning a trade, and at least one yeoman wrote that the navy's commitment to the physical health and strength of its sailors "increases his life 10 years."[27] This system relied on the extensive infrastructure and personal networks developed over decades by the bureau to allow for a targeted and personalized view of naval service.

Developing relationships with local press had two purposes: most obviously, it could allow for the dissemination of positive publicity; but these contacts could also prevent news that ran counter to the desired clean, masculine image from making it into the local papers. This was especially important when sailors found themselves involved in criminal activity. In November 1928, the navy learned that a local judge in Bay Shore, New York, gave a local criminal a choice between jail time or enlistment in the service. The judge did so because he believed his own prior naval service had helped him tremendously, but the navy did not want the public to believe that men entered the service in such a manner. The judge apologized and the local recruiting officer persuaded other local papers not to run stories on the matter so as not to embarrass the navy or harm its recruiting efforts.[28]

The efforts at promoting a masculine image of sailors during the 1920s met with mixed to disappointing results. The service met its manpower goals, but scores on aptitude tests given to new recruits and retention rates of existing servicemen both remained low throughout the decade, suggesting that the navy was not competitive with the strong civilian economy for young men. Furthermore, some in the navy still believed that the public viewed sailors as little more than "riffraff" even after all this PR work. These results clearly showed the limits of publicity in completely reversing widely held perceptions.[29]

The navy's relationship with Hollywood, however, opened up an entirely new medium through which to project an appealing, masculine image of sailors. The creation of the Motion Picture Board in 1929 put the Recruiting Bureau and the Information Section into closer contact with one another while giving the latter more overt responsibility in generating positive publicity. Still, developing a relationship with Hollywood required some finessing as the low- and middle-brow films that made up the bulk of studios' output often relied on spectacle and lurid—by late 1920s standards, at least—content to attract audiences. Finding common ground between the needs of the navy and Hollywood often required negotiation through the script and screening process, but both parties proved willing to work together. The film studios certainly used the navy's prestige in their quest to appeal to more middle-class, respectable audiences. This had been a long-running concern of the industry dating back to the 1910s, and the creation of the MPPDA in 1922 by the studios was a further move toward institutional legitimacy and acceptance.

Meanwhile, the navy gained the clear and immediate benefit of controlling content that appeared on American movie screens. Most importantly, by taking Hollywood's proven and lucrative models of storytelling and applying them to stories the navy desired be told on-screen, the navy had essentially outsourced its public relations to masters of image building. Given the priority the service placed on recruiting and building a positive image of its sailors, this model of collaboration proved especially beneficial in promoting the benefits of service to American men by presenting stories of young men whose naval service allows them to fulfill their masculine potential.

With the release of some of the first films produced under the new navy-Hollywood partnership, these positive narratives of self-fulfillment reached national audiences. Thanks to Hollywood, the Naval Academy football team remained in the spotlight even when it failed to duplicate the success of the 1926 team. John Ford's *Salute* (1930) established the pattern for several later Naval Academy football films by incorporating an athletic storyline into a plot that became a staple of interwar navy films: namely, the transformation of new midshipmen into budding naval officers. In the film, Paul Randall, a physically slight young man, lives in the shadow of his older brother, John, a cadet at West Point, and his grandfather who served alongside Adm. George Dewey at Manila Bay. Paul participates in the athletic activities offered at the Naval Academy, including crew, but believes that only through success on the football field can he achieve a sense of independent manhood. His drive and determination win over two upperclassmen who had previously hazed him but who then assist Paul in his quest to become a valuable player for the team. In the film's climax, Paul comes into direct competition with his brother John during the annual Army–Navy game and helps the team battle to a tie score. The film reinforces the excitement and the prestige of these games by including numerous shots of the thousands of excited and cheering spectators in the stands who try to will their team to victory. While *Salute* and other films afforded the studios the opportunity to vary the settings of football pictures, they provided a new means for the navy to publicize the value it placed on athletics and to remind audiences that an aspiring servant to the nation existed under every Naval Academy football helmet.[30]

The navy's establishment of athletic events for officers and men certainly encouraged the growth and development of sailors, but it also helped sailors maintain their competitive spirit. Throughout the interwar period, navy officials would call attention to other means of instilling this spirit among the fleet. During the fleet concentration periods that occurred during the winter and spring months, the navy held a variety of target and engineering competitions among the ships and crews of the fleet. Successful crews could then proudly display their "E" pennants for the next calendar year in recognition of their achievements. The navy attempted to promote the results of these annual competitions and impart a sense of pride in what the victorious crews accomplished. The navy had issued press releases announcing the results of these competitions as early as 1922, but they eventually provided fodder for Hollywood films. In the 1930 comedy *True to the Navy*, "Bull's Eye" McCoy is an extraordinarily accurate gunner aboard the battleship *Mississippi* who commands respect for his ability to aim his turret crew's shots. Even though McCoy's basic concern in the film is his desire to marry his sweetheart, the fleet's annual gunnery contest drives the plot of the film. In fact, this spirit of competition pervades the entire fleet and helps raise the personal and professional stakes of the contest, so much so that gamblers are depicted as having a financial interest in which battleship earns the coveted "E." This competitiveness is also depicted as having healthy limits as some of McCoy's potential rivals save him from a bar brawl and eventually help get him back aboard the *Mississippi* to win the contest.[31] *True to the Navy* was a minor film, yet rare for showcasing how the competitive spirit hitherto identified with navy athletics translated into the fleet.

Another John Ford film, *Men without Women* (1930), touched on many of the themes that had defined naval recruiting and publicity about sailors for years. Released prior to the implementation of the Production Code (better known as the Hays Code, which led to tight restrictions on morally acceptable film content into the 1960s), the film opens with the enlisted men from an American submarine in a Shanghai bar replete with prostitutes and other seedy characters. Surprisingly, the Motion Picture Board had approved the film for release in spite of its depiction of the men in a depraved environment, presumably allowing the project to go forward because the film did not explicitly show the men partaking in these vices. The film overtly portrays Shanghai as a polyglot city with numerous native Chinese and foreign citizens, but also as a place where white men could invent entirely new personas and identities and thus leave their old lives in the West behind. One of the film's central characters, Chief Burke, is recognized by a British officer early in the film as a former Royal Navy officer named Quartermain, who was reputed to have given information to the Germans that allowed his submarine to be sunk during the war. Burke eventually admits his true identity to a shipmate, Ensign Price; proclaims his innocence for the past transgression; and heroically sacrifices himself by remaining on board to control the torpedo tube valves and thus allow the other men to escape their doomed submarine.[32] In most respects, the film traded on well-worn images and stereotypes about the behaviors of enlisted men, the allure of China, and selflessness, but it combined these elements in a single piece the *Film Daily* described as being "out of the ordinary" while "manag[ing] to hold the audience in gripping suspense."[33]

A later submarine film, *Hell Below* (1933), highlighted one of the potential strengths of relying on commercial films to promote a masculine image of sailors. Unlike brief accounts in the press, mentions in newsreels, or depictions in recruiting posters, Hollywood films could add compelling narratives to flesh out the lives of navy men. Juvenile fiction had once served this purpose, but the industry had avoided navy settings for most of the 1920s. Commercial films, however, could incorporate more adult themes, especially the idea of a noble sacrifice. In the *Hell Below*'s climactic scenes, Lt. Thomas Knowlton is a troubled officer who, through the example of his commanding officer, finally begins to embrace the concepts of service and sacrifice to a larger cause. Nearing the end of a suicide mission intended to destroy a German submarine base, Knowlton pushes his CO overboard so that he can helm his explosive-laden submarine, the *AL-14*, into a concrete bastion protecting the base. Knowlton completes the mission despite receiving three separate wounds from German machine guns and shore batteries. The film's closing shot dramatizes his death by showing the machine-gunning of his cap floating on the surface of the water. While personally tragic, the sacrifice of his life and of his boat allowed the Allies to maintain control of the sea lanes in the region.[34]

The benefit of narrative as expressed by *Hell Below* carried through to other films too. While many films satisfied the navy's basic hopes by incorporating existing themes of publicity about sailors, this compatibility ran much deeper. Oftentimes, the basic cultural elements of a film the studios produced would dovetail with the goals of naval publicity. Films required a basic narrative arc of plot or character to drive the story, and among the most common character arcs in Hollywood films regardless of their setting or subject matter has been the maturation of characters from a figurative childhood into adulthood. Screenwriting expert Syd Field describes this narrative of personal transformation as depicting "an essential aspect of our humanity."[35] Many of the films set in the navy featured arcs of personal growth and maturation and thus reinforced the notion that naval service could benefit those who took advantage of the opportunity. These stories fit extremely well with the navy's recruiting messages and remained one of the most important reasons the service continued to develop and maintain working relationships with the studios.

Furthermore, these narratives of masculine self-fulfillment stood out against the chaos in the civilian job market of the 1930s. Unemployment in 1929 had stood at approximately 3 percent, indicating the extremely tight labor market in which the navy had competed for recruits for much of the decade.[36] Unemployment figures rose rapidly in the years afterward, however, peaking at approximately 25 percent in 1933. The desire of men to take control over their own destinies noted by gender theorist Joe Dubbert in the 1920s had been shattered, as had the ability of many men to maintain themselves as breadwinners.[37] As Michael Kimmel argues, some of the best-known cultural expressions of the period, such as the novels of Ernest Hemingway and F. Scott Fitzgerald, depicted men cut off from the American dream, while John Steinbeck and the early gangster films displayed a strong interest in "self-made men."[38] These more abstract concerns had noticeable effects because those seeking to stop the spread of unionization and even the passage of unemployment insurance often deployed the language of masculinity to make their case.[39]

In an environment of social dislocation and broken men, the notion of boys becoming men through naval service took on added importance. Few, if any, of the navy-Hollywood collaborations directly acknowledged the existence of the Depression, but the narrative thrust of so many of these films touched on these social currents. The 1934 Warner Brothers film *Here Comes the Navy* serves as perhaps the most direct expression of Field's assertion about plots showing boys becoming men. The film depicts rough-and-tumble shipyard worker Chesty O'Connor becoming a dependable, if still rough-around-the-edges, enlisted man. Chesty's motives for enlisting are far from pure. Following several encounters with petty officer Biff Martin, including a brawl outside of a dance hall, Chesty decides to enlist to get back at Biff and prove that the navy made a mistake in accepting Biff as a man. Chesty fails to take heed of his ex-girlfriend's warning, "They only take men in the Navy," and finds the transition to naval discipline difficult. Like many other naval films of the period, *Here Comes the Navy* uses shots of men marching in formation to represent the orderliness and attractiveness of naval service, but Chesty openly disdains the discipline necessary to become a sailor. Following an incident in which Chesty circumvents his orders denying him further liberty, Chesty is court-martialed and shunned by the other enlisted men. Even after receiving the Navy Cross for putting out a fire in the gun turret of his ship, the battleship *Arizona*, the honor and significance of the decoration is lost on Chesty. Amidst a grand ceremony with the crew of the ship looking on and an admiral in attendance, Chesty visibly smirks at the level of attention focused on him. Chesty finally proves himself to the navy and receives the respect of Biff when he rescues Biff from certain death as he is caught up in the trailing lines of the airship *Macon* as it hovers above an air show. The film depicts the extreme risk Chesty assumes by selflessly lowering himself down a rope and then carrying Biff to the ground via parachute. While not explicitly stated at the end of the film, it is strongly implied that Chesty, now fully conformed to the naval lifestyle and discipline, will remain in the service for the duration of his career.[40]

Most often, publicity for sailors depicted enlisted men reaching their potential within the confines of their rank, but they could also deepen their commitment by attending the Naval Academy. In yet another of Daniels's programs at the Navy Department, enlisted men were allowed to take an exam to measure their qualifications and for entry to the Naval Academy. Intended as a means of "democratizing" the navy—twenty-five men would be admitted each year—and narrowing the gulf between officer and enlisted man, the program proved immediately successful as the first man to graduate from the academy under such terms did so at the top of his class. The modest number of appointments available perhaps limited the real-world impact of the program, but its small size did not prevent it from factoring into navy publicity. Both *Midshipman Jack* (1933) and *Shipmates Forever* (1935) prominently featured the transition faced by enlisted men who rotated out of the fleet and into life at Annapolis. The characters, Russell Burns and Johnny "Coxswain" Lawrence, are both shown as bright, knowledgeable men, but each one's strongest asset is his personal character. In *Midshipman Jack*, Burns's self-discipline wears off on his superior, Jack Austin, who had to repeat his fourth year at the academy due to a "conduct problem." Similarly, in *Shipmates Forever*, Johnny upbraids the protagonist, Richard Melville, for his disregard for a naval career, thus leading Melville to rededicate himself toward succeeding. In fact, both Austin and Melville become so transformed by their relationships with the former enlisted men that they nearly sacrifice their careers and lives to protect them when tragedy strikes.[41] In these instances, the enlisted men–turned-midshipmen thus served as models of personal discipline and reverence for naval tradition that many of their peers lacked. On a broader level, they continued to echo Daniels's stated belief that democratizing the navy by breaking down the cultural barriers between officers and enlisted men would benefit both the service and the nation.

Salute, *Midshipman Jack*, *Shipmates Forever*, and other films set at the Naval Academy created an unintended dilemma for the navy. While these films often incorporated many elements drawn from the lives of midshipmen at the academy and depicted aspiring officers fulfilling their masculine potential, the plots and character arcs displayed many similarities to the films with enlisted men as their protagonists. Officers had been showcased in publicity for athletic events, but the films set at the academy appeared to be, for all intents and purposes, recruiting films. The Naval Academy remained the primary entry point for an overwhelming majority of the officer corps of the 1930s, but it also remained open only to those who received an appointment from a U.S. senator or a member of the House of Representatives. This admissions process never factored into these films, meaning the public—especially anyone aspiring to be a naval officer—had been left with a startlingly incomplete picture of how one gained entry to the academy.

Even as the navy partially had ceded to Hollywood the constructing and disseminating of a normative masculine image of sailors on the industry's terms, the navy still sought to develop and maintain other sources of publicity. In Frank Martinek's various "Don Winslow of the Navy" products that first appeared in 1934, the character battles the forces of the nefarious Scorpion. The Scorpion uses any method imaginable, including torture, murder, and black magic, to try to destroy Western civilization in order to create a global dictatorship.[42] To counter this subversive threat and live up to the conventions of juvenile fiction, Martinek imbued Don Winslow with high moral standards to serve as a model for young men. Even while combating the Scorpion, Don Winslow remains "skilled in the art of the righteous endeavor" and refuses to take the life of either humans or animals in his quest to stop his arch nemesis. He consistently refrains from drinking, smoking, and other miscreant behaviors. As further evidence of his high and incorruptible moral standards, Winslow lives a chaste lifestyle free of any romantic attachment. With the exception of Mercedes, the daughter of his commanding officer, Adm. Michael Splendor, Winslow views women with suspicion and as potential threats to operational security. In *Don Winslow, U.S.N., in Ceylon with Kwang, Celebrated Chinese Detective* (1934), Winslow asks his loyal but dimwitted sidekick, Red Pennington: "Haven't you learned enough about women decoys or 'come-on girls'? With their synthetic and glamorous charms they have destroyed many men and nations as well."[43]

While the navy's encouragement of Martinek's work aided in the image-building of sailors, the service's leaders sought to protect the image of the men against any perceived slight. With funding from the Public Works of Art Project of the Works Progress Administration, artist Paul Cadmus created an oil painting entitled *The Fleet's In* in 1934. The painting contains numerous ribald images, including a pair

Paul Cadmus, *The Fleet's In,* 1934. Oil on canvas, 30 × 60 inches.
Naval History and Heritage Command, NH 92806-KN, Photographic Section.

of drunken sailors flirting with two transvestites, a woman angrily rebuffing a third sailor's advances as he gropes her, and two marines in the company of a homosexual man. The Corcoran Art Gallery in Washington, D.C., displayed *The Fleet's In* as part of an exhibition of Public Works of Art Project paintings in the spring of 1934, but the display of this artwork prompted complaints from the public. The *Washington Evening Star* printed a letter of complaint regarding the painting, and Secretary of the Navy Claude Swanson said of it that "it was right artistic but not true to the navy. It shows all the derelictions of the Navy and none of its virtues." Swanson ordered Assistant Secretary of the Navy Henry L. Roosevelt to remove the painting from the exhibition.[44]

Secretary Swanson was not the only naval official angry about the painting. Adm. Hugh Rodman publicly condemned it, but the *Washington Post* used Rodman's attack to question the navy's attempt to suppress Cadmus's work. The *Post* rebuked the navy's actions and attacked the service for attempting to censor the painting. More damningly, the *Post* implied that the painting's portrayal of sailors carried some truth, while dismissing as "far from the life of a sailor" those stock navy pictures of "fronded palms lift[ing] branches to a cloudless sky" or "slim boys wander[ing] through foreign parks, snapping their Kodaks at distinguished statues, 'seeing the world.'" Two months later, the *Post* returned to the controversy surrounding *The Fleet's In* when sailors from the battleships *Arkansas* and *Wyoming* attacked a woman and started riots while on shore leave in Nice, France. When comparing the actions of the sailors overseas to those depicted in the painting, the *Post* editorialized that "the orgy staged in this Riviera city made Paul Cadmus's second-rate painting appear like a sketch of a tea party." The painting was removed from public exhibition for the next year.[45] The *Post*'s editorial strongly suggested that the navy had gone too far in attempting to sanitize the image of sailors for recruiting purposes and had invited a backlash any time sailors misbehaved.

The concern over *The Fleet's In* also showed that many of the core themes that Josephus Daniels had instilled in the Navy Department after World War I had lingered for well over a decade. As further evidence of this, the Recruiting Bureau continued to issue posters emphasizing its core themes such as travel. A pair of recruiting posters issued by the bureau in 1935 highlighted the beauty and ruggedness of the territories of Hawaii and Alaska, promising men visits to picturesque Waikiki Beach on Oahu or cruises along the dramatic peaks of the Alaskan coast. In using these posters, coincident with an increase in tensions abroad, the navy attempted to highlight the possibilities for service in breathtaking, if not exactly exotic, locales safely within the confines of American territory.[46]

An additional legacy of Josephus Daniels's tenure and the Progressive Era would resurface the following year in 1936 when the Recruiting Bureau made an extremely rare pitch to entice African Americans to join the navy as messmen and stewards. Nearly every piece of media about sailors in the interwar period focused on the actions and exploits of white officers and enlisted men. This is unsurprising given that the interwar navy was comprised overwhelmingly of white officers and men with only a small and low-ranking contingent of racial minorities. The navy still counted a few Filipinos among its number and briefly recruited new men from the Philippines in the early 1930s, but these efforts occurred out of sight of the American public. African Americans, meanwhile, had once enjoyed some opportunity for advancement in naval service, but since the 1890s, the navy had segregated blacks into steward and mess ratings. Making matters worse, the navy further whitened its enlisted force after World War I by prohibiting the recruitment of African Americans from 1919 to 1931. The navy went to great lengths to enforce this ban; in 1922, the Bureau of Navigation ordered the New Orleans Recruiting Station to ensure that a visiting floatplane did not land near the "overwhelmingly negro" parts of the city neighboring Lake Pontchartrain for fear that the African Americans would believe that the navy once again welcomed their service.[47]

When the navy resumed recruiting African Americans, it designed materials that offered none of the benefits intended for white sailors. Instead, these campaigns

"On the Sand at Waikiki," 1935.
Naval History and Heritage Command, NH 86427, Photographic Section.

explicitly showed African American sailors serving their white officers in a manner akin to the paternalistic racism endemic to the South. Given the limited tasks the navy allowed African Americans to perform and the far fewer resources expended to bring black men into the service, the navy clearly viewed nonwhites an as afterthought within the service and projected a remarkably circumscribed image to attract new recruits.[48]

The campaign to add more African Americans to the enlisted force began concurrently with the first increase of the navy's authorized personnel since 1922. The navy needed more men to man the new ships entering service as a result of the National Industrial Recovery Act of 1933 and the Vinson-Trammell Act of 1934. These ships arrived as German and Japanese aggression prompted the navy's leaders to talk more explicitly about national security, but, at least initially, these tensions had little noticeable effect on the portrayals of sailors in Hollywood films. In fact, many of the films produced echoed the same themes and ideas seen in previous films. *The Devil's Playground* (1937) was a remake of Frank Capra's *Submarine*

Still frame from a film trailer intended for the recruitment of African Americans, 1936.
National Archives and Record Administration, Box 65, Entry 22, Record Group 80, NAB.

(1928) and kept the core themes of the earlier film intact, including showing how the bond between sailors could not be broken by a disreputable woman. *Navy Blue and Gold* (1937) recycled many of the ideas first seen *Salute* seven years earlier and focused on the exploits of midshipmen and football at the Naval Academy. John Ford's *Submarine Patrol* (1938) echoed plot elements seen in *Hell Below*, *Shipmates Forever*, and other previous films in depicting a wealthy young playboy enlisting during World War I and leading the motley crew of a wooden subchaser into a very dangerous mission. Not all of these films were financial successes, and, in fact, their respective studios classified both *The Devil's Playground* and *Navy Blue and Gold* as B-movies. While the recurring elements of the films may speak more to the formulaic nature of Hollywood at the height of the studio system, they also showed the degree to which films about the navy and its men inevitably touched on many themes the navy itself found appealing and beneficial to its image.

On balance, the partnerships with Hollywood and Martinek had led to portrayals of the navy as an institution where young, white men could reach a masculine ideal

"Service Afloat," 1939.
Naval History and Heritage Command, NH-76806, Photographic Section.

through adventure and both physical and moral growth. In fact, these media had mostly ignored the messages of the 1920s that emphasized the development of skills that would become useful in the private sector. There were good narrative reasons for this: the prospect of Don Winslow or many of the protagonists of Hollywood films abandoning their hard-won success within the navy for a civilian career would undercut the messages of many of these works. Furthermore, linking naval service to success in the civilian job market would seem out of touch given that the Great Depression had eviscerated the civilian job market and had led to the navy serving as a refuge for those seeking to escape economic deprivation. In October 1939, even as the economy remained stagnant and war had begun in Europe, the Recruiting Bureau curiously issued a poster claiming that the service trained men suitable for civilian employment by teaching a "useful trade" for young men wishing to join the service.[49] The curious timing and message of this poster suggests that the navy's allies in the mass media continued to have a better understanding of what might create an appealing image and narrative for sailors than the service itself.

It is difficult to ascertain whether the image projected by the Public Relations Branch, the Recruiting Bureau, and their allies appreciably changed Americans' opinions about the service and its sailors. As the navy developed new sources of publicity through the film studios and Frank Martinek, the social ravages of the Great Depression had led to a major spike in the retention rate of enlisted men, who wisely thought a navy career—even as Congress refused to authorize full pay for soldiers and sailors—better than braving the civilian job market. With retention rates high, the navy needed only small numbers of men and could afford to be highly selective as to who was accepted into the service. In effect, the Depression had solved many of problems the navy had encountered with its enlisted force in the previous decade. Yet, despite decades of reform and publicity to the contrary, even sailors themselves described the areas around their bases as "dirty and sleazy," meaning that the public still had reason to link the modern bluejacket to the stereotype of the transient sailor.[50]

Still, by the end of the interwar period, the navy had improved its ability to project a positive image of sailors by relying greatly on the complicity and support of external actors. These external media, including books and feature films, broadened the narrative scope and helped provide deeper motivations for joining naval service beyond those conveyed in posters and brief, internally produced recruiting films. Even though the navy had opened up new media sources through which to disseminate publicity about its sailors, the themes expressed through these new outlets continued to reflect the themes first expanded on by Secretary Daniels just after World War I. The navy could allow men to achieve their full potential and find success in a postservice civilian career or as a career navy man. Daniels's legacy in this arena remained in place for nearly two decades, and the themes he developed remained remarkably durable even through a profound period of social change and upheaval. Reliance on those themes had allowed the navy to fill its ranks and maintain itself as the nation's "first line of defense."[51]

◄ 6 ►

REPLACING THE FAMILIAR WITH THE NEW

PUBLIC PERCEPTIONS OF NAVAL TRANSFORMATION, 1919–1939

On the foggy night of 8 September 1923, the eighteen ships of Destroyer Squadron 11 under the command of Capt. Edward H. Watson turned eastward to enter the Santa Barbara Channel during a high-speed run from San Francisco to San Diego. The captain of the lead destroyer, the USS *Delphy*, Lt. Cdr. Donald T. Hunter, had assumed primary navigational responsibilities for the voyage, essentially sidelining his own navigator, Lt. (junior grade) Lawrence Blodgett. At 2104 hours, the third ship in the column formation, the USS *Young* (DD 314), struck underwater rocks that tore a large gash in the hull and quickly capsized the destroyer. Within minutes, eight more destroyers—including the *Delphy*—ran aground along the coastline near Honda Point well north of the entrance to the channel. Two ships suffered damage but remained under their own power, while the rest found themselves beached against the rough coastline. Through the herculean efforts of the ships' crews to save one another, only twenty-three men died in the terrible accident.[1]

Even after such a devastating accident, the navy stood officially silent on the matter for five days. Only on 13 September did the Information Section issue its first press release about the tragedy. New information continued to trickle out to the press for days afterward, leading the *New York Times* to criticize the navy's seemingly slothful and opaque public response. The delay in a full report stemmed from Captain Watson's sensible decision to delay submitting a full account until he had received complete damage reports from each of his ships, but this was not

The Honda Point disaster, 1923, showing the USS *S.P. Lee* (*right*) and USS *Nicholas* (*left*). *Naval History and Heritage Command, NH 84820, Photographic Section.*

communicated to the public.[2] Only in the face of overwhelming criticism did the navy decide to open up its court of inquiry to the press.

The well-covered inquiry revealed a startling fact: the accident had been caused by a mistrust of technology. Hunter had navigated by "dead reckoning" the ships' positions and ignored the radio compass bearings that showed the formation had not yet entered the Santa Barbara Channel before making their fateful turn.[3] The *New York Times* quoted at length from the court of inquiry's report, which castigated the captains and navigators of the trailing ships for blindly following Hunter and the *Delphy*. The report bluntly stated: "Dead reckoning alone can never be depended upon."[4]

The revelation of Hunter's decisions ran counter to a dominant theme of interwar navy publicity: the service's ability to develop and safely employ cutting-edge technology. Brig. Gen. William Mitchell publicly questioned the interwar U.S. Navy's ability to innovate. By the early 1920s, the navy's hierarchy clearly understood that the force structure must include aircraft and submarines in their most likely war scenario: a naval war in the western Pacific against Japan. Since, for obvious reasons, the navy refused to publicly identify Japan as its most likely enemy, the need and value of these weapons was explained to the public as the "three-plane" navy: it would dominate the surface of the ocean, the air above it, and the depths beneath it.

The public relations of naval aviation and submarines in the interwar period would evolve in very different ways despite their common organizational roots. First, the creation of the Bureau of Aeronautics gave aviation a single, powerful champion in Rear Admiral Moffett, who willingly used publicity to further his goals, even to the point of creating spectacles with his aircraft that attracted public attention but added little to the development of aviation as a tool of naval warfare. Meanwhile, the submarine force lacked a single advocate with Moffett's power and ability to generate the same public goodwill. Furthermore, submarines lacked the capability of generating the visual spectacle that attracted public attention, an important consideration as media grew more visually oriented. Second, the public held very different attitudes toward aviation and submarines that could be traced to World War I: aviators had become heroes while submariners were a scourge upon the seas.

In spite of these differences, both technologies pushed naval warfare into relatively new domains, which required sometimes painful development processes. Inevitably, these new technologies and their users failed. In addition to the Honda Point disaster, the navy suffered numerous high-profile accidents during the interwar period that resulted in the loss of men and machines, as well as public confidence in the service's ability to innovate. Moffett would modify his approach to public relations in the latter 1920s in the wake of some of these tragedies. These accidents also forced the service to develop a means of responding to specific incidents and crises. The navy needed to convince the public that it valued the lives of its aviators and submariners by working to make them safe despite the dangers these men faced when venturing into unforgiving seas and skies.

The struggle to safely incorporate aviation and submarines into the fleet represented a significant shift in how the navy thought it would achieve control of the seas. At the end of World War I, the battleship remained the dominant weapon in naval warfare. The vessel had sat atop the hierarchy of naval warfare since the days of the ship-of-the-line, and, to many, the conduct of the war had done little to shake faith in a proven technology. The U.S. Navy had benchmarked each construction program authorized by Congress by the number of battleships. The growing number of ever larger and more advanced battleships allowed the service to gain credibility with the public and with foreign competitors. The wartime construction boom, most notably the 1916 authorization for ten battleships and six battle cruisers that passed just after the Battle of Jutland, solidified the battleship's status within the navy.

Yet, even as the battleship remained the pinnacle of naval warfare and Secretary Daniels pressed for the completion of the battleships and cruisers authorized in 1916, the navy sought to promote its nascent aviation arm after the war. Still, the principal advocate for aviation was the director of naval aviation, an adviser to the CNO who had only a small staff. In spite of aviation's marginal bureaucratic status, the navy acted on a recommendation from Cdr. John Towers in May 1919 and sent a group of three large Curtiss NC flying boats on a transatlantic flight. Two of the flying boats encountered mechanical difficulties en route, but the third, the NC-4, completed its journey from Newfoundland to Lisbon in a mere eleven days. This achievement placed the navy and the crew of the plane, led by pilot Lt. A. C. Read, on the front pages of newspapers around the country, becoming a cornerstone of navy public relations for several years. But in the pantheon of long-distance flights, the NC-4 quickly lost significance when, two weeks later, British aviators John Alcock and Arthur Whitten-Brown completed a nonstop transatlantic flight from Newfoundland to Ireland. In spite of the difficulties encountered during the flight of the NC-4, Daniels encouraged more long-distance flights and suggested that long-range flying boats attempt a distance flight at least once every quarter.[5]

Air racing offered another outlet to publicize naval aviation. The first official air races had begun in France in 1909, and, by 1914, *New York Herald* publisher James Gordon Bennett and airplane enthusiast Jacques Schneider were financing competitions designed to develop land-based aviation and seaplanes, respectively. The races had paused during the war, but their revival and growing popularity after the war helped showcase the capabilities of naval aircraft to public audiences and the press. In 1920, the navy entered craft into the National Balloon Races and competed for the Pulitzer Trophy. The Navy News Bureau sought to temper public expectations for victory via its press releases, but the races proved important enough that Secretary Daniels attended them and foretold a greater commitment of military resources into such competitions.[6]

Even as Secretary Daniels raised public visibility for naval aviation, General Mitchell's increasingly strong denouncements of the navy forced Daniels to defend the viability of the surface fleet and downplay the potential importance of aviation. Daniels, citing a recent General Board study, argued in February 1921 that the lack of battleship engagements during the war had only reinforced the notion that battleships constituted the "basis of sea power." Later that year, during the bombing trials off the Virginia Capes, the navy claimed that these tests had done little to shake its faith in the battleship; for the remainder of the interwar period, the navy continued to define the battleship as the final arbiter of naval warfare. This would lead to the perception that a "Gun Club" of battleship officers dominated the navy and inhibited the development of alternative weapons systems. This perception masked the navy's status as a progressive institution desiring to integrate the latest technologies into its arsenal. The officer corps could ill afford to be publicly viewed as inhibiting innovation.[7]

Criticism leveled by the navy's leaders against the results of the 1921 bombing tests did not prevent the Recruiting Bureau from attempting to capitalize on the publicity surrounding them and highlight the service's commitment to innovation. A poster issued later that year depicted the ability of aircraft to sink warships. Released under the "What the Navy Is Doing" series, the poster entitled "Naval Vessels Sunk by Aerial Bombs" showed the German destroyer *G-102* struggling to stay afloat following an attack by army aircraft. While the poster noted that the army and navy jointly conducted the tests, the fact remains that the *G-102* was attacked only by army aircraft; it was the first vessel attacked and sunk after Brigadier General Mitchell became personally involved in the tests. For unknown reasons, the navy decided not to use photographs of the German light cruiser *Frankfurt* that was sunk later during the round of tests by aircraft from both services.[8] The baffling choice made by the Recruiting Bureau coincides with the brief period between the dissolution of the Navy News Bureau and the establishment of the Information Section; there was simply no public relations office with which the bureau could coordinate a coherent policy.

The Recruiting Bureau's poster, however, at least provided rhetorical support for the "three-plane" navy. The service had recognized from its experience in World War I that aircraft and submarines—both recent inventions compared with the battleship—could have profound effects on naval warfare. As the navy emerged from the war, however, its capabilities in both of the new technologies lagged in comparison to the major European powers. The battleship-building holiday consented to at the Washington Conference allowed resources to be channeled into aviation and submarines. Given that the service had measured its strength by the size of its battleship fleet since the turn of the century, reorienting the fleet to incorporate new technologies would not be easy. Analyses of these potential changes in the force structure began to appear in the press, arguing that the navy needed to replace "the familiar" with the new and to stay abreast of these new technologies. While the public may have agreed that the balanced fleet was a desirable outcome, it needed to be convinced that the navy could develop and effectively utilize these new technologies.[9]

WHAT THE NAVY IS DOING

"Naval Vessels Sunk by Aerial Bombs," ca. 1921.
Naval History and Heritage Command, NH 76739-KN, Photographic Section.

With battleship construction frozen, a space opened up for the new technologies and their advocates to fill. While the Navy News Bureau had issued press releases to promote naval aviation prior to 1921, the degree of public exposure to naval aviation increased exponentially with the creation of the Bureau of Aeronautics in June of that year and the appointment of Rear Admiral Moffett as its chief. As discussed in chapter 2, Moffett had a distinguished career and demonstrated an aptitude for public relations prior to his term at the bureau. Moffett would quickly expand many of the activities already in place and use those to increase public interest in naval aviation.

The navy had already invested in air racing prior to Moffett's appointment in 1921, but, as his biographer William Trimble has noted, he viewed it as a critical tool to attract more attention to the branch and devoted even more resources to it. During air racing's peak in the 1920s, the navy focused its energies on competing in three different races: the Pulitzer Trophy, the Schneider Cup; and the Curtiss Marine

Trophy. The navy enjoyed its most significant successes in 1923; in late September, a team of naval aviators captained by Lt. Frank "Spig" Wead represented the United States during the Schneider Cup races in Cowes, England. Lt. David Rittenhouse and Lt. Rutledge Irvine finished in first and second place, and Rittenhouse set a seaplane speed record of 177 miles per hour. A week later, Lt. Alford J. "Al" Williams flew at a record speed of 243 miles per hour to win the Pulitzer Trophy. In early November, Lt. H. B. Brow flew an aircraft in excess of 265 miles per hour during an exhibition over Mitchell Field in New York with Williams close behind.[10]

These events provided several opportunities for the navy and for the Bureau of Aeronautics in particular to trumpet the advancement of naval aviation. Whereas previously press releases issued by the Navy News Bureau sought to keep expectations of experimental flights in check, the tone markedly changed after Moffett's arrival. In the weeks leading up to the 1923 races, navy press releases predicted that existing speed records would be "shattered" at the upcoming competitions. When speaking with reporters after his record-setting Pulitzer Trophy run, Lieutenant Williams reported that the physical strains were so immense that he slipped in and out of consciousness during the tight, high-speed turns and that his "damned legs were asleep" due to the lack of blood flow. The press eagerly covered these races and other record-setting events in a variety of sports for subscribers to marvel at, and these records were consistently identified as being broken by navy aircraft. Editorialists speculated on the top speeds possible with propeller-driven aircraft. The usually enthusiastic Brig. Gen. William Mitchell claimed that speeds could top out at 300 miles per hour, while others argued that 500 mph remained attainable. Due to the nature of the flight course, which involved several tight turns, Williams's Pulitzer Trophy achievement would be seen as a "freak" feat of human progress for years to come, and he would be held up as one of a select group of "speed champions." In September 1925, Williams set another speed record. He surpassed Mitchell's threshold when he piloted his Curtiss racer to a speed of 302 miles per hour, making the front page in numerous prominent newspapers.[11]

The constant striving for speed drew attention to the air racing program, and naval officials reasoned that the development had also had practical effects on aeronautical progress. As previously stated, Moffett justified air racing efforts to further the performance of combat aircraft. Air races showcased "radical innovations in aircraft design" guaranteed to improve naval aircraft, such as the use of monoplanes or retractable landing gear. To reinforce this point further, the navy argued after the 1923 Schneider Cup competition that seaworthiness and speed were the most desirable characteristics of seaplanes. The maintenance of these racing teams allowed the navy to develop stronger ties with aircraft manufacturers, even though the aircraft used in the races typically bore little technical resemblance to machines used in operational settings.[12]

Beginning in 1924, one of Moffett's primary motivations for participating in air racing—to demonstrate the effectiveness of naval aircraft in relation to those of the Army Air Corps—disappeared by mutual agreement. The army and navy withdrew their teams from the fall 1924 Pulitzer Trophy race. The following spring, Assistant Secretary of the Navy Theodore Roosevelt Jr. proposed to Gen. Mason Patrick that the two services cooperate in future races. After initially balking at this suggestion, the army relented weeks later when it appeared that funding cuts would limit future participation in air races. The navy revealed these changes in a 30 March 1925 press release that described the plan for the army and navy to collaborate during upcoming racing events that fall. The team sent to the Schneider Cup races in 1925 included fliers from both services, but army lieutenant James Doolittle bested his navy counterparts in winning the trophy for the United States.[13] The racing success had brought positive attention to the navy, but continued investment seemed likely to result in diminishing returns.

In addition to racing, Admiral Moffett also used the navy's rigid airships for PR work. During the 1920s, when the development of fixed-wing aircraft stagnated, Moffett increasingly viewed the airship as a vital weapon of war. He emerged as the most outspoken advocate for airships within the navy and proved instrumental in spurring the development of progressively larger vessels. For Moffett, the endurance of the airship made it an ideal scouting craft for the fleet.[14]

The navy's first domestically built rigid airship, the *ZR-1*, entered service in late 1923 and instantly became an asset in Moffett's public relations campaigns as the craft attracted prominent media coverage. The maiden flight of the "dreadnought of the air" on 4 September 1923 over Lakehurst, New Jersey, attracted fifteen thousand spectators eager to catch a glimpse of the large, silver-doped airship. The following week the *ZR-1* flew over New York City and Philadelphia to great fanfare and intense media coverage. The airship would later fly to Washington, D.C., and then journeyed to St. Louis on a trip timed to coincide with the International Air Races. Moffett, who attended the races, returned to Lakehurst aboard the *ZR-1*. The publicity blitz during the fall of 1923 ended with the airship, rechristened as the *Shenandoah*, making Navy Day overflights of Washington and Baltimore.[15]

During the next two years, Moffett tasked the *Shenandoah* with a seemingly never-ending series of promotional flights as he believed that additional appropriations for airships would be forthcoming from Congress if the public could witness the mighty craft. Of the *Shenandoah*'s fifty-nine flights undertaken between 1923 and 1925, those with a clear public relations function (nineteen) outnumbered the flights in which it operated as a member of the fleet (thirteen). Though the public and members of Congress had opportunities to view this technological marvel, this came at a price. Moffett had not sought to include the *Shenandoah* in exercises and thus failed to gain the operational experience necessary to turn the dirigible from a novelty into a proven asset.[16]

In October 1924, the *Shenandoah* undertook its longest journey yet when Moffett sought to demonstrate the reliability of rigid airships by sending the craft on a cross-country, round-trip flight. Flights across the continental United States proved troublesome because the warm, turbulent air over land wreaked havoc on a craft designed to function in the cool, relatively stable air masses found over much of the world's oceans. Moffett accepted these substantial risks so that the navy could publicly respond to the recent around-the-world flight undertaken by the Army Air Service. To Moffett, the *Shenandoah* needed to prove that it was not just a "fair weather ship" and that it could successfully fly for long distances as would be necessary during scouting missions over the Pacific. Moffett personally flew aboard the *Shenandoah* as it crossed the country and, although it encountered some difficulties over the southern Rockies, it survived without damage and completed the trip in only forty hours.[17]

As Moffett worked to develop enthusiasm among private industry and the general public for aircraft, the navy's submarine force assumed a lesser position in the public framing of the desired force structure. World War I aviators had drawn notice for their flamboyance and their individuality—both of which traits contrasted sharply with the horrific war of attrition on the ground—whereas Germany's unrestricted submarine warfare had associated the craft with the unjust killing of civilians and sailors. Since submarines of the day were essentially torpedo boats with a rudimentary capability to submerge for short periods of time, their relatively small size and reliance on stealth made them ideal weapons for commerce raiding. The vulnerability of submarines forced their captains to attack surface ships without following the rules of naval warfare, which required notifying the targeted vessel prior to firing on it and allowing its crew and passengers to leave the ship safely. The German U-boats sparked a major international incident after the 1915 sinking of the liner *Lusitania*, and Germany's decision to resort to unrestricted submarine warfare two years later finally precipitated U.S. intervention into the conflict. The very factors that made submarines effective in these roles, however, led the Allies to view the German submarine threat as a "scourge" unleashed upon the Atlantic Ocean.

This moral outrage over German submarines carried over into popular depictions of the war effort. In the book *Dave Darrin and the German Submarines* (1919), the titular hero listens to survivors of a sunken freighter report that the "brutes shelled us" even after they had escaped to their lifeboats. Darrin maintains his professional demeanor until he learns that an enemy submarine had torpedoed a vessel carrying his wife, then declares that "now he HATED those German fiends!" In their wartime service, the titular heroes of the *Navy Boys* book series frequently find themselves on missions where they uncovered German submarine nests on small islands in the eastern Atlantic or off the shores of Maine. The Germans show little compunction to abide by the niceties of war, even managing to disguise a submarine as a surface steamer to avoid detection by Allied ships. The threat the Germans posed could be found anywhere, and only the determined efforts of the Allies eliminated the peril.[18]

These and other negative perceptions of the submarine led to many public discussions of its being banned through international agreement. Representatives from Great Britain took the lead in proposing such a ban. This idea factored into the debates over the fate of the U.S. 1916 and 1919 naval construction programs and continued to influence the negotiating process at Washington in 1921. The notion of a ban on submarines gained some traction in the United States concurrent with the public support for naval arms limitation, among many of the same groups and individuals who had helped push for the Washington Conference in 1921. Senator William Borah of Idaho believed that all submarines should be scrapped, and he held fast to this position throughout the disarmament era. As the debate raged in Washington, the *New York Times* came out in favor of a total ban on submarines and argued that "if the conference were to agree to scrap all the submarines in commission and building, the whole world would applaud, in such abhorrence is submarine warfare held." By this time, the idea of banning submarines appeared to gain support within influential policymaking circles.[19]

The clamor against the submarine eventually amounted to nothing. The navy viewed a possible ban as a political issue, not a public relations matter. At the Washington Conference, every participant, save for Britain, saw a need for the submarine. In light of the 5:5:3 ratio, some argued a submarine ban would only have tilted the treaty even more heavily in Britain's favor. Dudley Knox predicted that submarines would eventually grow dependent on guns rather than torpedoes as their main armament, thus losing their "ruthless" character and becoming a more accepted weapon of war.[20] Indeed, the United States and other powers experimented with designing and building "cruiser" submarines during the interwar period, but the type never caught on, thus leaving submarines to continue relying on torpedo attacks.[21]

As the roles and missions for submarines remained unsettled, press coverage of submarines focused on safety and reliability. Concern over the ability of submarines to perform their missions without error became the theme defining their public image. As early as 1920, Secretary Daniels complained, "Our submarine builders have never quite gotten up to the place I think they ought to be." Others in the navy lamented that even the most advanced American submarine class, the S-class boats, paled in comparison both in size and in capability to the German U-boats that had nearly strangled Britain during the war. A series of highly publicized accidents plagued the navy's submarine force in the 1920s and complicated any attempt to create a coherent public relations strategy for submarine construction. The first major accident to occur after World War I happened on 1 September 1920 when the *S-5* attempted a test dive as it steamed near Cape May, New Jersey. A crewman left the submarine's main induction valve open as it slid beneath the waves, causing the boat to flood rapidly. The flow of water concentrated in the forward torpedo room, and the submarine settled bow first on the bottom. Fortunately for the crew, the submarine's stern protruded above the waves and a passing freighter eventually sighted the stricken craft. Rescuers from a second ship eventually cut a hole in the submarine and freed the entire crew.[22]

The press published a stream of articles on the incident describing the initial rescue operations and the desperate measures the men aboard the submarine resorted to when attempting to signal the freighter as it passed by the sunken vessel. While the men's conduct was seen as beyond reproach, editorials lamented that the technological progress of the age had found its limits. One editorial stated, "None of the new and wonderful inventions that are supposed to make this age so far ahead of all of its predecessors in human history" played a role in securing the rescue of the men of the *S-5*. While hyperbolic, the editorial expressed some unease on two fronts: submarines could potentially consign dozens of men to their death in an instant, and the navy appeared to have no means of responding to such an emergency. This concern that the navy could not adequately safeguard the lives of its submarine crews foreshadowed problems in the years ahead for the service.[23] The navy, perhaps buoyed by the successful rescue of the *S-5*'s crew, never made publicizing submarine safety a priority in the years that followed.

This proved a poor choice because a series of relatively minor accidents plagued the submarine force in succeeding years. In December 1921, the *S-48* sank off the coast of Connecticut while on builder's trials, but its crew brought the bow of the flooded submarine to the surface to facilitate rescue and all escaped unharmed. The *O-5* sank in October 1923 near the Atlantic entrance to the Panama Canal after being rammed by a steamer, and three of the submarine's crew drowned. Finally, the hapless *S-48* ran aground off the coast of New Hampshire on the night of 29 January 1925. The submarine suffered heavy damage due to a storm, but rescuers saved the entire crew and the navy salvaged the submarine in early February. None of these accidents attracted as much public attention as the *S-5*'s sinking because the loss of life was minimal to nonexistent. The crew of the next submarine would not be so lucky.[24]

The fates of the navy's aviation and submarine programs converged in the dark month of September 1925. As mentioned in chapter 2, the airship *Shenandoah* crashed on 3 September just as news broke that a PN-9 piloted by Cdr. John Rodgers disappeared between California and Hawaii. The press lauded Rodgers and his crew for their heroism after their successful rescue, and they remained in the public eye for many weeks, most notably when Rodgers became a featured Navy Day speaker the following month.[25] In spite of the laudatory coverage, the twin crashes had opened the navy to a torrent of press criticism questioning its ability to manage its advanced technological assets. Some news outlets speculated that a radical overhaul of naval aviation policy lay ahead and that the navy's airship program would come to an end with the crash of the *Shenandoah*. Others debated whether naval aviation "need[ed] advertising badly enough" to justify the risks associated with lengthy flights and argued that senior officials should show "prudence" and watch out for the pilots' safety. Secretary of the Navy Curtis Wilbur responded to the criticism by stating that senior officers had issued the orders "lawfully," that the motivations for the flights did not stem from "political maneuverings," and that Rodgers and Lansdowne both had the right and opportunity to cancel their respective missions and failed to do so.[26] Moffett's strategy had worked well at gathering attention, but the *Shenandoah* crash had exposed his extreme willingness to use aircraft and airships for publicity purposes at the expense of safety and training. This had the potential to completely undermine the base of public and political support he had fostered since 1921.

As the furor continued, on the night of 25 September—just three weeks after the crash of the *Shenandoah*—the merchant steamer *City of Rome* encountered the *S-51* off Block Island, but the low silhouette of the submarine caused confusion among the steamer's lookouts and officers when determining proper right-of-way. When the *City of Rome* finally caught sight of the smaller *S-51*'s stern running lights, it was too late to change course and the steamer collided with the smaller vessel, striking it amidships. Of the thirty-six men aboard the *S-51*, only three escaped.[27]

The navy quickly dispatched vessels to the scene, but initial dives on the *S-51* wreck revealed the ship to be a total loss and the remaining crew dead. Coming so quickly on the heels of the *Shenandoah* and PN-9 disasters, the *S-51*'s demise only worsened the public relations crisis. Prominent newspapers such as the *New York World* and the *Baltimore Sun* editorialized that the recent spate of disasters likely occurred because of mismanagement and insisted that Secretary Wilbur resign. The *Brooklyn Eagle* also argued that the navy's inability to get a salvage derrick to the *S-51* quickly represented a "scandal of inefficiency" and that the service "showed nothing but an eagerness to hush everything up." Wilbur responded by refusing to resign, but, in an apparent attempt to revive public confidence in his leadership, he ordered that rescue operations on the *S-51* continue long after divers maintained there was no hope of recovering survivors.[28] The entire response and especially the last-minute attempt at face saving showed that the navy had never developed any plan to implement in case of tragedy and harked back to the days before omnipresent press coverage became an everyday fact of life.

The effects of both disasters loomed over the navy for many months afterward. The press and Brigadier General Mitchell, upset at the loss of his friend and commander of the *Shenandoah*, Cdr. Zachary Lansdowne, continued to disparage the navy and Secretary Wilbur for their handling of the affair. Commander Lansdowne's widow spoke openly about her husband's reservations, given that he originally hailed from Greenville, Ohio (a town two hundred miles west of the *Shenandoah*'s crash site), and knew the unpredictability of Midwestern weather. In the initial aftermath of the crash and during the board of inquiry hearings in October, Lansdowne's widow stated that her husband opposed making a flight with no obvious military purpose. President Calvin Coolidge stood by his cabinet secretary during the crisis, which did abate the criticism.[29]

The fatal crash of the *Shenandoah* and other airships worldwide sparked a debate concerning their practicality and the publicity efforts surrounding them, and Moffett and the Information Section struggled to control the narrative. Moffett's lofty promises of airships blazing new trails for civilian-controlled craft and the usefulness of the type in naval warfare remained hypothetical. The *Shenandoah* crash underscored the dangers airships confronted in rough weather. On 3 October, Moffett insisted in his speech made during the launching of the new aircraft carrier *Lexington* that the navy would move forward and continue airship development, but his proclamation did not end the criticism. One editorial argued, "If the *Shenandoah* could not make a daylight flight over peaceful country fairs, what could the Navy expect of her in a wartime flight at night over enemy bases spouting shrapnel?"[30]

Moffett's strategy of using public relations appeared to have backfired, but the Morrow Board created by President Coolidge following the *Shenandoah*'s disaster sought both the secretary's and Mitchell's testimony in order to craft an aviation policy. Moffett availed himself of the opportunity to articulate practical benefits for the flights and, more importantly, present a more coherent plan for aviation than Mitchell. Thanks in part to his performance and his ability to court powerful political allies, Moffett suffered remarkably little publicly or politically for the crash of the *Shenandoah*. Meanwhile, Mitchell's allegations of negligence made against the senior leadership of both the army and the navy led to a court-martial that attracted significant media attention. The trial turned into a public examination of military aviation, and Mitchell eventually lost his case. He chose to resign rather than accept a five-year suspension from the army.[31]

Even with the *Shenandoah*'s crash, the Bureau of Aeronautics continued to believe in the viability of airships and remained steadfast in its efforts to procure more of these crafts for the navy. The Morrow Board recommended expanding the navy's air arm and led Congress to authorize two new mammoth airships. Moffett continued to argue that the navy's development of airships for military purposes would spark the development of a vast fleet of commercial airships that would transport cargo and passengers across the United States and around the globe. He went on to label the crew of the *Shenandoah* "builders of a new age and a new freedom for the human race."[32] With these new authorizations, Moffett's use of lofty rhetoric and touting of commercial benefits to airship development constituted his public campaign to restore faith in his maligned craft.

Moffett had used the power of his position to capitalize on the practicality and visibility of aircraft in building up the Bureau of Aeronautics and to politically survive the *Shenandoah* affair, but the submarine force still lacked a single public champion to lead it beyond the *S-51* disaster. Once again, safety concerns appeared to overwhelm the operational value of submarines. Rehabilitating the image of the submarine force proved difficult because the *S-51* sinking had briefly reignited talk in the United States of supporting a ban on submarines at the next disarmament conference. The renewed calls for the ban originated in Britain, which had just lost one of its own submarines, the *M-1*, in an accident that killed its crew. Supporters of a ban also revived the humanitarian issues posed by submarines during World War I and the seemingly inordinate risks endured by the officers and men assigned to such vessels. Supporters of the ban ironically conceded, however, that the risk to the crews did not provide a significant enough reason for nations to ban submarines.[33] In essence, submarine ban advocates had seized on the accidents to renew their cause but stopped short of extending their concern for human life to submarine crews.

As talk of a ban circulated in the press, the navy wrestled with what to do about the sunken hulk of the *S-51*. Initially, the navy planned to contract with civilian firms to raise the submarine, but Lt. Edward Ellsberg, a diver stationed at the New York Navy Yard, helped persuade officials in Washington to use the service's own ships and men for the task. The operation, led by Capt. Ernest J. King, turned into an extended ordeal as the ocean depths, weather, and technical hurdles all limited the progress of the divers and salvagers. Overly optimistic articles continued to appear in the nation's newspapers, and officers on the scene promised a quick resolution to the operation. It then came as a bitter disappointment when the onset of winter weather forced a postponement of the salvage operations until spring, thus leaving the issue unresolved.[34] Thus, these first few months of the salvage operation seemed to bring the navy no credit for deciding to raise the submarine itself.

When the salvage vessels returned to the *S-51* site in April 1926, the navy finally gained praise and respect for its handling of the affair. Lieutenant Ellsberg's suggestion that the navy manage its own salvage operation—while potentially risky and, according to Ellsberg, motivated by a sense of duty and professionalism rather than a desire to court public opinion—proved valuable in rehabilitating the service's image. After further difficulties, the navy finally brought the *S-51* to the surface using pontoons in July 1926 and towed it to the New York Navy Yard in Brooklyn for inspection. In an outpouring of grief, respect, and morbid curiosity, more than fifty thousand people filed by the dry dock at the yard that housed the *S-51* to catch a glimpse of the submarine that had served as a watery grave for its crew. Newspapers lauded the navy's "spirit to carry on" in spite of the dangers and hoped that the service learned valuable lessons that would prevent future disasters. The media also praised Lieutenant Ellsberg and the rest of the divers who made the salvage of the *S-51* possible. Ellsberg became a national celebrity, and his recounting of the salvage operations in various press outlets led to the publication of his memoir of the incident, *On the Bottom*, in 1928.[35]

King's and Ellberg's efforts brought them and the navy acclaim and temporarily ended the debates on the viability of submarines, but this situation was fleeting. Just two years later, on 17 December 1927, the *S-4* collided with the U.S. Coast Guard cutter *Paulding* while attempting to surface after a short dive near Provincetown, Massachusetts. Initially thought to be a total loss, the submarine settled on the bottom partially intact, and six men in the forward torpedo room survived the incident. The navy rushed vessels to the scene and recalled many of the veterans of the *S-51* operation, including Captain King and a retired Commander Ellsberg. When divers reached the *S-4* on 19 December, they communicated with the survivors trapped within the submarine by tapping on the hull. Bad weather delayed the rescue efforts, and the six men died of asphyxiation before divers could attach an air hose to the stricken submarine.[36]

The Information Section worked to issue daily press releases as the scale of the tragedy unfolded. Compared to the slow trickle of press releases after the Honda Point accident, this represented a significant improvement and a step toward transparency. The personnel on the scene of the S-4 sinking, however, did not match the professionalism of the officers in Washington. When a tugboat carrying newspaper correspondents attempted to close in on the site, men aboard the salvage vessels so disdained their presence that they trained a firehose on the boat to ward it off. With the sailors off Provincetown doing little to aid in the flow of information, the only news was what came from Washington or from district headquarters at the Portsmouth Navy Yard.[37]

The navy's inability to rescue the survivors of the collision created a storm of criticism in the press and rekindled many of the same issues debated during the aftermath of the S-51 sinking. Secretary Wilbur came under fire yet again for his apparent lack of energy and inability to properly administer the Navy Department. Editorials questioned whether the navy had learned anything from the S-51 disaster or took seriously any of the suggestions it received to develop a reliable means of rescuing submariners. Wilbur quickly responded to the criticism by releasing a letter from Adm. George H. Rock of the Bureau of Construction explaining the various means considered and rejected by the bureau to improve the safety of submarines. This letter failed to stem the tide of advice from "experts" and suggestions from members of the public published in the press. As a result, it appeared that the navy lacked the ability to learn from its mistakes or properly care for its sailors. Some press articles even resurrected the idea of banning submarines altogether due to the dangers their crewmen routinely faced.[38]

More problematic were charges that "red tape" clogged the navy's bureaucracy and made the service ill-suited to respond to crisis situations like the accidental ramming of the S-4. The flap over Rear Adm. Thomas Magruder's September 1927 *Saturday Evening Post* article, discussed in chapter 2, which had raised numerous charges of inefficiency, had only been settled weeks prior to the sinking of the S-4, and the navy's apparent tardiness during the rescue operation resurrected many of the charges made in 1925 and repeated by Magruder. Even the news of King and Ellsberg's recall failed to stem the flood of negative press. The press labeled Secretary Wilbur's visit to the salvage site a week after the S-4's sinking a fit of "belated energy." Ellsberg, still held in high regard as an expert on such matters, defended the Navy Department's efforts in attempting to rescue the crew of the S-4, but he would later argue that several feasible means existed for the navy to improve the safety of submarines without compromising their operational utility.[39]

USS *S-4* in dry dock at Boston Navy Yard after salvage, 19 March 1928.
Naval History and Heritage Command, NH 41826, Photographic Section.

As the submarine force continued to grapple with concerns over safety, Moffett evolved his approach to public relations by limiting his aviators' exposure to risk for publicity. Up until the *Shenandoah* crash, Rear Admiral Moffett and the Bureau of Aeronautics relied on "manufactured" events to draw attention to naval aviation. In other words, the bureau called attention to events designed to maximize public interest but of questionable military value. During the debates over an independent air service, such activities demonstrated that the navy could operate aircraft effectively and develop types equivalent to those produced for the Army Air Corps. The navy had successfully staved off the threat of unification in part because Moffett had kept naval aviation in the public eye.

Mitchell's professional demise and the promise of increased resources thanks to the Morrow Board finally eased the pressure on Moffett to generate publicity that had little or no military value. The evident cutbacks in air racing in 1925 continued in the years thereafter as Moffett curtailed the navy's involvement in the sport. In February 1927, the navy issued a press release explaining its pilots' absence from the upcoming Schneider Cup race, arguing that the service "has fostered racing as far as it [could] under present conditions." Naval officials hoped that civilian manufacturers would maintain an American presence in competitive air racing, and after 1929, the navy's involvement in races would be confined to events involving standard service aircraft or balloons. The navy would enter aircraft for the Curtiss Marine Trophy during the next few years, but these races involved aircraft not specifically designed or modified for racing. During a speech in 1931, David S. Ingalls, the assistant secretary of the navy for the air, repudiated previous statements regarding the factors shaping the design of naval aircraft when he stated that current planes, while fast, are designed for "cruising radius," the ability to carry weapons and equipment, and the "extreme ruggedness" needed to survive carrier landings. When discussing the end of the navy's involvement in racing, Moffett argued that the funds expended on developing high-speed aircraft was "money well spent."[40]

Surprisingly, the drawdown of the navy's racing program dismayed Congress and also the navy's most prominent pilot: Lt. Al Williams. During the late 1920s, the navy allowed Williams to spend much of his time developing the Mercury Racer at the Naval Aircraft Factory in anticipation of future races, but the plane Williams helped design failed to make a single flight in the 1929 Schneider Cup due to technical issues. Members of the House Naval Affairs Committee publicly claimed that they could not understand why the navy, which had long touted the benefits of entering major racing competitions, suddenly lost interest in racing and appeared to allow foreign rivals to gain a technological edge. Williams selfishly complained to the navy for revoking his special status and ordering him to sea duty. Congress debated a resolution to promote Williams to captain and to place him on the retired list, but the navy opposed the move, believing that it had unfairly favored Williams over other prominent racers, such as Rittenhouse. Congress dropped the proposed resolution, and Williams resigned his commission; he later joined the Marine Corps with the rank of captain and served in that branch until 1940 when he was forced to resign for advocating an independent air force. In hindsight, the 1930 imbroglio over Williams signaled the end of the navy's interest in international aircraft racing.[41]

Even as the Bureau of Aeronautics ceased sending aircraft to races in the late 1920s, Moffett sought to maintain a presence at air shows and air races. Instead of racing, the aircraft demonstrated formation flying and other types of maneuvers to the large crowds in attendance. As early as 1928, navy pilots established informal flight demonstration teams; the first of these was known as the Three Sea Hawks. The group consisting of pilots from the carrier *Saratoga* flew at several public gatherings on the West Coast, the most prominent of these being the 1928 National Air Races in Los Angeles. The team disbanded in 1929 when its members received new orders. While the navy did not create permanent teams until the post–World War II creation of The Blue Angels, the service sent aircraft to the National Air Races each year to stage exhibition flights. The exhibitions provided excellent fodder for newsreel cameras as navy aircraft performed complicated maneuvers for delighted spectators below. The navy only insisted that any air show in which its aircraft participated *not* also feature dangerous stunt flights, lest the public link the service with daredevil maneuvers. Even if the navy's actual participation in air races remained limited to exhibition flights, popular works of entertainment continued to associate the service with racing. The 1939 film *Tail Spin*, written by Frank Wead, focused on the activities of female pilots as they competed in transcontinental races based on a real event, the Women's Air Derby. To add color to the proceedings, Wead included a character who was a naval aviator participating in the races.[42] Taking part in more routine flights at races and shows kept naval aviation visible without having to devote the huge resources that had once defined its participation in the Schneider Cup and other competitions.

Moffett and others in the Bureau of Aeronautics sought to keep naval aviation in the public eye, and two developments at the end of the decade aided this goal. First, the navy finally commissioned its new aircraft carriers, the *Lexington* and *Saratoga*. The ships themselves were technological marvels; constructed on the unfinished hulls of battle cruisers authorized in the 1916 program, they reigned as the largest aircraft carriers in the world until 1945. In comparison to the navy's first aircraft carrier, the diminutive and lumbering *Langley*, these two carriers represented a monumental leap forward. The ships' power plants generated 180,000 horsepower via turboelectric motors and endowed the ships with very high steaming speeds of up to thirty-five knots. The sheer size of the new ships and their large complements of aircraft—usually between seventy-five and eighty-five planes, but capable of a hundred or more—could attract attention simply by operating with the fleet.[43]

Both ships would spend much of 1928 as crews learned to operate aircraft from their much larger decks, finally joining the fleet by the end of the year. Their first major exercise with the fleet, Fleet Problem IX in January 1929, resulted in much publicity about their remarkable capabilities. Reports published prior to the commencement of the exercise speculated that outside interest among naval powers would be high because Fleet Problem IX would be the first operational test of carriers of that size. Newspapers dispatched special correspondents to the event, with the *New York Times* employing a former Royal Navy officer, and the

Los Angeles Times using an active-duty officer, Lt. Arthur Ageton. The climax of the exercise occurred on 26 January when the *Saratoga* approached the Panama Canal from the south and launched an eighty-three-plane attack on the Pedro Miguel and Miraflores Locks on the Pacific side of the canal. The raid caught the defenders by surprise, and umpires ruled the locks destroyed, although planes from the *Lexington* and gunfire from battleships "sank" the *Saratoga* while its aircraft were away. The attack, masterminded by Rear Adm. Joseph M. Reeves, was the subject of press articles for weeks afterward. These news articles reinforced the idea that the new carriers, with their high speeds and large air groups, constituted a significant step forward for naval aviation.[44]

Fleet Problem IX brought favorable press coverage, and this would be reinforced with the premiere of *The Flying Fleet* in New York just weeks after the end of the exercise. The film, for which Wead earned his first story credit, told the story of young aviators training at Pensacola, Florida, and North Island, California, and climaxed with a loose retelling of the PN-9 saga from September 1925. Wead's expertise proved vital in crafting the first story set among naval aviation. Of the flying sequences, *New York Times* film critic Mordaunt Hall appreciated how "they roll and turn as one machine, the pilots being apparently as much at home in the clouds as cavalrymen on terra firma. And although there have been seen on the screen World War air duels and various other exciting airplane activities, nothing quite as stirring or as beautiful as some of these scenes has so far been pictured in animated photography."[45]

The opportunities to showcase aviation on-screen certainly bolstered Moffett's efforts, but the new carriers could sometimes generate headlines for reasons other than standard fleet operations. By November 1929, a severe drought in Washington State had dried up the rivers and shut down hydroelectric plants, causing the city of Tacoma to ration its electricity. After an appeal from civic officials, Secretary of the Navy Charles F. Adams overruled the advice of the Bureau of Engineering and transferred the *Lexington*—undergoing a refit at the nearby Puget Sound Navy Yard—to Tacoma so that the city could tap directly into the carrier's turboelectric drive. Crowds of onlookers watched as the tugs maneuvered the *Lexington* into position on 15 December, and the ship generated 20,000 kilowatts of electricity two days later following the construction of temporary transmission lines from the ship to the city's electrical grid. While in port, the navy encouraged greater contact with the public and invited a group of more than five hundred Boy Scouts from all over the state of Washington to come aboard the ship. Dudley Knox used the incident to argue that the utilization of the *Lexington* in this role constituted "a proper naval function and one of the by-products of the national investment in a Navy." After rains finally restored the water flow to nearby rivers, the *Lexington* left Tacoma on 17 January 1930 after supplying Tacoma's electricity for an entire month.⁴⁶

Still, the most reliable means of attracting attention to the carriers came through air operations, but, because the navy denied all requests for coverage of Fleet Problems X and XI in 1930, the next major public test of the carriers did not occur until 1931. Fleet Problem XII called for the *Lexington* and *Saratoga* to defend a hypothetical canal in Nicaragua from the Black fleet, which consisted of the navy's battleships and the carrier *Langley*. Immediately, the press seized on the exercise as a test of naval aviation and a revival of the "airplanes versus battleships" debate. The exercise was an operational disappointment due to the complete imbalance of the fleets and the inability of the two carriers to concentrate their strength against a single enemy force, which allowed Black to safely achieve its objectives and end the exercise. Analyses of the exercise concluded not that naval aviation was weak or flawed in failing to prevent Black success, but that the navy simply needed more carriers to have a solid "naval air force." In the *New York Times*, Hanson Baldwin argued that the maneuvers proved that aircraft had the potential to revolutionize naval warfare, and he believed "the influence of airpower upon naval history" existed to make fleets dependent on strong air forces in combat situations.⁴⁷ Even in this moment of supposed failure, Baldwin and other writers pressed the case for expansion that furthered the goals of the Bureau of Aeronautics.

The mix of operational experience and Hollywood spectacle that drew attention to naval aviation offered Moffett a safer template for promoting the resurgent airship program. In a marked departure from the experience with the *Shenandoah*, Moffett and the navy limited the amount of publicity surrounding its mammoth new airship, the *Akron*. The board of inquiry for the *Shenandoah* crash had questioned the value of its publicity flights but fell short of rebuking the admiral. Although Moffett had paid no political price for the *Shenandoah*'s crash, his treatment of the *Akron* showed an unwillingness to expose the new airship to unnecessary risk. Whereas the commissioning of the *Shenandoah* in 1923 had been a spectacle staged by Moffett, he intended for the *Akron*'s commissioning in 1931 to be out of the public eye; only the Goodyear Corporation's pleas reluctantly led the navy to grant press access to the ceremony. Some of the *Shenandoah*'s first flights had occurred over New York City and generated headlines, but Moffett kept the press away from the *Akron* until after the completion of its initial tests. The *Akron* would embark on a transcontinental flight in May 1932 with no press aboard, which again differed markedly from the previous approach with the *Shenandoah*.⁴⁸

Moffett's limits on publicity for the *Akron* in no way diminished his enthusiasm for the airship program nor meant that he would heretofore reject all publicity for it. Instead, Hollywood helped Moffett give the program public visibility. The commissioning of the *Akron* coincided with the release of the Wead-penned film *Dirigible* (1931), which showcased the navy's airship program. Starring Jack Holt as Jack Bradon and Ralph Graves as "Frisky" Pierce, the film focused on the friendly rivalry between lighter- and heavier-than-air pilots in competition to fly to the South Pole and notably featured an airship rescuing downed fixed-wing aviators. The film highlighted many key elements of the airship program, including the massive shed hangars that stored the navy's airships at Lakehurst and the recently tested capability to launch and retrieve aircraft by means of a "trapeze" system fitted to the underside of an airship's hull. These details required the construction of extensive models and location shooting, making it the most expensive film produced by Columbia Pictures at that time. Upon its release, *Dirigible* became both a critical and box office success.[49]

The same opportunities afforded the airship program by Hollywood also applied to the carrier fleet. Wead again provided a platform for publicity by writing the screenplay for *Hell Divers*, released in December 1931 by MGM. As mentioned in chapter 4, the fraught development process for *Hell Divers* had produced a visually impressive film that conveyed much about the current state of naval aviation and depicted the delicate choreography characteristic of flight deck operations aboard a carrier. Several overhead shots of the *Saratoga* emphasize the size of the carrier and its large complement of aircraft. The aviation sequences stunned critics and audiences, leading Mordaunt Hall, who wrote, "It takes one through the curriculum of Uncle Sam's sailors of the air, from a naval base on land to wonderful sights of pilots bringing their machines down on the deck of the *Saratoga*." The sight of aircraft landing on the deck aroused spontaneous applause from the audience. Hall noted that "there [were] flashes of dozens of machines in the air at one time and others of these same machines safely at rest on this specially constructed warship."[50] The *New York Evening Post* glowingly wrote that the navy had not put on a "first class" show since the Great White Fleet until the release of *Hell Divers*. The *Post*'s review further added that *Hell Divers* was "worth its weight in gold in keeping alive in the young men—and the young women, too—of this country their historic pride in their Navy."[51]

Moffett and his subordinates had perfected a new public relations paradigm by the early 1930s that portrayed aviation as effective and safe, but the submarine accidents of the 1920s continued to shape portrayals of the latter. Released three

USS *Saratoga* during fleet review in New York City, 31 May 1934.
Naval History and Heritage Command, NH 681, Photographic Section.

months after the sinking of the *S-4*, Frank Capra's motion picture *Submarine* (1928) prominently features a submarine sinking to the ocean floor with many of its crew still alive and trapped beneath the waves. At the film's climax, the navy diver implausibly rescues the crew by attaching an air hose to the stricken submarine. To its credit, the navy refused to shy away from allowing depictions of such tragedies to reach movie screens, but the method that enabled the crew's rescue in the film was based on an unrealistic feat of derring-do.[52] If audiences actually believed this was a viable solution to submarine accidents, this posed a serious problem for the navy because it lacked a realistic solution to the problem.

In the months and years after the *S-4* disaster, the navy publicized several concurrent efforts to improve submarine safety. In 1928, the navy began work on two devices intended to allow men trapped aboard submarines to reach safety. The first of these, the Momsen lung, was developed by Lt. Charles "Swede" Momsen in 1929. Attached to the Submarine Safety Test Unit, Momsen and his assistants utilized the salvaged *S-4* to test their new device. Men successfully escaped from the submarine at depths of more than two hundred feet, or nearly twice the depth at which the submarine had sunk in 1927. The navy publicized the tests and the successful result, leading to very positive press assessments of the service's ability to solve this urgent problem. Concurrent with these tests, the navy announced that it would permanently attach a submarine salvage ship with a crew of divers to each of the navy's fleets to allow for rapid responses to accidents. To further promote these advances, in August 1930, a Hearst Metrotone newsreel featured footage of "thrilling" and successful tests of the Momsen lung conducted aboard the *S-22* off New London, Connecticut. At one point, the navy even arranged for an officer attached to its diving unit to give a public lecture at the YMCA in Washington, D.C., that included the screening of several films made during the testing of the new rescue equipment.[53]

While the navy may have been working to correct deficiencies in submarine rescue equipment, the release of *Men without Women* (1930) failed to correct any falsities regarding submarine disasters. Like that of *Submarine*, the plot of John Ford's film climaxes with the sinking of an American submarine, this time off the coast of China. The crew of the submarine ultimately escapes by swimming out of the torpedo tubes without any sort of breathing device, a scenario even more implausible than that seen in the preceding *Submarine*. As the eminent film historian Laurence Suid notes, these films conveyed false impressions to the public of the feasibility of rescuing men from trapped submarines while the navy lacked this capability.[54] Even though the navy had already begun testing better rescue equipment by the time of *Men without Women*'s release, the film continued to give audiences unrealistic expectations of survival the next time a submarine accident occurred. The navy was perhaps fortunate that another submarine accident didn't occur in the wake of these films that would have exposed these feats of rescue as Hollywood mythmaking rather than a credible solution to a crisis.

The questions of safety dogged submarines more than aircraft at least in part because the navy's concept of submarine operations remained unsettled. The service definitely valued submarines, but it remained unclear exactly what missions they might undertake in war. In iterations of War Plan Orange, submarines would act as advance scouts for the fleet as it steamed across the Pacific to meet the Imperial Japanese navy in battle. The navy also employed submarines to deny the enemy sea control in major exercises such as Grand Joint Exercise 4 held in Hawaiian waters in February 1932. Gradually, the navy began employing its submarines in independent offensive operations and, in an experience comparable to that of the aircraft carriers, "freed" submarines from being tied to the battle line. Reflective of this shift in usage, the navy began working toward a standard submarine design capable of transpacific voyages and of operating independently in an offensive capacity. Only in 1939 did the navy begin internally discussing the utilization of the submarines in a *guerre de course* campaign against enemy merchant shipping.[55]

However important these developments were, these doctrinal and technical debates took place out of public view. The lack of agreement on the utility of submarines and the technical requirements to build boats prevented the creation of any public relations campaigns similar to those for naval aviation. Moreover, submarines faced the simple fact that their most distinctive quality—the ability to submerge—meant they could not capitalize on highly visible public events. While surfaced, their relatively small size, combined with the design considerations that allowed submarines to submerge, meant that the type would be dwarfed if placed alongside other ships. Given that newsreels tended to include only visually interesting subjects, submarines rarely factored into this form of media. When they did appear, it was usually in a relatively unexciting way, although *Universal Newsreel* once touted the dangers involved for a cameraman as he operated a camera mounted on a submarine's mast as it dove beneath the waves. As such, the doctrinal change toward independent operations received only scant publicity during the 1930s.[56]

These isolated instances of publicity and the internal debates over submarine roles and missions continued to mask that the lack of a clear advocate for these craft created a vacuum of public perception. Within this space, Ellsberg, in spite of his junior rank, remained perhaps the most influential figure in publicizing the submarine force. After participating in the salvage operations of the *S-51* and *S-4* and writing a memoir, he turned his hand to fiction and published a World War I submarine novel titled *Pigboats* in 1931. MGM released a film adaptation of the novel, retitled *Hell Below*, in April 1933. Set aboard the fictional *AL-14*, *Hell Below* depicted the submarine conducting offensive operations against German ships and, in the film's climax, port facilities on the Adriatic Sea. Notably, the film focused on submarines in combat and never addressed any safety issues. The navy assisted in the production of the film, but it failed to make much of an impression with critics and audiences because of its "jarring" mix of farce and melodrama.[57]

Submarines, like the beleaguered airship program, remained inextricably linked to their safety records. Despite all the precautions taken by Moffett in the years since the *Shenandoah* crash, the effort to prove the dirigible's worth ended in tragedy. On 4 April 1933, the *Akron* crashed while en route from Washington to Lakehurst. Admiral Moffett, along with seventy-two crew and passengers, died when the airship broke up during a heavy storm off the New Jersey coast. The navy responded quickly to the accident, but ships in the vicinity rescued only three survivors.

Adding to the tragedy, the blimp *J-3* crashed while searching for wreckage and survivors, killing two crewmen . The navy did not discourage access to the accident scene, thus allowing American filmgoers to watch footage of both wrecks and the convalescing survivors via newsreel.[58] Unlike with the *Shenandoah*, *S-51*, and *S-4*, the press found little to criticize with the navy's release of information about the accident; that the crash occurred during a routine training flight rather than a tour of state fairs certainly had something do with it, meaning that Moffett's restraint in promoting the *Akron* had been successful.

Instead, most analyses of the accident focused on the future of the airship in naval service. Articles and editorials argued the airship had a "checkered career" in every foreign and domestic military service and questioned whether the *Akron*'s crash would cause the demise of the U.S. airship program. Some still believed that "if the rigid airship was of use before this disaster, it cannot be argued now that the disaster has destroyed it." The new head of the Bureau of Aeronautics, Rear Adm. Ernest J. King, confirmed that the navy would continue to operate the *Akron*'s sister ship, the USS *Macon*, and that he expected it to have a long life of "usefulness."[59]

The *Macon* operated with the fleet over the next two years, but the craft failed to succeed in its scouting mission during Fleet Problem XV in 1934. During a flight from California to Florida in April 1934, the *Macon* began to show signs of structural defects near its tail fins. These defects eventually proved fatal to the *Macon*, causing it to crash on 12 February 1935 when a strong gust of wind struck it as it flew near Point Sur, California. The lessons learned from the *Akron*—namely, the inclusion of proper survival gear—contributed to saving the lives of all but two men out of a crew of eighty-three. While the navy still possessed the old USS *Los Angeles* in reserve, the press immediately recognized that the crash of the *Macon* marked the end of the navy's experimentation with rigid airships.[60] With Moffett, their primary champion, now deceased, no one wanted to advocate for a craft with such a dubious operational record.

King's appointment to succeed Moffett as chief of the Bureau of Aeronautics heralded another shift in the bureau's public relations priorities. The demise of the airship program notwithstanding, the bureau still had an expanding carrier fleet at its disposal with the U.S. navy's first purpose-built carrier, the *Ranger*, entering service in 1934. The *Ranger* ultimately proved a disappointment, but the larger, more capable *Yorktown* and *Enterprise* entered into service in 1937 and 1938, respectively. These ships, combined with a steadily increasing number of planes and pilots, meant that the bureau was no longer in the organizationally precarious position of its formative years because the navy better understood the value that the carriers brought to the fleet. Only on rare occasions did the carriers engage in pure publicity work, such as in 1934 when aircraft from the *Lexington* staged a mock dive-bombing attack on a destroyer in full view of New York City as the carrier departed the city after a large fleet review that spring. As such, media coverage of naval aviation mostly ceased to view it as a novelty but rather as an integral part of fleet operations.[61]

As aviation's role cemented into place, the image of the submarine force remained unsettled. Hollywood films continued to propagate the notion that submarines remained unsafe, but a pair of films released in 1937 finally showcased some of the new rescue equipment developed in the intervening years. As mentioned in chapter 4, that year Columbia released its remake of Frank Capra's *Submarine* retitled as *The Devil's Playground*. The plot remained unchanged from the original film, but the remake included a scene where many of the submarine's crew used Momsen lungs to ascend to the surface after an accident. Curiously, the Motion Picture Board had objected to the accuracy of the filmmaker's use of the lungs in addition to many other elements of the story, but it is likely that the desire to give the lungs more publicity ultimately helped the film secure approval.[62] The cooperation, however, did little to attract notice of the new technology or the film itself, which one review labeled as "B product at its unimportant best."[63]

Several months later, Warner Brothers released *Submarine D-1*, based on a Wead screenplay and directed by Lloyd Bacon. Wead's story fictionalized the development of the other major submarine rescue device, the McCann Rescue Chamber, which could attach to a submarine's hull and rescue eight crewmen at a time. As with the earlier *Hell Divers*, the navy's familiarity with Wead and the obvious potential for positive publicity outweighed the numerous security concerns raised by allowing the crew to film aboard a navy submarine. This access proved essential for the film's financial success, and reviewers claimed the film's accuracy and effects "held the attention of the preview audience in a vise-like grip."[64] The film proved successful enough that Warner Brothers adapted it into a radio play that aired on the *Jack Benny* program.

By the late 1930s, the navy had attempted to convince the public of the importance and the effectiveness of its aviation arm and of its submarine force. The expiration of the battleship building holidays agreed to at the Washington Conference, however, changed the equation somewhat as the service needed to justify capital ship new construction. Many officers argued that only the battleship could attain "real command of the sea" and that the type was "still supreme" in the pantheon of naval weapons systems. Articles in the popular press argued that aviation, even after the rapid developments of the past decade, could only harass the battleship and not sink it in combat. The navy itself added to the confusion in 1938 when the chief of naval operations, Adm. William D. Leahy, remarked that the battleship remained "the bulwark of offensive and defensive power upon which all other types must depend for support when driven back by superior forces." These speeches and articles dismissing the new upstart technologies in favor of the battleship did not entirely repudiate the effort to develop aviation and submarines, but rather demonstrated that naval officials altered their messages depending on specific circumstances.[65]

Interwar publicity struggled to reflect the ideal of the "three-plane" navy that had encompassed the service's efforts to build a balanced fleet. Reflective of the "transformational" nature of the period, Moffett and officers such as Ellsberg attempted to show the public that the service had committed itself to modifying its conception of naval warfare. This process was not always a smooth one, nor was it entirely consistent. Moffett used his bureaucratic position to craft a high-risk public relations strategy that could have backfired on him and the entire Bureau of Aeronautics, but he survived and transitioned into a new era of publicity built around the carrier fleet and Hollywood. Concurrently, the submarine fleet lacked the coherent vision of the bureau, and publicity often struggled merely to portray the boats as safe, let alone as moral and useful implements of naval warfare. Unfortunately, the elements of the "three-plane" navy often appeared in isolation to one another and never truly reflected the idea of naval combined arms. Ironically, safety emerged as one of the few commonalities between aviation and submarine publicity, forcing the Information Section/Public Relations Branch to learn, at the cost of many men and machines, how to better manage publicity when tragedy struck. This was challenging because the circumstances and context of each accident made it extremely difficult to fully control the coverage. By 1939, these basic safety questions continued to dog the submarine force's image even as aviation had become an accepted part of the fleet, just as Moffett had hoped.

◄ 7 ►
"THE FIRST LINE OF DEFENSE"
PUBLIC DEFINITIONS OF THE INTERWAR NAVY'S MISSION

For a world scarred by a brutal and costly war, the Washington Naval Conference offered a new vision of hope and cooperation. In his farewell address to the conference delegates, President Harding said, "The faith plighted here today will mark the beginning of a new and better epoch in human progress. . . . You have written the first effective expression of the great Powers in the consciousness of peace and the utter futility of war." The editors of the *Philadelphia Inquirer* echoed Harding's sentiments by asserting, "The pessimist, the prophet of evil, and the gloom peddler had a rotten day" when the nine nations signed the agreements that had come from months of negotiations. Given that the pressure for disarmament had arisen at least in part because of a groundswell of public support, the *New York Evening Mail* declared that the conference "proved the power of enlightened public opinion when it chooses to assert itself."[1] This sense of peaceful accomplishment created a mood of euphoria that profoundly rejected the assertions made by the former secretary of the navy Josephus Daniels and others that a lasting peace required an enlarged fleet.

In this environment, naval leaders could not easily justify the greater force structure that they considered vital to American security. In previous years, navalists argued that a fleet could defend U.S. interests abroad and deter foreign naval threats against North America. The famous phrase justifying the Naval Act of 1916—"a navy, second to none"—claimed that simple supremacy was a worthwhile goal unto itself. Now none of those appeals seemed to hold any weight with the public. As a result, the U.S. Navy, an institution that viewed itself as the nation's "first line of defense," would resort to justifying its value without focusing on national security. This seemed intuitive to a generation of naval officers well versed in the works of Alfred Thayer Mahan who understood that sea power had a significant role to play in maintaining a prosperous peace. Communicating the navy's peacetime value, however, proved much more difficult in practice. Making matters perhaps more difficult was the fact that the Information Section (and its successor, the Public Relations Branch) had a much more limited role in this specific realm because so much of what became fodder for debate came from the press and official statements from senior officers and civilians that mostly bypassed its control. Still, the office could help frame the debate, and, during the 1920s and 1930s, it helped publicize the nonmilitary benefits of the navy to the nation, including its role in fostering the growth of American commerce and the provision of humanitarian relief. In doing so, appeals for naval expansion often utilized indirect arguments, frequently relying on historical analogies to connect to contemporary policy concerns. As the 1930s wore on and the international situation deteriorated, however, the navy began to adjust its message and put national security at the forefront of naval policy.[2]

In the aftermath of the Washington Conference of 1921–22, the navy and its supporters developed two distinct rationales for justifying naval expenditures. One path was to directly challenge the legitimacy of arms limitation. Most senior naval officers opposed the treaty terms, although Capt. William Veazie Pratt, who later served as both the commander in chief of the United States Fleet and the chief of naval operations, became one of the few notable proponents of disarmament within the navy because he believed the Five-Power Treaty set clear and reasonable goals for appropriations and construction.[3] Since many sources of publicity and lobbying, such as William Randolph Hearst, the Navy League, and, to some degree, Dudley W. Knox, were outsiders to the Navy Department, they could more freely state their opinions on disarmament and whether they believed it good for the navy or the nation as a whole. Knox had hoped his *The Eclipse of American Sea Power* would trigger a backlash against the treaties, but this never came to pass.

The effects of the treaties spilled over into other policy debates. In the spring of 1922, as Congress debated a new appropriations bill that threatened to reduce the navy's enlisted personnel strength to 65,000—a reduction of nearly half and 31,000 shy of the Navy Department's estimated manpower needs—prominent officials attempted to raise public awareness on the issue. Members of Congress argued that any further decline in naval efficiency threatened to turn the United States into "the third naval power" behind Great Britain and Japan and alleged that more than one-third of American battleships would need to remain out of commission should the personnel bill pass. In a public appearance, Capt. Luke McNamee, the head of the Office of Naval Intelligence, pointed out, "A modern Navy is not something that one can take out of one's pocket when war breaks out and then toss merrily on the scrap heap when it is over." Naval officers, he argued, genuinely desired peace and hoped that another war would never come but recognized that only through the maintenance of an efficient naval establishment could American security be guaranteed, now or in the future.[4]

Many of the small group of officers who had advocated for the creation of the Information Section in 1922, including Knox and Captain McNamee, unsurprisingly made public calls to renew construction in the years after the Washington Conference. Knox's *Eclipse of American Sea Power* made an extended plea for new ships, and McNamee echoed that sentiment in a speech before the Women's Republican Club of Massachusetts in January 1923. There he contended that coming global instability and resource competition required a navy and that a strong fleet remained the best instrument capable of ensuring American economic sufficiency. As part of the sea control triad, McNamee maintained that the navy could successfully enforce national policy through the maintenance of trade routes, the protection of overseas territories, and the enforcement of American diplomatic policy, of which he stated, "It is a sad commentary on human nature to note what an emphasis a battleship adds to diplomatic note." McNamee argued that "disarmament by example" was a foolish policy resulting from falsehoods found in foreign-based propaganda. Without the navy, he asserted, there would be no way to maintain American prestige in the international system or to "guard our families and firesides."[5]

The Navy League agreed with many of the arguments made by Knox and likewise believed that the Washington treaties left much to be desired, yet league officials feared that an open and forceful denouncement of the treaties would lead to ruin for both the organization and its cause. The league's recent return from near ruin left its leaders reluctant to appear publicly to fan the flames of conflict, especially since the treaties had defused a possible arms race. Instead, many of the league's press releases advocated building the fleet to the limits specified as part of the Five-Power Treaty. Since building to the treaty limits constituted expansion in an absolute sense, it provided the Navy League with the rhetorical cover to continue to advocate for construction. The Five-Power Treaty contained no minimum construction requirements for the signatories to uphold. Thus, no new ships were necessary to uphold the terms of the treaty, but the league believed that some construction was necessary to enable the navy to fulfill American security commitments. Beginning just after the Washington Conference adjourned, but lasting well into the 1930s, the Navy League would issue press releases highlighting the ratios of fleet strengths as they existed to make the case for new rounds of naval construction.[6]

The problem for the navy with developing an explicit message of preparedness in the 1920s lay in the lack of an apparent threat to U.S. security on the horizon. Germany and Russia were continental powers, but the Treaty of Versailles and recovery from a civil war, respectively, limited their ability to adversely affect international security. The public also showed little enthusiasm for a rivalry between the United States and Great Britain despite suspicion of British motives from some quarters. The interwar navy incorporated British (color-coded Red) fleets into battle simulations performed at the Naval War College and even into some early 1920s Fleet Problems, but, beyond these measures and a few halfhearted and grossly underdeveloped war plans, the navy agreed with public sentiment.[7]

In the eyes of the Navy Department, only Japan possessed the means to endanger American territorial or economic security. War planning against Japan began around the turn of the century after Japanese military victories over China and czarist Russia. During World War I, Japan seized several island groups formerly held by Germany and attempted to impose a series of demands on China, causing American policymakers to fear that Japan coveted the Philippines.

While the Washington Conference brought calm to the Pacific Rim, new sources of tension soon appeared. The rise of nativist sentiments after the war led to a congressional debate over the exclusion of non–northern European immigrants into the United States for both racial and political reasons. West Coast citizens and legislators successfully pressed for the inclusion of a total ban on Japanese immigration in the Immigration Act of 1924 that President Calvin Coolidge signed into law on 9 May. Press outlets, particularly in Japan but in other countries as well, expressed outrage at the creation of racial quotas and speculated on the dire future of American-Japanese relations.[8]

A confluence of events reluctantly brought the navy into a public debate over national security. By happenstance, the navy's fleet concentration during the winter of 1924–25 was scheduled to take place in Hawaiian waters, a noteworthy event since most of the recent concentrations had focused on areas near Panama and the Caribbean. Further exacerbating matters, the Battle Fleet planned an extensive cruise to Australia and New Zealand following the conclusion of Fleet Problem V and Grand Joint Exercise 3. Press speculation ran rampant as to the intent of the maneuvers and the potential provocation that could result from holding the exercises in the central Pacific. Editorials, however, defended the navy's need for extensive training so that it could maintain a high level of readiness and resented the implications made by domestic pacifist groups or their media counterparts in Japan. In response to claims by a Tokyo newspaper that war would be inevitable should the planned maneuvers occur, the *Baltimore Sun* labeled the statement as a "stupid outburst" and argued that the American news media did not react in fear each time the IJN trained in Pacific waters. In December 1924, Congress briefly debated a resolution calling on the navy to cancel the exercises, an event that inspired more invective on the issue, but discussion ended without a vote. Japanese leaders ended the brief flap the following month when they publicly declared the American maneuvers a nonthreat to their nation.⁹

When they began in April, the maneuvers received extensive media coverage at home that emphasized the vulnerability of the Hawaiian Islands to attack. The Black force defending the islands accurately anticipated the method of approach utilized by Blue yet found itself completely unable to stop the advance. To some reporters, this demonstrated that the navy and the combined power of the battle line could effectively defend American interests in the Pacific. Also garnering attention was the subsequent cruise of the Battle Fleet to Australia and New Zealand, which intended to show the fleet's ability to execute operations far removed from its home ports and to develop closer political and military ties with the Commonwealth nations. The *Sydney Morning Herald* believed that "no other power today could so lightly face the cost of this far cruise of so great a naval force." The visit of the fleet was well received in Australia as thousands of onlookers greeted its arrival at Sydney and led to a glowing exchange of messages between officers of the fleet and the Australian prime minister.¹⁰ After this triumphant cruise, the fleet was to return home and soon celebrate Navy Day, which, coincidentally, had a diplomatic and defensive theme: "Our Navy—a Messenger of Peace."¹¹

Yet, just as the fleet returned to American waters in August 1925, a new potential source of inflammation between the United States and Japan appeared with the publication of *The Great Pacific War: A History of the American-Japanese Campaign of 1931–1932*. Its author, Hector Bywater, based the novel on the knowledge he had acquired writing on naval affairs for the *Baltimore Sun* since the Washington Conference. Since the conclusion of the conference, he had grown increasingly skeptical of Japanese intentions, and in 1923 he wrote a column titled "America Not to Blame If Arms Treaty Fails," in which he critiqued Japanese proposals to build up its treaty-exempt auxiliary forces, especially cruisers, destroyers, and submarines. The worsening of tensions in the months following the passage of the Immigration Act of 1924 led Bywater to conclude that a war between the United

NAVY DAY

★

Tuesday, October 27, 1925

That the importance of our Navy to the success of our National Government and to the Peace of the World, may be generally known and understood, the Navy League of America has requested that special observance be given on this day, the

Birthday of Theodore Roosevelt

who said *"The United States Navy is the greatest guarantee of Peace which this country possesses."*

★

A special evening program from the Westinghouse Radio Station KDKA, and Station WCAE of the Pittsburgh Press and Kaufmann & Baer Co. will be a feature of the Navy Day observance.

"Perhaps the day will come when nations will employ no armed force. Until such a day comes we shall find our assurance in a Navy of the first rank." —WARREN G. HARDING

"A powerful Navy we have always regarded as our proper and national means of defense." —WOODROW WILSON

It is suggested that we fly American flags from our respective homes on Tuesday, October 27th, and that small flags be worn in appreciation of

Our Navy—A Messenger of Peace

WEAR A SMALL FLAG, TUESDAY

"Navy Day," 1925.
National Archives and Record Administration, Box 24, Entry 89, Record Group 24, NAB.

States and Japan, while certainly not inevitable, was more likely than many persons cared to admit. Bywater then set out to write a speculative account of how a war between the two powers might unfold.[12]

Bywater's prescient, well-informed analysis of Pacific affairs provided a remarkable view of modern naval warfare. The fictional war results from Japanese overpopulation and a fear of growing Chinese strength, which causes Japan's leaders to see the necessity of a war to cement its position in East Asia. After disabling the Panama Canal, the numerically and technologically superior Japanese fleet forces the United States to abandon the Philippines and Guam and drives the fleet back to the West Coast. The fleet then struggles to defend the coast from Japanese raids and suffers defeat in a counteroffensive in the Bonin Islands. After a period of regrouping that finally sees the full integration of carriers and submarines into the fleet, the navy initiates a slow, cautious advance across the Pacific similar to the real-life War Plan Orange, seizing island bases and eventually forcing the Japanese to a climactic battle near Yap Island. The Japanese finally surrender in the face of air attacks on the Home Islands and China's expulsion of Japanese forces from the Asian mainland.[13]

Bywater demonstrated the depth of his knowledge of naval affairs in *The Great Pacific War* and received abundant praise for his work, particularly in reviews by Dudley Knox and Nicholas Roosevelt, a first cousin of Theodore and writer for the *New York Times*. Knox was particularly struck by the immense cost incurred by the United States to fight the war compared to the seemingly small return it eventually received on that investment when drawing up the peace terms after the Japanese surrender. Others, however, questioned the timing of the book's release and its effect on American-Japanese relations. An editorial in the *Chicago Tribune* roundly criticized the book's appearance on the heels of recent discord between the United States and Japan, calling it "most unpleasant" in its timing and apparent determination to inflame tensions. The *Los Angeles Times* argued that the book unfairly painted Japan as an aggressor nation and contended that its leaders no longer considered war a viable policy option. The press and the public had no penchant for a new American war in the 1920s and resented the suggestion that one could break out in the near future.[14]

Bywater recognized that the shortfalls in naval construction could imperil the U.S. Navy's ability to fulfill its commitments in the Pacific, a message echoed in the mid-1920s by Knox and others, but this message failed to resonate with the public. Instead, the service began developing alternative methods of justifying its value to the nation. A strong fleet capable of an effective national defense composed just one part of Mahan's triad of sea control. The navy and other sources of public relations support began expending much effort pointing out the more benign and beneficial aspects of naval development and of being a true sea power. This included linking the navy to commercial prosperity, peaceful scientific developments, and missions of relief and humanitarian aid that the service could perform on account of its considerable physical reach.

One way the service responded to the lean years of the 1920s was to demonstrate its commitment to administrative and financial efficiency. Soon after the

Washington Conference, Secretary of the Navy Edwin Denby stated before Congress that the navy would immediately begin selling old ships and surplus material left over from the war in an effort to lighten its financial burden. He followed this by publicizing a directive calling for greater supervision of supplies and accounts in order to streamline efficiency; he also ordered officers aboard ship to manage their expenses "on a strictly business basis." To counter the image of hidebound naval officers bent on maximizing the amount of funds received and spent each fiscal year, the navy sought to emphasize that its Supply Corps used modern business practices to aid in administering the hundreds of millions of dollars appropriated to the service each year. One Information Section press release praised the Supply Corps for its "freedom from red tape" and ability to maximize financial efficiency within the Navy Department. The navy also sought to publicize changes to disembarkation procedures for discharged men to save money on unnecessary travel.[15] These minor measures, however, seemed unlikely to resonate with the public no matter how reasonable or effective.

While the publicizing of these efficiency measures was designed to convey to the public the navy's commitment to frugality, one action aimed at lowering administrative costs actually led to a major political scandal. Over the protest of officers within the Navy Department, President Warren G. Harding allowed the Department of the Interior to assume jurisdiction over the navy's oil reserves at Teapot Dome, Wyoming, and lease any of the lands to private companies or individuals. After taking control of the reserves, Secretary of the Interior Albert Fall accepted gifts and considerable sums of money to lease the land to oilmen Harry F. Sinclair and Edward Doheny; these transactions sparked a Senate investigation and consequent scandal. The order transferring the reserves required that Navy Secretary Denby agree to the transfer of the reserves, which he did without taking any bribes. Before Congress, Denby defended the leases authorized by Fall and himself as protective measures to ensure that nonlicensed private concerns did not drain the reserves before the navy could utilize them. Most of the wrongdoing rested in Fall's hands, but Denby's having acquiesced to the leases eventually forced him to announce his resignation on 18 February 1924, while blaming his fate on "partisan trickery." Fortunately for the Navy Department, the controversy remained confined to Denby alone and eventually resulted in the restoration of navy control over the oil reserves in 1927.[16]

The navy's publicizing of its efficiency measures demonstrated its commitment to adaptation in difficult times, but the service needed to promote more active and far-reaching ways in which it could aid the nation. Reflective of Mahan's linkage of maritime supremacy to economic health, the navy in the mid-1920s frequently linked the strength of the service to the development and maintenance of American commercial and industrial prosperity. This seemed a timely course correction given the relatively strong state of the economy during the 1920s. Furthermore, it allowed the navy to argue in favor of an enlarged force structure capable of overseas commitments without ever needing to identify any specific threat to those interests. These efforts first began in 1920 with the News Bureau issuing press releases on the use of aircraft from naval air stations to perform "fish patrols" that relayed information to local fishermen to increase daily hauls. Overseas, the navy's role in protecting American commerce created opportunities for additional publicity. For instance, in 1927, the leaders of Standard Oil praised the navy for protecting the company's personnel and assets from "greater financial loss" during the Chinese unification crisis in 1926–27.[17]

To further the image of the navy as an agent of economic prosperity, the service and its allies also devoted time to promoting the growth of the American merchant marine, the size of which had been in steady decline since the Civil War. As the navy's thinking during the interwar period on present and future conflicts rarely deviated from basic Mahanian theory, neither did its publicity. Making up the triad on which sea power was based were three legs: a strong merchant marine, overseas bases, and a strong battle fleet. This translated to interwar naval leaders and advocates arguing that the fleet must protect and support maritime trade for the nation to remain wealthy and secure. In doing so, the navy and, particularly, the Navy League, spent much effort educating the public on the value of seaborne commerce and the protection of sea lanes.

Promoting the merchant marine began in earnest in 1922 as elements of the Navy Department increasingly came to view their own fate as intertwined with that of maritime commerce. The Morale Division of the Bureau of Navigation issued a bulletin warning of the consequences should the navy's funding be drawn down too far by Congress in the midst of the public debate over disarmament. To remedy the problem, the bureau recommended that naval officers educate themselves on the value of the merchant marine because it was imperative that officers tell the public "how the Navy can be made to effectively advance the business of our citizens." This emphasis ran completely counter to the "silent service" ethos and threatened to turn every officer into an unofficial publicist, but the plan was never implemented. Still, the merchant marine had its public advocates. Dudley Knox, for example, argued that the volume of foreign trade factored heavily into America's economic well-being and that only the navy and a strong American merchant marine could guarantee continued growth.[18]

Even though the Navy Department sought to link its growth to the merchant marine soon after the Washington Conference, the issue did not begin to receive sustained attention for several more years. Only in 1926 did the Navy League begin accentuating the importance of a strong merchant marine during the annual Navy Day celebration. To enhance the publicity of this cause, Knox distributed a memo intended to guide the speeches of those appearing at Navy Day events across the country. The memo provided speakers with specific statistics to cite in their talks, such as the decline of the volume of trade carried in American hulls to 34 percent in 1925. Knox also advised that speeches include a section arguing that the United States was not economically self-sufficient and that foreign trade constituted the lifeblood of American prosperity. By 1928, Navy Day organizers were specifically instructed that a balanced fleet and an "adequate Merchant Marine" should constitute the goals of each Navy Day.[19]

Yet another way the navy sought to promote itself as more than a mere tool for national defense came through publicizing the service's humanitarian and disaster relief missions, both abroad and at home. The 1923 Recruiting Bureau film *The Navy and the Near East* showcased the navy's movement of refugees from Smyrna during the Greco-Turkish War the previous year, but this was far from the only time the navy intervened in such a crisis. The Asiatic Fleet responded rapidly to the 1923 earthquake in Japan that killed more than 100,000 in Tokyo and the surrounding areas. In all, more than a dozen ships and several aircraft helped bring much needed aid to the Japanese people. The relief briefly led to hopes of increased goodwill between the two nations, as did the navy's donation of complete sets of charts and maps as a gift to the Japan's navy to replace those lost in the earthquake.[20]

The navy also promoted its relief work inside the continental United States. The most prominent instance of domestic disaster relief occurred during the 1927 flooding of the Mississippi River. Heavy rains beginning in 1926 were followed by record single-day rainfalls on 15 April 1927, flooding thousands of square miles of land in the river basin. The navy played a key role in the relief efforts coordinated by Secretary of Commerce Herbert Hoover and others when it mobilized tugs and other small craft to navigate the troubled waters. The CNO, Adm. E. W. Eberle, suspended training operations at the air station at Pensacola so that thirty-one seaplanes, the bulk of the force stationed there, could assist in the relief operations. The press praised the navy's seaplanes as "winged messengers of mercy" for assistance they rendered to marooned families and reminded readers that the service "[did] its full share" when disaster struck.[21]

Surveys and expeditions conducted for both scientific and commercial purposes became another frequent source of nondefense publicity for the navy. One geographic area the navy spent much effort exploring during the 1920s and 1930s was the Arctic. The navy had first become linked to Arctic exploration in 1909 when Rear Adm. Robert E. Peary claimed to be the first person to reach the North Pole, leading to widespread praise and fame for the achievement. While the war years delayed further expeditions to the region, the interwar navy revived its interest in the Arctic. Rear Admiral Moffett planned for several years to have one of the navy's new airships, the *Shenandoah*, become the first craft to fly over the North Pole. The navy asserted that polar exploration was not a publicity stunt and that missions dispatched to the region could provide numerous scientific benefits. Most importantly, the navy argued that the expeditions into the Arctic Ocean would foster a greater understanding of weather systems that formed in the cold air masses and descended on the temperate climate zones of the Northern Hemisphere. The service also hoped that polar exploration by air could open up new travel routes over the Arctic that would save thousands of miles and large amounts of fuel. Some naval leaders believed that valuable mineral resources might lay hidden beneath the ice sheet—like those recently discovered in Spitsbergen, Norway, and in Alaska. The service also pointed out several other lesser ancillary benefits of Arctic exploration, including the surveying of more than half a million square miles of completely uncharted territory, investigating any landmasses known to be locked in by the polar ice sheet, and the charting of tides in the region.[22]

Due to the high costs and risks involved, President Calvin Coolidge cancelled the proposed airship flight over the North Pole in 1924, but this did not prevent the navy from associating itself with further exploration of the region. In a series of privately funded ventures, Lt. Cdr. Richard E. Byrd—on leave from the navy—achieved celebrity for claiming to overfly both the North and South Poles during expeditions that received some assistance from the navy. The first of Byrd's highly publicized flights took place in May 1926 when Byrd and copilot Floyd Bennett overflew the North Pole, an accomplishment that brought Byrd widespread glory in the United States and led Adm. E. W. Eberle to remind the public of Byrd's commission by claiming that he measured "up to the highest and best traditions of the American Navy."[23]

In the weeks after Byrd's flight over the North Pole, he spoke openly of his desire to explore the Antarctic region by air, but before doing so he set his sights on crossing the Atlantic Ocean. In June 1927, Byrd successfully flew from the United States to France in a Fokker trimotor aircraft, but, although Byrd had successfully reached Paris, he found the airfield too crowded with traffic and the plane eventually crashed near the Normandy coast. Thankfully, the crash resulted in only minor injuries for Byrd's crew. Parisians celebrated Byrd's achievement, but the flight had the unfortunate distinction of coming just weeks after Charles Lindbergh had successfully reached Paris in his nonstop solo flight.[24]

In 1928, Byrd's long-discussed plan to explore Antarctica finally came to fruition, with the navy again reaping publicity rewards from his privately financed venture. The navy provided Byrd with equipment, namely radio transmitters and a ground sonar unit capable of penetrating the dense ice to determine the topography of the land below. En route, Byrd also received navigational assistance from the navy, but easily the grandest declaration of support came from Rear Admiral Moffett on 26 October 1929. During a radio broadcast, Moffett promised that the airship *Akron* would be made available to Byrd for Antarctic exploration should he desire it—an offer that never was never fulfilled. The remainder of Byrd's expedition brought him further acclaim when, on 28 November 1929, he flew in a Ford Trimotor piloted by Bernt Balchen and crewed by two other men over the South Pole in an accomplishment labeled a "splendid feat." The press also partially attributed this exploit to the navy as it credited George Washington Littlehale with providing the navigational data Byrd needed to determine when he had passed over the pole. The expedition returned home the following year to public fanfare, and Byrd received a promotion to rear admiral for his feats. He would return to the Antarctic in 1933 and 1939.[25]

During the 1920s as the navy sought to emphasize the nonmilitary benefits the service provided to the country, it found ways to more subtly remind the public of the value of sea power in national defense. Examples drawn from naval history allowed the service to remind the public of its past successes while avoiding any bellicose rhetoric in the present. No symbol of naval history and preparedness loomed larger than the USS *Constitution*, and the navy drew attention to the ship's restoration. In early 1926, as the "Save Old Ironsides" fund began to accumulate, Secretary of the Navy Curtis Wilbur referred to the donations from thousands of New York City schoolchildren as giving "proof [of] their young faith in the ideals for which that ship fought and which it now represents." Such references continued over the next year as the fund-raising drive collected enough money to fund the ship's full restoration at the Boston Navy Yard. During a visit to the yard in July 1927, Wilbur explicitly linked the aged warship to the contemporary cause of preparedness by comparing the microbes that had rotted the wooden hulk of the old frigate to antinavalist forces doing much the same to the modern naval establishment—both threats lay hidden beneath the surface but had the potential to destroy the afflicted.[26]

To a Navy Department attempting to rally support among a divided public for valuable appropriations, the ship stood as "a great national instrument" that had inspired "patriotism and national unity at a critical time in the country's development." In 1931, Secretary of the Navy Charles F. Adams used a speech delivered aboard the *Constitution* to defend President Herbert Hoover's record on naval preparedness. Adams argued that the president believed in "preparedness as a safeguard of peace" and linked this claim to the ship's history as a symbol of America's commitment to protect itself from any potential threat. The *Constitution*'s victories in combat, he argued, had laid the foundation for years of peace.[27]

The navy expended much effort promoting its peacetime missions, but as had happened at the time of the Immigration Act of 1924, external events forced naval leaders to directly address controversial contemporary issues. The Geneva Conference commanded much press coverage that remained beyond the direct influence of the Information Section. The Robert R. McCormick–edited *Chicago Tribune* remained a reliable opponent to naval arms limitations and published many editorials excoriating the conference's purpose, with one dreading another meeting of "American idealists [and] European realists."[28] Meanwhile, other papers, such as the *Des Moines Register*, appeared much more skeptical of the claims of American weakness and reprinted a British editorial from Archibald Hurd that claimed American ignorance and hypocrisy about U.S. naval construction programs.[29] Ultimately, the Geneva Conference failed to resolve the disputes over the "cruiser issue" between the United States, Great Britain, and Japan.[30]

The press took the failure of the Geneva Conference as a sign that naval construction would soon begin anew. *The Literary Digest*'s survey of postconference press coverage found editorials in pro-navy newspapers such as the *Tribune* blaming the conference's failure on British perfidy. The more sanguine coverage from the *Baltimore Sun* and other newspapers recognized that naval construction may be likely or even necessary but dreaded the fiscal and political consequences that would arise from a major building program.[31] These words proved prophetic because, in December, Representative Thomas Butler used the results of a General Board study to introduce a bill that called for the construction of seventy-one ships. This prompted denunciations in the press and a massive outpouring of public criticism that rivaled the coalescence of opposition to naval expansion prior to the Washington Conference. The public opposition to the bill was so strong and widespread that even Butler himself admitted that it ran well beyond the work of "professional pacifists."[32] To alleviate the public's concern, a new bill was introduced in the House on 28 February 1928 that called for the construction of fifteen cruisers and a single aircraft carrier. This more palatable cruiser bill, however, still generated much public debate for the remainder of the year and only passed Congress in February 1929.[33]

Even in the wake of the 1929 cruiser bill, some naval officers continued to rely on historical examples to argue a public case for expanding the fleet. Later that year, Lt. Cdr. Holloway H. Frost published *We Build a Navy*, a series of episodic descriptions of naval battles from the days of the Continental Navy up to the War of 1812 that, in unabashed fashion, called for contemporary construction. From the outset, Frost acknowledged that his work should not be taken as a definitive history of the United States Navy nor should readers expect any lengthy discussion of naval policy in that era. In explaining the episodic structure of the book, Frost stated in the preface that his "volume is a story, not a history. It recounts those chapters of our early naval annals which I conceive to be the most interesting, the most dramatic, and the most instructive." Frost alluded to contemporary ambivalence toward the navy when he wrote of the navy after the War of 1812, "It is difficult for us in these days to realize the place our Navy then had in the hearts of Americans." In light of such statements, Frost hoped that the book would explain to its readers the "vital necessity of a Navy . . . and of a vigorous national policy."[34] Whereas Mahan's earliest works had supported American naval expansion through subtext couched in a broader discussion of military principles, Frost completely foregrounded his purpose and explicitly linked his retelling of the American past to inform present policy. In this way, history could correct the public's view that an enlarged fleet was unnecessary.

Yet again, no matter how compelling and subtle the argument for construction was, it was not easy for this peripheral public relations strategy to gain traction. In this instance, Frost's indirect call for a larger fleet was overshadowed by the larger firestorm of controversy caused by the William Shearer flap discussed in chapter 3. The lingering political and public resentment of the failure at Geneva had kept arms limitation in the public mind well after the conclusion of the conference and led directly to President Hoover declining to place any naval officers in the delegation to the London Conference in 1930. Instead, as had occurred at the Washington Conference, officers were relegated to adviser status only, which left Hoover's Secretary of State, Henry L. Stimson, in charge of the proceedings. Furthermore, many of the negotiations occurred in advance and out of the public eye so as to prevent the buildup of outside pressure on specific negotiating platforms. This combination of measures allowed the conference's attendees to produce a new agreement that extended the battleship building holiday for five years to 1936; set cruiser tonnage between the United States, Great Britain, and Japan at a 10:10:7 ratio; and capped destroyer tonnage at 150,000 tons for the United States and Britain.[35]

Only after the conference did naval leaders begin to speak out about the proceedings. Most press outlets supported ratification of the London treaty, but William

Randolph Hearst made personal, and ultimately unsuccessful, pleas with senators to "exercise their own judgment" and block ratification. Hearst's newsreels provided platforms for congressional naval affairs committee chairmen Representative Fred Britten and Senator Fred Hale to denounce the treaty, with the former declaring that it would spur a new naval race and that the "British have us hamstrung and hogtied and there they will keep us long as limitations of armament are the order of the day." The navy's civilian heads and Rear Admiral Moffett defended the results of the conference for different reasons. Moffett, an adviser to the delegation in London, was pleased by the lack of reductions on carrier tonnage and the allowances in American cruiser tonnage to construct "flying deck cruisers" or hybrid warships that could greatly increase the number of carrier decks without counting against the carrier tonnage limits set out in the Five-Power Treaty. Assistant Secretary of the Navy Ernest Lee Jahncke, by contrast, spoke out in favor of the treaty because it committed the United States "to an orderly and normal advance" in the coming years.[36]

By the time of the London Conference, the effects of the Great Depression had begun to be felt across the country. As the economic crisis worsened, it forced the navy to have to adjust its publicity. That same spring, public calls to reduce government expenditures began to circulate. As it had done during the lean years after the Washington Conference, the navy's public relations apparatus once again argued that the service could streamline its operations so as to limit its financial burden to the country. Press releases touted the implementation of economy measures that included reusing the steel intended for use in the battleships scrapped under the terms of the Five-Power Treaty and increasing the use of arc welding in shipyards. The navy also promoted the "rigid economy" practiced in flight operations that limited the number of practice flights and practically forbade familiarization flights, which had no discernible operational purpose. Fortunately for the navy, more extreme reductions, including the placement of the *Lexington* and *Saratoga* in rotating reserve whereby only one of the ships would be in commission at a time, were never implemented.[37] Given that aviation had drawn much public attention to the fleet, withdrawing one of the carriers from regular service could have had disastrous public relations consequences.

Even though the navy quickly responded to the possible threats to its budget, not all publicity accounted for the changed economic conditions. Some efforts continued to assert the service's value in maintaining peacetime prosperity. In 1931, the ONI issued a publication entitled *The United States Navy in Peacetime: The Navy in Relation to the Industrial, Scientific, Economic, and Political Developments of the Nation*. The publication added few new ideas to the public debate, instead elaborating on many of the themes of navy public relations over the previous ten years. In it, the authors argued that the navy was an inherently "progressive institution" with "industrial, social, scientific, and diplomatic" responsibilities to the nation. The book used a mixture of contemporary and historical examples to highlight the diverse contributions the navy made to the nation's betterment. Its authors maintained that trade protection was the navy's primary mission, but they pointed to other domestic benefits of naval expansion, including the subsidization of the domestic steel industry in the late nineteenth century to produce armor plating or the more recent examples of the assistance provided to the radio and aviation industries during their formative years. The book chronicled the histories of the Hydrographic Office, the Naval Observatory, and the Navy Communications Service and pointed out their contemporary tasks of facilitating the easy movement of commerce by air and sea through the distribution of navigational aids and the broadcasting of weather reports. The book also touched on other missions, including exploration, the navy's role in international diplomacy, and the execution of humanitarian relief. Emphasizing this last mission proved especially timely as the Information Section sought press coverage of the *Lexington*'s relief work following the Nicaraguan earthquake on 31 March 1931 that killed more than two thousand people.[38] Still, it is not clear how widely the ONI distributed this booklet, meaning that only a small audience likely read this detailed explanation of the navy's various missions. Trying to sell the public on the peacetime value of the navy had proven difficult enough, and relying on small, ineffective ways of promoting that message only exacerbated the shortcomings of navy public relations.

Soon, a new PR challenge emerged that stood the navy's claim to be a benevolent agent of peacetime prosperity completely on its head. In early 1932, Harper released a new book from progressive historian Charles Beard. Known for his classist reevaluations of bedrock American beliefs, his latest volume, *The Navy: Defense or Portent?*, fired an intellectual broadside into the purported array of self-interested naval officers and greedy business interests that perpetrated on America the interrelated afflictions of preparedness and navalism. In a volume that relied on recent history and analysis of contemporary events, Beard vociferously attacked the basis for American naval policy, its advocates, and the rhetoric used to support that policy. As Beard saw it, the nexus of business and political interests reflected by William Shearer and the Navy League had allowed the navy to expand beyond its absolute needs. To remedy this problem, Beard called for clearer statements of naval policy and, more importantly, implored the American people to assert themselves as the driving force behind naval policy and to not surrender that power to the supposed expertise of individuals, including naval officers, with a vested stake in naval expansion. As Beard put it, the "naval program cannot be left to the Navy League, to the Navy Department, or to naval officers alone."[39] This seemed perhaps a strange case to make given that public pressure had created and sustained the naval arms limitation movement for a decade, but Beard felt that these shadowy forces might well undermine that consensus.

The ONI and the Public Relations Branch took a dim view of Beard's book and, as had occurred previously with Shearer and others, investigated the author.[40] They found little usable information, but the DNI, Capt. Hayne Ellis, prompted district commandants to devise methods to respond to what he described as a "particularly vicious attack on the Navy."[41] Dudley Knox joined the fray and roundly criticized a seed article Beard had published in *Harper's Weekly*.[42] The attention given Beard's book and the responses to it eventually died down, but Beard's attack on navalism and preparedness struck a chord with the ONI for two interrelated reasons. First, the ONI resented the association with Shearer, who had been a thorn in the navy's side for many years. Second, Beard's allegations of warmongering and profiteering ran against the grain of naval publicity that portrayed the service as a responsible and effective public institution.

Ironically, Beard's book appeared as the worsening effects of the Great Depression led to calls for more radical solutions to the crisis, including increased spending on naval construction. Finally, the service found a more effective rhetorical response to the Depression than simply touting efficiencies. In a speech to the American Legion in June, Rear Admiral Moffett publicly claimed that constructing new ships for the fleet could alleviate some of the nation's economic ills. Only with the change in presidential administrations, however, did the navy's strategy for procuring more funds and ships begin to change. After the inauguration of Franklin Roosevelt in 1933, the navy officially promoted its value as an agent of economic recovery and a provider of promotional assistance for the New Deal agencies created during Roosevelt's "first hundred days." In October 1933, the Recruiting Bureau released a poster showing the crew of the carrier *Saratoga* posed in formation on the flight deck in the shape of the letters "NRA" and the ubiquitous Blue Eagle logo, thus signaling the navy's support for the ambitious National Recovery Administration.[43]

The legislation passed by Congress during FDR's first months in office provided many direct benefits for the navy. The National Industrial Recovery Act, which created the NRA, also created the Public Works Administration, through which more than $238 million were appropriated for naval construction, financing the carriers

Men of the Airplane Carrier U. S. S. SARATOGA Forming the Insignia of the National Recovery Act on the Wide Landing Deck of their Ship.

"Navy Adopts 'Blue Eagle,'" 1933.
Naval History and Heritage Command, NH 76793, Photographic Section.

Yorktown and *Enterprise*, among other projects. To better spread the economic benefits of such work, the navy contracted half of the construction to be paid for with these funds to private yards and performed the rest in its own shipyards.[44]

Naval officials justified the construction as a "start" toward building the navy to treaty limits and linked this idea to using naval construction as an economic stimulus to maintaining employment for thousands of Americans. The navy also strongly associated preparedness and industrial recovery when discussing the Vinson-Trammell Act of 1934, the largest construction bill passed by Congress since 1916. Passed by Congress in March, the new act eventually allowed for the construction of one carrier, four cruisers, fifty-one destroyers, and twenty-eight submarines. Assistant Secretary of the Navy Henry L. Roosevelt stated in nationally broadcast radio addresses that the new construction closed a significant gap between the present size of the fleet and the tonnage allowed by the limitation treaties and that it constituted a method by which the United States could achieve its "legitimate naval aspirations." Of perhaps greater interest to the public, Roosevelt also stated that the new building could lead to the hiring of as many fourteen thousand workers over the next year just to maintain the desired pace.[45]

The navy coupled the creation of jobs with the need for preparedness to gain public and congressional support for building the navy up to "treaty limits." Recruiting posters used the dramatic image of a battleship's guns firing at night at some unseen target, making clear its slogan that the navy is "Always Alert."[46]

The strong political support for the Vinson-Trammell Act was hardly universal, however, and the navy's demands for preparedness only continued to stoke the mistrust of navalism that Beard had inflamed. His writings had struck the chord of suspicion that long endured after World War I that the American munitions industry had engaged in profiteering against the national interest before and during U.S. involvement in the conflict. By April 1934, enough public pressure motivated Congress to launch a formal investigation into what critics called the "merchants of death." The Women's International League for Peace and Freedom's president, Dorothy Detzer, joined forces with Senator Gerald P. Nye of North Dakota, and the latter formed the Special Committee on Investigation of the Munitions Industry, which popularly became known as the Nye Committee. The committee did not solely represent pacifistic interests; Senator Arthur Vandenberg, a noted proponent of preparedness, lent his support to the committee's proceedings. The committee studied ties between the navy and the private shipyards and the steel industry seeking to determine whether or not the navy grossly overpaid for construction assigned to private shipyards. The committee believed that the so-called "Big Three" shipyards—Newport News Shipbuilding and Drydock, Bethlehem Shipbuilding, and New York Shipbuilding—colluded to prevent other companies from receiving significant building contracts from the navy. Senior naval officers involved in the bidding process often went to work for these same private shipbuilders soon after their retirement from the service. In addition, Nye also explored charges that the Electric Boat Company, the DuPont Corporation, and other companies pooled profits and supported lobbying efforts to prevent disarmament. Only circumstantial evidence existed to prove the charges leveled by the committee against the navy and its corporate partners. In the end, although the committee conducted hearings for two years, from 1934 to 1936, its final report failed to offer specific allegations of wrongdoing.[47]

Interestingly, as the navy's leaders and publicists sought to fine-tune their message regarding its value to the nation, the relationship with Hollywood did not factor greatly into the equation. The studios had remained profitable during the

"Always Alert," 1933.
Naval History and Heritage Command, Navy Art Gallery.

Depression even as attendance declined by 25 percent, but this forced the studio heads to seek more, and riskier, external financing for their films. This then left the studios unwilling to imperil their status as the dominant player in the world's film market and potentially lose their overseas profits. Europe was the largest and most profitable region, but the studios could also count on thousands of theaters in Latin America and Asia to screen their films. The moguls feared that inflaming political tensions could prompt a reaction from censorship and customs officials overseas and hurt their profits. Thus, they consciously avoided producing films that might create controversy.[48]

These overarching financial concerns filtered down into the film collaborations between the navy and the studios. To be fair, many of the films that the Navy Department Motion Picture Board reviewed and recommended for cooperation, or at least those not set within the confines of the Naval Academy, included scenes depicting their protagonists undertaking some kind of training exercise to maintain readiness and efficiency. Frank Capra's *Submarine* (1928) showed its titular craft participating in a fictionalized Fleet Problem before its accident. The first naval aviation film, Wead's *The Flying Fleet* (1929), shows two of its primary characters engaging in a mock dogfight against one another over the air station at North Island, adjacent to San Diego. Wead's later *Hell Divers* (1933) depicts numerous operational training sequences, which included dogfighting, a live-fire dive-bombing attack against a radio-controlled battleship, and a search problem that pitted fixed-wing aircraft against the airship *Macon*. Even the comedy *Son of a Sailor* (1933) climaxes with the film's protagonist, Handsome, inadvertently foiling an international espionage plot and parachuting onto a target ship just as it is bombed by aircraft from the *Saratoga*.[49] Within the confines of comedies, melodrama, or disaster films, the navy's commitment to preparedness appeared on the nation's movie screens, yet these elements always remained backgrounded in each of these films. The Motion Picture Board, much like the industry it worked with, had steered the service clear of controversy by rejecting scripts that commented on current events. As such, Hollywood was not a major factor in communicating a naval preparedness message to the American people for much of the 1930s.

The continual struggle for the navy and its leaders was how to ask for preparedness without identifying any clear threats to national security. Oftentimes, the press would do this themselves, but the dilemma forced naval leaders into many uncomfortable public debates. Service leaders publicly refused to identify Japan as its most likely enemy into the 1930s, but the press still encouraged speculation about the possibility of conflict between the two nations. This was especially the case after Japan invaded Manchuria in September 1931, which led to repeated U.S. demands that Japan withdraw from the region. When Japan refused, Secretary of State Henry Stimson suggested to President Hoover that portions of the Asiatic Fleet proceed to Shanghai to demonstrate American resolve. Hoover rejected the advice but allowed Grand Joint Exercise 3 and Fleet Problem XIII to occur as scheduled in February 1932. While the exercise had been planned long in advance, some members of the media assumed that the timing of the maneuvers in Hawaii was not a coincidence. An ominous article that appeared in the *New York Times* just before the Battle Force sailed for Hawaiian waters on 30 January denied any change in plans had been made as a result of the crisis, yet it included a statement from Admiral Leigh that the fleet would be "fully prepared for any contingency."[50]

The 1932 crisis quickly passed, but it presaged a similar incident in 1935 when the navy scheduled Fleet Problem XVI for the waters of the northern Pacific between Midway Atoll and the southern coast of Alaska. When first announced in September 1934, the press assumed that the location of exercise—the first held west of

Hawaii—held greater significance, including American interest in an Alaskan naval base or regarding the recent Japanese demands for naval parity at the upcoming limitation conference in London. Further complications occurred on 29 December when Japan announced its withdrawal from the Washington treaties. The Japanese protested the maneuvers occurring so far into the Pacific, but American commentators, including Navy League president Nelson Macy, noted that Japan planned its own similar exercises in the central Pacific. As in 1925 and 1932, the crisis abated with the end of the maneuvers, but it left many worried that such deployments by the navy could lead to an unintended war.[51]

Fleet Problem XVI came on the heels of the announcement in late 1934 by the Japanese government that it intended to withdraw from the Washington treaties. Along with the increased concern for security discussed in chapter 4, this upsetting of the international order led the navy to emphasize further the need for expansion and preparedness. It also dramatically altered both press and public attitudes toward the 1935 London Naval Conference. Commentators on both sides of the Atlantic viewed the possibility of reaching a settlement equitable to all parties, including the Japanese, to be dim at best.[52] President Roosevelt strongly and publicly supported the continued construction programs under way, calling the navy "not only the first line of defense, but the most important line of defense."[53] Coverage during and after the conference grimly noted the likelihood of a Japanese buildup in fleet strength and even the possibility of lesser powers such as Brazil and Turkey entering the fray with their own battleship construction.[54]

The terms of the 1936 London Naval Treaty maintained many of the existing limits on ship construction but included an "escalator clause" that granted signatories the right to exceed either the tonnage or the armament limits if another power did so. Rumors of Japanese construction only increased the likelihood that the United States or Britain could invoke that clause. These growing troubles overseas allowed the Roosevelt administration and the large Democratic majorities in Congress to continue to push forward naval construction programs. To align with the begrudging yet growing public support for construction, naval publicity attempted to allay concerns that new American construction would only worsen the international situation. In a Navy Day address, Rear Adm. Charles Train openly expressed sympathy for those worried that the navy would be built to excess, but the remainder of his speech indicated that a strong navy was needed to protect the "national welfare."[55]

Despite these many diplomatic incidents and press speculation, the navy continued to shy away from using the growing Japanese intransigence to justify construction. Instead, as before, historical analyses that avoided the present-day naval situation remained a preferred medium for delivering a message of preparedness to the American public. In September 1936, just months after the end of the London Conference, Dudley Knox published his single-volume *History of the United States Navy*. The introduction, authored by Adm. William L. Rodgers, argued that the book provided an "accurate narrative" record of naval events that illustrated the value of the Navy and inspired the Navy itself. Unlike Frost's earlier naval history, Knox incorporated analysis of peacetime naval policy into the narrative and argued that sea power had decided every conflict the United States had fought. Knox frequently criticized civilian meddling in naval policy, particularly President Jefferson's gunboat policy, Assistant Secretary of the Navy Gustavus Fox's demand for a direct Union naval assault on Charleston in 1863, and President Wilson's decision to prevent the navy from preparing for war in 1914. Knox ended his narrative in contemporary times and offered yet another lamentation on the navy in the disarmament era similar to that in *The Eclipse of American Sea Power*. Reviews called Knox's work a "plea for naval preparedness," and Hanson Baldwin, while critical of Knox's lack of objectivity, argued that "all Americans will do well to weigh the lesson Captain Knox draws for us."[56]

Occasionally, ancillary missions performed by the navy outside of the preparedness framework garnered publicity during the latter 1930s. In 1937, the navy aided in the search for aviator Amelia Earhart and her navigator, Fred Noonan, who disappeared during the final leg of their circumnavigational flight when they attempted to reach their refueling point near the remote Howland Island some three thousand miles southwest of Hawaii. This kind of search was not without precedent as the navy had participated in the search for French aviators Charles Nungesser and Francois Coli after their failed attempt to fly nonstop from Paris to New York in May 1927. Naval officials, upon discovering that Earhart's plane had gone missing, felt that "it was incumbent upon the Navy to render whatever aid practicable in the interest of humanity." Consolidated PBY Catalina patrol planes from Pearl Harbor launched their first searches on 3 July, and within three days, the navy dispatched several ships to the area, including the battleship *Colorado* and the carrier *Lexington*. Planes from the *Lexington* continued to search for Earhart until the navy called off the search on 18 July after searching more than ninety thousand square miles of ocean and countless isolated islets.[57]

While the value or conduct of the navy's previous humanitarian efforts had never been questioned, the search for a single missing plane prompted public criticism of the time and, especially, the expense involved in mounting such operations. The fifteen-day search cost an estimated $4 million in fuel oil and aviation gasoline, the use of both of which had often been limited in recent years. On the final day of searching, Representative Byron Scott broached the idea of passing legislation ensuring that the navy could only be used for search purposes if the flight had any "scientific value." Three days later, the president responded to such criticism by noting that naval aircraft needed to remain aloft for a certain number of hours per day and that the *Lexington* steamed no faster during the search than it would have during a Fleet Problem. President Roosevelt declared the navy's actions above reproach and argued that the search would have occurred regardless of who had been behind the controls of the aircraft.[58]

The Earhart incident notwithstanding, the navy's rhetoric only grew more strident in supporting preparedness and framing the service as an agent of national defense. Officers publicly asserted that "passive defense" should be rejected by all right-thinking citizens and that pre–World War I Germany should have taught everyone that "there is little or no use in having an inferior navy." The bombing of the gunboat *Panay* on 12 December 1937 by Japanese aircraft as it steamed down the Yangtze River prompted Hearst to describe Japan as an "aggressive, belligerent, militaristic, ambitious and impudent nation, intoxicated by its continual success in predatory warfare." The navy did not directly capitalize on the incident to further promote preparedness, but the language employed by officials over the next year in support of preparedness became ever more ominous. In a statement in February 1938, Adm. William D. Leahy argued that the navy "does not have in mind any particular possible enemy," but that the world looks upon the United States with "covetous eyes" because of the nation's wealth and prestige. Naval officers concluded that "wars and near wars, the remaking of maps, and general chaotic conditions that prevail over large areas of the earth" necessitated an increase of naval construction and alterations to the nation's defense posture. In March 1939, Leahy asserted that "vigilance within, vigilance without" must be practiced to keep America safe from "antagonistic" governing philosophies currently dragging the world into chaos.[59]

As the preparedness drive reached new heights in 1939, it received further historical justification from a pair of differing sources seeking to revive interest in Mahanian theory. In April, Yale University Press published *Mahan: The Life and Work of Captain Alfred Thayer Mahan, U.S.N.*, by William D. Puleston, a retired navy captain and former head of the ONI. Intended to show how circumstance and background influenced the thinking of the "exponent of sea power, the apostle of expansion," Puleston analyzed Mahan's most significant writings and their intended effect to advance the study of naval warfare but also to serve as a guide for American policymakers. The same month that Puleston's biography appeared, Harold and Margaret Sprout published *The Rise of American Naval Power*, a chronicle of U.S. naval policy from the days of the Revolution to the end of World War I that used Mahan's ideas as a framework for its analysis. To complete their volume, the Sprouts received some assistance and cooperation from the ONI.[60]

Reviewers of both books hoped that policymakers and members of the public wanting to understand contemporary military and naval affairs would take to heart the lessons prescribed therein. Dudley Knox found the Sprouts more capable than most civilian authors in interpreting "semi-technical material dealing with naval policy and operations" and especially praised their having performed a "national service" for illuminating the process through which civilians and senior officers formulate said policies. Hanson Baldwin, who reviewed both books for the *New York Times*, praised Puleston for his frequent allusions in the text to contemporary affairs, while expressing regret that Puleston did not spend more time analyzing Mahan's relevance to present-day naval affairs. In contrast, Baldwin found the work of the Sprouts of greater value because they explained the origins of American naval policy in a clear and cogent manner. Regarding its contemporary significance, Baldwin stated, "No book could be more timely today when the doctrines of Mahan are again influencing the destiny of man." He observed that the Sprouts downplayed "the power of propaganda" and the importance of groups such as the Navy League in disseminating the navalist message, but Baldwin's tone suggests that the use of propaganda—a term that had acquired decidedly negative connotations after World War I—was necessary and proper to the furthering of naval expansion. Moreover, he hoped that civilians and military officials alike would learn from the book's historical examples. In particular, Baldwin cited the effects of the European balance of power on American national security and the historical record of the United States entering wars militarily unprepared.[61] In an increasingly unsettled world, Baldwin believed that the Sprouts' take on the recent past offered a guide for present-day concerns.

Consistently communicating the navy's value and a responsible message of preparedness during the interwar period proved especially challenging for the service. More so than in recruiting or touting specific technologies, this task was quite difficult because events well beyond the navy's control often influenced how the public viewed it. Statements of senior officers that circumvented the press releases of the Information Section/Public Relations Branch further relegated that office to the background in its own arena. In addition, both the navy and Hollywood remained reluctant—for good reason—to use their relationship to directly influence contemporary politics and policy, thus effectively negating the value of the service's most important public relations ally. Naval leaders also believed many Americans saw no need for a navy or believed that economic conditions rendered a navy unaffordable. Within these constraints, naval publicity attempted to compensate for these difficulties by promoting such missions as humanitarian relief and the benefits of constructing and maintaining a modern navy, such as the jobs created in steel plants and shipyards during the 1920s and 1930s. Even as the world moved closer and closer to war during the 1930s, the service sought ways to use historical analogies in order to sidestep thorny contemporary issues. At a time when the press and public seemed reluctant to embrace a full drive for preparedness, the navy's conservative public relations strategy prevented it from becoming a lightning rod for controversy or a catalyst for war.

CONCLUSION

EVALUATING THE EFFECTIVENESS OF
NAVY PUBLIC RELATIONS ON THE EVE OF WAR

On 29 April 1939, twenty-eight navy vessels arrived in New York Harbor to participate in a fleet review to commemorate the opening of the World's Fair. The arrival of these American ships was to be followed by visits of British, Canadian, Argentinian, and Mexican vessels over the next several months. The navy had not made a large-scale visit to New York since President Franklin Roosevelt reviewed the fleet there in 1934. The size and scope of the fair, which included historical exhibits, radio broadcasts, and pictorials for *Life* magazine, prompted navy and local officials to begin preparing for the event months in advance. In January 1939, some three months before the visit, the Chief of Naval Operations ordered ComThree, Rear Adm. Clark Woodward, to liaise between the service and the mayor of the city, Fiorello LaGuardia. The Public Relations Branch assigned Lt. Cdr. Bernard L. Austin and civilian staffer Helene Philbert to work with World's Fair organizers over a period of several weeks. Austin's task was to coordinate and plan the various activities in which the navy would participate from the opening of the fair on 30 April to Navy Day the following October. To highlight the navy's presence, local officials promoted the arrival of ships at the port and printed a series of posters entitled "The Fleet's In" so that potential visitors knew the correct times and locations to view and go aboard the ships.[1]

The navy's participation in the World's Fair turned out to be one of the last truly peacetime public relations events the service staged before World War II. Due to the ongoing troubles in both Europe and Asia, the navy gradually reduced its level of participation in the fair during the weeks leading up the event. Initially, plans called for the ships of both the Scouting Force and the Battle Force, 119 in all, to visit New York Harbor and participate in the ceremonies. Decreased to 86 in March, President Franklin Roosevelt further reduced the contingent by two-thirds when, on 15 April 1939, he ordered the bulk of the U.S. Fleet to return immediately to Pacific waters. By the time Roosevelt issued the order, several vessels had already arrived in New York. The suddenness of Roosevelt's decision prompted Admiral Woodward to broadcast a message on local radio to recall the 20 percent of men on either liberty or leave. Two battleships, the *West Virginia* and the *Tennessee*, which had arrived at the New York Navy Yard for scheduled overhauls, likewise had their stays cut short. These sudden departures came as a blow to the organizers of the fair, who had estimated that as many as one million people would visit the fleet during its stay.[2]

Although Roosevelt gave no explanation for his ordering of the Battle Force back to the Pacific, the move came just two weeks after Japan had annexed the Spratly Islands in the South China Sea to help facilitate its expansion in Southeast Asia. The departure of the ships certainly came as a disappointment given the huge effort expended on preparing the city for the fleet's arrival, but it also served as an unpleasant reminder of the increasingly dangerous situation overseas. This disruption failed, however, to completely dampen the mood for the navy's visit as the city hosted balls on 1 and 2 May for the officers and enlisted men of the fleet, respectively, and coordinated several smaller events, including athletic competitions at the New York Athletic Club. The remaining ships welcomed visitors aboard every day from 1 P.M. until 5 P.M. Over the next several months, more than eight million people viewed a navy display in the Federal Building depicting the lives of sailors and naval policy, and more than 360,000 attended a special Navy Day celebration at the World's Fair that fall.[3]

As thousands of visitors viewed the navy's exhibits in New York, a sudden crisis erupted off the coast of New England. On 23 May, the crew of the USS *Squalus* commenced the nineteenth of a series of dives designed to test the seaworthiness of the nearly three-month-old submarine. The previous eighteen dives had occurred without incident, giving the submarine's CO, Lt. Oliver Naquin, and the other fifty-eight officers and men every confidence that the next would result in the same. This nineteenth dive, however, proved different as water began pouring into the submarine's engine room through the main induction valve while the boat was submerged. When all efforts to blow out the ballast tanks failed, Lieutenant Naquin ordered the submarine's watertight doors closed to prevent the water aft in the engine room from flooding the entire boat. The submarine sank to the bottom in approximately 240 feet of water with only thirty-three of the original fifty-eight men alive aboard the sunken hulk. In the hours that followed, the navy drew on lessons learned in the aftermath of the losses of the *S-51* and *S-4* more than a decade earlier and mounted a rapid rescue effort to save the submariners. The navy quickly dispatched the salvage vessel *Falcon* to the scene with a McCann Rescue Chamber aboard. In a matter of hours, the chamber made a series of dives to the *Squalus* and brought all survivors to the surface. The efforts vindicated the efforts made over the preceding years to develop rescue gear for downed submariners.

The successful rescue helped turn the accident into a stunning public relations success because it proved that many hard lessons had been learned. The *Squalus* incident became the first test of 1936 additions to the *Intelligence Manual* on "Emergencies" that had built upon lessons learned from previous incidents and also a recent policy directive issued by the commander in chief of the U.S. Fleet, Adm. Claude C. Bloch, on 18 May that called for quicker releases of information. The Public Relations Branch not only followed this new guidance during the crisis but also implemented new practices that evidenced just how far the branch had come since the clumsy responses that had marked previous accidents. Lieutenant Commander Austin, fresh from his work at the World's Fair, had received permission directly from the CNO, Admiral Leahy, to work from the scene at Portsmouth Navy Yard, where he established a makeshift information center capable of receiving radio traffic from the rescue vessel *Falcon*, which he then quickly conveyed to the correspondents gathered at the base. In addition, the Navy established a room in its telegraph office at the headquarters building in Washington to handle all of the traffic coming from Portsmouth. Within three days of the accident, the Public Relations Branch had issued a flurry of press releases detailing each step of the rescue operations, the identities of the survivors and the known deceased, and information on the development, earlier in the decade, of the rescue equipment being utilized.[4]

Press outlets touted the effectiveness of the Public Relations Branch in handling the crisis. The *Christian Science Monitor* reported on the unprecedented amount of access granted by the branch ashore as well by as the officers of the *Falcon*. Sailors at the *S-4* site in 1927 had used a firehose to ward off approaching reporters, but the *Squalus*'s salvagers actively encouraged cameramen to close within a hundred yards to film the rescue operations.[5] Associated Press reporter E. Harry Crockett offered even more effusive praise for the navy, claiming that "the United States Navy knows how to meet newspaper 'deadlines.'" At the information center in Portsmouth, Crockett reported that officers would enter the room and ask the assembled newsmen, "How long before your next deadline, boys? Will an interview by 10:30 satisfy most of you?"[6]

The Public Relations Branch's cooperation with the World's Fair and its work after the *Squalus* accident revealed much about the development of navy public relations in the preceding seventeen years. The plans for the fair showed that the navy intended to put on a big public spectacle in the nation's largest city. Yet, long before the establishment of the Information Section or the first Navy Day in 1922, the service had demonstrated an ability to organize large public events. Dating back to the late nineteenth century, these events allowed citizens to gain a close-up view of a service that remained oftentimes isolated and hidden from view. Furthermore, although the navy's presence at the World's Fair was never a secret, the elaborate planning for the event took place out of the public eye and allowed the service to piggyback onto an event guaranteed to attract public attention. Thus, the fair represented a more traditional publicity opportunity, organized in ways similar to Navy Day and many other public exhibitions, albeit on a larger scale.

The *Squalus* incident, however, revealed an entirely new capacity for navy public relations. By their nature, crises create uncertainty, forcing officials to make quick decisions that put public relations organizations through a stress test. The staff of the Information Section/Public Relations Branch had faced many problems in formulating effective responses to the tragedies of the interwar period. The service's civilian and uniformed leaders likewise did the office few favors by sometimes exacerbating these accidents through their unhelpful actions and statements. By establishing an information center, encouraging much greater physical access, and rapidly disseminating reports to the press on the scene, the Public Relations Branch demonstrated a clear capacity for organizational learning. Through many growing pains, the branch had finally found an effective formula for communicating with the press in the most urgent of circumstances.

An academic study from the period likewise confirmed the organizational and policy development that the fair and the *Squalus* accident had demonstrated. A month after the *Squalus* sank, James McCamy's *Government Publicity: Its Practice in Federal Administration* appeared, offering, for the first time, an objective, quantifiable study of how federal agencies used public relations. Based on his doctoral research in political science conducted in 1937 and 1938, McCamy used several measures to gauge the relative effectiveness of each department and agency, including content studies of periodicals and the *New York Times* during random intervals to determine the levels of coverage each department received. The navy polled well in the newspaper study, placing eighth out of nearly forty government agencies surveyed. The periodical study showed that discussions of policy and personnel were few, but articles on the work of sailors and equipment were quite numerous. This suggests that the Public Relations Branch had been far more successful in promoting stories on technological transformation than on either manpower or national defense.[7]

In addition to content analyses, McCamy also devoted considerable space to the process and organization of public relations within government agencies. His findings showed that the problems experienced by the Public Relations Branch were not unique. The New Deal agencies aggressively promoted themselves using the latest theories and methods, but many other agencies including the navy still developed their policies based on intuition and, according to McCamy, did not devote nearly enough resources to measuring their effectiveness. More importantly, McCamy discovered that many agencies found it difficult both to coordinate the various public relations activities within their agency and to bridge the gap between "operators" and public relations personnel.[8] These related problems had plagued the Public Relations Branch for years, but McCamy's research confirmed that the navy was far from alone in building an effective public relations establishment.

A far more damning assertion made by McCamy was that the navy, along with many other government agencies, lacked a true public relations strategy and any long-term public relations campaigns to accomplish strategic goals. As McCamy's study proved, the navy could generate significant amounts of publicity, but the policies set down by both civilian and uniformed leaders mostly governed the structure and policy of public relations and attached only one priority to the release of information: that it not reveal classified information. The dearth of public relations experience within the navy, the inability of the Public Relations Branch to control all public relations responsibilities, and the branch's position within the bowels of the service's bureaucracy likely caused this situation. Thus, in a strict sense, the branch did not have the opportunity to manage the type of public relations campaigns then becoming more common in the more sophisticated government agencies or in the private sector.

Yet, what the branch in particular and the navy as a whole oversaw was more akin to modern-day strategic communications, which includes advertising and public relations, rather than PR, strictly defined.[9] The branch disseminated its own publicity while also collaborating with and enabling the campaigns of the Recruiting Bureau and Rear Admiral Moffett's Bureau of Aeronautics, both of which had clear strategic goals. The Recruiting Bureau sought to attract enough worthy young men into the service using recruiters, posters, and films, a goal that it consistently met throughout the interwar period. Whereas the Recruiting Bureau projected a positive image of the service, the work of the Information Section/Public Relations Branch often involved limiting negative press coverage of the service's enlisted force.

Rear Admiral Moffett, like the Recruiting Bureau, had his own bureaucratic power base from which to single-handedly initiate his own PR campaigns on behalf of the bureau. Moffett could see to it that ships and aircraft moved to locations or participated in events designed to attract the maximum amount of attention, and he possessed direct control over aviation personnel, many of whom had their own publicity value thanks to their professional accomplishments. The Information Section provided support for Moffett's work by issuing press releases in advance of many of these events and coordinating press coverage.

Beyond those specific campaigns, however, the policy guidance given to the Information Section/Public Relations Branch makes it clear that the navy intended the office to develop effective relationships with the media. The initial guidance emphasized the print press, but the office quickly expanded into radio even though a firm policy to govern the latter was not forthcoming. The navy had enjoyed occasional ties to the film industry dating back to before World War I, but these early interactions had always been handled on an ad hoc basis by the navy's leadership. The creation of the Motion Picture Board in 1929 gave the navy's small public relations office access to the largest remaining form of mass media not under its purview and thus significant power to shape the navy's public image. Furthermore, the board gave the officers of the Information Section/Public Relations Branch more influence and oversight over the work of the Recruiting Bureau and the Bureau of Aeronautics. Both of these entities had their own representatives on the board by 1931, but the Public Relations Branch arguably had the most control since it maintained the official link to Hollywood studios.

McCamy's analysis of navy public relations occurred as the international system devolved into chaos as Adolf Hitler's Germany upended the European order and as Japan invaded China. Just months later, the world was plunged into war. On 1 September, forces from Nazi Germany invaded neighboring Poland, prompting Great Britain and France to declare war on Germany two days later. On 8 September, President Roosevelt declared a national emergency and initiated a series of measures designed to prepare the United States for a potential conflict. The outbreak of war quickly began to affect the navy's public relations practices.

The security crisis brought an increase in naval manpower and a corresponding growth in capability. By 1939 the ONI's Public Relations Branch had eight staffers: the officer-in-charge, Cdr. Leland P. Lovette; an assistant for press relations, Lieutenant Commander Austin; an assistant for photography, Lt. W. G. Beecher Jr., as well as two civilian assistants, two stenographers, and a marine orderly. The onset of war overseas spurred an expansion of navy public relations as the service

Acting Secretary of the Navy Charles Edison holding a press conference, 14 September 1939. Lt. Cdr. Bernard L. Austin (*standing, right*) and Cdr. Leland P. Lovette (*seated, right*).
Naval History and Heritage Command, NH 56939, Photographic Section.

expanded the staff to thirteen in July 1940. An enlarged staff allowed for a dramatic increase in the number of press releases issued by the branch from 1939 to 1941, giving matters of national defense even greater prominence among the forms of print media.

The enlarged staff helped, but even more important was the increase in public relations experience in the branch. Commander Lovette had been among the most active heads of the branch in its history, and he remained in his position until July 1940. Cdr. Harry Thurber replaced Lovette, but this was not his first public relations assignment. As a lieutenant, Thurber had previously served in the Information Section from 1925 to 1926. His appointment indicates that the navy had finally understood that public relations constituted a distinct career track and required certain skills. Thurber's staff included several reservists whose civilian careers had given them experience in newspapers and radio. Lt. Cdr. William Galvin had prior experience as the secretary of the Navy League as a civilian, while another officer, Lt. Cdr. E. John Long, applied his previous experience at *National Geographic* to head the branch's Pictorial Section.[10] Film director and reserve lieutenant commander John Ford also helped train a number of photographers and cameramen for public relations duty. The officers who had worked in the Information Section/Public

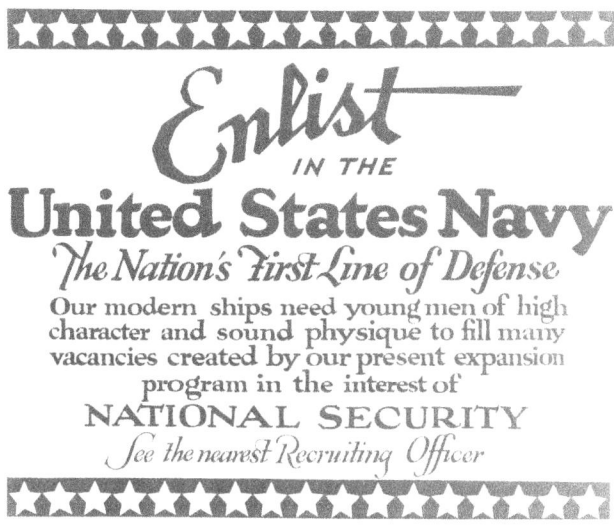

"Enlist in the United States Navy," 1940.
Naval History and Heritage Command, NH 77222, Photographic Section.

Relations Branch prior to 1939 had often shown the ability to learn public relations on the job, but few had any previous familiarity with media or public relations. Thurber and his staff were easily the most experienced group of officers and civilians the navy had applied to public relations work to that time.

This larger, more experienced office continued to produce publicity in the areas that had dominated interwar navy public relations—manpower, technology, and the value of the navy to the nation—but a message of preparedness clearly took precedence. Whereas preparedness had been one message among many put forth by the navy and its supporters in the 1920s and 1930s, the need for an enlarged navy to protect national security became the dominant theme in the two years prior to American entry into World War II.[11]

This message of preparedness spilled over into recruiting. Recruiters continued to tout the benefits of naval service, but by June 1940, posters issued by the Recruiting Bureau melded the themes that had typified interwar recruiting, such as foreign travel and physical development, with the need for enhanced national security. Whereas the interwar navy, with its posters calling on "young men of high character and sound physique," had sold itself as an institution capable of turning boys into men for the benefit of the nation, the present emergency did not allow for such

"The United States Navy has a job to do for America: Join up and fight," 1940. *Naval History and Heritage Command, NH 77227, Photographic Section.*

niceties. Instead, the largest and boldest text of its advertisements was reserved for statements regarding "national security."[12]

A poster issued in October 1940 explicitly called attention to the national emergency and showcased the navy's newest weapons. The images of sleek, modern monoplanes, which had only recently entered service, and surface craft combined served to not only reinforce the idea of the balanced fleet but to clearly call attention to the service's national defense mission. Any mention of learning a trade or of self-improvement was abandoned.[13]

Hollywood continued to occupy a central place in providing public relations support for the navy, and the films produced by the studios with service cooperation further underscored the preparedness message. Several movies emphasized the growth of naval aviation, including *Flight Command* (1940) and a short entitled *Eyes of the Navy* (1940), culminating in the 1941 Warner Brothers film *Dive Bomber*. Starring popular box office draw Errol Flynn and with a screenplay authored by Frank Wead, *Dive Bomber* contained a number of features setting it apart from the films that had preceded it. First, Warner Brothers made the expensive decision to use Technicolor film, which drove the film's budget to the then-considerable sum of $1,038,000. Second, it was unique among the aviation pictures for focusing on the development of flight medicine and the stresses that newer, high-performance aircraft placed on the human body. The film underwent strict scrutiny as the navy became "triply careful" to ensure that no material that could be construed as a breach of security reached the screen.[14]

A significant financial success, *Dive Bomber* became the seventh-highest-grossing film of 1941 in a field led by Walt Disney's *Fantasia* and the World War I story of *Sergeant York*. *Dive Bomber* also helped arouse one of the last bursts of isolationist sentiment prior to U.S. entry into World War II. In 1941, Senator Gerald P. Nye, who had previously launched the investigations into the so-called merchants of death, claimed that Hollywood studios intended their films, including *Dive Bomber*, to goad the nation into going to war. Congress had occasionally inquired about the connection between the navy and Hollywood during the mid-1930s, but the depth of this relationship seemingly took on new urgency as films increasingly emphasized preparedness even while the United States remained officially neutral. During a series of hearings that fall, film producers denied the allegation made by Nye and other isolationist senators. The hearings never produced any solid evidence to justify the charges, and, not surprisingly, the Senate and the rest of the nation quickly lost interest in the proceedings after the Japanese attacked Pearl Harbor on 7 December.[15]

The growth of the Public Relations Branch after 1939 led to a decline in the importance of the navy's external allies that had proven instrumental during the lean years of the 1920s and 1930s. The Navy League of the United States resumed publishing its journal *Sea Power* in 1939, but the group's poor financial state and a drop in memberships limited its participation in preparedness drives. The growing public support for a strong national defense by 1940, especially after the fall of France that June, and the continued enlargement of the navy's own public relations capabilities meant that the Navy League and other like-minded groups diminished in importance.[16]

The decline in the importance of the Navy League occurred as the Public Relations Branch expanded in 1939 and 1940, but even more dramatic changes loomed over the horizon. In 1940, as a nod to bipartisanship in the growing crisis, President Roosevelt appointed former newspaper publisher Frank Knox to become secretary of the navy. Knox's politics and demeanor differed greatly from the last navy secretary to have newspaper experience, Josephus Daniels, but they both shared an understanding of the value of effective publicity. The Public Relations Branch had grown considerably over the years in both manpower and effectiveness, but it remained an autonomous entity within the Office of Naval Intelligence and several steps removed from the secretary's office. On 1 May 1941, Knox folded the Public Relations Branch into the new Office of Public Relations and, in the months ahead, expanded the staff to thirty-seven officers, thirty civilians, and ten enlisted men.[17]

Establishment of the new office demonstrated three significant advances, the first of which was the decision to place it directly under the authority of the secretary of the navy. The old Navy News Bureau had been a civilian office that reported directly to Secretary Daniels, but Secretary Knox instead maintained the predominantly military character of the Public Relations Branch. Knox's restoration of the public relations function to the secretary's office promised to significantly increase its importance and power within the Navy Department. Second, as he increased the staff to seventy-seven over the next several months, Knox filled many key positions with capable individuals he knew from his newspaper days. No longer did the navy's public relations office suffer from a fundamental lack of manpower and resources. Finally, Knox appointed a flag officer, Rear Adm. Arthur J. Hepburn, as the director of public relations. This was a step up from past practice, as commanders headed the old Information Section. These three enhancements clearly signaled Knox's commitment to improving the navy's public relations capabilities.

These developments between 1939 and 1941 affirmed the navy's traditional willingness to mobilize public relations during times of crisis, and the service's PR capabilities underwent a dramatic transformation, for which a true peacetime public relations establishment had laid the foundation. The mobilization of navy public relations during the latest national emergency built on nearly a quarter century of PR development dating back to the establishment of the Navy News Bureau in 1917 and carried on through the Information Section and the Public Relations Branch. These organizations, at times in cooperation with the Recruiting Bureau, Rear Admiral Moffett, Dudley Knox, and the Navy League, had developed ties to the mass media that allowed the navy to enhance its image.

The interwar navy was, to use a modern concept, a "closed system" of public relations. Such a system only reacts when an external issue threatens organizational viability. In reaction to stimuli from outside, a closed system tends to call attention to the organization with little clear design or motivation behind publicity efforts beyond maintaining a presence in the public sphere. The organization in question develops its policies and needs internally and seeks little outside input on how those goals might be met. Such systems assume that the public's mind can always be changed on an issue, thus leading to attempts to gain public acquiescence for the organization's goals.[18] This is quite an ambitious goal, and one that early public relations pioneer Edward Bernays thought impossible. In *Propaganda* (1928), Bernays argued that even successful public relations campaigns could, at best, only modify public opinion and had little or no hope of completely reversing the public's stance on an issue. He may have waged dramatically successful PR campaigns even at that early stage of his life and career, but he also recognized that the profession he thought had the power to shape public consciousness had finite limits.[19]

Several years before Bernays had made his point about the limits of public relations, the navy had learned this lesson firsthand. The Navy News Bureau established by Secretary Daniels enjoyed his full support. In addition, Daniels staffed the bureau wholly with civilians possessing extensive news experience. Despite these advantages, the Navy News Bureau could do little to stem the tide of the widespread social and political movement favoring naval arms limitation. By the time of the disbanding of the bureau in September 1921, the Washington Conference had already been scheduled to convene two months later, with little chance for the navy to affect the proceedings. The Navy News Bureau also had no effective response to the charges leveled against the service by army general Mitchell and other supporters of a unified air service who believed the navy and its separate aviation arm hindered both national security and the development of aviation. Bernays would likely have assessed this situation as too bleak for a PR campaign to solve on its own because it would have to run completely against the prevailing public mood. Thus, the navy's first public relations office—which increasingly lacked internal and external support for its mission by 1921—had no hope of adequately addressing this crisis brought on by the postwar push for arms limitation.

A key feature of modern public relations campaigns is the need for direct, detailed, and consistent research to gauge public attitudes toward a product, group, or issue. Data of that type, for the most part, does not exist for the interwar era, which reflects how the navy guided PR policies by intuition without relying on collected information. Many factors affected the growth of the navy in the 1930s, including the election of Democratic politicians to the executive and legislative branches who were committed to naval expansion, especially as a means of economic stimulus. The advent of new foreign threats in both Europe and Asia likewise increased the need for a strong navy to protect the nation and its interests. Civilian public relations campaigns of the interwar period also relied much more on the intuition of its practitioners than on scientific analysis of carefully researched information. These practitioners rarely received clear, direct feedback from the general public.[20]

The data collected by the navy and other media outlets during the interwar period that might help measure any public relations successes are both incomplete and can at best suggest corollary effects. For instance, the navy met its manpower targets throughout the interwar period, and the chief of the Bureau of Navigation reported in 1928 that the quality of recruits had increased in recent years. This is perhaps borne out through higher General Classification Test scores, but this overlaps with a small rise in the number of disciplinary incidents, from 1.5 to 1.8 percent, thought to be insignificant by the chief of BuNav. These trends occurred in a relatively strong economy, but the collapse of the job market that began in 1930 and the navy's ability to recruit and retain only the best men given the high rate of civilian unemployment complicates any attempt at measuring the success of any recruiting and manpower publicity.[21]

Analyzing trends in naval spending also reveals no causal effects attributable to the navy's public relations efforts. The navy's budgets reflected the priority placed on naval spending by Congress, and during the interwar period the navy's allocation waxed and waned. From a high of $1.97 billion in 1919, naval spending fell to $768 million two years later, and, in the immediate aftermath of the Washington Conference, to less than half that—just over $300 million per fiscal year, from 1923 until 1925. With some variation, annual spending remained constant at approximately $350 million until 1933 when President Franklin Roosevelt and the heavily Democratic Congress began increasing spending, until it reached $673 million in 1939.[22]

By the latter 1930s, some firms and individuals began conducting public opinion polling with some scientific rigor, which offers more clues about the public's attitude toward the interwar navy. Polls from 1935 onward showed that significant majorities of the American public—usually more than 75 percent—supported an increase in naval construction, but this did not mean the service enjoyed unequivocal support. Only 57 percent of those polled in 1938 supported tax increases to pay for an enlarged fleet. In a poll taken in July 1940 that asked males under forty-six years of age which branch of the military they preferred to serve in if the country was directly attacked, the navy lagged behind both the army and the "air forces," with only 24 percent of all respondents compared to 44 percent for the army. Interestingly, respondents under the age of thirty showed more interest in naval service, with the army and air forces tied at 34 percent and the navy lagging by only five percentage points.[23]

Poll results indicate that the public overwhelmingly supported a vigorous naval construction program by the latter 1930s, while a smaller majority supported tax hikes to pay for the fleet. To interpret these polls as a victory for the navy's public relations campaigns, however, is a stretch due to the absence of the necessary items found in the questionnaires themselves, such as why respondents supported an increase in naval appropriations. The shift could easily have been attributable to the growing international instability of the mid-1930s given the rise of the militarist faction in Japan and the Nazis in Germany. In any case, the continued public reluctance to serve revealed in 1940 polling also suggests that support and admiration of the navy only ran so deep.

Polls from later in the decade show that much had changed since the immediate aftermath of World War I, when the Navy News Bureau could not conceivably counter the overwhelming public support for policies in opposition to the navy's interests. The impact of the Great Depression and growing instability in Europe on the prevailing public mood completely changed, leading to increased backing for pro-navy policies. This shift created new public relations opportunities, such as Commander Lovette's assistance provided to Kendall Banning's books in 1939. Furthermore, as private media companies believed they could somehow profit from association with the navy, this likewise made life easier for the staff of the Public Relations Branch.

The effect of these developments was that the concerns of other entities became increasingly intertwined with navy public relations. Media outlets needed to distinguish themselves from their competitors and often played up spectacle and controversy to attract audiences. The gathering of a fleet for review, a new technical feat accomplished by Moffett's growing aviation branch, or the achievements of navy personnel fit well within those parameters. Hollywood films and studio-owned newsreels, in particular, often relied on visual spectacles, whether by using filmed model works to depict mock aerial attacks or submarine-mounted cameras to dive beneath the waves. William Randolph Hearst may have been an outlier case in this regard by combining those tendencies with extreme jingoism, but only the latter made him exceptional relative to his competitors. This emphasis on spectacle and entertainment dominated films and newsreels, and, when combined with the navy's emphasis on accuracy, meant that the navy devoted comparatively little creative energy to devising a popular message of naval expansion prior to the international crises of the late 1930s.

This was a critical deficiency, but it should not completely mask the growth of navy public relations in the 1920s and 1930s. In replacing the civilian-staffed Navy

News Bureau with the officer-manned Information Section, Secretary Denby had committed the service to managing its own public image for the first time. The early years of this transition proved rocky, and identifying experienced personnel was quite difficult. By the 1930s, however, the personnel of the Public Relations Branch had exercised the authority it did possess to create a network of contacts in the newspaper, radio, publishing, and film industries who often solicited support and information from the branch in crafting their respective projects. Designing an effective policy to manage radio eluded the branch because of the geographic localization of radio combined with the ephemeral nature of the broadcasts, but the navy and the Navy League always found stations willing to air speeches they deemed important. The service enjoyed far more success with Hollywood and used its clout to gain control over the editing of feature films that received official cooperation. Through its close relationship with former aviator Frank Wead, the navy even occasionally enjoyed the opportunity to shape a film project from initial concept to release.

Media exposure helped to continue normalizing the navy as a public institution and to overcome the decades of isolation experienced by the service when it was a small, forward-deployed, squadron-organized service. It is telling that the first public relations policies crafted during the interwar period and the debates surrounding them often assumed that merely explaining what the navy did in a clear fashion to the public would alleviate this cultural deficit. The "silent service" culture combined with a misunderstanding that the rise of the mass media meant that organizations, whether public or private, would need to compete for space had informed this worldview. Establishing relationships with outside parties helped surmount these problems.

The relationships forged during the interwar period endure to this day, having survived sweeping changes in American society and culture, and in the forms of media the public consume. Just as the interwar navy maximized the public relations benefit of Hollywood films, the service reaped the benefits of its positive portrayal in *Top Gun* (1986), reporting an increased interest in naval service on the part of young men. The Navy League, too, survived its own ups and downs and continues to occupy an important role within navy public relations. In 2008, the league sponsored a series of meetings entitled "Conversations with the Country" that helped formulate and propagate the *Cooperative Strategy for 21st Century Seapower*, a maritime strategy developed jointly by the U.S. Navy, Marine Corps, and Coast Guard. In addition, as the interwar navy sometimes relied on pithy slogans such as "the first line of national defense" or the "three-plane" navy to describe its goals, the modern navy has used such slogans as "A global force for good" to promote its value to the public.[24]

In October 1941, Gerald Beskin of the Office of Public Relations, a reserve lieutenant, argued that the navy, having mastered the air, the sea, and the ocean's depths, needed to enter "the fourth dimension of modern naval tactics": public consciousness. Doing so meant "interpret[ing] the Navy to the public and the public to the Navy, serving to draw them together for the common good of all."[25] This dire international situation made Beskin's plea a necessary one, yet, in fairness to him, the service had heeded Captain McNamee's desperate clarion call to learn how to "sell the Navy to the people" two decades earlier. The interwar navy had, for the first time, recognized a need to reach out to the public and to communicate its actions and strategic goals to a wider audience. To do so, the navy developed a public relations office that remained understaffed and underresourced, and whose personnel often lacked essential experience in the field. Despite these serious handicaps, the reach of navy publicity spread into new forms of media and laid the foundation for future expansion. This structure proved readily adaptable to the outbreak of war in Europe in 1939 by addressing many of the inadequacies of the interwar period, and Secretary Knox's creation of the Office of Public Relations in May 1941 finally acknowledged the central importance of public relations to the institutional health of the navy. When war came in December 1941, there was no need to create a PR organization from scratch because, unlike any other time in the navy's history, navy public relations had long since been mobilized.

NOTES

Introduction

1. Quoted in Vincent Davis, *Postwar Defense Policy and the U.S. Navy, 1943–1946* (Chapel Hill: University of North Carolina Press, 1962), 46–47.
2. For some of the titles that address interwar transformation, see Craig C. Felker, *Testing American Sea Power: U.S. Navy Strategic Exercises, 1923–1940* (College Station: Texas A&M University Press, 2006); Norman Friedman, Thomas Hone, and Mark D. Mandeles, *American and British Aircraft Carrier Development, 1919–1941* (Annapolis, Md.: Naval Institute Press, 1999); Joel Ira Holwitt, *"Execute against Japan": The U.S. Decision to Conduct Unrestricted Submarine Warfare* (College Station: Texas A&M University Press, 2009); and David John Ulbrich, *Preparing for Victory: Thomas Holcomb and the Making of the Modern Marine Corps, 1936–1943* (Annapolis, Md.: Naval Institute Press, 2011).
3. Lawrence C. Hoag, *Preface to Preparedness: The Washington Disarmament Conference and Public Opinion* (Washington, D.C.: American Council on Public Affairs, 1941), 89–123. Although dated, the book provides an excellent survey of the different groups formed to support disarmament and of the newspaper editorials written on the issue; George F. Baer, *One Hundred Years of American Sea Power: The U.S. Navy 1890–1990* (Stanford, Calif.: Stanford University Press, 1993), 39–40, 48, 59–61, 86–87.
4. "Air Bombing Tests," *New York Times*, 29 July 1921, 8; James J. Cooke, *Billy Mitchell* (Boulder, Colo.: Lynne Rienner Publishers, 2002), 127–28.
5. Scott M. Cutlip, *Public Relations History: From the 17th to the 20th Century; the Antecedents* (Hillsdale, N.J.: Lawrence Erlbaum Associates, 1995), xiv–xv; F. Donald Scovel, "Helm's a Lee: A History of the Development of the Public Affairs Function in the United States Navy, 1861–1941" (master's thesis, University of Wisconsin–Madison,

1968), ii–iii, vii; R. Dale Klinkerman, "From Blackout at Pearl Harbor to Spotlight on Tokyo Bay: A Study of the Evolution in U.S. Naval Public Relations Policies and Practices during World War II" (Ph.D. diss., University of Wisconsin–Madison, 1972), 10; Frederick Harrod, *Manning the New Navy: The Development of the Modern Naval Enlisted Force* (Wesport, Conn.: Greenwood Press, 1978), 45–46; William F. Trimble, *Admiral William A. Moffett: Architect of Naval Aviation* (Washington, D.C.: Smithsonian Institution Press, 1994), 120–24; Lawrence Suid, *Sailing on the Silver Screen: Hollywood and the Navy* (Annapolis, Md.: Naval Institute Press, 1996), x, 55.

6. Peter Karsten, *The Naval Aristocracy: The Golden Age of Annapolis and the Emergence of Modern American Navalism* (New York: Free Press, 1972), 362, 367–71.

7. Captain Luke McNamee to William Howard Gardiner, 28 July 1922, 1, I32, William Howard Gardiner Papers [hereafter cited as Gardiner Papers], Houghton Library, Harvard University, Cambridge, Mass. [hereafter cited as HL].

8. Glen T. Cameron and Dennis L. Wilcox, *Public Relations: Strategies and Tactics*, 9th ed. (Boston: Person, Allyn, and Bacon, 2009), 161–64.

9. Scott M. Cutlip, Allen H. Center, and Glen M. Broom, *Effective Public Relations*, 8th ed. (Upper Saddle River, N.J.: Prentice Hall, 2000), 15–17.

10. Rosa Brooks, "Confessions of a Strategic Communicator," *Foreign Policy*, 6 December 2012, http://foreignpolicy.com/2012/12/06/confessions-of-a-strategic-communicator/.

11. Ivy Lee, "Declaration of Principles," in Sherman Morse, "An Awakening in Wall Street," *American Magazine* 62 (September 1906): 457–63.

12. Richard West, "The Navy and the Press during the Civil War," *U.S. Naval Institute Proceedings* [hereafter cited as *Proceedings*] 63, no. 1 (January 1938): 38–41.

13. Captain Robert F. Stockton was one of the few naval officers who actively sought press coverage for his accomplishments prior to the Civil War, although this backfired with the disastrous explosion of a heavy gun aboard his command, the USS *Princeton*, in 1844. See Harold D. Langley, "Robert F. Stockton: Naval Officer and Reformer," in *Quarterdeck and Bridge: Two Centuries of American Naval Leaders*, ed. James C. Bradford (Annapolis, Md.: Naval Institute Press, 1997), 77–102; and Ann Blackman, "Fatal Cruise of the USS *Princeton*," *Naval History* 19, no. 5 (October 2005): 37–41.

14. Mark Shulman, *Navalism and the Emergence of American Sea Power, 1882–1893* (Annapolis, Md.: Naval Institute Press, 1995), 14–21, 23–25.

15. William E. Livezey, *Mahan on Sea Power*, rev. ed. (Norman: University of Oklahoma Press, 1986), 335–37.

16. Davis, *Postwar Defense Policy*, 251.

17. Paul E. Pedisich, *Congress Buys a Navy: Politics, Economics, and the Rise of American Naval Power, 1881–1921* (Annapolis, Md.: Naval Institute Press, 2016), 53–122.

18. Calvin DeArmond Davis, *The United States and the Second Hague Peace Conference: American Diplomacy and International Organization, 1899–1914* (Durham, N.C.: Duke University Press, 1975), 4–9, 24–25, 139–42; Henry J. Hendrix, *Theodore Roosevelt's Naval Diplomacy: The U.S. Navy and the Birth of the American Century* (Annapolis, Md.: Naval Institute Press, 2009), xiv–xv.

19. Armin Rappaport, *The Navy League of the United States* (Detroit: Wayne State University Press, 1962), 1–4. See also Dirk Bonker, *Militarism in a Global Age: Naval Ambitions in Germany and the United States before World War I* (Ithaca, N.Y.: Cornell University Press, 2012).
20. Rappaport, *Navy League*, 17; Richard L. Wright, *The Navy League of the United States: Civilians Supporting the Sea Services for More Than a Century* (Arlington, Va.: Navy League of the United States, 2006), 45.
21. Harrod, *Manning the New Navy*, 11–12, 15–17, 34–44.
22. Rappaport, *Navy League*, 17–43; Wright, *Navy League*, 53–54.
23. Deidre Johnson, *Edward Stratemeyer and the Stratemeyer Syndicate* (New York: Twayne Publishers, 1993), 1–14; a representative sample of the youth-oriented naval literature includes Irving H. Hancock, *Dave Darrin's First Year at Annapolis; or, Two Plebe Midshipmen at the United States Naval Academy* (Philadelphia: Altemus, 1910); Frank Gee Patchin, *The Battleship Boys at Sea; or, Two Apprentices in Uncle Sam's Navy* (Philadelphia: Altemus, 1910); and Yates Stirling, *A United States Midshipman Afloat* (Philadelphia: Penn Publishing, 1908).
24. Lawrence H. Suid, *Guts and Glory: The Making of the American Military Image in Film*, 2nd ed. (Frankfort: University Press of Kentucky, 2002), 12.
25. Russell Merritt, "Nickelodeon Theaters, 1905–1914," in *The American Film Industry*, ed. Tino Balio (Madison: University of Wisconsin Press, 1985), 91; Robert Anderson, "The Motion Picture Patents Company: A Reevaluation," in Balio, *American Film Industry*, 133–52.
26. Scovel, "Helm's a Lee," 31–32.
27. Heather Pace Marshall, "'There's Nothing a Marine Can't Do': Publicity and the Marine Corps, 1911–1917" (paper presented at the Naval History Symposium, Annapolis, Md., 10 September 2009). See also Heather Pace Marshall, "'It Means Something These Days to Be a Marine': Image, Identity, and Mission in the Marine Corps, 1861–1918" (Ph.D. diss., Duke University, 2010); and Heather Pace Venable, *Deliberate Heroes: The Making of the Corps' Warrior Ethos* (Naval Institute Press, forthcoming).
28. Helene Philbert, "History of Navy Public Relations" (talk given at the Navy Public Relations Course in Washington, D.C., 23 July 1945), Box 121; Office of Information Subject Files, 1940–1958; Entry P 3 [hereafter cited as EP 3]; Records of the Office of Information; General Records of the Department of the Navy, 1947–, Record Group [RG] 428, National Archives and Records Administration, College Park, Md. [hereafter cited as NACP].
29. Suid, *Guts and Glory*, 13; Suid, *Sailing on the Silver Screen*, 4–5.
30. Harrod, *Manning the New Navy*, 28–31, 47.
31. Mordecai Lee, *Congress vs. the Bureaucracy: Muzzling Agency Public Relations* (Norman: University of Oklahoma Press, 2011), 19–26, 30, 52–53, 84; Scovel, "Helm's a Lee," 53–54, 57, 61.
32. Hoag, *Preface to Preparedness*, 38; Scovel, "Helm's a Lee," 56; Baer, *American Sea Power*, 59–60; *Congressional Record*, 64th Cong., 1st Sess., 17 July 1916, 11167–94.

Chapter 1. The Limits of Public Relations

1. Scovel, "Helm's a Lee," 53–54, 57, 61.
2. Clayton R. Koppes and Gregory D. Black, *Hollywood Goes to War: How Politics, Profits, and Propaganda Shaped World War II Movies* (New York: Macmillan, 1987), 48–49; Larry Wayne Ward, *The Motion Picture Goes to War: The U.S. Government Film Effort during World War I* (Ann Arbor, Mich.: UMI Research Press, 1985), 1; Larry Tye, *The Father of Spin: Edward L. Bernays and the Birth of Public Relations* (New York: Crown, 1998), 16–21.
3. Philbert, "History of Navy Public Relations," 1–2; Scovel, "Helm's a Lee," 61–62.
4. Scovel, "Helm's a Lee," 61–62.
5. Albert W. Fox, "Navy Officers and Creel in Feud; Censor's Methods Are Resented; Navy's Publicity Success Envied," *Washington Post*, 14 October 1917, 10.
6. Suid, *Sailing on the Silver Screen*, 7–8.
7. Wright, *Navy League*, 55–56; Rappaport, *Navy League*, 70–74.
8. Jerry W. Jones, *U.S. Battleship Operations during World War I* (Annapolis, Md.: Naval Institute Press, 1998), vii–viii, 27–28.
9. Baer, *American Sea Power*, 73–74, 83–85.
10. "Navy Week," *New York Times*, 18 December 1918, 14; Scovel, "Helm's a Lee," 72; "Bad Weather Delays Arrival of Fleet," *New York Times*, 19 December 1918, 3; "Daniels Lauds Navy as Fleet Nears Home Port," *New York Times*, 25 December 1918, 1; "Ovation to Sea Fighters," *New York Times*, 27 December 1918, 1; "Rodman Pictures the Fleet's Work: The 'New York' Rammed by U-Boat," *New York Times*, 27 December 1918, 1; "Night Ashore for Sailors," *New York Times*, 27 December 1918, 5; "Men from Warships Get Shore Leave," *New York Times*, 28 December 1918, 18.
11. Scovel, "Helm's a Lee," 63; "To Launch 'Tennessee' Soon," *New York Times*, 21 April 1919, 14; "Throng at Launch of the 'Tennessee,'" *New York Times*, 1 May 1919, 16; Jonathan G. Utley, *An American Battleship at Peace and War: The USS Tennessee* (Lawrence: University Press of Kansas, 1991), 2.
12. Hoag, *Preface to Preparedness*, 22–24; Josephus Daniels, *The Navy and the Nation: Wartime Addresses* (New York: George H. Doran Company, 1919), 295–301; "Navy First in World," *Washington Post*, 31 December 1918, 2; "Cable Still a Secret," *Washington Post*, 5 February 1919, 3.
13. Hoag, *Preface to Preparedness*, 24–25; Stephen Roskill, *The Period of Anglo-American Antagonism, 1919–1929*, vol. 1 of *Naval Policy between the Wars* (New York: Walker, 1968), 91.
14. "Sees War If League Fails," *New York Times*, 16 October 1919, 3.
15. Allan R. Millett and Peter Maslowski, *For the Common Defense: A Military History of the United States of America*, 2nd ed. (New York: Free Press, 1994), 91, 124, 248–49.
16. Dudley W. Knox, "Our Post War Mission," *Proceedings* 45, no. 8 (August 1919): 1293–1302; quotations on 1294, 1295, 1296, and 1298.
17. Cooke, *Billy Mitchell*, 13, 49–51, 66–67.
18. Tami Davis Biddle, *Rhetoric and Reality in Air Warfare: The Evolution of American and British Ideas about Strategic Bombing, 1914–1945* (Princeton, N.J.: Princeton University Press, 2002), 30–34.

19. Thomas Wildenberg, *Billy Mitchell's War with the Navy: The Interwar Rivalry over Air Power* (Annapolis, Md.: Naval Institute Press, 2013), 38–42; "The Neglect of Aviation," *New York Times*, 21 August 1919, 10; "Air Rule Vital in War," *Washington Post*, 19 October 1919, 2.
20. C. Vann Woodward, *The Strange Career of Jim Crow* (New York: Oxford University Press, 2002), 91. Daniels exhibited many of the traits common to southern progressives from the period, including strong support for temperance and support for racial segregation. Daniels, *Navy and the Nation*, 302; Baer, *American Sea Power*, 58–59; Mary Klachko, "William Shepherd Benson: Naval General Staff American Style," in *Admirals of the New Steel Navy*, ed. James C. Bradford (Annapolis, Md.: Naval Institute Press, 1990), 320–22.
21. Klachko, "William Shepherd Benson," 300–304; "Congress Inquiry into Navy Awards," *Washington Post*, 24 December 1919, 1; Elting Morison, *Admiral Sims and the Modern American Navy* (Boston: Houghton Mifflin, 1942), 434–38.
22. Morison, *Admiral Sims*, 441–62; "Sims Arraigns Navy Department," *New York Times*, 18 January 1920, 1; Paolo E. Coletta, *Admiral Bradley Fiske and the American Navy* (Lawrence: Regents Press of Kansas, 1979), 200–206.
23. Lawrence R. Murphy, *Perverts by Official Order: The Campaign against Homosexuals by the United States Navy* (New York: Haworth Press, 1988), 11–36, 69–103, 154–57; George Chauncey Jr., "Christian Brotherhood or Sexual Perversion: Homosexual Identities and the Construction of Boundaries in the World War I Era," in *Hidden from History: Reclaiming the Gay and Lesbian Past*, ed. Martin Baum Duberman, Martha Vicinus, and George Chauncey Jr. (Markham, Ont.: New American Library Books, 1989): 294–317.
24. Murphy, *Perverts by Official Order*, 158–273; Ted Morgan, *FDR: A Biography* (New York: Simon & Schuster, 1985), 245; "Lay Navy Scandal to F. D. Roosevelt," *New York Times*, 20 July 1921, 4.
25. John R. Ferris, "The Symbol and the Substance of Sea Power: Great Britain, the United States, and the One-Power Standard, 1919–1922," in *Anglo-American Relations in the 1920s: The Struggle for Supremacy*, ed. B. J. C. McKercher (Edmonton: University of Alberta Press, 1990), 65–66, 79; Lawrence Sondhaus, *Navies of Europe, 1815–2002* (New York: Longman, 2002), 196. In October 1921, on the eve of the Washington Conference, the British ordered four "super-*Hood*" fast battleships, see Roskill, *Anglo-American Antagonism*, 227.
26. "Budget of the U.S. Navy: 1794 to 2014," https://www.history.navy.mil/research/library/online-reading-room/title-list-alphabetically/b/budget-of-the-us-navy-1794-to-2004.html; Baer, *American Sea Power*, 98.
27. John Whiteclay Chambers II, ed., *The Eagle and the Dove: The American Peace Movement and United States Foreign Policy, 1900–1922* (New York: Garland, 1976), 519; "Borah Offers Plan to Reduce Navies," *New York Times*, 15 December 1920, 1; E. David Cronon, *The Cabinet Diaries of Josephus Daniels, 1913–1921* (Lincoln: University of Nebraska Press, 1963), 575.
28. Hoag, *Preface to Preparedness*, 41, 45–49.
29. Wildenberg, *Billy Mitchell's War*, 49–50.

30. Charles Melhorn, *Two-Block Fox: The Rise of the Aircraft Carrier, 1911–1929* (Annapolis, Md.: Naval Institute Press, 1974), 61, 63; Wildenberg, *Billy Mitchell's War*, 52–60.
31. William Mitchell, "Has the Airplane Made the Battleship Obsolete?," *World's Work*, April 1921, 550–55; "The March of Events: An Editorial Interpretation," *World's Work*, April 1921, 534–36; Lee P. Warren, "The Battleship Still Supreme," *World's Work*, April 1921, 556–59.
32. Millet and Maslowski, *For the Common Defense*, 272–76; William Mitchell, *Our Air Force: The Keystone to National Defense* (New York: E. P. Dutton and Company, 1921), 27.
33. Mitchell, *Our Air Force*, xviii–xx, xxiv–xxvi, 160; quotation on xxi.
34. Melhorn, *Two-Block Fox*, 70–72; "Army Planes Sink Destroyer in Twenty Minutes," *New York Times*, 14 July 1921, 1.
35. "Bombs Fail to Sink the 'Ostfriesland,'" *New York Times*, 21 July 1921, 1; "Bombing Aircraft Sink the 'Frankfurt,'" *New York Times*, 19 July 1921, 1.
36. "2,000 Pound Bombs from Army Planes Sink 'Ostfriesland,'" *New York Times*, 22 July 1921, 1.
37. "Air Bombing Tests," *New York Times*, 29 July 1921, 8; Cooke, *Billy Mitchell*, 127–28.
38. Melhorn, *Two-Block Fox*, 56–57.
39. Hoag, *Preface to Preparedness*, 74–77.
40. Phillips Payson O'Brien, *British and American Naval Power: Politics and Policy, 1900–1936* (Westport, Conn.: Praeger, 1998), 158–59.
41. Joyce Blackwell, *No Peace without Freedom: Race and the Women's International League for Peace and Freedom, 1915–1975* (Carbondale: Southern Illinois University Press, 2004), 4–5; Hoag, *Preface to Preparedness*, 89–92.
42. Hoag, *Preface to Preparedness*, 47, 113–20.
43. O'Brien, *British and American Naval Power*, 158–59; Roskill, *Anglo-American Antagonism*, 301.
44. Hoag, *Preface to Preparedness*, 100–106, 120–23.
45. "Lists Arms Advisers," *Washington Post*, 2 November 1921, 1; Hoag, *Preface to Preparedness*, 126–31.
46. Assistant Secretary of the Navy to the Secretary of the Navy, "Intelligent Publicity for the Navy," 8 March 1921, Box 12 [hereafter cited as B12], Entry 19—General Correspondence, 1913–1926 [hereafter cited as E19], Records of the Office of the Secretary of the Navy, Records of the Navy Department, 1798–1947, RG 80, National Archives Building, Washington, D.C. [hereafter cited as NAB]. Senior Member Present, General Board to SecNav, "Intelligent Publicity for the Navy," 18 April 1921, B12, E19, RG 80, NAB; Admiral William S. Sims to SecNav, "Intelligent Publicity for the Navy," 4 April 1921, B12, E19, RG 80, NAB; Chief of the Bureau of Navigation to SecNav, "Intelligent Publicity for the Navy," 13 May 1921, B12, E19, RG 80, NAB.
47. Scovel, "Helm's a Lee," 79; Officer in Charge to BuNav, "Publicity," 17 May 1919, B395, General Correspondence, 1917–1925, Entry 89—General Records of the Bureau of Naval Personnel and Its Predecessors, 1801–1966 [hereafter E89], Records of the Bureau of Naval Personnel, 1798–1991, RG 24, NAB; Officer in Charge, Navy Recruiting

Bureau to BuNav, "Utilizing the Services of Ex-service Men for Publicity for the Navy," 1 October 1919, B396, E89, RG 24, NAB; Harrod, *Manning the New Navy*, 45.
48. M. E. Montgomery to Brooks, 20 October 1919, B315, E89, RG 24, NAB; Officer in Charge, St. Louis Recruiting Station, to Josephus Daniels, 23 October 1919, B315, E89, RG 24, NAB.
49. Memo for Capt. Courtney, 9 November 1922, B316, E89, RG 24, NAB; Officer in Charge, Navy Recruiting Bureau, to Chief of BuNav, 10 November 1922, B316, E89, RG 24, NAB; Jeffrey Vance and Suzanne Lloyd, *Harold Lloyd: Master Comedian* (New York: Henry N. Abrams, 2002), 64–72. The film confirmed Lloyd's status as a comedy star and propelled him to new heights in his Hollywood career.
50. Rappaport, *Navy League*, 77–78; Wright, *Navy League*, 74.
51. Herbert F. Hill, "The Navy League, Past, Present, and Future," *Sea Power* 5, no. 6 (December 1918): 365–66; AENAV Twenty One, 7 March 1921, B200, E89, RG 24, NAB.
52. Wright, *Navy League*, 75–76; Rappaport, *Navy League*, 89–90.
53. Roskill, *Anglo-American Antagonism*, 310–12, 328.
54. Baer, *American Sea Power*, 99–101; Roskill, *Anglo-American Antagonism*, 316–17. A more recent take on the Washington Conference and its place within the long arc of Anglo-American relations is Kori Schake, *Safe Passage: The Transition from British to American Hegemony* (Cambridge, Mass.: Harvard University Press, 2017), 235–53.

Chapter 2. Publicity and Propaganda

1. William O. Stevens, "The Naval Officer and the Civilian," *Proceedings* 47, no. 11 (November 1921): 1725–39; quotation on 1733.
2. C. K. Blackburn, "Mistaken Publicity," *Proceedings* 48, no. 1 (January 1922): 77–79; quotation on 77.
3. Karsten, *Naval Aristocracy*, 277–317.
4. Director, War Plans Division, to the Chief of Naval Operations, "Press Relations," 12 January 1922, B12, E19, RG 80, NAB.
5. Memorandum for the CNO, "Press Relations," 14 January 1922, B12, E19, RG 80, NAB; Rear Admiral Luke McNamee to Hasbrouck, 3 December 1921, B10, Entry 79—Formerly Security Classified Correspondence (General Subject CAP Files) 1901–1927 [hereafter E79], RG 38, NAB; Rear Admiral Luke McNamee to Captain E. H. Watson, 11 February 1922, B10, E79, RG 38, NAB.
6. SecNav to All Bureaus and Offices, "Navy Department Information Section under the Office of Naval Intelligence," 21 February 1922, B2617, E19, RG 80, NAB; Scovel, "Helm's a Lee," 85–86; Klinkerman, "Blackout at Pearl Harbor," 17.
7. Captain Ralph A. Koch, Officer Bio File, Naval History and Heritage Command [hereafter cited as NHHC].
8. Philbert, "History of Navy Public Relations," 2.
9. Ibid., 2–3.
10. J. W. McElroy, *Office of Naval Records and Library, 1882–1946* (Washington, D.C.: Navy Department, 1946).

11. Dudley W. Knox to Thomas T. Craven, 20 January 1922, Box 2, Papers of Dudley W. Knox [hereafter cited as Knox Papers], Library of Congress, Washington, D.C. [hereafter LOC].
12. Dudley W. Knox to H. S. Kimball (CEO, Emergency Fleet Corporation), 8 February 1922, Box 1 [B1], Knox Papers, LOC.
13. Dudley Knox, *The Eclipse of American Sea Power* (New York: Army and Navy Journal, 1923), v, 14–15.
14. Ibid., 41–42.
15. Ibid., 1–15, 23, 132–40.
16. Ibid., 140.
17. Jeffrey M. Dorwart, *Conflict of Duty: The U.S. Navy's Intelligence Dilemma, 1919–1945* (Annapolis, Md.: Naval Institute Press, 1983), 24.
18. Rappaport, *Navy League*, 91–92.
19. McNamee to Robert W. Kelley, 17 June 1922, B11, Entry 78—Confidential Subject and General Correspondence Files, 1913–1926 [hereafter E78], RG 38, NAB.
20. Robert W. Kelley to McNamee, 28 June 1922, B11, E78, RG 38, NAB; McNamee to Robert W. Kelley, 1 July 1922, B11, E78, RG 38, NAB.
21. Rappaport, *Navy League*, 91–92.
22. Gardiner to Theodore Roosevelt Jr., "Memorandum on Naval Publicity," 19 September 1921, 3, I32, Gardiner Papers, HL; Gardiner to Henry Breckenridge, 26 May 1921, I31, Gardiner Papers, HL.
23. Scovel, "Helm's a Lee," 1, 29–30; Rappaport, *Navy League*, 92–94; Wright, *Navy League*, 78.
24. Theodore Roosevelt Jr., 6 July 1922, 331, Box 1 [B1], Theodore Roosevelt, Jr. Papers, LOC.
25. Theodore Roosevelt Jr., 10 July 1922, 333, B1, Theodore Roosevelt, Jr. Papers, LOC.
26. Memorandum for Colonel Roosevelt from Rear Admiral William Veazie Pratt, "Notes on a Naval Day and Naval Clubs," 15 July 1922, Box 9, Papers of Admiral William V. Pratt, NHHC.
27. McNamee to Gardiner, 28 July 1922, 1, I32, Gardiner Papers, HL.
28. Ibid.
29. Gardiner to McNamee, 2 August 1922, I32, Gardiner Papers, HL; Gardiner to McNamee, 8 August 1922, I32, Gardiner Papers, HL.
30. Edwin Denby to Gardiner, 17 October 1922, B19, E19, RG 80, NAB.
31. McNamee to Hussey, 15 September 1922, B10, E79, RG 38, NAB.
32. SecNav to All Ships and Stations, "Navy Day," 12 September 1922, B19, E19, RG 80, NAB.
33. Memorandum for Officers in the Bureau, "Navy Day," 18 September 1922, B361, E89, RG 24, NAB; CNO to Commandant, Thirteenth Naval District, "Radio Telephone Broadcasts," 14 October 1922, B19, E19, RG 80, NAB; S. S. McClure, "Admiral Sims," *McClure's*, November 1922, 26–31; William S. Sims, "Roosevelt and the Navy: Recollections, Reminiscences, and Reflections," *McClure's*, November 1922, 32–41; William S. Sims, "Roosevelt and the Navy," *McClure's*, December 1922, 56–62; William S. Sims, "Theodore Roosevelt at Work," *McClure's*, January 1923, 61–66, 95–101.

34. "Navy Day," *Chicago Tribune*, 24 October 1922, 8; Memo for the Press for Release Morning Papers, 23 October 1922, B5, Entry 113—Press Releases and Transcripts of Press Conferences and Speeches, 1917–36 [hereafter E113], RG 80, NAB; "Navy Day: A Summons to Patriotic Thought," *Chicago Tribune*, 27 October 1922, 8.
35. Information Section of the Office of Naval Intelligence to Recruiting Officers and Inspectors for Material Bureaus, Etc., "Suggestions for Navy Day," 24 September 1923, B361, E89, RG 24, NAB.
36. Grafton Wilcox, "Admiral Tells Why U.S. Must Have Big Fleet," *Chicago Tribune*, 22 October 1922, 12; Hugh M. Rodman, "A Navy Day Address," 27 October 1922, E113, RG 80, NAB.
37. "Keeping the Spotlight on War," *Christian Science Monitor*, 27 October 1922, 20.
38. Lt. Paul P. Spaulding, USNRF, to SecNav, "Report on Navy Day," 7 December 1922, B316, E89, RG 24, NAB.
39. Gardiner to Roosevelt Jr., "Introduction of Civilian Writers at the NWC," 18 January 1923, 2–3, I32, Gardiner Papers, HL; AsstSecNav to SecNav, "Intelligent Publicity for the Navy," 8 March 1921, E19, RG 80, NAB.
40. Gardiner to Roosevelt Jr., "Introduction of Civilian Writers at the NWC," 18 January 1923, 3–4, I32, Gardiner Papers, HL.
41. Gardiner to Roosevelt Jr., "Memo, Periodic Confidential Communiqués to Retired Naval Officers," 19 January 1923, I32, Gardiner Papers; Gardiner to Roosevelt Jr., 14 February 1923, I32, Gardiner Papers, HL.
42. Rappaport, *Navy League*, 98; Robert W. Kelley to SecNav, 25 August 1923, B361, E89, RG 24, NAB; Roosevelt Jr. to Kelley, 28 August 1923, B361, E89, RG 24, NAB.
43. Samuel Gompers to Roosevelt Jr., 20 September 1923, B361, E19, RG 80, NAB; Kelley to McNamee, 17 August 1923, B1, Walter Bruce Howe Papers [hereafter cited as Howe Papers], Naval War College Library, Newport, R.I. [hereafter cited as NWCL]; Howe to Marion Eppley, 11 August 1923, B1, Howe Papers, NWCL.
44. CNO to Commander in Chief, U.S. Fleet, "Navy Day," 14 September 1923, B19, E19, RG 80, NAB; Memo for the Press for Immediate Release, 25 October 1923, B6, E113, RG 80, NAB; Rappaport, *Navy League*, 99.
45. Commanding Officer, Seventh Division, Twelfth Naval Reserve Brigade, "Navy Day at Fresno, California, October 27th, 1923," 29 October 1923, B361, E89, RG 24, NAB; W. J. Confer to SecNav and BuNav, "Navy Day—participation in—report of," 2 November 1923, B361, E89, RG 24, NAB; H. W. Brooks to BuNav, "Navy Day," 30 October 1923, B361, E89, RG 24, NAB.
46. CNO to CinCBat, "Navy Day," 30 August 1926, 1–2, B433, Entry 22—General Correspondence 1926–1940 [hereafter E22], RG 80, NAB; CNO to the Commander, Scouting Fleet, et al., 24 September 1926, B433, E22, RG 80, NAB; CNO to the Commanding Officer, Naval Air Station, San Diego, and ComEleven, 27 September 1926, B433, E22, RG 80, NAB; Memo to Howe, "Navy Day 1926," ca. October 1926, B1, Howe Papers, NWCL.
47. SecNav to the Naval Service, "Press Relations," 3 February 1923, B44, EP 3, RG 428, NACP; Memorandum for the Chief of BuNav from Luke McNamee, 27 September 1922, B55, E78, RG 38, NAB.

48. Captain Halsey Powell, Office Bio File, NHHC; Paul R. Kemberger to Catheryn Seckler-Hudson, "Case study of the Office of Public Relations, Executive Office of the Secretary, Department of the Navy," 27 January 1948, Box 121, EP 3, RG 428, NACP; H. R. Thurber to Hersey, 20 July 1931, B141, Entry 81—Classified General Correspondence 1929–1942 [hereafter E81], RG 38, NAB.
49. Memo to All Bureaus and Offices, 27 August 1924, B2617, E19, RG 80, NAB; Office of Naval Intelligence, *Instructions for Naval Officers, May 1923* (press releases issued by the Navy News Bureau, the Information Section of the Office of Naval Intelligence, and the Office of Public Relations reside in Entry 113 of RG 80, NAB); Henry H. Douglas, "Public Relations, United States Navy," *Proceedings* 67, no. 10 (October 1941): 1433.
50. The Marine Corps' Publicity Bureau did not consider itself bound by any such constraints in marketing its service to the public. See Venable, *Deliberate Heroes*.
51. Memo to All Bureaus and Offices, 27 August 1924, B2617, E19, RG 80, NAB.
52. Knox to S. M. Reynolds, 21 January 1925, B1, Knox Papers, LOC.
53. Scovel, "Helm's a Lee," 90–91.
54. Captain Halsey Powell, Officer Bio File, NHHC.
55. Knox to S. M. Reynolds, 21 January 1925, B1, Knox Papers, LOC.
56. J. H. Adams to Knox, 14 January 1927, B2, Knox Papers, LOC.
57. Planners involved with drafting War Plan Orange concluded that the United States could not adequately defend its possessions in the western Pacific prior to the Washington Conference. See Edward S. Miller, *War Plan Orange: The U.S. Strategy to Defeat Japan* (Annapolis, Md.: Naval Institute Press, 1991), 53–56, 111–13; Knox to Wat T. Cluverius, 20 January 1922, B1, Knox Papers, LOC; Knox to Thomas C. Frothingham, 24 April 1925, B9, Knox Papers, LOC; and Knox to James T. Williams Jr., 14 September 1925, B1, Knox Papers, LOC.
58. Knox to Orson Munn, 23 November 1926, B2, Knox Papers, LOC. Knox to Munn, 23 October 1926, Munn to Knox, 29 October 1926, and Knox to James P. Baxter, 7 February 1929, all in B2, Knox Papers, LOC.
59. "Mr. Bywater's Articles," *Baltimore Sun*, 11 November 1921, 8. The only full-length biography of Bywater is William H. Honan, *Visions of Infamy: The Untold Story of How Journalist Hector C. Bywater Devised the Plans That Led to Pearl Harbor* (New York: St. Martin's, 1991); Hector C. Bywater, *Sea Power in the Pacific: A Study of the American-Japanese Naval Problem* (New York: Houghton Mifflin, 1921); Hector C. Bywater, *The Great Pacific War: A History of the American-Japanese Campaign of 1931–1933* (London: Constable and Co., 1925); Hector C. Bywater, *Navies and Nations* (New York: Houghton Mifflin, 1927).
60. Knox to Capt. Leonard M. Cox, 12 May 1924, B1, Knox Papers, LOC; Hector C. Bywater, "US Is Told Bluntly to Review Own Record," *Baltimore Sun*, 15 July 1926, 14; Dudley W. Knox, "Replies to Bywater's Criticism of America," *Baltimore Sun*, 21 July 1926, 11; Hector C. Bywater, "US Is Told Bluntly to Review Own Record," *Baltimore Sun*, 22 August 1926, 7; Dudley W. Knox, "Capt. Knox Criticizes the Sun's Naval Views," *Baltimore Sun*, 8 January 1927, 7; Hector C. Bywater, "Bywater Meets Attack Made by Captain Knox," *Baltimore Sun*, 18 January 1927, 15; Dudley W. Knox, "Capt.

Knox Returns to Battleship Question," *Baltimore Sun*, 21 January 1927, 9; Dudley W. Knox, "Captain Knox Reviews 'Great Pacific War,'" *Baltimore Sun*, 21 September 1925, 7; Dudley W. Knox, "Bywater's New Book Provokes Criticism," *Baltimore Sun*, 2 October 1927, 9.

61. Dudley W. Knox, "Our Vanishing History and Traditions," *Proceedings* 52, no. 1 (January 1926): 15–25; "Naval Foundation Selects Officers and Receives Gift," *Washington Post*, 4 April 1926, sec. S, 2.

62. Trimble, *Admiral William A. Moffett*, 53–54; Jimmy Wayne Dyess, "A History of the United States Navy Band, Washington, D.C." (Ph.D. diss., University of Houston, 1988): 20–23.

63. Trimble, *Admiral William A. Moffett*, 7–10.

64. Ibid.

65. Eugene E. Wilson, *Slipstream: The Autobiography of an Air Craftsman* (New York: Whittlesey House, 1950), 9–10.

66. Davis, *Postwar Defense Policy*, 46–47.

67. Chief of the Bureau of Aeronautics to Chief of BuNav, "Recommending Temporary Additional Duty Orders for Rear Admiral W. A. Moffett, USN," 17 December 1923, B4148, General Correspondence, 1925–1942, Entry 62—General Records of the Bureau of Aeronautics, 1917–1961 [hereafter E62], Records of the Bureau of Aeronautics, 1911–1972, RG 72 [hereafter RG 72], NAB; BuAer to the Honorable Clark Burdick, 25 June 1923, B4148, E62, RG 72, NAB.

68. Chief of BuAer to CNO, "USS *Langley*—Movements of," 2 May 1923, B202, E50, RG 72, NAB. Commanding Officer USS *Langley* to CNO, "USS *Langley*, Schedule of Employment; Recommendation, re," 30 June 1923, B202, General Correspondence, 1917–1926, Entry 50—Records of Predecessors, 1911–1930 [hereafter E50], Records of the Bureau of Aeronautics, 1911–1972, RG 72, NAB; Trimble, *Admiral William A. Moffett*, 106–7.

69. Trimble, *Admiral William A. Moffett*, 120–25.

70. BuNav to Moffett, "Orders of 26 September 1923, Modified," 16 October 1923, B4148, E62, RG 72, NAB.

71. CINCUS to CNO, "Proposed Flight from Honolulu to Australia," 27 December 1924, B141, E62, RG 72, NAB.

72. "Army, Navy and the Airplane," *Literary Digest*, 14 March 1925, 71–72; CINCUS to CNO, "Proposed Flight from Honolulu to Australia," 27 December 1924, B141, E62, RG 72, NAB; A. H. Ford to Moffett, 2 October 1924, B141, E62, RG 72, NAB; Navy Department, Immediate Release, 24 August 1925, 1–3, B8, E113, RG 80, NAB.

73. Douglas H. Robinson and Charles L. Keller, *Up Ship! A History of the U.S. Navy's Rigid Airships, 1919–1935* (Annapolis, Md.: Naval Institute Press, 1982), 104–9; Navy Department, Immediate Release, ca. September 1925, 1–3, B8, E113, RG 80, NAB.

74. Navy Department, Immediate Release, 2 October 1925, 1–6, B8, E113, RG 80, NAB; Address by CMDR John Rodgers over WCAP radio, Washington, D.C., 27 October 1925, 1–4, B8, E113, RG 80, NAB.

75. Venable, *Deliberate Heroes* (forthcoming).

76. Quoted in Harrod, *Manning the New Navy*, 48; Bureau of Navigation Circular Letter No. 101–19, 19 July 1919, B396, E89, RG 24, NAB.
77. Officer in Charge, Navy Publicity and Morale, to BuNav, "Paid Advertising Campaign," 4 August 1920, B396, E89, RG 24, NAB; Memo for Commander Culp, 7 June 1919, Box 395, General Correspondence, 1917–1925, RG 24, NAB; Richard H. Leigh to Josephus Daniels, "Bids for advertising in periodicals and newspapers for recruiting purposes," 17 June 1919, B395, E89, RG 24, NAB; James O'Shaughnessy to Daniels, 18 September 1919, B395, E89, RG 24, NAB, 1–8; F. M. Poteet to BuNav, "Paid Advertising Campaign," 13 January 1920, B396, E89, RG 24, NAB.
78. C. E. Courtney to BuNav, "Sales Management Doctrine," 31 July 1920, B396, E89, RG 24, NAB; Chief of BuNav (Thomas Washington) to the Navy Recruiting Service, "Competition in Recruiting," 10 November 1922, B901, E89, RG 24, NAB; Harrod, *Manning the New Navy*, 38.
79. Recruiting Bureau to Navy Recruiting Station, St. Louis, Mo., "Motion Picture Film Publicity," 10 July 1919, B396, E89, RG 24, NAB; Harrod, *Manning the New Navy*, 44.
80. Officer in Charge, Navy Recruiting Bureau, to Chief of BuNav, "Motion Picture Publicity," 4 August 1922, B316, E89, RG 24, NAB; Film 24.24, *Our Navy in the Near East* (1923), Records of the Navy Recruiting Bureau, RG 24, NACP; Film 24.12, *Crossing the Line* (1920), Records of the Navy Recruiting Bureau, RG 24, NACP; Officer in Charge, Navy Recruiting Station, Providence, R.I., to the Chief of BuNav, "Exhibition of Pictures," 2 May 1923, B316, E89, RG 24, NACP; Officer in Charge, Baltimore Recruiting Station, to BuNav, 19 March 1920, B315, E89, RG 24, NAB.
81. BuNav to Josie Henderson, 6 August 1921, B315, E89, RG 24, NAB; Officer in Charge, Navy Recruiting Bureau, to Chief of BuNav, "Lending of Navy Property," 8 July 1922, B316, E89, RG 24, NAB; Inspector of Recruiting, Central Division, to BuNav, "Moving Picture Machines," 24 February 1920, B315, E89, RG 24, NAB; Officer in Charge, U.S. Navy Recruiting Station, St. Louis, to BuNav, "Use of Motion Pictures and Kodaks," 6 April 1923, B316, E89, RG 24, NAB.
82. Chief of BuNav to All Ships and Stations, "Recruiting Publicity," 25 June 1931, Box 65, Entry 90—General Correspondence 1925–1940 [hereafter E90], General Records of the Bureau of Naval Personnel and Its Predecessors, 1801–1966, RG 24, NAB; Chief of BuNav to All Ships and Stations, "Recruiting Publicity," 1 December 1927, B64, E90, RG 24, NAB; Chief of BuNav to All Ships and Stations, "Recruiting Publicity," 25 June 1931, B65, E90, RG 24, NAB; Chief of BuNav to the Officer in Charge, Navy Recruiting Station, Salt Lake City, "Radio Publicity," 16 August 1929, B64, E90, RG 24, NAB.
83. Chief of BuNav to the Officer in Charge, Navy Recruiting Station, Cincinnati, "Naval Publicity," 26 June 1925, B64, E90, RG 24, NAB; Officer in Charge, Navy Recruiting Station, Cincinnati, to Chief of BuNav, "Navy Publicity," 19 June 1925, B64, E90, RG 24, NAB; Wade Mountfortt to Curtis Wilbur, 20 June 1925, B64, E90, RG 24, NAB.
84. H. R. Thurber to Hersey, 20 July 1931, B141, E81, RG 38, NAB.
85. Thomas P. Magruder, "The Navy and Economy," *Saturday Evening Post*, 24 September 1927, 6–7; "Disciplining Magruder," *Literary Digest*, 5 November 1927, 9; "Navy and Army Waste," *Nation*, 12 October 1927, 354; Scovel, "Helm's a Lee," 48, 117–18; SecNav

to Magruder, "Article on 'The Navy and the Economy' *Saturday Evening Post*, of 24 September 1927," 1 October 1927, 1–10, B411, E22, RG 80, NAB; Wilbur to Magruder, "Article on 'The Navy and Economy,' *Saturday Evening Post*, of 24 September 1927," 3 October 1927, B411, E22, RG 80, NAB.
86. Richard Fanning, *Peace and Disarmament: Naval Rivalry and Arms Control, 1922–1933* (Lexington: University Press of Kentucky, 2015).

Chapter 3. A Sustained Publicity

1. Dudley W. Knox, "The Navy and Public Indoctrination," *Proceedings* 55, no. 6 (June 1929): 479–90.
2. Arthur Sears Henning, *Government by Propaganda* (Chicago: Chicago Tribune Public Service Office, 1927), 8, 16–18, 29–32, 47–52.
3. Hanson W. Baldwin, "Newspapers and the Navy," *Proceedings* 56, no. 12 (December 1930): 1085–90.
4. Capt. Macgillivray Milne to Capt. William Baggaley, 31 December 1930, Box 2, Entry UD 1—Officer of the Director Official Correspondence 1929–1943 [hereafter cited as EUD 1], RG 38, NAB.
5. Rear Adm. Philip Andrews to Adm. Charles F. Hughes (CNO), 31 July 1929, B1, EUD 1, RG 38, NAB.
6. Capt. A. W. Johnson (DNI) to Rear Adm. Philip Andrews (ComOne), 23 October 1929, B1, EUD 1, RG 38, NAB.
7. Director of Naval Intelligence to Commandants of Naval Districts, "The Supply of Naval Information to the Press—Public Relations," 18 March 1930, B44, EP 3, RG 428, NACP; Scovel, "Helm's a Lee," 108–9, 117.
8. SecNav to All Bureaus and Offices, "Information Section, Office of Naval Intelligence—Duties of, and Assistance to be Given to," 17 November 1930, B2098, E22, RG 80, NAB.
9. F. E. M. Whiting, "A Further Application of Our Publicity Policy," *Proceedings* 57, no. 9 (September 1931): 1169.
10. Ibid., 1170.
11. Philip T. Rosen, *The Modern Stentors: Radio Broadcasters and the Federal Government, 1920–1934* (Westport, Conn.: Greenwood Press, 1980), 21–57, 62–63; Jim Cox, *American Radio Networks: A History* (Jefferson, N.C.: McFarland, 2009), 16–25, 45–55. See also Memo for CMDR Farquhar from H. E. Fisher, "The United States Navy and Radio," 7 May 1929, B415, E22, RG 80, NAB.
12. "Radio Program Today," clipping from *Syracuse Post-Standard*, 22 June 1922, B1, Entry 40—Newspaper Clippings and Miscellaneous Publications, 1911–1923 [hereafter E40], RG 38, NAB; BuNav to All Retired Officers above Commander, "Navy Day," 8 October 1924, B361, E89, RG 24, NAB; William M. Galvin to Howe, 11 July 1927, B2, Howe Papers, NWCL; Howe to Gardiner, 6 August 1927, 1–2, B2, Howe Papers, NWCL.
13. Dyess, "United States Navy Band," 32–35.
14. Ibid., 35–36, 39–40, 45–47.
15. Ibid., 50–61, 64.

16. CinCBat to CNO, "Radio Broadcasts from Ships," 15 April 1930, E22, RG 80, NAB.
17. Lt. Cdr. J. G. Ware to William J. McGinley, 17 April 1920, 1–6, B857, E89, RG 24, NAB; W. D. Puleston to Will Hays, 3 October 1925, B1359, E90, RG 24, NAB; BuNav to All Ships, Stations, and Marine Corps Posts, "Navy Film Service," 16 June 1924, B859, E89, RG 24, NAB.
18. Puleston to Hays, 3 October 1925, B1359, E89, RG 24, NAB; BuNav to Commanding Officer, US Naval Air Station, San Diego, "Navy Film Service," 4 September 1924, B859, E89, RG 24, NAB.
19. Douglas Gomery, *The Hollywood Studio System: A History* (London: British Film Institute, 2005), passim; Eileen Bowser, *The Transformation of Cinema, 1907–1915* (Berkeley: University of California Press, 1994), 112–13.
20. Gomery, *Hollywood Studio System*, 27–70, 175–76; Tino Balio, "A Mature Oligopoly, 1930–1948," in Balio, *American Film Industry*, 256; Garth Jowett and James M. Linton, *Movies as Mass Communication*, 2nd ed. (New York: Sage, 1989), 19, 118–19.
21. Suid, *Guts and Glory*, 29, 32, 39.
22. Suid, *Sailing on the Silver Screen*, 9–11; William R. Shoemaker to E. W. Creecy, 24 February 1925, B859, E89, RG 24, NAB.
23. Slavoj Zizek, *Welcome to the Desert of the Real* (New York: Verso, 2002), 13–14; Jowett and Linton, *Movies as Mass Communication*, 120–21; Neal Gabler, *Life: The Movie: How Entertainment Conquered Reality* (New York: Vintage Books, 1998), 57–58; Nick Roddick, *A New Deal in Entertainment: Warner Brothers in the 1930s* (London: British Film Institute, 1983), 11–12.
24. Suid, *Sailing on the Silver Screen*, 18.
25. William R. Shoemaker to Frederick James Smith, 14 August 1925, B859, E89, RG 24, NAB; Smith to the Navy Department, 5 August 1925, B859, E89, RG 24, NAB; G. R. O'Neill to F. H. Poteet, 17 October 1928, B1360, E90, RG 24, NAB; Chief of BuNav to Commandants, 1st to 13th Naval Districts et al., "Cooperation with Motion Picture Theaters," 17 October 1928, B1360, E90, RG 24, NAB; Officer in Charge, Navy Recruiting Station, Baltimore, to Chief of BuNav, "Motion Picture 'Annapolis,'" 2 January 1929, B1389, E90, RG 24, NAB.
26. ComBatFlt to the Officer in Charge, Navy Recruiting Station, Los Angeles, "Motion Picture 'Annapolis,'" 28 November 1928, B1390, E90, RG 24, NAB; Officer in Charge, Navy Recruiting Station, San Francisco, to BuNav, "Motion Picture 'Annapolis,' Report on as to Its Value as Navy Publicity," 23 November 1928, B1390, E90, RG 24, NAB; Officer in Charge, Navy Recruiting Station, St. Louis, to BuNav, "Cooperation with Motion Picture Theaters," 19 November 1928, B1360, E90, RG 24, NAB.
27. Officer in Charge, Navy Recruiting Station, Newark, to Chief of BuNav, "Review of Motion Picture 'Salute,'" 1 October 1929; Officer in Charge, Navy Recruiting Station, New York, to Chief of BuNav, "Cooperation with Motion Picture Theaters, Re: Motion Picture 'Salute,'" 18 October 1929; Officer in Charge, Navy Recruiting Station, Richmond, to Chief of BuNav, "Motion Picture 'Salute,' Report on," 13 September 1929; and Officer in Charge, Navy Recruiting Station, Baltimore, to Chief of BuNav, "Motion Picture 'Salute,'" 19 September 1929—all in B1367, E90, RG 24, NAB.

28. DNI to Chief of BuNav, "Approval of Scenario 'The Big Gun' by Lt. D. L. McCarthy, US Navy," 6 December 1928; Leigh to McCarthy, 15 December 1928; Lt. D. L. McCarthy to Leigh, 25 July 1928—all in B1360, E90, RG 24, NAB.
29. Memo for the CNO from the Chief of the BuNav, 18 December 1928; SecNav to the CNO and the BuNav, "Motion Picture Plays of Naval Subjects," 15 January 1929—both in B412, E22, RG 80, NAB.
30. SecNav to All Bureaus and Offices, "Review of Motion Picture Scenarios and Screenplays," 5 August 1931, B432, E22, RG 80, NAB.
31. Suid, *Sailing on the Silver Screen*, 17–18; CNO to All Ships and Stations, "Policy Concerning Cooperation with Motion Picture Producers," 29 June 1937, B431, E22, RG 80, NAB.
32. Memorandum for the CNO, "Navy Cooperation in the Production of Motion Pictures," 5 August 1931, B432, E22, RG 80, NAB.
33. M. L. Hersey Jr. to Irene C. Crisp, 29 August 1931, B432, E22, RG 80, NAB; Navy Department Motion Picture Board to the Chief of Naval Operations, "Paramount Publix proposed photoplay—'The Devil and the Deep,'" 23 April 1932, B431, E22, RG 80, NAB.
34. Suid, *Sailing on the Silver Screen*, 19–20; Samuel Goldwyn to the Senior Member, Standing Board to Review Motion Picture Plays, 3 June 1932, B431, E22, RG 80, NAB; Goldwyn to the Senior Member, Standing Board to Review Motion Picture Plays, 8 June 1932, B431, E22, RG 80, NAB; Navy Department Motion Picture Board to CNO, "United Artists proposed photoplay—'U-Boat,'" 13 June 1932, B431, E22, RG 80, NAB.
35. A directoscope was an optical device used to aim naval artillery pieces. Herbert A. Jones to William A. Orr, 21 January 1931, B1362, E90, RG 24, NAB.
36. Cdr. Lucius Dunn to CNO, "Minority Report on moving picture scenario 'Shipmates' (Metro-Goldwyn-Mayer)," 10 January 1931, B181, E81, RG 38, NAB.
37. Rear Adm. John Halligan (Acting CNO) to Orr, 31 January 1931, B181, E81, RG 38, NAB.
38. Suid, *Sailing on the Silver Screen*, 18; William V. Pratt to Irene C. Crisp, 24 December 1931; Irene C. Crisp to CNO, 15 December 1931—both in B432, E22, RG 80, NAB.
39. Roddick, *New Deal in Entertainment*, 24–25. In 1955, John Ford would direct a film about Wead's life titled *The Wings of Eagles*. The best printed source for information on Wead's life is Harvey M. Beigel, "'Spig' Wead: Naval Aviator and Screenwriter," *American Aviation Historical Society Journal* (Winter 1997): 302–9.
40. Beigel, "'Spig' Wead," 307.
41. Orr to Cdr. Herbert A. Jones, 27 September 1930, B182, E81, RG 38, NAB.
42. Orr to SecNav Adams, 22 January 1931, B181, E81, RG 38, NAB.
43. Rear Adm. John Halligan (Acting CNO) to Orr, 31 January 1931; Rear Adm. John Halligan (Acting CNO) to Orr, 4 February 1931—both in B181, E81, RG 38, NAB.
44. Hersey to Orr, 24 April 1931, B181, E81, RG 38, NAB; Senior Member, Navy Standing Motion Picture Board (Gearing), to CNO via DNI, "Metro-Goldwyn-Mayer Photoplay 'Sea Eagles,'" 5 August 1931, B181, E81, RG 38, NAB.
45. Orr to Hersey, 20 June 1931, B181, E81, RG 38, NAB.

46. CNO to William A. Orr, 22 July 1931, B181, E81, RG 38, NAB.
47. William A. Orr to Adm. Wyatt R. Sexton, 4 August 1931, B181, E81, RG 38, NAB; Senior Member to CNO, "Sea Eagles"; ibid.; Hersey to Orr, 6 August 1931, B181, E81, RG 38, NAB.
48. William A. Orr to Cdr. Mark L. Hersey, 7 August 1931, B181, E81, RG 38, NAB.
49. Hersey to Wead, 24 December 1931, B182, E81, RG 38, NAB.
50. Friedman, Hone, and Mandeles, *Aircraft Carrier Development*, 135–84.
51. Memorandum for the DNI from Cdr. Mark L. Hersey, "Metro-Goldwyn-Mayer photoplay 'Hell Divers,'" 12 April 1932, B181, E81, RG 38, NAB; Orr to CNO, 26 December 1931, B183, E81, RG 38, NAB; William A. Orr to CNO, 31 December 1931, B181, E81, RG 38, NAB.
52. Memorandum for Hersey, "Hell Divers."
53. Adison Delaney to SecNav, 4 October 1932, B181, E81, RG 38, NAB.
54. ComAirUSFleet to CINCUS, "Publication of confidential information," 25 April 1932, B179, E81, RG 38, NAB.
55. Hugh Byas, "Film Notes from Tokyo," *New York Times*, 2 October 1932.
56. Leigh to Maud C. Stockwell, 25 April 1930; Stockwell to President Herbert Hoover, 2 April 1930—both in B1360, E90, RG 24, NAB.
57. ComBatFor to CNO, "RKO Pathe Corporation, Ltd.—Cooperation with, in Production of Photoplay 'Mystery Ship,'" 18 July 1931, B432, E22, RG 80, NAB; ComBatFor to CNO, "Motion Picture 'Summerville Number Four,' Naval Cooperation with Universal Pictures Corporation in Production of," 16 August 1931, B432, B425, E22, RG 80, NAB.
58. CNO to ComBatFor via CINCUS, "Policy with Respect to Naval Cooperation in Production of Photoplays," 8 September 1931, 1–3, B432, E22, RG 80, NAB.
59. Adam G. King to the Officer in Charge, Navy Recruiting Station, Los Angeles, 28 May 1931, B1362, E90, RG 24, NAB; Officer in Charge, Navy Recruiting Station, Los Angeles, to the Recruiting Inspector, Western Division, "Paramount Moving Picture 'The Lawyer's Secret,'" 29 May 1931, B1362, E90, RG 24, NAB; Recruiting Inspector, Western Division, to Chief of BuNav, "Paramount Moving Picture 'The Lawyer's Secret,'" 1 June 1931, B1362, E90, RG 24, NAB; Memo, "Conference between representatives for the Navy Department and Mr. Will Hays in connection with R.K.O. photoplay 'Sailor Be Good,'" 10 March 1933, B431, E22, RG 80, NAB.
60. Raymond Fielding, *The American Newsreel: A Complete History 1911-1967, Second Edition* (Jefferson, North Carolina: McFarland and Company, 2006), 45-46, 63-76.
61. Fielding, *The American Newsreel*, 86, 147; for examples of each naval newsreel subject see "First of US Navy's "Pocket Battleships" Launched on Coast," *Universal Newsreel*, 27 Mar. 1933; "Uncle Sam Gets 403 'Future Admirals' at Middy Graduation," *Universal Newsreel*, 8 June 1930; "Seas Sweep Decks as Cruiser Battles Gale in Speed Test," *Universal Newsreel*, 12 Mar. 1930, all from Universal Newsreel Catalog, RG 200 UN, NACP.
62. Rep. Burton French to SecNav Curtis Wilbur, 26 December 1924, B1, EUD 1, RG 38, NAB.
63. William B. Shearer, *The Cloak of Benedict Arnold* (Washington, D.C.: National Capitol Press, 1928), 1.

64. Ibid., 9.
65. Ibid., 45.
66. Memorandum from Capt. A. W. Johnson, "Telephone Conversation with Mr. Shearer," 12 January 1929, B103, Entry UD 84—Central Administrative Correspondence, 1930–1948 [hereafter EUD 84], RG 38, NAB; William Shearer to Herbert Hoover, 8 February 1929, B148, E81, RG 38, NAB.
67. Lt. Cdr. A. S. Merill to Lt. Cdr. Paul F. Foster, 9 February 1929, B148, E81, RG 38, NAB.
68. "Shearer, 'Big Navy Man,' in Pay of Warship Builders," *Baltimore Sun*, 22 August 1929, 1; "Hearst Disclaims Shearer Lobbying," *Washington Post*, 3 October 1929, 2; "Shearer Says 4 Admirals Urged Him to Conduct Big Navy Propaganda," *Baltimore Sun*, 9 September 1929, 1; "Admiral Jones Not Thought of as Aiding Shearer," *Chicago Tribune*, 10 September 1929, 18.
69. "Why Was This Story Told?," *Washington Post*, 1 October 1929, 8; "Naval Officers Face Charge of Aiding Shearer," *Christian Science Monitor*, 27 September 1929, 1; "Closes Shearer Matter," *New York Times*, 12 June 1930, 3.
70. Howe to Gardiner, 29 May 1931, 1–2, B2, Howe Papers, NWCL; "Memorandum to Present in Obtaining Financial Support for Navy Day," n.d., [ca. August 1925], B3, Howe Papers, NWCL; Howe to Gardiner, 8 April 1927, 1–4, B1, Howe Papers, NWCL; Memorandum, "Navy Day 1928," 16 May 1928, B3, Howe Papers, NWCL; Minutes of the Meeting of the Executive Committee of the Navy League of the United States, 23 June 1931, I30, Gardiner Papers, HL.
71. Rappaport, *Navy League*, 135; Howe to Gardiner, 6 October 1930, 1–10, B2, Howe Papers, NWCL; Howe to John Stapler, 7 November 1930, B2, Howe Papers, NWCL; "Summary Report—Navy Day 1930," 12 January 1930 [1931], B3, Howe Papers, NWCL; Minutes of the Meeting of the Executive Committee of the Navy League of the United States, 23 June 1931, B2, Howe Papers, NWCL.
72. James W. Wadsworth to Howe, 6 July 1931, B2, Howe Papers, NWCL; Rappaport, *Navy League*, 137–38; Minutes of the Meeting of the Executive Committee of the Navy League of the United States, 23 June 1931, B2, Howe Papers, NWCL; Howe to Wadsworth, 10 July 1931, B2, Howe Papers, NWCL.
73. In 1924, the Navy League scrapped a proposed release attacking Secretary of State Charles Evans Hughes's decision to ignore the advice of his naval advisers at the Washington Conference, and in 1926 the organization refrained from criticizing President Calvin Coolidge for his failure to support naval expansion. See Howe to Gardiner, 26 November 1924, B1, Howe Papers, NWCL; Howe to Gardiner, 7 January 1926, B1, Howe Papers, NWCL; "Hoover Held Ignorant on Naval Affairs," *Washington Post*, 29 October 1931, 1; Rappaport, *Navy League*, 100–106, 113–22, 144–49; Wright, *Navy League*, 87–88; Report of the Recorder General, 6 November 1931, B2, Records and Papers of the Naval Order of the United States, 1890–2005, Cushing Library, Texas A&M University, College Station [hereafter cited as NOUS Papers].
74. Walter Bruce Howe's papers at the Naval War College Library in Newport, R.I., contain no references to the dispute. Gardiner's collection, however, contains numerous

pieces of correspondence detailing the height of the dispute in late 1932 and early 1933. Gardiner to Walter C. Cole, 9 February 1932, I30, Gardiner Papers, HL; Gardiner to Wadsworth, 30 December 1932, I30, Gardiner Papers, HL; Minutes of the Meeting of the Board of Directors of the Navy League of the United States, 20 January 1933, I31, Gardiner Papers, HL; Rappaport, *Navy League*, 146–55.
75. "Secretary's Notes," *Proceedings* 55, no. 5 (May 1929): 475.
76. "USS *Lexington*, Press and Photographic Policy," n.d.; CNO to Commandant, 5th Naval District et al., "USS *Lexington*, Press and Photographic Arrangements for Exhibition Flights for Congressional Party—April 26, 1930," 22 April 1930; CNO to CinCBat, "Radio broadcasting from ships—Radio publicity offer from OUR NAVY Magazine and Station WGBS," 5 April 1930; Stephen T. Early to Adm. William H. Standley, 18 March 1930; and Commanding Officer, Lakehurst Station, to CNO, "Non-rigid airship—sound picture recordings from," 1 April 1930—all in B44, EP 3, RG 428, NACP.
77. Albert A. Nofi, *To Train the Fleet for War: The U.S. Navy Fleet Problems, 1923–1940* (Newport, R.I.: Naval War College Press, 2010), 154.
78. Capt. C. M. Austin to SecNav via ComBatFor, "Service as correspondent of newspaper service," 30 January 1932, B35, Entry 85—Division of Naval Intelligence Administrative Files, 1927–1944 [hereafter E85], RG 38, NAB; Captain C. M. Austin, "For Release, for Morning Papers, 3 February," 3 February 1932, B35, E85, RG 38, NAB.
79. Director of Naval Communications (S.C. Hooper) to DNI, "Publicity with regard to decrypting activities," 10 February 1932, B35, E85, RG 38, NAB.
80. Captain C.M. Austin to SecNav via ComBatFor, "Service as newspaper correspondent," 25 February 1932, B35, E85, RG 38, NAB; Captain C.M. Austin, "For Release, morning papers," 14 March 1932, B35, E85, RG 38, NAB; DNI (Ellis) to CNO, "Articles submitted to the Press by Captain C.M. Austin, USN," 7 April 1932, B35, E85, RG 38, NAB.
81. DNI (Ellis) to CNO, Chief BuAer to DNI, "USS *Akron*—Press Release Concerning," 31 March 1932, B35, E85, RG 38, NAB.
82. No formal announcement was made concerning the name change, but the earliest documents referring to the PR Branch appeared in July 1931. See H. R. Thurber to Hersey, 20 July 1931, B141, E81, RG 38, NAB.

Chapter 4. Compatible with Military Secrecy

1. CINCUS (Reeves) to CNO, "Warner Bros. Pictures, Inc., request cooperation preparation scenario, present day Submarine Force activities," 22 November 1935, B184, E81, RG 38, NAB.
2. Chief of Naval Operations to Hal Wallis, 6 December 1935, B427, E22, RG 80, NAB; Cdr. F. G. Reinicke to Spig Wead, 9 December 1936, B184, E81, RG 38, NAB.
3. Richard W. Steele, *Propaganda in an Open Society: The Roosevelt Administration and the Media, 1933–1941* (Westport, Conn.: Greenwood Press, 1985), 5–16, 35–36, 44–52, 62–65.
4. Minutes of the Meeting of the Board of Directors of the Navy League of the United States, 20 January 1933, I31, Gardiner Papers, HL; Rappaport, *Navy League*, 153–65.

5. Office of Naval Intelligence, *Intelligence Manual* (19), 5 October 1933, B2, Entry UD 83A—Officer of Naval Intelligence Monographs [hereafter EUD 83A], RG 38, NAB.
6. Ibid., 3018.
7. Ibid., 3019.
8. Ibid.
9. Ibid., 3002, 3018.
10. "A History of Band Music in the Navy and the United States Navy Band," n.d., B10, F.P. 3, RG 428, NACP; ibid., 65–69, 73–75, 81–82; Navy Press Room, For Immediate Release, 4 May 1933, B10, F.P. 3, RG 428, NACP.
11. David Nasaw, *The Chief: The Life of William Randolph Hearst* (New York: Houghton Mifflin, 2000), 453; Reader Report submitted by A. Cunningham, 14 January 1933, Production Code Authority Papers [hereafter cited as PCA Papers], Margaret Herrick Library, Hollywood, Calif. [hereafter cited as MHL]; Joseph Breen to Will Hays, 10 February 1933, PCA Papers, MHL; Hearst to Louis B. Mayer, 25 March 1933, B38, William Randolph Hearst, Sr., Papers [hereafter cited as Hearst Papers], BANC MSS 77/121 c, Bancroft Library, University of California–Berkeley [hereafter cited as BL].
12. "Gabriel over the White House," *Motion Picture Herald*, 8 April 1933, 26; Matthew Bernstein, *Walter Wanger: Hollywood Independent* (Minneapolis: University of Minnesota Press, 1994), 434.
13. "Mr. Hearst Outlines How His Newspapers Should Be Made" (1922), B4, Hearst Papers, BL; Ian Mugridge, *The View from Xanadu: William Randolph Hearst and United States Foreign Policy* (Buffalo, N.Y.: McGill-Queen's University Press, 1995), 100–102; Nasaw, *Chief*, 53, 69–70, 74–80, 100, 152. The *Journal* was renamed the *New York Journal and American* in 1901 and eventually became just the *New York American*. Gabler, *Life: The Movie*, 66–69.
14. Nasaw, *Chief*, 322; Mugridge, *View from Xanadu*, 19.
15. Nasaw, *Chief*, 386, 426–29; Mugridge, *View from Xanadu*, 20–23.
16. Thomas Joseph Wren to Hearst, 25 June 1941, B6, Hearst Papers, BL; Mugridge, *View from Xanadu*, 41–42, 57–58, 90, 103–5; Memo to Editors All Hearst Morning Papers and Afternoons Where No Mornings, 6 November 1932, B4, Hearst Papers, BL.
17. Louis Pizzitola, *Hearst over Hollywood: Power, Passion, and Propaganda in the Movies* (New York: Columbia University Press, 2002), x, 29–36, 86–89, 174–75, 217; Nasaw, *Chief*, 209, 278–80, 314.
18. Nasaw, *Chief*, 305–8, 350; Agreement between Warner Brothers, Inc. and Cosmopolitan Corporation, 31 October 1934, Box Cosmopolitan Legal File 1 of 2, Warner Brothers Archive, University of Southern California, Los Angeles [hereafter cited as WB Archive]; Hal Wallis to McCord, 3 October 1938, Box Wings of the Navy 1 of 1, WB Archive; Einfield to Wallis, 26 October 1938, Box Wings of the Navy 1 of 1, WB Archive; R. J. Obringer to Jack Warner, 8 June 1936, Box Cosmopolitan Legal File 1 of 2, WB Archive; Obringer to Warner, 8 May 1938, Box Cosmopolitan Legal File 1 of 2, WB Archive.
19. Raymond Fielding, *The American Newsreel: A Complete History, 1911–1967* (Norman: University of Oklahoma Press, 1972), 110, 167; "What the London Pact Really Means,"

Hearst Metrotone News, 7 June 1930; "Navy Treaty Fight Stirs the Capital," *Hearst Metrotone News*, 16 July 1930; and "America Warned Navy Is Weak," *Hearst Metrotone News*, 10 February 1932—all in Hearst Metrotone News Collection, Film and Television Archive, University of California–Los Angeles [hereafter cited as FT Archive].

20. Nasaw, *Chief*, 470–77, 504.
21. Cdr. Jonas Ingram to Cdr. W. D. Kilduff (4th ND), 3 January 1934, B143, E81, RG 38, NAB.
22. Cdr. Jonas Ingram to Cdr. S. M. Kraus (Naval Aircraft Factor), 6 January 1934, B143, E81, RG 38, NAB.
23. Rear Adm. W. T. Cluverius to Rear Adm. E. J. King, 15 October 1934, B143, E81, RG 38, NAB.
24. Capt. W. D. Puleston (DNI) to Lt. Walter Winchell, USNR, 19 October 1934, B143, E81, RG 38, NAB.
25. Cdr. S. A. Clement to Harry C. Butchur (CBS), 20 March 1936, B143, E81, RG 38, NAB.
26. Coulton Waugh, *The Comics* (New York: Macmillan, 1947), 126–27; Martin Sheridan, *Comics and Their Creators: Life Stories of American Cartoonists* (Westport, Conn.: Hyperion Press, 1977), 227.
27. Sheridan, *Comics and Their Creators*, 227; Waugh, *Comics*, 128.
28. Sheridan, *Comics and Their Creators*, 227; Wendell A. Link to Senator George McGill, 3 February 1938, B258, E22, RG 80, NAB; William H. Standley to Senator George McGill, 18 February 1938, B258, E22, RG 80, NAB; Frank Martinek, *Don Winslow, U.S.N., in Ceylon with Kwang, Celebrated Chinese Detective* (Chicago: Rosenow, 1934), 5–6; Waugh, *Comics*, 128. Martinek received positive recognition for his work from Secretary of the Navy Frank Knox in September 1941, and the navy would cooperate with the production of a *Don Winslow* film serial the following year. See Knox to Martinek, n.d. [ca. September 1941], B28, Office File of Secretary of the Navy Frank Knox, RG 80, NACP.
29. Lt. D. A. Frost to Louis F. Edelman, 26 November 1937, B184, E81, RG 38, NAB.
30. Cabanne had attended the Naval Academy during the 1910s, and Bacon served in the navy's Photo Department during World War I. See Suid, *Sailing on the Silver Screen*, 9–11; William R. Meyer, *Warner Brothers Directors: The Hard-Boiled, the Comic, and the Weepers* (New Rochelle, N.Y.: Arlington House Publishers, 1978), 17–24; Hal Wallis to William Guthrie, 3 March 1941, Box Navy Blues 1 of 1, WB Archive; and Joseph McBride, *Searching for John Ford: A Life* (New York: St. Martin's Press, 2001), 67, 98, 138, 171–74, 203–5, 266.
31. Suid, *Sailing on the Silver Screen*, 17.
32. Swanson to Senator Elbert D. Thomas, 28 January 1935, B429, E22, RG 80, NAB; CNO to Thomas R. Amlie, 11 March 1936, B427, E22, RG 80, NAB; Thomas to Swanson, 18 January 1935, B429, E22, RG 80, NAB; Thomas R. Amlie to the SecNav, 2 March 1935, B427, E22, RG 80, NAB; SecNav to Rep. Arthur P. Lemneck, 10 March 1936, B180, E81, RG 38, NAB.
33. Scovel, "Helm's a Lee," 153–55.

34. Orr to Claude Swanson, 8 February 1935; Navy Department Motion Picture Board to CNO, "Metro-Goldwyn-Mayer Photoplay—'Murder in the Fleet,'" 19 February 1935; CNO to Orr, 2 March 1935, and F. H. Bastedo to C. H. Baker, 29 August 1935—all in B429, E22, RG 80, NAB.
35. CNO to William Orr, 25 March 1935, B181, E81, RG 38, NAB.
36. CNO to Lucien Hubbard, 2 May 1935, B429, E22, RG 80, NAB.
37. CNO to Major General Commandant, Marine Corps, "Marine Orderly Detailed to Duty in the Navy Press Room," 17 April 1935, B2098, E22, RG 80, NACP; Major General Commandant to CNO, "Withdrawal of Marine on duty in the Navy Press Room," 9 April 1935, B2098, E22, RG 80, NACP.
38. Scovel, "Helm's a Lee," 117–18; "General Order No. 32," 13 May 1935, B1, EP 3, RG 428, NACP; "General Order No. 36," 13 May 1935, B1, EP 3, RG 428, NACP.
39. Lt. A. D. Blackledge to Rutgers Neilson (RKO), 2 October 1935, B184, E81, RG 38, NAB.
40. Memorandum for Lieutenant Blackledge from C. E. Van Hook, 18 September 1935, B429, E22, RG 80, NAB.
41. Memorandum for the CNO from Paul H. Bastedo, 3 October 1935, B184, E81, RG 38, NAB.
42. CNO to Anthony Muto, 7 October 1935, B427, E22, RG 80, NAB; Pandro S. Berman to CNO, 23 October 1935, B427, E22, RG 80, NAB.
43. Office of Naval Intelligence, *Naval Intelligence Manual*, 101, 18 April 1936, B2, EUD 83A, RG 38, NAB.
44. Ibid., 215.
45. Ibid., 174.
46. O. R. Pilat, "Navy Activity Hedged by War-Time Secrecy," *Brooklyn Eagle*, 16 September 1936, B133, E81, RG 38, NAB.
47. CNO to Commandants, All ND, "Security," 22 October 1936, B133, E81, RG 38, NAB.
48. ComThree to CNO (DNI), "Censorship of Motion Pictures," 14 October 1936, B180, E81, RG 38, NAB; "History of 'Let's Join the Navy,'" ca. October 1936, B180, E81, RG 38, NAB.
49. OIC, Recruiting Bureau (F. E. M. Whiting) to Chief of BuNav via ComThree, "Censorship of Motion Pictures," 14 October 1936, B180, E81, RG 38, NAB.
50. CNO (Puleston by direction) to Chief BuYards and Docks, "Floating Drydock ARD-1; Request for photograph of, by Republic Steel Corporation," 12 April 1935, B44, E85, RG 38, NAB.
51. CNO to ComThree, "Magazine article relating to and artist's drawings of the USS ARD-3," 5 January 1937, B43, E85, RG 38, NAB; Chief BuYards and Docks (Rear Adm. Norman M. Smith) to CNO (ONI), "Magazine article relating to and artist's drawings of the floating dry dock ARD-3," 8 January 1937, B43, E85, RG 38, NAB.
52. Chief BuYards and Docks to CNO (ONI), "Magazine article relating to and artist's drawing of the floating dry dock ARD-3," 15 January 1937, B43, E85, RG 38, NAB; ComEleven (Sinclair Gannon) to CNO (DNI), "Floating Dry-Dock ARD-1 to participate in maneuvers, newspaper publicity concerning," 6 February 1937, B44, E85, RG 38, NAB.

53. Memorandum for Commander Leighton from C. E. Taylor, "L. U. Reavis, articles by," 12 October 1936, B147, E81, RG 38, NAB; Memorandum for Capt. Leighton from C. E. Taylor, "L. U. Reavis, report on interview with, 3:30–5:30 P.M., 22 July 1937," 22 July 1937, B147, E81, RG 38, NAB.
54. CNO to Capt. Jonas H. Ingram via Commandant, NY Navy Yard, "L. U. Reavis, Commercial Artist, Contact with, report on," 19 February 1938, B 148, E81, RG 38, NAB.
55. Memo to the Navy Department Motion Picture Board from H. A. Badt, "Script of film 'The Depths Below'—Comments on Script of," 4 August 1936; Memo for Rear Adm. Sinclair Gannon from H. A. Jones, 2 September 1936; CNO to Harry Cohn, 12 August 1936, and C. Young to Alfred Bolton, 25 September 1936—all in B425, E22, RG 80, NAB.
56. Memorandum for the U.S. Navy Motion Picture Board of Review from Lt. Cdr. C. E. Taylor, "Saturation of Public Interest in Motion Pictures of Naval Activities by Reason of Numerous Second Rate Productions," ca. September 1937, B180, E81, RG 38, NAB.
57. Memorandum to Senior Member, Navy Department Motion Picture Board, from Lt. Cdr. S. H. Hurt, "Monogram Pictures—'The Marines Have Landed,' Review of," 20 May 1938, B183, E81, RG 38, NAB.
58. CNO (Leahy) to J. S. Harrington (Monogram), 27 May 1938, B183, E81, RG 38, NAB.
59. Frank Wead, "Submarine Story, Revised Temporary Script," 28 July 1936, B426, E22, RG 80, NAB; Frank Wead to Cdr. F. G. Reinicke, 24 November 1936, B184, E81, RG 38, NAB; Memorandum for Lieutenant Bolton from F. T. Leighton, "Manuscript—'Submarine Story,'" 13 November 1936, B424, E22, RG 80, NAB.
60. G. W. D. Dashiell to Cdr. F. G. Reinicke, 12 March 1937, B184, E81, RG 38, NAB.
61. Cdr. F. G. Reinicke to Capt. Richard S. Edwards, 14 December 1936, B184, E81, RG 38, NAB.
62. Capt. R. S. Edwards (ComSubSquadSix) to Cdr. F. G. Reinicke, 15 March 1937, B184, E81, RG 38, NAB.
63. Lt. A. J. Bolton to Louis F. Edelman, 1 March 1937, B184, E81, RG 38, NAB; Chief of Naval Operations to Hal Wallis, 4 November 1937, B425, E22, RG 80, NAB.
64. DNI to CNO, "Metro-Goldwyn-Mayer requests assignment of officer to assist in preparing motion picture scenario," 31 October 1931, B432, E22, RG 80, NAB; William Goetz to William D. Leahy, 2 May 1938, B419, E22, RG 80, NAB; CNO to the Commanding Officer, Naval Air Station, San Diego, "Cooperation with Warner Brothers Pictures, Inc.," 8 October 1938, B423, E22, RG 80, NAB.
65. Louis F. Edelman to Lt. D. A. Frost, 11 January 1938; Lt. D. A. Frost to Louis F. Edelman, 14 January 1938—both in B184, E81, RG 38, NAB.
66. Memorandum to Capt. Frank T. Leighton from Lt. Cdr. C. E. Taylor, 14 January 1938, B184, E81, RG 38, NAB.
67. Memorandum for Lt. Daniel A. Frost from Lt. Cdr. S. H. Hurt, "Warner Brothers rough notes on 'Pensacola' story," 15 January 1938, B184, E81, RG 38, NAB.
68. Lt. Cdr. Lovette to Rear Adm. W. F. Halsey, 17 February 1938, B184, E81, RG 38, NAB.

69. Lovette to Charles A. Peters (NPS), 12 January 1939, B184, E81, RG 38, NAB.
70. "Wings of the Navy," *Motion Picture Herald*, 21 January 1939, 38.
71. Memo to Senior Member Navy Department Motion Picture Board from S.H. Hurt, "Motion Picture Script 'Heroes Come High' dated 28 June 1938,—Columbia Pictures," 12 July 1938, B419, E22, RG 80, NAB. Irene Muto to Leahy, 25 April 1938, B419, E22, RG 80, NAB.
72. ComThree to SecNav, "Radio Talks to be given by Lieutenant Commander Elliott Ranney, SC, US Naval Reserve," 1 September 1937, B164, E81, RG 38, NAB; Memorandum to the DNI via Capt. Frank T. Leighton from Lt. Cdr. Courtney E. Taylor, "Radio Talks by Naval Personnel," ca. 25 September 1937, B164, E81, RG 38, NAB.
73. Capt. Frank T. Leighton to DNI, "Radio Talks by Naval Personnel," 25 September 1937, B164, E81, RG 38, NAB.
74. Wright, *Navy League*, 96–102; Rappaport, *Navy League*, 155–76; Minutes of the Meeting of the Board of Directors of the Navy League of the United States, 16 January 1936, B3, Howe Papers, NWCL.
75. Douglas, "Public Relations, United States Navy," 1433.
76. Leland Pearson Lovette, *Naval Customs, Traditions, and Usage* (Annapolis, Md.: Naval Institute Press, 1933).
77. Bernard L. Austin, *The Reminiscences of Vice Admiral Bernard L. Austin, U.S. Navy, Retired* (Annapolis, Md.: U.S. Naval Institute, 1971), 70–71.
78. Scovel, "Helm's a Lee," 118–19; Wyman H. Packard, *A Century of U.S. Naval Intelligence* (Washington, D.C.: Department of the Navy, 1996), 332; Austin, *Reminiscences of Vice Admiral Austin*, 55–57.
79. Kendall Banning to Lovette, 20 November 1938, B141, E81, RG 38, NAB.
80. Lovette to Kendall Banning, 5 December 1938; Lovette to Cdr. James Fife (U.S. Submarine Base New London), 19 January 1939; Lovette to Kendall Banning, 13 December 1938; Kendall Banning to Lovette, 12 January 1939; CNO to Chief of BuNav, "Kendall Banning, writer—transportation aboard USS *Wyoming*," 22 June 1939—all in B141, E81, RG 38, NAB.
81. Lovette to Cdr. James Fife (US Submarine Base New London), 19 January 1939, B141, E81, RG 38, NAB.
82. Kendall Banning, *The Fleet Today* (New York: Funk and Wagnalls, 1940), xi.
83. Lt. B. L. Austin to Hanson Baldwin, 26 November 1938, B42, E85 RG 38, NAB; Cdr. Leland P. Lovette to Hanson Baldwin, 20 December 1938, B42, E85, RG 38, NAB; Lovette to Cdr. F. E. M. Whiting (Recruiting Bureau), 2 June 1938, Box 34, E85, RG 38, NAB.

Chapter 5. "The Finest Qualities of American Manhood"

1. "United States Public Health Service," *Bismarck Tribune*, 8 January 1919, 2.
2. R. W. Connell, *Masculinities* (Berkeley: University of California Press, 1995), 68–71.
3. Frank Martinek, *Don Winslow Saves the Secret Formula* (New York: Grosset and Dunlap, 1941), 2–3.

4. Harrod, *Manning the New Navy*, 11–13; quotation on 11.
5. Allan M. Brandt, *No Magic Bullet: A Social History of Venereal Disease in the United States since 1880* (New York: Oxford University Press, 1987), 73; Elizabeth C. MacPhail, "When the Red Lights Went Out in San Diego: The Little Known Story of San Diego's 'Restricted District,'" *Journal of San Diego History* 20, no. 2 (Spring 1974), https://sandiegohistory.org/journal/1974/april/stingaree/; Timothy J. Gilfoyle, *City of Eros: New York City, Prostitution, and the Commercialization of Sex, 1790–1920* (New York: W. W. Norton & Company, 1994), 222.
6. Daniels, *Navy and the Nation*, 56–69; Harrod, *Manning the New Navy*, 28–31, 135–36.
7. Directorate of Information Operations and Reports, *Department of Defense: Selected Manpower Statistics—Fiscal Year 1997* (Washington, D.C.: Government Printing Office, 1997), 50; Harrod, *Manning the New Navy*, 30, 37–38.
8. For more on the emphasis the navy placed on athletic competitions, see Robert Shenk, ed., *Playships of the World: The Naval Diaries of Admiral Dan Gallery, 1920–1924* (Columbia: University of South Carolina Press, 2008), 7, 69–77.
9. Halsey Davidson, *Navy Boys behind the Big Guns; or, Sinking the German U-Boats* (New York: G. Sully, 1919), frontispiece.
10. "Navy Eight Wins Trip to Antwerp," *New York Times*, 25 July 1920, 19; Navy News Bureau, Immediate Release, 3 September 1920, 1–2, B2, E113, RG 80, NAB; Robert Shenk, "To the 1920 Olympics by Cruiser," *Naval History Magazine* 22, no. 4 (August 2008): 34–39; Navy News Bureau, Immediate Release, 12 March 1920, 1–4, B1, E113, RG 80, NAB; Navy News Bureau, Immediate Release, 6 July 1920, 1–4, B1, E113, RG 80, NAB; Navy News Bureau, Release Monday Morning, 20 September 1920, B2, E113, RG 80, NAB.
11. "Comfort, Courtesy, Safety, and Speed," *Smithsonian Institute*, accessed 20 November 2017, http://americanhistory.si.edu/onthewater/exhibition/5_3.html.
12. H. Irving Hancock, *Dave Darrin's South American Cruise; or, Two Innocent Young Naval Tools of an Infamous Conspiracy* (Philadelphia: Altemus, 1919), 134–36. For more on the imperialistic overtones in turn-of-the-century children's literature, see Brian Rouleau, "Childhood's Imperial Imagination: Edward Stratemeyer's Fiction Factory and the Valorization of American Empire," *Journal of the Gilded Age and Progressive Era* 7, no. 4 (October 2008): 479–512.
13. Halsey Davidson, *Navy Boys on Special Service; or, Guarding the Floating Treasury* (New York: G. Sully, 1920), 203.
14. C. E. Courtney to BuNav, "Sales Management Doctrine," 31 July 1920, B396, E89, RG 24, NAB; Chief of BuNav (Thomas Washington) to the Navy Recruiting Service, "Competition in Recruiting," 10 November 1922, B901, E89, RG 24, NAB.
15. Photo NH 76765-KN, Photographic Section, Washington Navy Yard, Washington, D.C. [hereafter referred to as Photographic Section], NHHC; Navy News Bureau, Release Afternoon Papers, 2 June 1922, B4, E113, RG 80, NAB.
16. Kemp Tolley, *Yangtze Patrol: The US Navy in China* (Annapolis, Md.: Naval Institute Press, 1971), 81–267; Photo NH 76751-KN, Photographic Section, NHHC.
17. *A Sailor Made Man*, directed by Fred C. Newmeyer, Hal Roach Studios, 1921.

18. Karsten, *Naval Aristocracy*, 187–93; BuNav to Officer in Charge, Navy Recruiting Station, Parkersburg, W.Va., "Gratuitous Advertising," B396, E89, RG 24, NAB.
19. Josephus Daniels, "Training Men for the Navy and the Nation," *Saturday Evening Post*, 9 April 1921, 21–24, 78–83.
20. Directorate of Information Operations and Reports, *Department of Defense*, 50–51.
21. Navy News Bureau, Release Afternoon Papers, 2 June 1922, B4, E113, RG 80, NAB. The rhetoric of Americanism was also adopted by a resurgent Ku Klux Klan during the 1920s. See Joe L. Dubbert, *A Man's Place: Masculinity in Transition* (New York: Prentice Hall, 1979), 200–201; for an example of a speech by a naval officer explicitly acknowledging and supporting Americanism, see address by William H. Standley to the Daughters of the American Revolution, Washington, D.C., 22 April 1936, 1–10, B26, E113, RG 80, NAB; see also Mugridge, *View from Xanadu*, 28, 90–91; Herbert Hoover, *American Individualism* (Garden City, N.Y.: Doubleday, Page, and Co., 1922), 1–14.
22. Film 24.24, *Our Navy in the Near East* (1923), Records of the Navy Recruiting Bureau, RG 24, NACP.
23. Photo NH 76783-KN, Photographic Section, NHHC.
24. For a detailed account of the Point Honda disaster, see Charles Lockwood and Hans Christian Adamson, *Tragedy at Honda: One of America's Greatest Naval Disasters* (Philadelphia: Chilton, 1960). For additional detail and a discussion of the navy's handling of news of the accidents, see chap. 6; and Charles G. Ross, "Untold Stories of High Heroism in Recent Destroyer Disaster," *St. Louis Post-Dispatch*, 2 December 1923, 13, B114, EP 3, RG 428, NACP.
25. Hanson W. Baldwin, *The Reminiscences of Hanson Weight Baldwin, U.S. Navy Retired* (Annapolis, Md.: Naval Institute Press, 1976), 2:152–56.
26. Navy News Bureau, Immediate Release, 29 November 1920, B2, E113, RG 80, NAB; Walter Eckersall, "Army–Navy Game to Stay Forever in Fans' Memory," *Chicago Tribune*, 29 November 1926, 21; "A Great Game and Its Meaning," *Chicago Tribune*, 30 November 1926, 10; "Army–Navy Elevens to Play in Chicago," *New York Times*, 23 January 1926, 1; Genevieve Forbes Herrick, "$100,000 Paid for Army–Navy Box Seats," *Chicago Tribune*, 2 October 1926, 1; Walter Eckersall, "Army–Navy Game in Chicago May Decide U.S. Grid Title," *Chicago Tribune*, 1 November 1926, 29; "Navy Is to Broadcast Play-by-Play Story of Army Game to U.S. Fleet the World Over," *New York Times*, 18 November 1926, 21; Walter Eckersall, "Army-Navy Thrill; All Even," *Chicago Tribune*, 28 November 1926, 1, 4.
27. Officer in Charge, Navy Recruiting Station, Boston, to BuNav, "Newspaper Publicity," 12 May 1930, B65, E90, RG 24, NAB.
28. W. F. Newton to Judge Frank A. Page, 2 November 1928; Page to Newton, 5 November 1928; and Officer in Charge, Navy Recruiting Bureau, to Chief of BuNav, "Clippings from the Bay Shore Journal of 25 October 1928—'Youth Charged with Disorderly Conduct is Permitted to Join Navy,'" 21 November 1928—all in B64, E90, RG 24, NAB.
29. Utley, *American Battleship*, 62. Congress officially authorized the navy to have approximately 86,000 enlisted personnel after the passage of a personnel bill in 1923. In 1928,

the secretary of the navy reported a shortage of two thousand men due to funding shortages and the need to provide men for naval aviation. *Annual Report of the Secretary of the Navy for the Fiscal Year 1928* (Washington, D.C.: GPO, 1929), 166; M. MacKaye, "Modern Bluejacket, No Longer Recruited from the Nation's Riffraff," *Outlook and Independent*, 31 July 1929, 532–33.

30. "Sport: Army vs. Navy," *Time*, 26 December 1927, 25. The two academies had different age restrictions on who could enter and also different rules regarding the length of eligibility for players; Navy Press Room, Immediate Release, 8 January 1932, B19, E113, RG 80, NAB; "Salute, Dialogue Taken from the Screen," 30 July 1929, Box 776, Performing Arts Collections, University of California–Los Angles; later football films set at the Naval Academy included *Hold 'Em Navy*, directed by Kurt Neumann, Paramount Pictures, 1937; and *Navy Blue and Gold*, directed by Sam Wood, Metro-Goldwyn-Mayer, 1937.

31. Navy Department, Memo for the Press, 14 August 1922, 1–2, B4, E113, RG 80, NAB; Utley, *American Battleship*, 62; *True to the Navy*, directed by Frank Tuttle, Paramount Pictures, 1930.

32. *Men without Women*, directed by John Ford, Fox Film Corporation, 1930.

33. "Men without Women," *Film Daily*, 2 February 1930, 11.

34. *Hell Below*, directed by Jack Conway, Metro-Goldwyn-Mayer, 1933.

35. Syd Field, *Screenplay: The Foundations of Screenwriting*, rev. ed. (New York: Delta Trade Paperbacks, 2005), 63, 68.

36. Bureau of Labor Statistics, "Labor Force, Employment, and Unemployment, 1929–1939: Estimating Methods," *Monthly Labor Review* (July 1948): 51–52.

37. Dubbert, *Man's Place*, 198–99.

38. Michael S. Kimmel, *Manhood in America: A Cultural History*, 2nd ed. (New York: Oxford University Press, 2006), 141–45.

39. Alice Kessler-Harris, "Measures for Masculinity: The American Labor Movement and Welfare State Policy during the Great Depression," in *Masculinities in Politics and War: Gendering Modern History*, ed. Stefan Dudink, Karen Hagerman, and John Tosh (New York: Manchester University Press, 2000), 220–35.

40. *Here Comes the Navy*, directed by Lloyd Bacon, Warner Brothers Studios, 1934.

41. Navy Department, Hold for Release, 30 September 1926, B86, EP 3, RG 428, NACP; *Midshipman Jack*, directed by Christy Cabanne, RKO Radio Pictures, 1933; *Shipmates Forever*, directed by Frank Borzage, Warner Brothers Pictures, 1935.

42. Martinek, *Don Winslow in Ceylon*, 9–14.

43. Ibid., 15, 63; Sheridan, *Comics and Their Creators*, 227; Waugh, *Comics*, 126–28.

44. "The Post Impressionist," *Washington Post*, 24 April 1934, 8; Memorandum from Gale Munro to File, 17 November 1998, Navy Art Collection Files, Washington Navy Yard, Washington, D.C. The transvestites in the painting have noticeable Adam's apples visible in the plunging necklines of their dresses, and the prominently displayed red tie of the man in the suit was, during the 1930s, an open display of homosexuality.

45. "The Fleet's In," *Washington Post*, 20 April 1934, 8; "The Fleet's In," *Washington Post*, 8 July 1934, sec. B, 4.

46. "On the Sand at Waikiki," 12 July 1935, Navy Art Gallery, Washington Navy Yard, Washington, D.C. [hereafter cited as Navy Art Gallery]; "Picturesque Alaska," 27 April 1935, Navy Art Gallery.
47. Officer in Charge, Navy Recruiting Station, New Orleans, to BuNav, "Trip of aircraft from Pensacola to Chicago about 1 August 1922," 25 July 1922, B396, E89, RG 24, NAB; Charles Hughes Williams III, "'We have . . . kept the negroes' goodwill and sent them away': Black Sailors, White Dominion in the New Navy, 1893–1942" (master's thesis, Texas A&M University, 2008), 5, 25–26, 29–30, 74–76, 94; Robert M. Jiobu, *Ethnicity and Assimilation: Blacks, Chinese, Filipinos, Japanese, Koreans, Mexicans, Vietnamese, and Whites* (New York: SUNY Press, 1991), 50.
48. Officer in Charge, Navy Recruiting Bureau, to Chief of BuNav, "Trailers for Motion Picture Films," 28 January 1936, B65, E90, RG 24, NAB.
49. Photo NH-76806, Photographic Section, NHHC.
50. *Annual Report of the Secretary of the Navy for the Fiscal Year 1932* (Washington, D.C.: GPO, 1933), 22; Theodore C. Mason, *Battleship Sailor* (Annapolis, Md.: Naval Institute Press, 1982), 42.
51. Hugh M. Rodman, "A Navy Day Address," 27 October 1922, B5, E113, RG 80, NAB.

Chapter 6. Replacing the Familiar with the New

1. Lockwood and Adamson, *Tragedy at Honda*, 4–156.
2. Navy Department, Immediate Release, 13 September 1923, B114, EP 3, RG 428, NACP.
3. Lockwood and Adamson, *Tragedy at Honda*, 168–69.
4. "Navy Inquiry Board Orders Trials of 11 in Destroyers' Loss," *New York Times*, 1 November 1923.
5. Clark G. Reynolds, *Admiral John H. Towers: The Struggle for Naval Air Supremacy* (Annapolis, Md.: Naval Institute Press, 1991), 127–66; Navy Department, Memo for the Press, 3 October 1922, B5, E113, RG 80, NAB; "Alcock and Brown Fly across Atlantic," *New York Times*, 16 June 1919, 1; Navy News Bureau, Immediate Release, 25 March 1920, B1, E113, RG 80, NAB.
6. Don Berliner, *Airplane Racing: A History, 1909–2008* (Jefferson, N.C.: McFarland, 2010), 9–46; Navy News Bureau, Immediate Release, 23 November 1920, B2, E113, RG 80, NAB; Navy News Bureau, Immediate Release, 24 November 1920, 1–8, B2, E113, RG 80, NAB; ibid.
7. Navy News Bureau, Release Noon Thursday, 3 February 1921, 8, B12, EP 3, RG 428, NACP. The "Gun Club" factors heavily into Clark G. Reynolds's *The Fast Carriers: The Forging of an Air Navy* (New York: McGraw Hill, 1968) and Robert O'Connell's *Sacred Vessels: The Cult of the Battleship and the Rise of the U.S. Navy* (Boulder, Colo.:Westview Press, 1991).
8. Photo NH 76739-KN, Photographic Section, NHHC.
9. F. G. Lowry, "Three-Plane Navy," *Saturday Evening Post*, 11 June 1921, 16. The effect of the Washington Conference development is explored in several books, including John T. Kuehn, *Agents of Innovation: The General Board and the Design of the Fleet That Defeated the Japanese Navy* (Annapolis, Md.: Naval Institute Press, 2008); and Friedman, Hone, and Mandeles, *Aircraft Carrier Development*.

10. Navy Department, For Release, 19 July 1923, B5, E113, RG 80, NAB; "Americans First in Cowes Air Race," *New York Times*, 29 September 1923, 2; Navy Department, Immediate Release, 28 September 1923, B5, E113, RG 80, NAB; "World Record Made by Flyer in Race," *Baltimore Sun*, 7 October 1923, 1; "Fastest Flight Just Cuts Five Miles a Minute," *Boston Globe*, 3 November 1923, 1.
11. Navy Department, For Release, 19 July 1923, B5, E113, RG 80, NAB; "High Speed Hazards in Aviation," *New York Times*, 7 November 1923, 16; Navy Department, Immediate Release, 31 October 1923, 1–2, B6, E113, RG 80, NAB; Robert Edgren, "Speed Champions Found Are Found in Numbers," *Baltimore Sun*, 15 March 1925, sec. S, 2; "Navy Plane Goes Five Miles a Minute," *Boston Globe*, 19 September 1925, 1. The *Washington Post*, *New York Times*, and *Los Angeles Times* likewise ran front-page stories detailing Williams's flight.
12. Navy Department, Memo for the Press, 11 September 1922, B4, E113, RG 80, NAB; Navy Department, Immediate Release, 28 September 1923, B5, E113, RG 80, NAB; Trimble, *Admiral William A. Moffett*, 121–22.
13. Mitchell attempted to frame the interservice collaboration on air racing as revelatory during his court-martial in late 1925. See James O'Donnell Bennett, "Economy Plan Blamed for Air Service Fiasco," *Chicago Tribune*, 12 November 1925, 2; Navy Department, Release Morning Papers, 7 November 1926, 1–6, B10, E113, RG 80, NAB.
14. Friedman, Hone, and Mandeles, *Aircraft Carrier Development*, 22–23.
15. "American Dreadnought of the Air Takes Trial Flight," *Christian Science Monitor*, 4 September 1923, 1; "ZR-1 Encircles City in a 12-Hour Flight over Three States," *New York Times*, 12 September 1923, 1; BuNav to Moffett, "Orders of 26 September 1923, Modified," 16 October 1923, B4148, E62, RG 72, NAB; "Shenandoah, New Giant Dirigible, to Fly over Baltimore Navy Day," *Baltimore Sun*, 23 October 1923, sec. SS, 24.
16. Robinson and Keller, *Up Ship!*, 71.
17. Navy Department, Immediate Release, 22 September 1923, B5, E113, RG 80, NAB; "Story of the Trip by Wireless from Airship," *New York Times*, 8 October 1924, 1; "Shenandoah Makes Pacific Coast Goal," *New York Times*, 11 October 1924, 1.
18. H. Irving Hancock, *Dave Darrin and the German Submarines; or, Making a Clean-Up of the Hun Sea Monsters* (Philadelphia: Altemus, 1919), 230; Halsey Davidson, *Navy Boys after the Submarines; or, Protecting the Giant Convoy* (New York: G. Sully, 1918), 151–206; Halsey Davidson, *Navy Boys at the Big Surrender; or, Rounding Up the German Fleet* (New York: G. Sully, 1919), 95–146.
19. "Outlaw the Submarines," *New York Times*, 17 November 1921, 15.
20. Knox, *Eclipse of American Sea Power*, 69, 79–82; quotation on 79.
21. Norman Friedman, *U.S. Submarines through 1945: An Illustrated Design History* (Annapolis, Md.: Naval Institute Press, 1995), 168–80.
22. Transcript of Afternoon Press Conference by Josephus Daniels, 16 December 1920, 6, B3, E113, RG 80, NAB; Gary E. Weir, *Building American Submarines, 1914–1940* (Washington, D.C.: Naval Historical Center, 1991), 28–38; "Rescuing the Crew Imprisoned Hours in Submarine S-5," *New York Times*, 3 September 1920, 1.
23. "This Rescue without a New Feature," *New York Times*, 6 September 1920, 6.

24. "S-48," *Dictionary of American Naval Fighting Ships*, accessed 15 June 2010, http://www.history.navy.mil/DANFS/s2/s-48.htm; "O-5," *Dictionary of American Naval Fighting Ships*, accessed 15 June 2010, http://www.history.navy.mil/DANFS/o1/o-5.htm.

25. Address by CMDR John Rodgers over WCAP radio, Washington, D.C., 27 October 1925, 1–4, B8, E113, RG 80, NAB; "Heroes of the PN-9," *Washington Post*, 12 September 1925, 6. Rodgers recounted the tale of survival for himself and his crew in "First PN-1 Story by John Rodgers," *Los Angeles Times*, 12 September 1925, sec. A, 1.

26. "Terrible Risks," *Boston Globe*, 5 September 1923, 16; Navy Department, Press Release, 9 September 1925, 1–2, B8, E113, RG 80, NAB; "Loss of Two Ships Expected to Force Change in Program," *Washington Post*, 4 September 1923, 1; Navy Department, Immediate Release, 2 October 1925, 1–6, B8, E113, RG 80, NAB.

27. Edward Ellsberg, *On the Bottom* (New York: Dodd, Mead and Co., 1928), 1–6.

28. "Two Other Newspapers Join in Demand for Wilbur's Scalp," *Baltimore Sun*, 30 September 1925, 1, 8; "Wilbur Unwilling to End Efforts to Rescue Crew," *Boston Globe*, 2 October 1925, 13.

29. "Widow Claims Lansdowne Declared Journey Unsafe," *Boston Globe*, 4 September 1925, 1; "Mrs. Lansdowne in Repetition of Charge," *Boston Globe*, 12 October 1925, 1; "Now Another Naval Tragedy," *Literary Digest*, 10 October 1925, 7–9.

30. "The Impracticable Dirigible," *Chicago Tribune*, 12 October 1925, 8; Address of William A. Moffett at Launching of USS *Lexington*, Quincy, Mass., 3 October 1925, 1–6, B8, E113, RG 80, NAB; Howard Mingos, "Shenandoah Disaster a Costly Lesson to Aviation," *New York Times*, 6 September 1925, sec. XX, 1.

31. Trimble, *Admiral William A. Moffett*, 162–66. An even-handed account of Mitchell's trial can be found in Cooke, *Billy Mitchell*, 187–224.

32. Navy Department, Release Evening Papers, 11 June 1926, 3, B9, E113, RG 80, NAB.

33. R. L. Duffus, "Submarine Again Becomes a World Issue," *New York Times*, 22 November 1925, sec. XX, 3.

34. Ellsberg, *On the Bottom*, 12–15; Thomas Buell, *Master of Sea Power: A Biography of Fleet Admiral Ernest J. King* (Boston: Little, Brown, 1979), 57–58; "Hope to Raise S-51 within Ten Days," *Hartford Courant*, 13 November 1925, 1.

35. "Raising the S-51," *Washington Post*, 12 July 1926, 4; "Sea Yields Death Ship," *Los Angeles Times*, 6 July 1926, 1; "Salvaging S-51," *New York Times*, 25 July 1926, sec. E, 6.

36. "More S-51 Divers Called to the S-4," *New York Times*, 20 December 1927, 3; Navy Department, Immediate Release, 4 January 1928, 1–2, B11, E113, RG 80, NAB; Navy Press Room, Immediate Release, 5 January 1928, 1–4, B11, E113, RG 80, NAB.

37. Navy Press Room, Immediate Release, 20 December 1927, 1–4, Box 11, E113, RG 80, NAB; Navy Press Room, Immediate Release, 21 December 1927, 1–2, Box 11, E113, RG 80, NAB; Austin, *Reminiscences of Vice Admiral Austin*, 60–61.

38. "Who Is to Blame for Our Submarine Disasters?," *Literary Digest*, 7 January 1928, 5–7; "The S-4 Disaster," *Los Angeles Times*, 26 December 1927, sec. A, 4; "Wilbur Answers Criticism of Navy," *New York Times*, 23 December 1927, 1; "Invent Device for Raising Submarine," *Norfolk New Journal and Guide*, 14 January 1928, 1; "Germans Offer Way to Raise S-4," *Washington Post*, 15 January 1928, sec. M, 14; "Plans Submarine Derrick,"

New York Times, 15 January 1928, 18; "Urges End of Submarines," *New York Times*, 25 December 1927, 12.
39. "Mr. Wilbur's Belated Energy," *Baltimore Sun*, 25 December 1927, 6; "Justifiable Criticism," *Chicago Tribune*, 18 January 1928, 8; Edward Ellsberg, "A Grapple with Death on the Ocean Floor," *Los Angeles Times*, 1 April 1928, sec. K, 12.
40. Navy Department, Immediate Release, 9 February 1927, B10, E113, RG 80, NAB; Navy Press Room, Immediate Release, 24 June 1931, B18, E113, RG 80, NAB; Navy Press Room, Immediate Release, 23 July 1931, 1–2, B18, E113, RG 80, NAB.
41. Navy Press Room, For Release Wednesday Morning, 7 August 1929, 1–3, B13, E113, RG 80, NAB; "Navy Air Work Inquiry Called," *Los Angeles Times*, 16 March 1930, 12; Navy Press Room, For Information, 31 March 1930, B14, E113, RG 80, NAB; Report on Senate Resolution 235, 27 May 1930, B15, E113, RG 80, NAB; "Alford Williams, Aviation Expert," *New York Times*, 16 June 1958, 23.
42. John Fry, *USS Saratoga CV-3: An Illustrated History of the Legendary Aircraft Carrier, 1927–1946* (Atglen, Pa.: Schiffer Publishing, 1996), 27; Gordon Swanborough and Peter M. Bowers, *U.S. Navy Aircraft since 1911* (Annapolis, Md.: Naval Institute Press, 1976), 71; Paul R. Matt and Bruce Robertson, *United States Navy and Marine Corps Fighters, 1918–1962* (Fallbrook, Calif.: Aero Publishers, 1962), 39–43; "Throngs Cheer Vikings of the Air," *Los Angeles Times*, 15 September 1928, sec. A, 1. Information on one of the earliest nonracing appearances at the National Air Races can be found in the following: Navy Press Room, Immediate Release, 12 August 1929, B13, E113, RG 80, NAB; Navy Press Room, Immediate Release, 10 August 1928, B12, E113, RG 80, NAB; and *Tail Spin*, directed by Roy Del Ruth, Fox Film Corporation, 1939.
43. Navy Department, Release Sunday Papers, 6 November 1927, 1–10, B11, E113, RG 80, NAB.
44. "Fleet Leaves for Isthmus," *Los Angeles Times*, 15 January 1929, 1; Lewis Freeman, "Commander's Story of Saratoga Raid," *New York Times*, 19 February 1929, 14. The 1949 film *Task Force*, directed by Delmer Daves, would reference the events of Fleet Problem IX and even included a partially fictionalized Rear Admiral Reeves as one of its central characters.
45. Mordaunt Hall, "The Screen," *New York Times*, 11 February 1929, 26.
46. Knox to Kendall Banning, 15 September 1931, B3, Knox Papers, LOC; "Tacoma Cuts Down Use of Electricity," *Los Angeles Times*, 21 November 1929, 9; "Ask That Plane Ship Feed Power to Two Cities," *New York Times*, 21 November 1929, 44; "Lexington Ties Up at the Tacoma Dock," *New York Times*, 16 December 1929, 4; "Navy Goes to Rescue of Tacoma, Wash., in Serious Power Shortage," *Los Angeles Times*, 19 December 1929, sec. A, 8; "500 Boy Scouts Visit Plane Carrier in Dock," *New York Times*, 12 January 1930, 51.
47. "Naval Air Force," *Washington Post*, 1 March 1931, sec. S, 1; Hanson Baldwin, "Navy Revises Its Technique," *New York Times*, 12 April 1931, sec. MS, 3; "Planes to Get Big Test in War Game," *Baltimore Sun*, 16 February 1931, 1.
48. CNO to ComFour et al., "USS *Akron*—Press relations on flight to Pacific Coast," 26 April 1932, B4211, E22, RG 80, NAB.

49. Trimble, *Admiral William A. Moffett*, 166; *Dirigible*, directed by Frank Capra, Columbia Pictures, 1931; Michael Paris, *From the Wright Brothers to "Top Gun": Aviation, Nationalism, and Popular Cinema* (Manchester: Manchester University Press, 1995), 111.
50. Mordaunt Hall, "The Screen: Fun and Thrills Are Interwoven in Picture of Amazing Flying Feats by Uncle Sam's Air Sailors; Love vs. Tradition," *New York Times*, 23 December 1931.
51. Memorandum for Captain Neyes, 13 January 1932, B1362, E90, RG 24, NAB.
52. *Submarine*, directed by Frank Capra, Columbia Pictures, 1928.
53. "Metrotone Films Undersea Escapes from Submarine," *Hearst Metrotone Newsreel*, 19 August 1930, FT Archive; Navy Department, Hold for Release, 4 April 1929, 1–17, B13, E113, RG 80, NAB; CNO to the CINCUS et al., "Submarine Rescue Vessels and Training of," 21 May 1929, B13, E113, RG 80, NAB; "Submarine Rescue Work to Be Shown," *Washington Post*, 13 March 1932, sec. S, 10.
54. *Men without Women*, directed by John Ford, Fox Film Corporation, 1930; Suid, *Sailing on the Silver Screen*, 25–27.
55. Felker, *Testing American Sea Power*, 61–75; Holwitt, *"Execute against Japan,"* 76–78.
56. One of the rare exceptions to the lack of coverage of submarine operations is Lewis Freeman, "Submarines' Value Shown at Panama," *New York Times*, 1 February 1929, 9; "Cameraman Risks Life to Film Dive of Huge US Sub," *Universal Newsreel*, 18 October 1933, Universal Newsreel Catalog, RG 200 UN, NACP.
57. Mordaunt Hall, "Walter Huston, Robert Montgomery and Jimmy Durante in a Mixture of Farce and Melodrama," *New York Times*, 26 April 1933, 13.
58. "Mighty Akron Lost at Sea! 73 Perish!," *Hearst Metrotone Newsreel*, 8 April 1933, FT Archive.
59. Reginald M. Cleveland, "Record of the Airship: Disasters and Victories," *New York Times*, 9 April 1933, sec. XX, 8; "The Akron Tragedy," *New York Times*, 5 April 1933, 18; Navy Press Room, Immediate Release, 24 June 1933, B22, E113, RG 80, NAB.
60. Robinson and Keller, *Up Ship!*, 186–92; "Macon's Loss Scraps U.S. Airship Plans," *Christian Science Monitor*, 13 February 1935, 1; "Capital Sees End of Airship Plans," *Washington Post*, 13 February 1935, 1; "The Macon Disaster," *Los Angeles Times*, 14 February 1935, sec. A, 4.
61. "Wings of Navy Dip in Salute at Sea," *New York Times*, 1 June 1934, 13; Address by Arthur B. Cook at Air Defense Day Program, Cleveland, Ohio, 2 September 1937, 1–3, B29, E113, RG 80, NAB.
62. *The Devil's Playground*, directed by Erle C. Kenton, Columbia Pictures, 1937; C. Young to Alfred Bolton, 25 September 1936, B425, E22, RG 80, NAB.
63. "The Screen," *New York Times*, 15 February 1937, 12.
64. "Submarine D-1," *Motion Picture Daily*, 11 November 1937, 3.
65. Jonas H. Ingram, "Why the Battleship?," *Scientific American*, August 1934, 82–84; Navy Press Room, Immediate Release, 8 February 1938, 1–2, B30, E113, RG 80, NAB; J. Lincke, "Airplanes Can't Sink Battleships," *Saturday Evening Post*, 10 April 1937, 12–13, 83–86.

Chapter 7. "The First Line of Defense"

1. All statements quoted from "What the Arms Parley Accomplished," *Literary Digest*, 18 February 1922, 7–10.
2. Edward L. Bernays, *Crystallizing Public Opinion* (New York: Boni and Liveright, 1923), 152. Hugh M. Rodman, "A Navy Day Address," 27 October 1922, B5, E113, RG 80, NAB.
3. Pratt was later ostracized by the naval officer corps for his contrarian viewpoints. See Gerald E. Wheeler, *Admiral William Veazie Pratt, U.S. Navy: A Sailor's Life* (Washington, D.C.: GPO, 1974), 185–86, 342, 355.
4. Navy Department, Released for Publication, 31 March 1922, 2, B4, E113, RG 80, NAB; Address Delivered by Luke McNamee to National Council for Reduction of Armament, 4 April 1922, 2, B4, E113, RG 80, NAB; Radio Talk by Capt. Luke McNamee, 8 November 1922, B157, EP 3, RG 428, NACP.
5. "Keep Our Navy Strong," Address Delivered by Capt. Luke McNamee to the Women's Republican Club of Massachusetts, 22 January 1923, 6, 14, B5, E113, RG 80, NAB.
6. Navy League Press Release, 27 November 1922, Item 31, Gardiner Papers, HL; Rappaport, *Navy League*, 89–90.
7. William Braisted, "On the American Red and Red-Orange Plans, 1919–1939," in *Naval Warfare in the Twentieth Century, 1900–1945: Essays in Honour of Arthur Marder*, ed. Gerald Jordan (New York: Crane Russak, 1977), 167–82; Thomas Wildenberg, *All the Factors of Victory: Admiral Joseph Mason Reeves and the Origins of Carrier Air Power* (New York: Brassey's, 2003), 110–15; Felker, *Testing American Sea Power*, 114.
8. Gerald E. Wheeler, *Prelude to Pearl Harbor* (Columbia: University of Missouri Press, 1963), 31–35.
9. "A Stupid Outburst," *Baltimore Sun*, 16 November 1924, 10; "Japanese Paper Sees War Threat in U.S. Maneuvers," *Baltimore Sun*, 15 November 1924, 1; Wheeler, *Prelude to Pearl Harbor*, 36–37.
10. "Plane and Subsea Craft Fail to Save Hawaii from 'Foe,'" *Washington Post*, 28 April 1925, 1; "The American Fleet," *Sydney Morning Herald*, 26 June 1925, 8; "Sydney Welcomes the U.S.A.," *Sydney Morning Herald*, 24 July 1925, 12; "Link of Friendship," *Sydney Morning Herald*, 7 August 1925, 8; "Warm Thanks," *Sydney Morning Herald*, 7 August 1925, 9.
11. Navy Day poster, B24, E22, RG 24, NAB.
12. Hector C. Bywater, "Japan: A Sequel to the Washington Conference," *Atlantic Monthly*, February 1923, 240–49; Hector C. Bywater, "America Not to Blame If Treaty Fails," *Baltimore Sun*, 25 March 1923, 8. Bywater had taken the position during the crisis over the exercises that Japan had nothing to fear from the American plans. See Hector C. Bywater, "Tokio Criticism of Maneuvers by U.S. Navy Held Unjustified," *Baltimore Sun*, 16 November 1924, 1; Bywater to Ferris Greenlet, 1–3, 28 August 1924, B6, William H. Honan Papers, NWCL.
13. Bywater, *Great Pacific War*, 1–304. In his biography of Hector Bywater, Honan argues that Bywater's book convinced American war planners to alter the details of War Plan Orange. See Honan, *Visions of Infamy*, 196–97, 268–69.

14. Dudley W. Knox, "Capt. Knox Reviews 'Great Pacific War,'" *Baltimore Sun*, 21 September 1925, 7; Nicholas Roosevelt, "If War Comes in the Pacific," *New York Times*, 13 September 1925, sec. BR, 5; "Calling Our Next Unpleasantness," *Chicago Tribune*, 18 August 1925, 8; *Los Angeles Times*, "Trouble Breeders," 21 September 1925, sec. A, 4.
15. Navy News Bureau, Immediate Release, 4 March 1922, 1, B4, E113, RG 80, NAB; Address by Rear Adm. David Potter, Atlantic City, N.J., 6 May 1922, 5, B4, E113, RG 80, NAB; Statement by Edwin Denby before the House Naval Affairs Committee, 13 February 1922, 5–7, B4, E113, RG 80, NAB. The navy continued to list several ships, including the USS *Rochester* (ex–*New York*, ex-*Saratoga*), dating to the 1880s and the early years of the "new" steel navy on the active list. The *Rochester* itself would remain on active duty until its decommissioning in 1933.
16. "Denby Resigns as Navy Head; Retires March 10," *Baltimore Sun*, 19 February 1924, 1; Layton McCartney, *The Teapot Dome Scandal: How Big Oil Bought the Harding White House and Tried to Steal the Country* (New York: Random House, 2009), 83–84, 173, 215; "Insists Oil Reserves Are Being Drained," *New York Times*, 5 May 1922, 33; *San Francisco Examiner*, 4 February 1924, clipping in B114, EP 3, RG 428, NACP; Navy Department, Memo for the Press, 18 February 1924, 1–3, B6, E113, NAB.
17. Navy News Bureau, Immediate Release, 3 September 1920, B2, E113, RG 80, NAB; Navy Department, Immediate Release, 28 June 1927, B10, E113, RG 80, NAB.
18. BuNav, Morale Division, "Bulletin No. 2," 16 February 1922, B1, Knox Papers, LOC; Knox to Lt. Cdr. Emmet, 29 September 1922, B1, Knox Papers, LOC.
19. McNamee to J. G. Harbord, 25 September 1928, B254, E22, RG 80, NAB; "Skeleton Form for Use of Navy Day Speakers," October 1926, B2, Knox Papers, LOC.
20. Film 24.24, *Our Navy in the Near East* (1923), Records of the Navy Recruiting Bureau, RG 24, NACP; Navy Department, Memo for the Press, 4 September 1923, 1–3, B5, E113, RG 80, NAB. Among other effects, the earthquake irreparably damaged the Japanese battlecruiser *Amagi* as it lay in drydock, which prevented its conversion to an aircraft carrier. See Robert Gardiner, Randal Gray, and Przemyslaw Budzbon, *Conway's All the World's Fighting Ships, 1906–1921* (Annapolis, Md.: Naval Institute Press, 1985), 232; "Gives Charts to Japan," *New York Times*, 11 November 1923, sec. E, 14.
21. "Airplane Relief Work," *Washington Post*, 6 May 1927, 6; "H. M. Baker Dictator," *New York Times*, 24 April 1927, 1; "Flying 48 Planes for Flood Relief," *New York Times*, 5 May 1927, 2; John M. Barry, *Rising Tide: The Great Mississippi Flood of 1927 and How It Changed America* (New York: Simon & Schuster, 1998), 173–201.
22. Navy Department, Memo for the Press, 26 December 1923, B41, EP 3, RG 428, NACP.
23. "First News of Byrd's Great Feat as It Reached the 'New York Times,'" *New York Times*, 10 May 1926, 1; "Nation's Leaders Laud Byrd's Feat," *New York Times*, 10 May 1926, 3. Byrd later wrote a full-length account of the North Pole expedition entitled *Skyward* (New York: Putnam and Sons, 1928).
24. Edwin L. James, "Byrd Hurled through Window into Water," *New York Times*, 2 July 1927, 1; "All Paris Gives Byrd a Rousing Welcome; Acosta Found to Be Hurt, Chief Must Rest; Commander Writes of Perils of the Trip," *New York Times*, 3 July 1927, 1; P. J. Phillip, "Paris Receives Byrd as It Did Lindbergh," *New York Times*, 3 July 1927, 1.

25. "Air Officials Applaud Byrd," *Los Angeles Times*, 30 November 1929, 2; "Byrd Will Sound Ice in Antarctic," *New York Times*, 10 June 1928, 131; "Navy Sends Data to Guide Byrd," *New York Times*, 18 December 1928, 15; "Cmdr. Byrd Told Navy's Airship Will Aid Him," *Washington Post*, 27 October 1929, sec. M, 1; Russell Owen, "Start Is Made at 10:29 P.M. New York Time," *New York Times*, 29 November 1929, 1; "Naval Figures Told Byrd When He Was at Pole," *Christian Science Monitor*, 30 November 1929, 2; "Hoover's Pen Makes Byrd Rear Admiral for Polar Exploits," *New York Times*, 22 December 1929, 1.
26. Navy Department, Immediate Release, 4 February 1926, B9, E113, RG 80, NAB.
27. Address by Curtis Wilbur at Boston Navy Yard, 16 June 1927, 1, B11, E113, RG 80, NAB; Address by Ernest Lee Jahncke at the Ceremonies of Commissioning the United States Frigate *Constitution*, Boston Navy Yard, 1 July 1931, 1, B18, E113, RG 80, NAB; Navy Press Room, For Release after Delivery, 27 October 1931, 2, B19, E113, RG 80, NAB.
28. "A 'Trumpet Blast' to Halt Ruinous Naval Rivalry," *Literary Digest*, 26 February 1927, 7.
29. Archibald Hurd, "America's Increasing Armaments," *Des Moines Register*, 20 June 1927, 4.
30. William F. Trimble, "The United States Navy and the Geneva Conference for the Limitation of Naval Armament, 1927" (Ph.D. diss., University of Colorado, 1974), 3–6, 255–77, 386.
31. "What the Failure of the Naval Conference Means," *Literary Digest*, 20 August 1927, 8.
32. "The 'Big-Navy' Congressman Hears from Home," *Literary Digest*, 3 March 1928, 10.
33. President Coolidge himself remained critical of Britain for attacking American naval construction while pursuing its own building programs. See "Coolidge's 'Call Down' to Europe," *Literary Digest*, 1 December 1928, 8–10.
34. Holloway H. Frost, *We Build a Navy* (Annapolis, Md.: Naval Institute Press, 1929), vii, 411.
35. Wheeler, *Prelude to Pearl Harbor*, 164–76.
36. William Randolph Hearst, "The Senate Is the Treaty Making Power of the United States," in *Selections from the Writings and Speeches of William Randolph Hearst* (San Francisco: Private publisher, 1948), 198–200; "Navy Treaty Fight Stirs the Capital," *Hearst Metrotone News*, 16 July 1930, FT Archive; Address by Ernest Lee Jahncke over NBS radio, 28 July 1930, 1, B15, E113, RG 80, NAB; "What the London Pact Really Means," *Hearst Metrotone News*, 7 June 1930, FT Archive; Address by William A. Moffett, Akron, Ohio, 27 October 1930, 1–9, B16, E113, RG 80, NAB.
37. Navy Press Room, Immediate Release, 23 September 1930, 1, B16, E113, RG 80, NAB; Navy Press Room, Immediate Release, 19 August 1930, 1–7, B34, EP 3, RG 428, NACP; Wheeler, *Admiral William Veazie Pratt*, 313. Pratt, while serving as commander in chief of the U.S. Fleet, recommended such a plan to the CNO, Adm. Charles F. Hughes.
38. *The United States Navy in Peacetime: The Navy in Relation to the Industrial, Scientific, Economic, and Political Developments of the Nation* (Washington, D.C.: GPO, 1931), iii; Navy Press Room, Immediate Release, 31 March 1931, 1–2, B17, E113, RG 80, NAB;

Navy Press Room, Immediate Release, 4 April 1931, 1–2, B17, E113, RG 80, NAB; "Ships at Canal Rush to Nicaragua's Aid," *New York Times*, 1 April 1931, 2.
39. Charles A. Beard, *Navy: Defense or Portent?* (New York: Harper, 1932), 196.
40. Lt. Cdr. I. R. Allen to ComNine, 1 February 1932, B141, E81, RG 38, NAB.
41. DNI to Commandants, All Naval Districts, "Charles Beard's book,—'The Navy: Defense or Portent?,'" 4 March 1932, B10, E79, RG 38, NAB.
42. Knox to Editor, *Harper's Magazine*, 3 February 1932, B4, Knox Papers, LOC.
43. Address by William A. Moffett before American Legion, Macon, Ga., 23 June 1932, 1–7, B20, E113, RG 80, NAB; Photo NH 76793, 12 October 1933, Photographic Section, NHHC.
44. Navy Press Room, Immediate Release, 24 May 1933, 1–5, B22, E113, RG 80, NAB; Navy Press Room, Immediate Release, 13 June 1933, B22, E113, RG 80, NAB.
45. Address by Henry L. Roosevelt over NBC radio, 27 October 1934, 4, B25, E113, RG 80, NAB; James F. Cook, *Carl Vinson: Patriarch of the Armed Forces* (Macon, Ga.: Mercer University Press, 2004), 100–103; Address by Henry L. Roosevelt over NBC radio, 19 September 1934, 1–11, B25, E113, RG 80, NAB.
46. "Always Alert," 26 October 1933, Navy Art Gallery.
47. Paul A. C. Koistinen, *Planning War, Pursuing Peace: The Political Economy of American Warfare, 1920–1939* (Lawrence: University Press of Kansas, 1998), 253–65.
48. Koppes and Black, *Hollywood Goes to War*, 21–22.
49. Suid, *Sailing on the Silver Screen*, 38; *Submarine*, directed by Frank Capra, Columbia, 1928; "Submarine D-1, Final Script," 11 June 1937, Box Submarine D-1, WB Archive; *The Flying Fleet*, directed by George W. Hill, Metro-Goldwyn-Mayer, 1929; *Son of a Sailor*, directed by Lloyd Bacon, Warner Brothers Pictures, 1933; *Hell Divers*, directed by George W. Hill, Metro-Goldwyn-Mayer, 1931.
50. "Our Fleet Is Ready for Far East Call," *New York Times*, 30 January 1932, 2; Armin Rappaport, *Henry L. Stimson and Japan, 1931–1933* (Chicago: University of Chicago Press, 1963) 119–20.
51. "Navy to Hold 1935 War Game in Alaska Area," *Baltimore Sun*, 20 September 1934, 1; Elliott Thurston, "U.S. Decides on War Show by Fleet Off Pacific Coast," *Washington Post*, 20 September 1934, 1; "U.S. Churchmen in Japan Protest Navy Maneuvers," *Chicago Tribune*, 21 April 1935, 19; "Japan's Protest on U.S. Fleet Is Held Baseless," *Chicago Tribune*, 17 May 1935, 14.
52. "Gloomy Prospects for Naval Conference," *Literary Digest*, 2 November 1935, 9; "Sea Power and Parity around the Table," *Literary Digest*, 23 November 1935, 13–14.
53. "Sea Power—Bulwark of Peace," *Literary Digest*, 26 October 1935, 26.
54. "Bigger and Better 'Battle-Wagons,'" *Literary Digest*, 15 February 1936, 14.
55. "Your Navy of Today," Address by Rear Adm. Charles Russell Train, Cleveland, Ohio, 27 October 1936, 1–16, B27, E113, RG 80, NAB.
56. Dudley W. Knox, *A History of the United States Navy* (New York: G. P. Putnam and Sons, 1936), ix; "'History of Navy' Held Worth While in a Mad World," review of *A History of the United States Navy*, by Dudley W. Knox, *Chicago Tribune*, 17 October 1936, 17; Hanson Baldwin, "The Fighting Ships Pass in Review," review of *A History of*

the United States Navy, by Dudley W. Knox, *New York Times*, 20 September 1936, sec. BR, 5.
57. Statement by Worthington, n.d., B34, EP 3, RG 428, NACP; Robinson and Keller, *Up Ship!*, 151; Navy Press Room, Immediate Release, 3 July 1937, B34, EP 3, NACP; Navy Press Room, Immediate Release, 6 July 1937, B34, EP 3, RG 428, NACP; "63 Planes Poised for Earhart Hunt," *New York Times*, 13 July 1937, 12; "Navy to Stop Hunt for Miss Earhart," *New York Times*, 18 July 1937, 12.
58. "Navy to Stop Hunt for Miss Earhart," *New York Times*, 18 July 1937, 12; "President Defends Hunt for Earhart," *New York Times*, 21 July 1937, 23.
59. Address by Arthur B. Cook at Air Defense Day Program, Cleveland, Ohio, 2 September 1937, 1, B29, E113, RG 80, NAB; "Our Navy," Address of Hugh Rodman to Combined Service Clubs, Terre Haute, Ind., 27 October 1937, 4, B29, E113, RG 80, NAB; William Randolph Hearst, "The Japanese Menace," in *Writings and Speeches*, 282–83; Navy Press Room, Immediate Release, 7 February 1938, 1, B30, E113, RG 80, NAB; Address of William D. Leahy to the Society of Sponsors of the American Navy, Washington, D.C., 24 February 1938, 2, B30, E113, RG 80, NAB; Address by Rear Adm. A. F. Fairfield over WOL radio, 27 October 1938, 1, B31, E113, RG 80, NAB; Address by William D. Leahy at Army and Navy Dinner, Worcester, Mass., 29 March 1939, 6, B32, E113, RG 80, NAB.
60. William D. Puleston, *Mahan: The Life and Work of Captain Alfred Thayer Mahan* (New Haven, Conn.: Yale University Press, 1939), 93–136; Harold Sprout and Margaret Sprout, *The Rise of American Naval Power, 1776–1918* (Princeton, N.J.: Princeton University Press, 1939); Harold Sprout to Rear Adm. R. S. Holmes (DNI), 28 September 1937, B149, E81, RG 38, NAB.
61. Dudley W. Knox, review of *The Rise of American Naval Power, 1776–1918*, by Harold Sprout and Margaret Sprout, *Journal of the American Military Institute* 3 (Summer 1939): 122–23; Hanson Baldwin, "Captain Mahan, Spokesman of Sea Power," review of *Mahan: The Life and Work of Captain Alfred Thayer Mahan*, by William D. Puleston, *New York Times*, 30 April 1939, 110; Hanson Baldwin, "America as a Great Sea Power," review of *The Rise of American Naval Power, 1776–1918*, by Harold Sprout and Margaret Sprout, *New York Times*, 4 June 1939, sec. BR, 1.

Conclusion

1. Memorandum for the CNO from Leland Lovette, "Fleet Review and New York Visit; Suggestions for Press Arrangements," 5 April 1939; Report of the Meeting of the Public Relations Committee, ca. April 1939, 4–5; and poster from InterBorough Rapid Transit Company, April 1939—all in B99, EP 3, RG 428, NACP.
2. "Fleet for Fair Reduced," *New York Times*, 22 March 1939, 25; "Navy Aim Mystery," *New York Times*, 16 April 1939, 1; "Recall Navy Men to 3 Ships Here," *New York Times*, 16 April 1939, 36.
3. Sadao Asada, *From Mahan to Pearl Harbor: The Imperial Japanese Navy and the United States* (Annapolis, Md.: Naval Institute Press, 2006), 210; Naval Liaison Officer–New York World's Fair 1939, to CNO, "Report on US Naval Participation at New York World's Fair 1939," ca. May 1940, 1–14, B99, EP 3, RG 428, NACP.

4. Austin, *Reminiscences of Vice Admiral Austin*, 60–62; Office of Naval Intelligence, *Naval Intelligence Manual*, 174, 18 April 1936, B2, EUD 83A, RG 38, NAB; Scovel, "Helm's a Lee," 124; Navy Department, Immediate Release, 23 May 1939; Navy Department, Immediate Release, 24 May 1939, 1–3; Navy Department, Immediate Release, 24 May 1939, NAB; Navy Department, Immediate Release, 24 May 1939; Navy Department, Immediate Release, 25 May 1939; Navy Department, Immediate Release, 25 May 1939—all in B33, E113, RG 80, NAB; Carl LaVO, *Back from the Deep: The Strange Story of the Sister Subs Squalus and Sculpin* (Annapolis, Md.: Naval Institute Press, 1994), 51–52; "Naval Officials Commended for Aid to Newsmen," *Christian Science Monitor*, 26 May 1939, 10; "Squalus on Bottom Again in Dramatic Salvage Disaster," *Universal Newsreel*, 14 July 1939, Universal Newsreel Catalog, RG 200 UN, NACP.
5. "Naval Officials Commended for Aid to Newsmen," *Christian Science Monitor*, 26 May 1939, 10.
6. "U.S. Navy Helps Newsmen Meet Their Deadlines," *Atlanta Journal-Constitution*, 4 June 1939, 8A.
7. James L. McCamy, *Government Publicity: Its Practice in Federal Administration* (Chicago: University of Chicago Press, 1939), 63, 75; Mordecai Lee, "Herman Beyle and James McCamy: Founders of the Study of Public Relations in Public Administration, 1928–1939," *Public Voices* 11, no. 2 (2010): 26–46.
8. McCamy, *Government Publicity*, 159, 172–87, 190.
9. Kirk Hallahan et al., "Defining Strategic Communication," *International Journal of Strategic Communication* 1, no. 1 (March 2007): 3–35.
10. Klinkerman, "Blackout at Pearl Harbor," 25–28.
11. Ibid., 24.
12. Photo NH 77222, Photographic Section, NHHC.
13. Photo NH 77227, Photographic Section, NHHC.
14. Robert Lord to McCord, 28 July 1941, Box Dive Bomber 1 of 1, WB Archive; Budget, 18 March 1941, Box Dive Bomber 1 of 1, WB Archive.
15. Colin Shindler, *Hollywood Goes to War: Films and American Society, 1939–1952* (New York: Routledge, 1979), 27; Suid, *Sailing on the Silver Screen*, 54–55.
16. Rappaport, *Navy League*, 177–79.
17. Douglas, "Public Relations, United States Navy," 1433.
18. Cutlip, Center, and Broom, *Effective Public Relations*, 238–39.
19. Edward L. Bernays, *Propaganda* (New York: Liveright, 1928), 28.
20. Cutlip, Center, and Broom, *Effective Public Relations*, 125.
21. *Annual Report of the Secretary of the Navy for the Fiscal Year 1926* (Washington, D.C.: GPO, 1927), 142; *Annual Report of the Secretary of the Navy for the Fiscal Year 1927* (Washington, D.C.: GPO, 1928), 134, 164; *Annual Report of the Secretary of the Navy for the Fiscal Year 1928* (Washington, D.C.: GPO, 1929), 146; *Annual Report of the Secretary of the Navy for the Fiscal Year 1930* (Washington, D.C.: GPO, 1931), 23; *Annual Report of the Secretary of the Navy for the Fiscal Year 1932* (Washington, D.C.: GPO, 1933), 22, 142.

22. "Budget of the U.S. Navy, 1794–2004," https://www.history.navy.mil/research/library/online-reading-room/title-list-alphabetically/b/budget-of-the-us-navy-1794-to-2004.html.
23. Hadley Cantril and Mildred Strunk, eds., *Public Opinion, 1935–1946* (Princeton, N.J.: Princeton University Press, 1951), 923, 939–41. Thanks to Dr. Lisa Mundey for identifying this source.
24. Suid, *Sailing on the Silver Screen*, 234; "Conversations with the Country," accessed 24 May 2010, http://www.navy.mil/maritime/display.asp?page=cwtc.html; Mark D. Faram, "The Hunt for the Next U.S. Navy Slogan Is On," *Navy Times*, 29 April 2016, https://www.navytimes.com/news/your-navy/2016/04/29/the-hunt-for-the-next-u-s-navy-slogan-is-on/.
25. Gerald Beskin, "Public Relations: The Fourth Dimension of Modern Naval Tactics," *Proceedings* 67, no. 9 (September 1941): 1296.

BIBLIOGRAPHY

Archival and Manuscript Sources

Hearst Metrotone News Collection. Film and Television Archive. University of California–Los Angeles.
Library of Congress. Washington, D.C.
    Papers of Dudley W. Knox
    Theodore Roosevelt Jr. Papers
Margaret Herrick Library. Los Angeles, Calif.
    Paramount Script Collection
    Production Code Authority Papers
National Archives Building. Washington, D.C.
    Record Group 24—Records of the Bureau of Naval Personnel
    Record Group 38—Records of the Office of Chief of Naval Operations
    Record Group 72—Records of the Bureau of Aeronautics
    Record Group 80—Records of the Navy Department, 1798–1947
National Archives. College Park, Md.
    Record Group 24—Records of the Bureau of Naval Personnel
    Record Group 200 UN—Universal Newsreel Catalog
    Record Group 428—Records of the Navy Department, 1947–
Naval History and Heritage Command. Washington Navy Yard. Washington, D.C.
    Officer Bio Files
    Papers of Admiral William V. Pratt
Naval War College Library. Newport, R.I.
    Walter Bruce Howe Papers
    William H. Honan Papers

Performing Arts Collections. University of California–Los Angeles.
Records and Papers of the Naval Order of the United States. Cushing Library. Texas A&M University. College Station.
Warner Brothers Archive. University of Southern California, Los Angeles.
William Howard Gardiner Papers. Houghton Library. Harvard University, Cambridge, Mass.
William Randolph Hearst Papers. Bancroft Library. University of California–Berkeley.

Microfilm

Congressional Record: Proceedings and Debates of the United States Congress. Washington, D.C.: GPO, 1874.

Newspapers

Atlanta Journal-Constitution
Baltimore Sun
Bismarck Tribune
Boston Globe
Chicago Tribune
Christian Science Monitor
Des Moines Register
Film Daily
Hartford Courant
Literary Digest
Los Angeles Times
Motion Picture Herald
New York Times
Norfolk New Journal and Guide
St. Louis Post-Dispatch
Sydney Morning Herald
Washington Post

Print and Online Sources

Annual Report of the Secretary of the Navy for the Fiscal Year 1926. Washington, D.C.: GPO, 1927.
Annual Report of the Secretary of the Navy for the Fiscal Year 1927. Washington, D.C.: GPO, 1928.
Annual Report of the Secretary of the Navy for the Fiscal Year 1928. Washington, D.C.: GPO, 1929.
Annual Report of the Secretary of the Navy for the Fiscal Year 1930. Washington, D.C.: GPO, 1931.
Annual Report of the Secretary of the Navy for the Fiscal Year 1932. Washington, D.C.: GPO, 1933.
Asada, Sadao. *From Mahan to Pearl Harbor: The Imperial Japanese Navy and the United States.* Annapolis, Md.: Naval Institute Press, 2006.
Austin, Bernard L. *The Reminiscences of Vice Admiral Bernard L. Austin, U.S. Navy, Retired.* Annapolis, Md.: Naval Institute Press, 1971.
Baer, George. *One Hundred Years of Sea Power: The United States Navy, 1890–1990.* Stanford, Calif.: Stanford University Press, 1994.
Baldwin, Hanson W. "Newspapers and the Navy." U.S. Naval Institute *Proceedings* 56, no. 12 (December 1930): 1085–90.

———. *The Reminiscences of Hanson Weight Baldwin, U.S. Navy Retired*. 2 vols. Annapolis, Md.: Naval Institute Press, 1976.

Balio, Tino, ed. *The American Film Industry*. Rev. ed. Madison: University of Wisconsin Press, 1985.

Barry, John M. *Rising Tide: The Great Mississippi Flood of 1927 and How It Changed America*. New York: Simon and Schuster, 1998.

Beard, Charles A. *The Navy: Defense or Portent?* New York: Harper, 1932.

Beigel, Harvey M. "'Spig' Wead: Naval Aviator and Screenwriter." *American Aviation Historical Society Journal* (Winter 1997): 302–9.

Berliner, Don. *Airplane Racing: A History, 1909–2008*. Jefferson, N.C.: McFarland, 2010.

Bernays, Edward L. *Crystallizing Public Opinion*. New York: Boni and Liveright, 1923.

———. *Propaganda*. New York: Liveright, 1928.

Beskin, Gerald. "Public Relations: The Fourth Dimension of Modern Naval Tactics." U.S. Naval Institute *Proceedings* 67, no. 9 (September 1941): 1296–98.

Biddle, Tami Davis. *Rhetoric and Reality in Air Warfare: The Evolution of American and British Ideas about Strategic Bombing, 1914–1945*. Princeton, N.J.: Princeton University Press, 2002.

Blackburn, C. K. "Mistaken Publicity." U.S. Naval Institute *Proceedings* 48, no. 1 (January 1922): 77–79.

Blackman, Ann. "Fatal Cruise of the USS *Princeton*." *Naval History* 19, no. 5 (October 2005): 37–41.

Blackwell, Joyce. *No Peace Without Freedom: Race and the Women's International League for Peace and Freedom, 1915–1975*. Carbondale: Southern Illinois University Press, 2004.

Bonker, Dirk. *Militarism in a Global Age: Naval Ambitions in Germany and the United States before World War I*. Ithaca, N.Y.: Cornell University Press, 2012.

Bowser, Eileen. *The Transformation of Cinema, 1907–1915*. Berkeley: University of California Press, 1994.

Bradford, James C., ed. *Admirals of the New Steel Navy*. Annapolis, Md.: Naval Institute Press, 1990.

———. *Quarterdeck and Bridge: Two Centuries of American Naval Leaders*. Annapolis, Md.: Naval Institute Press, 1997.

Brandt, Allan M. *No Magic Bullet: A Social History of Venereal Disease in the United States since 1880*. New York: Oxford University Press, 1987.

Brooks, Rosa. "Confessions of a Strategic Communicator." *Foreign Policy*, 6 December 2012. http://foreignpolicy.com/2012/12/06/confessions-of-a-strategic-communicator/. Accessed 8 April 2018.

"Budget of the U.S. Navy, 1794–2004." https://www.history.navy.mil/research/library/online-reading-room/title-list-alphabetically/b/budget-of-the-us-navy-1794-to-2004.html.

Buell, Thomas B. *Master of Sea Power: A Biography of Fleet Admiral Ernest J. King*. Boston: Little, Brown, 1980.

Bureau of Labor Statistics. "Labor Force, Employment, and Unemployment, 1929–1939: Estimating Methods." *Monthly Labor Review* (July 1948): 51–52.

Byrd, Richard Evelyn. *Skyward*. New York: Putnam and Sons, 1928.

Bywater, Hector C. *The Great Pacific War: A History of the American-Japanese Campaign of 1931–1933*. London: Constable and Co., 1925.

———. "Japan: A Sequel to the Washington Conference." *Atlantic Monthly* 131 (February 1923): 240–49.

———. *Navies and Nations*. New York: Houghton Mifflin, 1927.

———. *Sea-Power in the Pacific: A Study of the American-Japanese Naval Problem*. New York: Houghton Mifflin, 1921.

Cameron, Glen T., and Dennis L. Wilcox. *Public Relations: Strategies and Tactics*. 9th ed. Boston: Person, Allyn, and Bacon, 2009.

Cantril, Hadley, and Mildred Strunk, eds. *Public Opinion, 1935–1946*. Princeton, N.J.: Princeton University Press, 1951.

Chambers, John Whiteclay, II, ed. *The Eagle and the Dove: The American Peace Movement and United States Foreign Policy, 1900–1922*. New York: Garland, 1976.

Coletta, Paolo E. *Admiral Bradley Fiske and the American Navy*. Lawrence: Regents Press of Kansas, 1979.

"Comfort, Courtesy, Safety, and Speed." *Smithsonian Institute*. http://americanhistory.si.edu/onthewater/exhibition/5_3.html. Accessed 20 November 2017.

Connell, R. W. *Masculinities*. Berkeley: University of California Press, 1995.

"Conversations with the Country." http://www.navy.mil/maritime/display.asp?page=cwtc.html. Accessed 24 May 2010.

Cook, James F. *Carl Vinson: Patriarch of the Armed Forces*. Macon, Ga.: Mercer University Press, 2004.

Cooke, James J. *Billy Mitchell*. Boulder, Colo.: Lynne Rienner Publishers, 2002.

Cox, Jim. *American Radio Networks: A History*. Jefferson, N.C.: McFarland, 2009.

Cronon, E. David, ed. *The Cabinet Diaries of Josephus Daniels, 1913–1921*. Lincoln: University of Nebraska Press, 1963.

Cutlip, Scott M. *Public Relations History: From the 17th to the 20th Century. The Antecedents*. Hillsdale, N.J.: Lawrence Erlbaum Associates, 1995.

Cutlip, Scott M., Allen H. Center, and Glen M. Broom. *Effective Public Relations*, 8th ed. Upper Saddle River, N.J.: Prentice Hall, 2000.

Daniels, Josephus. *The Navy and the Nation: Wartime Addresses*. New York: George H. Doran Company, 1919.

———. "Training Men for the Navy and the Nation." *Saturday Evening Post* (9 April 1921), 21–24, 78–83.

Davidson, Halsey. *Navy Boys after the Submarines; or, Protecting the Giant Convoy*. New York: G. Sully, 1918.

———. *Navy Boys at the Big Surrender; or, Rounding Up the German Fleet*. New York: G. Sully, 1919.

———. *Navy Boys behind the Big Guns; or, Sinking the German U-Boats*. New York: G. Sully, 1918.

———. *Navy Boys on Special Service; or, Guarding the Floating Treasury*. New York: G. Sully, 1920.

Davis, Calvin DeArmond. *The United States and the Second Hague Peace Conference: American Diplomacy and International Organization, 1899–1914*. Durham, N.C.: Duke University Press, 1975.

Davis, Vincent. *The Admirals Lobby*. Chapel Hill: University of North Carolina Press, 1967.

———. *Postwar Defense Policy and the U.S. Navy, 1943–1946*. Chapel Hill: University of North Carolina Press, 1962.

Dictionary of American Naval Fighting Ships. https://www.history.navy.mil/research/histories/ship-histories/danfs.html.

Directorate of Information Operations and Reports. *Department of Defense: Selected Manpower Statistics—Fiscal Year 1997*. Washington: Government Printing Office, 1997.

Dorwart, Jeffrey M. *Conflict of Duty: The U.S. Navy's Intelligence Dilemma, 1919–1945*. Annapolis, Md.: Naval Institute Press, 1983.

Douglas, Henry H. "Public Relations, United States Navy." U.S. Naval Institute *Proceedings* 67, no. 10 (October 1941): 1432–37.

Dubbert, Joe L. *A Man's Place: Masculinity in Transition*. Englewood Cliffs, N.J.: Prentice-Hall, 1979.

Duberman, Martin Baum, Martha Vicinus, and George Chauncey Jr., eds. *Hidden from History: Reclaiming the Gay and Lesbian Past*. Markham, Ont.: New American Library Books, 1989.

Dudink, Stefan, Karen Hagerman, and John Tosh, eds. *Masculinities in Politics and War: Gendering Modern History*. New York: Manchester University Press, 2000.

Dyess, Jimmy Wayne "A History of the United States Navy Band, Washington, D.C." Ph.D. diss, University of Houston, 1988.

Ellsberg, Edward. *On the Bottom*. New York: Dodd, Mead and Co., 1928.

Fanning, Richard. *Peace and Disarmament: Naval Rivalry and Arms Control, 1922–1933*. Lexington: University Press of Kentucky, 2015.

Faram, Mark D. "The Hunt for the Next U.S. Navy Slogan Is On." *Navy Times*, 29 April 2016. https://www.navytimes.com/news/your-navy/2016/04/29/the-hunt-for-the-next-u-s-navy-slogan-is-on/. Accessed 10 November 2017.

Felker, Craig C. *Testing American Sea Power: U.S. Navy Strategic Exercises, 1923–1940*. College Station: Texas A&M University Press, 2007.

Field, Syd. *Screenplay: The Foundations of Screenwriting*. Rev. ed. New York: Delta Trade Paperbacks, 2005.

———. *United States Submarines to 1945: An Illustrated Design History*. Annapolis, Md.: Naval Institute Press, 1995.

Fielding, Raymond. *The American Newsreel: A Complete History, 1911–1967*. Norman: University of Oklahoma Press, 1972.

Friedman, Norman. *U.S. Submarines through 1945: An Illustrated Design History*. Annapolis, Md.: Naval Institute Press, 1995.

Friedman, Norman, Thomas Hone, and Mark D. Mandeles. *American and British Aircraft Carrier Development, 1919–1941*. Annapolis, Md.: Naval Institute Press, 1999.

Frost, Holloway H. *We Build a Navy*. Annapolis, Md.: U.S. Naval Institute, 1929.

Fry, John. *USS Saratoga CV-3: An Illustrated History of the Legendary Aircraft Carrier, 1927–1946*. Atglen, Pa.: Schiffer Publishing, 1996.

Gabler, Neal. *Life the Movie: How Entertainment Conquered Reality*. New York: Vintage Books, 1998.

Gardiner, Robert, Randal Gray, and Przemyslaw Budzbon. *Conway's All the World's Fighting Ships, 1906–1921*. Annapolis, Md.: Naval Institute Press, 1985.

Gilfoyle, Timothy J. *City of Eros: New York City, Prostitution, and the Commercialization of Sex, 1790–1920*. New York: W. W. Norton & Company, 1994.

Gomery, Douglas. *The Hollywood Studio System: A History*. London: British Film Institute, 2005.

Hagan, Kenneth J., ed. *In Peace and War: Interpretations of American Naval History, 1775–1978*. Westport, Conn.: Greenwood Press, 1984.

Hallahan, Kirk, Derina Holtzhausen, Betteke van Ruler, Dejan Verčič, and Krishnamurthy Sriramesh. "Defining Strategic Communication." *International Journal of Strategic Communication* 1, no. 1 (March 2007): 3–35.

Hancock, H. Irving. *Dave Darrin and the German Submarines; or, Making a Clean-Up of the Hun Sea Monsters*. Philadelphia: Altemus, 1919.

———. *Dave Darrin's First Year at Annapolis; or, Two Plebe Midshipmen at the United States Naval Academy*. Philadelphia: Altemus, 1910.

———. *Dave Darrin's South American Cruise; or, Two Innocent Young Naval Tools of an Infamous Conspiracy*. Philadelphia: Altemus, 1919.

Harrod, Frederick. *Manning the New Navy: The Development of Modern Naval Enlisted Force, 1899–1940*. Westport, Conn.: Greenwood Press, 1978.

Hendrix, Henry J. *Theodore Roosevelt's Naval Diplomacy: The U.S. Navy and the Birth of the American Century*. Annapolis, Md.: Naval Institute Press, 2009.

Henning, Arthur Sears. *Government by Propaganda*. Chicago: Chicago Tribune Public Service Office, 1927.

Hill, Herbert F. "The Navy League, Past, Present, and Future." *Sea Power* 5, no. 6 (December 1918): 365–66.

Hoag, Lawrence C. *Preface to Preparedness: The Washington Disarmament Conference and Public Opinion*. Washington, D.C.: American Council on Public Affairs, 1941.

Holwitt, Joel Ira. *"Execute against Japan": The U.S. Decision to Conduct Unrestricted Submarine Warfare*. College Station: Texas A&M University Press, 2009.

Honan, William C. *Visions of Infamy: The Untold Story of How Journalist Hector C. Bywater Devised the Plans That Led to Pearl Harbor*. New York: St. Martin's, 1991.

Hoover, Herbert. *American Individualism*. Garden City, N.Y.: Doubleday, Page, and Company, 1922.

Ingram, Jonas H. "Why the Battleship?," *Scientific American* (August 1934): 82–84.

Jiobu, Robert M. *Ethnicity and Assimilation: Blacks, Chinese, Filipinos, Japanese, Koreans, Mexicans, Vietnamese, and Whites*. New York: SUNY Press, 1991.

Johnson, Deidre. *Edward Stratemeyer and the Stratemeyer Syndicate*. New York: Twayne Publishers, 1993.

Jones, Jerry W. *U.S. Battleship Operations during World War I*. Annapolis, Md.: Naval Institute Press, 1998.

Jordan, Gerald, ed. *Naval Warfare in the Twentieth Century, 1900–1945: Essays in Honour of Arthur Marder*. New York: Crane Russak, 1977.
Jowett, Garth, and James M. Linton. *Movies as Mass Communication*. 2nd ed. New York: Sage, 1989.
Karsten, Peter. *The Naval Aristocracy: The Golden Age of Annapolis and the Emergence of Modern American Navalism*. New York: Free Press, 1972.
Kimmel, Michael S. *Manhood in America: A Cultural History*. 2nd. Ed. New York: Oxford University Press, 2006.
Klinkerman, R. Dale. "From Blackout at Pearl Harbor to Spotlight on Tokyo Bay: A Study of the Evolution in U.S. Naval Public Relations Policies and Practices During World War II." Master's thesis, University of Wisconsin–Madison, 1972.
Knox, Dudley. *The Eclipse of American Sea Power*. New York: Army and Navy Journal, Inc., 1923.
———. *A History of the United States Navy*. New York: G. P. Putnam and Sons, 1936.
———. "The Navy and Public Indoctrination." U.S. Naval Institute *Proceedings* 55, no. 6 (June 1929): 479–90.
———. "Our Post-War Mission." U.S. Naval Institute *Proceedings* 45, no. 8 (August 1919): 1294–1302.
———. "Our Vanishing History and Traditions." U.S. Naval Institute *Proceedings* 52, no. 1 (January 1926): 15–25.
———. Review of *The Rise of American Naval Power, 1776–1918*, by Harold Sprout and Margaret Sprout. *Journal of the American Military Institute* 3 (Summer 1939): 122–23.
Koistinen, Paul A. C. *Planning War, Pursuing Peace: The Political Economy of American Warfare, 1920–1939*. Lawrence: University Press of Kansas, 1998.
Koppes, Clayton R., and Gregory D. Black. *Hollywood Goes to War: How Politics, Profits, and Propaganda Shaped World War II Movies*. New York: Macmillan, 1987.
Kuehn, John T. *Agents of Innovation: The General Board and the Design of the Fleet that Defeated the Japanese Navy*. Annapolis, Md.: Naval Institute Press, 2008.
LaVO, Carl. *Back from the Deep: The Strange Story of the Sister Subs Squalus and Sculpin*. Annapolis, Md.: Naval Institute Press, 1994.
Lee, Mordecai. *Congress vs. The Bureaucracy: Muzzling Agency Public Relations*. Norman: University of Oklahoma Press, 2011.
———. "Herman Beyle and James McCamy: Founders of the Study of Public Relations in Public Administration, 1928–1939." *Public Voices* 11, no. 2 (2010): 26–46.
Lincke, J. "Airplanes Can't Sink Battleships." *Saturday Evening Post* (10 April 1937): 12–13, 83–86.
Livezey, William E. *Mahan on Sea Power*. Rev. ed. Norman: University of Oklahoma Press, 1986.
Lockwood, Charles, and Hans Christian Adamson. *Tragedy at Honda: One of America's Greatest Naval Disasters*. Philadelphia: Chilton, 1960.
Lovette, Leland Pearson. *Naval Customs, Traditions, and Usage*. Annapolis: Naval Institute Press, 1933.
Lowry, E. G. "Three-Plane Navy." *Saturday Evening Post* (11 June 1921): 16–17, 72–78.

MacKaye, M. "Modern Bluejacket, No Longer Recruited from the Nation's Riffraff." *Outlook and Independent* (31 July 1929): 532–33.
MacPhail, Elizabeth C. "When the Red Lights Went Out in San Diego: The Little Known Story of San Diego's 'Restricted District.'" *Journal of San Diego History* 20, no. 2 (Spring 1974). https://sandiegohistory.org/journal/1974/april/stingaree/.
Magruder, Thomas P. "The Navy and Economy." *Saturday Evening Post* (24 September 1927): 6–7.
Marshall (Venable), Heather Pace. "'It Means Something These Days to be a Marine': Image, Identity, and Mission in the Marine Corps, 1861–1918." Ph.D. diss., Duke University, 2010.
———. "'There's Nothing a Marine Can't Do': Publicity and the Marine Corps, 1911–1917." Paper presented at the 2009 Naval History Symposium, Annapolis, Md., 10 September 2009.
Martinek, Frank. *Don Winslow Saves the Secret Formula*. New York: Grosset and Dunlap, 1941.
———. *Don Winslow, U.S.N., in Ceylon with Kwang, Celebrated Chinese Detective*. Chicago: Rosenow, 1934.
Mason, Theodore C. *Battleship Sailor*. Annapolis, Md.: Naval Institute Press, 1982.
Matt, Paul R., and Bruce Robertson. *United States Navy and Marine Corps Fighters, 1918–1962*. Fallbrook, Calif.: Aero Publishers, 1962.
McBride, Joseph. *Searching for John Ford: A Life*. New York: St. Martin's Press, 2001.
McCamy, James. L. *Government Publicity: Its Practice in Federal Administration*. Chicago: University of Chicago Press, 1939
McCartney, Layton. *The Teapot Dome Scandal: How Big Oil Bought the Harding White House and Tried to Steal the Country*. New York: Random House, 2009.
McElroy, J. W. *Office of Naval Records and Library, 1882–1946*. Washington, D.C.: Navy Department, 1946.
McKercher, B. J. C., ed. *Anglo-American Relations in the 1920s: The Struggle for Supremacy*. Edmonton, Canada: University of Alberta Press, 1990.
Melhorn, Charles. *Two-Block Fox: The Rise of the Aircraft Carrier, 1911–1929*. Annapolis, Md.: Naval Institute Press, 1974.
Meyer, William R. *Warner Brothers Directors: The Hard-Boiled, the Comic, and the Weepers* New Rochelle, N.Y.: Arlington House Publishers, 1978.
Miller, Edward S. *War Plan Orange: The U.S. Strategy to Defeat Japan, 1897–1945*. Annapolis, Md.: Naval Institute Press, 1991.
Millett, Allan R., and Peter Maslowski. *For the Common Defense: A Military History of the United States of America*. 2nd ed. New York: Free Press, 1994.
Mitchell, William. *Our Air Force: The Keystone to National Defense*. New York: E.P. Dutton and Company, 1921.
Morgan, Ted. *FDR: A Biography*. New York: Simon & Schuster, 1985.
Morison, Elting. *Admiral Sims and the Modern American Navy*. Boston: Houghton Mifflin, 1942.
Morse, Sherman. "An Awakening in Wall Street." *The American Magazine* 62 (September 1906): 457–63.

Mugridge, Ian. *The View from Xanadu: William Randolph Hearst and United States Foreign Policy*. Buffalo, N.Y.: McGill-Queen's University Press, 1995.

Murphy, Lawrence R. *Perverts by Official Order: The Campaign against Homosexuals by the United States Navy*. New York: The Haworth Press, 1988.

Nasaw, David. *The Chief: The Life of William Randolph Hearst*. New York: Houghton Mifflin, 2000.

O'Brien, Phillips Payson. *British and American Naval Power: Politics and Policy, 1900–1936*. Westport, Conn.: Praeger, 1998.

O'Connell, Robert. *Sacred Vessels: The Cult of the Battleship and the Rise of the U.S. Navy*. Boulder, Colo.: Westview Press, 1991.

Paris, Michael. *From the Wright Brothers to Top Gun: Aviation, Nationalism, and the Popular Cinema*. Manchester: Manchester University Press, 1995.

Patchin, Frank Gee. *The Battleship Boys at Sea; or, Two Apprentices in Uncle Sam's Navy*. Philadelphia: Altemus, 1910.

Pedisich, Paul E. *Congress Buys a Navy: Politics, Economics, and the Rise of American Naval Power, 1881–1921*. Annapolis, Md.: Naval Institute Press, 2016.

Pizzitola, Louis. *Hearst over Hollywood: Power, Passion, and Propaganda in the Movies*. New York: Columbia University Press, 2002.

Puleston, William D. *Mahan: The Life and Work of Captain Mahan*. New Haven, Conn.: Yale University Press, 1939.

Rappaport, Armin. *Henry L. Stimson and Japan, 1931–1933*. Chicago: University of Chicago Press, 1963.

———. *The Navy League of the United States*. Detroit: Wayne State University Press, 1962.

Reynolds, Clark G. *Admiral John H. Towers: The Struggle for Naval Air Supremacy*. Annapolis, Md.: Naval Institute Press, 1991.

———. *The Fast Carriers: The Forging of an Air Navy*. New York: McGraw Hill, 1968.

Robinson, Douglas H., and Charles L. Keller. *Up Ship! A History of the U.S. Navy's Rigid Airships, 1919–1935*. Annapolis, Md.: Naval Institute Press, 1982.

Roddick, Nick. *A New Deal in Entertainment: Warner Brothers in the 1930s*. London: British Film Institute, 1983.

Rosen, Philip T. *The Modern Stentors: Radio Broadcasters and the Federal Government, 1920–1934*. Westport, Conn.: Greenwood Press, 1980.

Roskill, Stephen. *The Period of Anglo-American Antagonism, 1919–1929*. Vol. 1 of *Naval Policy between the Wars*. New York: Walker, 1968.

Rouleau, Brian. "Childhood's Imperial Imagination: Edward Stratemeyer's Fiction Factory and the Valorization of American Empire." *Journal of the Gilded Age and Progressive Era* 7, no. 4 (October 2008): 479–512.

Schake, Kori. *Safe Passage: The Transition from British to American Hegemony*. Cambridge, MA: Harvard University Press, 2017.

Scovel, F. Donald. "Helm's a Lee: A History of the Development of the Public Affairs Function in the United States Navy, 1861–1941." Master's thesis, University of Wisconsin–Madison, 1968.

"Secretary's Notes." U.S. Naval Institute *Proceedings* 55, no. 5 (May 1929): 475.

Shearer, William B. *The Cloak of Benedict Arnold*. Washington, D.C.: National Capitol Press, 1928.

Shenk, Robert, ed. *Playships of the World: The Naval Diaries of Admiral Dan Gallery, 1920–1924*. Columbia: University of South Carolina Press, 2008.

———. "To the 1920 Olympics by Cruiser." *Naval History Magazine* 22, no. 4 (August 2008): 34–39.

Sheridan, Martin. *Comics and Their Creators: Life Stories of American Cartoonists*. Westport, Conn.: Hyperion Press, 1977.

Shindler, Colin. *Hollywood Goes to War: Films and American Society, 1939–1952*. Boston: Routledge, 1979.

Shulman, Mark. *Navalism and the Emergence of American Sea Power, 1882–1893*. Annapolis, Md.: Naval Institute Press, 1995.

Sims, William S. "Roosevelt and the Navy." *McClure's*, December 1922, 56–62.

———. "Roosevelt and the Navy: Recollections, Reminiscences, and Reflections." *McClure's*, November 1922, 32–41.

———. "Theodore Roosevelt at Work." *McClure's*, January 1923, 61–66, 95–101.

Smith, Isabel. Elliot Snow,."Historical Sketch of the Navy Department Library and War Records," March 1926. https://www.history.navy.mil/content/history/nhhc/research/library/about/history-of-the-navy-department-library-a-bibliography/historical-sketch-of-the-navy-department-library-and-war-records.html

Sondhaus, Lawrence. *Navies of Europe, 1815–2002*. New York: Longman, 2002.

Sprout, Harold, and Margaret Sprout. *The Rise of American Naval Power, 1776–1918*. Princeton, N.J.: Princeton University Press, 1939.

Steele, Richard W. *Propaganda in an Open Society: The Roosevelt Administration and the Media, 1933–1941*. Westport, Conn.: Greenwood Press, 1985.

Stevens, William O. "The Naval Officer and the Civilian." U.S. Naval Institute *Proceedings* 47, no. 11 (November 1921): 1725–39.

Stirling, Yates. *A United States Midshipman Afloat*. Philadelphia, Penn Publishing, 1908.

Suid, Lawrence. *Guts and Glory: The Making of the American Military Image in Film*. 2nd ed. Frankfort: University Press of Kentucky, 2002.

———. *Sailing on the Silver Screen: Hollywood and the U.S. Navy*. Annapolis, Md.: Naval Institute Press, 1996.

Swanborough, Gordon, and Peter M. Bowers. *U.S. Navy Aircraft since 1911*. Annapolis, Md.: Naval Institute Press, 1976.

Tolley, Kemp. *Yangtze Patrol*. Annapolis, Md.: Naval Institute Press, 1971.

Tompkins, E. F., ed. *Selections from the Writings and Speeches of William Randolph Hearst*. San Francisco: Private publisher, 1948.

Trimble, William F. *Admiral William A. Moffett: Architect of Naval Aviation*. Washington, D.C.: Smithsonian Institution Press, 1994.

Tye, Larry. *The Father of Spin: Edward L. Bernays and the Birth of American Public Relations*. New York: Crown, 1998.

Ulbrich, David John. *Preparing for Victory: Thomas Holcomb and the Making of the Modern Marine Corps, 1936–1943*. Annapolis: Naval Institute Press, 2011.

The United States Navy in Peacetime: The Navy in Relation to the Industrial, Scientific, Economic, and Political Developments of the Nation. Washington, D.C.: Government Printing Office, 1931.

Utley, Jonathan G. *An American Battleship at Peace and War: The USS Tennessee.* Lawrence: University Press of Kansas, 1991.

Vance, Jeffrey, and Suzanne Lloyd. *Harold Lloyd: Master Comedian.* New York: Henry N. Abrams, 2002.

Venable, Heather Pace. *Sergeant Strangelove: How the Marine Corps Convinced the Nation to Love It, 1874–1918.* Forthcoming.

Ward, Larry Wayne. *The Motion Picture Goes to War: The U.S. Government Film Effort during World War I* (Ann Arbor: UMI Research Press, 1985).

Waugh, Coulton. *The Comics.* New York: Macmillan, 1947.

Weir, Gary E. *Building American Submarines, 1914–1940.* Washington, D.C.: Naval Historical Center, 1991.

West, Richard. "The Navy and the Press during the Civil War." U.S. Naval Institute *Proceedings* 63, no. 1 (January 1938): 36–38.

Wheeler, Gerald E. *Admiral William Veazie Pratt, United States Navy: A Sailor's Life.* Washington, D.C.: Naval History Division, Department of the Navy, 1974.

———. *Prelude to Pearl Harbor.* Columbia: University of Missouri Press, 1963.

Whiting, F. E. M. "A Further Application of Our Publicity Policy." U.S. Naval Institute *Proceedings* 57, no. 9 (September 1931): 1169–72.

Wildenberg, Thomas. *All the Factors of Victory: Admiral Joseph Mason Reeves and the Origins of Carrier Airpower.* Washington, D.C.: Brassey's, 2003.

———. *Billy Mitchell's War with the Navy: The Interwar Rivalry over Air Power.* Annapolis, Md.: Naval Institute Press, 2013.

Williams, Charles Hughes, III. "'We Have . . . Kept the Negroes' Goodwill and Sent Them Away': Black Sailors, White Dominion in the New Navy, 1893–1942." Master's thesis, Texas A&M University, 2008.

Wilson, Eugene E. *Slipstream: Autobiography of an Air Craftsman.* New York: Whittlesey House, 1950.

Woodward, C. Vann. *The Strange Career of Jim Crow.* New York: Oxford University Press, 2002.

Wright, Richard L. *The Navy League of the United States: Civilians Supporting the Seas Services for More than a Century.* Arlington, Va.: Navy League of the United States, 2006.

Zizek, Slavoj. *Welcome to the Desert of the Real.* New York: Verso, 2002.

Filmography

Annapolis. Directed by Christy Cabanne. Pathé, 1928.
Annapolis Farewell. Directed by Alexander Hall. Paramount Productions, 1935.
Annapolis Salute. Directed by Christy Cabanne. RKO Pictures, 1937.
The Devil's Playground. Directed by Earl C. Kenton. Columbia Pictures, 1937.
Dirigible. Directed by Frank Capra. Columbia Pictures, 1931.
Dive Bomber. Directed by Michael Curtiz. Warner Brothers Pictures, 1941.

The Fleet's In. Directed by Michael St. Clair. Paramount Famous Lasky Corp., 1928.
Flight. Directed by Frank Capra. Columbia Pictures, 1929.
The Flying Fleet. Directed by George W. Hill. Metro-Goldwyn-Mayer, 1929.
Follow the Fleet. Directed by Mark Sandrich. RKO Radio Pictures, 1936.
Gabriel over the White House. Directed by Gregory LaCava. Metro-Goldwyn-Mayer, 1933.
A Girl in Every Port. Directed by Howard Hawks. Fox Film Corp., 1928.
Hell Below. Directed by Jack Conway. Metro-Goldwyn-Mayer, 1933.
Hell Divers. Directed by George W. Hill. Metro-Goldwyn-Mayer, 1932.
Here Comes the Navy. Directed by Lloyd Bacon. Warner Brothers Pictures, 1934.
Hit the Deck. Directed by Luther Reed. RKO Pictures, 1930.
Hold 'em Navy. Directed by Kurt Neumann. Paramount Pictures, 1937.
Men without Women. Directed by John Ford. Fox Film Corp., 1930.
Midshipman Jack. Directed by Christy Cabanne. RKO Radio Pictures, 1933.
Murder in the Fleet. Directed by Edward Sedgwick. Metro-Goldwyn-Mayer, 1935.
Navy Blue and Gold. Directed by Sam Wood. Metro-Goldwyn-Mayer, 1937.
Navy Blues. Directed by Ralph Straub. Republic Pictures, 1937.
Navy Blues. Directed by Lloyd Bacon. Warner Brothers Pictures, 1941.
A Sailor Made Man. Directed by Fred Newmeyer. Hal Roach Studios, 1921.
The Seas Beneath. Directed by John Ford. Fox Film Corp., 1931.
Shipmates Forever. Directed by Frank Borzage. Warner Brothers Pictures, 1935.
Son of a Sailor. Directed by Lloyd Bacon. Warner Brothers Pictures, 1933.
Submarine. Directed by Frank Capra. Columbia Pictures, 1928.
Submarine Patrol. Directed by John Ford. Fox Film Corp., 1938.
Suicide Fleet. Directed by Albert S. Rogell. RKO-Pathé, 1931.
Tail Spin. Directed by Roy Del Ruth. Fox Film Corp., 1939.
True to the Navy. Directed by Frank Tuttle. Paramount Pictures, 1930.
Wings of the Navy. Directed by Lloyd Bacon. Warner Brothers Pictures, 1939.

INDEX

Page numbers in *italics* indicate illustrations.

Adams, Charles F., 78, 179, 200
administrative reforms, 28–29
Admiral William A. Moffett (Trimble), 6
advance bases, 4
advertising, versus public relations, 8
Advertising Agencies Corporation, 68–69
advertising firms, 68–69
African Americans, 155–57
Ageton, Arthur, 179
aircraft carriers, 4, 40; arresting gear, 91; depiction in films, 91, 93–94; development of, 178, 185–86; in Fleet Problems, 101, 180; flight deck operations, 64–65, 181; in humanitarian missions, 179–80
aircraft design, 166–67
Air Force, 4
air racing, 65, 163, 165–67, 176–77
airships, 56, 65–67, 90, 103, 167–68, 180–81, 198
air shows, 177–78
Alcock, John, 163

American Advisory Committee, 36–37
American Black Chamber, The (Yardley), 102
American Expeditionary Force, 27
American Federation of Labor, 35, 56
Americanism, 143–44
American Legion, 37–38, 57
"America Not to Blame If Arms Treaty Fails" (Bywater), 192
American Review of Reviews, 31, 32
American Revolution, 26
Amlie, Thomas, 117–18
Anchors Aweigh (film), 87–88
Andrews, Philip, 77
Anglo-Japanese Alliance, 40
Annapolis (film), 84–85
Annapolis Salute (film), 126
Annapolis Today (Banning), 132–33
"Annapolites," 64, 68
Arctic exploration, 198–99
Argentina, 214
Armagnac, Alden Packard, 124

arms limitation movement. *See* naval arms limitation movement
Army Air Corps, 65, 114
Army-Navy games, 146, 148
Army Signal Corps, 21
Asiatic Fleet, 81, 197, 208
Associated Press, 102
Astaire, Fred, 120, 121
Astor Theater, 91, 93
athletic competitions, 138, 146, 149
Atlantic Monthly, 34
Austin, Bernard L., 131–32, 133, 214, 216, 219, *220*
Austin, Charles M., 102–3
Australia, 65, 192
Auxiliary Reserve Dock (ARD-1), 123–24
aviation accidents, 67, 171–76, 179, 184–85
aviation and air power: aerial bombing tests, 32–34, 163–64; British consolidation of, 27; carriers and, 180; distance flights, 65–67; Mitchell as advocate of, 4, 27–28; naval aviators and, 34; speed records and, 166; vulnerability of surface ships to, 31–33. *See also* naval aviation

Bacon, Lloyd, 113, 117, 129, 186, 250n30
Balchen, Bernt, 199
Baldwin, Hanson, 7, 74–75, 133, 180, 210, 212
Baltimore Sun, 26, 61, 74, 98, 172, 192, 200
Banning, Kendall, 132–33, 227
Barry, John, 52
Bastedo, Paul H., 120, 121–22, 126
battle "E" competitions, 149
Battle Fleet, 59–60, 81, 85, 89, 101, 140, 191, 192, 208, 215
Battle of Jutland, 23
Battle of Manila Bay, 13
Battleship Boys series (Patchin), 12
battleship-centric force, 4, 162–63, 163, 186–87
"Battleship Still Supreme, The" (Warren), 32
Beard, Charles, 203–4

Beecher, W. G., Jr., 219
Beery, Wallace, *92*
Belknap, Charles, Jr., 20
Bell Syndicates, 116
Bennett, Floyd, 198
Bennett, James Gordon, 163
Benson, William, 29
Berlin, Irving, 121
Bernays, Edward, 21, 108, 138–39, 225
Beroth, Leon, 116
Beskin, Gerald, 229
Bethlehem Shipbuilding, 206
"Big Gun, The" (screenplay), 85–86
Big Parade, The (film), 83, 85
Biograph Company, 13
Blackburn, C. K., 42
Blackledge, A. D., 120
Bloch, Claude C., 216
Blodgett, Lawrence, 160
Blue Angels, 178
B-movies, 125–26, 157
Bonaparte, Charles Joseph, 13, 50
book series, youth-oriented, 12, 138–40, 153
Borah, William, 30–31, 34, 35, 169
Boston Navy Yard, 199
Boy Scouts, 57
Brazil, 209
Breckinridge, Henry S., 39
Bright Lights (film), 38
Brisbane, Arthur, 117
Bristol, Arthur L., 128
Britain. *See* Great Britain
British Navy's Grand Fleet, 23
British propaganda, 60, 73
Britten, Fred, 113, 202
Broken Blossoms (film), 38
Brooklyn Eagle, 122, 172
Brooks, Rosa, 8
Brow, H. B., 166
Bureau of Aeronautics, 3, 7, 34, 91; air racing and, 166; film industry and, 128–29; Photographic Section, 44; public relations challenges for, 62–68

Bureau of Navigation, 86, 138; Morale Division, 44, 196; recruiting and, 68–71, 155
Bureau of Standards, 34
Butler, Thomas, 200
Byrd, Richard E., 198–99
Bywater, Hector, 48, 61, 192–93, 262n12

Cabanne, Christy, 117, 250n30
Cadmus, Paul, 153
Canada, 214
Capra, Frank, 89, 105, 125, 156, 182, 186, 207
Carter, Boake, 114–15
censorship, 13; of film industry, 83, 86, 92–94, 207; fleet reviews and, 102; of newsreels, 123
"Certain Naval Lessons of the Great War" (Sims), 28
Chamber of Commerce, 51
Chicago Daily News, 116
Chicago Tribune, 53, 62, 74, 146, 194, 200
children's literature, 138–40, 153
China, 191, 219
China Station, 140
Chinese unification crisis, 196
Christian Science Monitor, 54, 216
Church Peace Union, 36
Cincinnati Commercial Tribune, 71
Cincinnati Enquirer, 31
Cincinnati reserve center, 56–57
circumnavigational flights, 66–67
civilian job market, 142–43, 151, 158
Civil War, 8–9, 26, 52, 210
Classmates (film), 83, 84
Cloak of Benedict Arnold, The (Shearer), 97
Cluverius, Wat T., 114–15, 115–16, 119
Coli, Francois, 210
Columbia Broadcasting System, 79–80, 81, 115
Columbia Pictures, 89, 105, 125, 129, 181, 186
comic strips, 115–16

commerce raiding, 9
Committee on Public Information, 21, 22, 109
Connell, R. W., 136
content analysis of articles, 217–18
Continental Army, 26
Continental Navy, 26
"Conversations with the Country" meetings, 228
convoy escorts, 22
Coolidge, Calvin, 72, 80, 172, 191, 198, 264n33
Coontz, Robert E., 43, 64, 65–66
Cooperative Strategy for 21st Century Seapower, 228
Cosmopolitan magazine, 132
Cosmopolitan Pictures, 110, 112–13
Courtney, C. E., 69
Craven, Thomas T., 45
Creel, George, 21, 109
Crockett, E. Harry, 216
Crosley, Walter S., 14
Crossing the Line (film), 70
cryptology, 102
Crystallizing Public Opinion (Bernays), 108
Curtiss Marine Trophy, 165–66, 177
Cutlip, Scott M., 5

Daniels, Josephus, 15, 188, 224; administrative reforms and, 28–29; aerial bombing tests and, 32; air racing and, 163; film industry and, 14–15, 38, 81; on lifestyle of navy personnel, 135, 137–38; Mare Island explosion and, 23; medals controversy and, 28; "Men Must Live Straight If They Would Shoot Straight," 136; naval construction and, 4, 16, 24, 25–26, 30–31; Navy League and, 22–23, 38–39; Navy News Bureau and, 21, 22; navy public relations and, 14–16; Newport homosexuality investigation and, 29–30; press conferences and, 59;

Daniels, Josephus (*continued*)
  press releases and, 16; radio industry and, 79; Recruiting Service and, 15; on sea power, 163; on submarines, 170; "Training Men for the Navy and the Nation," 142–43; on venereal disease, 135
Dashiell, G. W., 127, 128
data collection, 225–26
Dave Darrin and the German Submarines (Hancock), 169
Dave Darrin series (Hancock), 12, 139
Dave Darrin's South American Cruise (Hancock), 139
Davidson, Halsey, 138, 139
Davies, Marion, 113
Davis, Vincent, 9
Decatur, Stephen, 52
Declaration of Principles (Lee), 8
De Lany, Walter S., 132
demobilization, 137
Denby, Edwin, 5, 23, 35, 39, 43–44, 48, 52, 57–60, 136, 195, 228
Department of Aeronautics, 27
Department of the Interior, 195
Detzer, Dorothy, 206
Devil Dogs of the Air (film), 113, 117
Devil in the Deep, The (film), 87
Devil's Playground, The (film), 105, 125, 156–57, 186
Dewey, George, 13
Dirigible (film), 89, 181
disarmament movement, 34–37, 72
district intelligence officers, 58, 108–9
District Press Branch, 109
district press officers, 146
Dive Bomber (film), 223
dive-bombers, 91
Doheny, Edward, 195
Don't Give Up the Ship (film), 57
Don Winslow, U.S.N., in Ceylon with Kwang, Celebrated Chinese Detective (Martinek), 153

Don Winslow of the Navy (comic strip), 115–16, 153
Don Winslow of the Navy (Martinek), 116
Don Winslow (radio show), 116
Doolittle, James, 167
Douglas, Henry H., 58–59
Doyle, S. H. R., 64
Dubbert, Joe, 151
Duckworth, H. S., *92*
DuPont Corporation, 206

Earhart, Amelia, 210
Eastern College Committee for the Limitation of Armaments, 36
Eberle, Edward W., 50, 56, 58, 59, 67, 197, 198
Eclipse of American Sea Power, The (Knox), 47–48, 60, 190, 210
economic agent, navy as, 195–97, 202–6
Edison, Charles, *220*
Edwards, Cliff, *92*
Edwards, Ralph, 127, 128
Electric Boat Company, 206
Ellis, Hayne, 93, 204
Ellsberg, Edward, 174, 175, 184
Emergency Fleet Cooperation, 46
enlisted personnel: improvement of life of, 15; at Naval Academy, 152–53; public perception of, 136; recruitment of, 11, 142–43; retention rate, 159. *See also* naval personnel
exploration missions, 197–99
Eyes of the Navy (film), 223

Fall, Albert, 195
Fantasia (film), 223
Farquhar, Allan, 76
Farragut, David, 52
feature films, 125–26
Federal Council of Churches, 36
Field, Syd, 150
Film Daily, 150
film directors, 117

film production process, 89–90
films and film industry, 5, 76; censorship and, 92–94; Congressional investigation of navy's cooperation with, 117–18; economic considerations in, 206–7; exhibition venues, 70; feature films and B-movies, 125–26; masculine image in, 147–48; naval aviation projects, 128–29; navy concerns over quality of, 126–27; Navy Day and, 57; navy in publicizing films, 84–85; Navy News Bureau and, 38; navy policy and, 86; objections to cooperation with, 94–95; preparedness depicted in, 207–8; recruiting and, 13, 69–70, 90; relationship with navy, 14–15, 81, 84; security restrictions on military cooperation with, 105–6; self-transformation narratives in, 150–51; social influence of, 83; as source for study of navy public relations, 6–7; technical advisors and, 88–89, 127–28; unfavorable depictions of navy by, 38; during World War II, 222–23. *See also specific titles*
Fiske, Bradley, 28–29, *29*
Fitzgerald, F. Scott, 151
Five-Power Treaty, 40, 43, 48, 53, 106, 111, 143, 189, 190–91, 202
Fleet Base Force, 81
fleet movements, 101
Fleet Problem V, 191–92
Fleet Problem IX, 101, 178–79
Fleet Problem XIII, 102–3, 208
Fleet Problem XV, 185
Fleet Problem XVI, 208–9
Fleet Problems, 59–60, 101, 191
fleet review of 1939, 214–15
fleet reviews, 24–25, 72, 101–2
Fleet's In, The (Cadmus), 153–55, *154*, 256n44
fleet training exercises, 42
Flight Command (film), 128, 223

flight deck operations, 64–65, 181
floating dry docks, 123–24
flying boats, 64, 66, 67, 163
Flying Down to Rio (film), 120
Flying Fleet, The (film), 88, 179, 208
Flynn, Errol, 223
Follow the Fleet (film), 120–22, 126, 128
Ford, Henry, 56
Ford, John, 117, 148, 149, 157, 183, 220
foreign influences and activities: British, on arms limitation movement, 97, 112; film depictions of military operations and, 105–6; pacifism and, 79; press and, 60–61; propaganda and, 60, 74
foreign travel, as recruiting inducement, 138–39, 143, 155
Forest Service, 15–16
Four Minute Men, 21
Four-Power Treaty, 40
Fox, Albert, 22
Fox, Gustavus, 210
Fox Film Corporation, 70, 83
Fox Movietone, 96
Fox Movietone News, 81
France, 40, 219, 223
Frankfurt (German cruiser), 33, 164
Freeman, Lewis, 101
French, Burton, 97, 99–100
"From Blackout at Pearl Harbor to Spotlight on Tokyo Bay" (Klinkerman), 5–6
Frost, Daniel A., 117, 210
Frost, Holloway H., 98, 201
Fullam, William, 29, 34
Funk and Wagnall's, 132
"Further Application of Our Publicity Policy, A" (Whiting), 78–79

Gable, Clark, *92*
Gabriel over the White House (film), 110–11, 113
Gallery, Daniel V., 138
Galvin, William, 220

Gardiner, William Howard, 49–50, 97, 99; civilian writers' course and, 54–55; criticism of navy policy by, 100–101, 107; Navy Day and, 51–52, 55–56
Gay Divorcee, The (film), 120
Gearing, Henry C., 90–91
General Board, 14, 24, 37
General Committee on the Limitation of Armaments, 36
General Electric, 79
General Orders on publicity, 120
Geneva Conference, 72–73, 98, 200
German Gotha bombers, 27
German High Seas Fleet, 23
Germany, 10, 87, 118, 164, 168, 191, 219
G-102 (German destroyer), 33
Gill, Charles C., 76, 104
Gillett Amendment, 8, 58–59
Gleaves, Albert, 100
"Goldfish Bowl, The" (screenplay), 88
Goldwyn, Samuel, 87
Gompers, Samuel, 35–36, 56
Government by Propaganda (Henning), 74
Government Publicity: Its Practice in Federal Administration (McCamy), 217–18
Grand Joint Exercise 3, 191–92, 208
Grand Joint Exercise 4, 102, 183
Graves, Ralph, 181
Great Britain, 10, 27, 30, 40, 47, 72, 91, 107, 112, 169, 173, 189, 191, 200, 201, 214, 219
Great Depression, 76, 83, 99, 151, 158, 159, 204; impact on Navy budget, 4–5; impact on Navy League, 17; naval construction and, 18
Great Lakes Training Center, 62
Great Pacific War, The: A History of the American-Japanese Campaign of 1931–1932 (Bywater), 61, 192–94
Great White Fleet, 10
Greco-Turkish War, 144, 197
Greece, 144, 197
guerre de course strategy, 9

Haislip, Harvey, 128
Hale, Frederick, 113, 202
Hall, Mordaunt, 179, 181
Hamilton, Mrs. William, 50
Hancock, H. Irving, 12, 139
Harding, Warren G., 23, 35–36, 36, 39, 80, 188, 195
Harper's Weekly, 204
Harrod, Frederick, 6, 136
"Has the Airplane Made the Battleship Obsolete?" (Mitchell), 32
Hawaiian Islands, 102, 192
Hawks, Wells, 37–38, 44, 68
Hays, Will, 56
Hays Code, 149
Hearst, William Randolph, 9, 72, 76–77, 110–14, 143, 189, 201–2, 211, 227
Hearst Metrotone, 81, 96
Hearst Metrotone News, 113, 114
hegemonic masculinity, 136
Hell Below (film), 150, 157
Hell Divers (film), 89–94, *92*, 105, 120, 181, 186, 208
"Helm's a Lee" (Scovel), 5–6
Hemingway, Ernest, 151
Henning, Arthur Sears, 74
Hepburn, Arthur J., 224
Here Comes the Navy (film), 151–52
"Heroes Come High" (script), 129
Hersey, Mark L., 91, 93
history of the navy, 61–62
History of the United States Navy (Knox), 210
Hitler, Adolph, 114
Hit the Deck (film), 120
HMS *Dreadnought*, 10
Holmes, Ralston S., 132
Holt, Jack, 181
homosexuality investigation, 29–30
Honda Point Disaster, 144–46, 160–61, *161*
Hoover, Herbert, 36, 94, 98, 99, 100, 101, 107, 143, 197, 200, 201, 208
House Committee on Appropriations, 31

House Naval Affairs Committee, 25, 177
Howe, Walter Bruce, 99, 100, 107
Hubbard, Nathaniel, 107, 130
Hughes, Charles Evans, 36, 39–40, 47–48, 77, 247n73
human interest stories, 7, 78
humanitarian missions, 144, 179–80, 197, 203, 210–11
Hunter, Donald T., 160–61
Hurd, Archibald, 200
Hurt, S. H., 126
Huston, Walter, 110
Hydrographic Office, 203

Immigration Act of 1924, 191, 192–93
Influence of Sea Power Upon History, 1660–1783, The (Mahan), 9
Information Section of ONI: counterintelligence activities and, 7; creation of, 5, 43–44, 190; film industry and, 87; Koch's rules for, 44–45; mass communication impact on, 79; Navy Day and, 57; obstacles to, 41; products disseminated by, 6; professional approach of, 58; Recruiting Bureau collaboration with, 68; reference files created by, 59; security concerns and, 59–60; in shaping image of sailors, 144–45; staffing of, 44, 59, 71–72, 73, 75–76; themes emphasized by, 7–8
Ingalls, David S., 86, 177
Ingram, Jonas, 114, 124
Instructions for Intelligence Officers, 58
Intelligence Manual, 77, 107–10, 122, 216
intelligence officers, district, 108–9
intelligence work: counterintelligence activities, 7, 8, 76; depiction in films, 119–20; district intelligence officers, 58, 108–9; public relations and, 17, 59–60, 76, 96–97, 104, 114–16; security concerns in film industry cooperation, 105–6. *See also* security concerns

"Intelligent Publicity" (Roosevelt), 37, 54–55
internationalism, 97
International Newsreel, 113
International News Service, 113
international system, 219
Irvine, Rutledge, 166
isolationism, 223
Italy, 40

Jack Benny program, 186
Jahncke, Ernest, 93, 202
Japan, 47, 72, 91, 94, 97, 189; attack on Pearl Harbor, 223; invasion of China, 219; invasion of Manchuria, 208; naval construction program, 30–31, 40, 118–19, 201; *Panay* incident and, 211; as potential adversary, 61, 112, 123, 156, 161–62, 183, 191–94, 208, 211; in Spratley Island annexation, 215; Washington Conference and, 40; withdrawal from Washington treaties, 209–10
Japanese earthquake of 1923, 197, 263n20
Jefferson, Thomas, 210
Jenkins, John Wilbur, 21, 22, 24
Johnson, Alfred W., 76–78, 98, 104
Jones, Hillary P., 50, 98
Jones, John Paul, 52
journalism course, 37
Jowert, Garth, 84

Karsten, Peter, 6, 9, 43, 64, 142
Kelley, Robert, 39, 48–49, 50, 56
Kellogg-Briand Pact, 94
Keystone Cops, 38
Kilduff, William D., 114
Kimmel, Michael, 151
King, Ernest J., 174, 185
Kiwanis Club, 57
Klinkerman, R. Dale, 5
Knight, Austin M., 62

Knox, Dudley W., 7, 17, 41, 43, *46*, 97, 189, 194, 204; on aircraft carriers, 179–80; Bywater debates and, 61; on dangers of anti-fleet propaganda, 60–61; *The Eclipse of American Sea Power*, 47–48, 60, 190, 210; *History of the United States Navy*, 210; on merchant marine, 196–97; on naval history, 61–62; on naval power, 212; "Our Post War Mission," 26–27; "Our Vanishing History and Traditions," 62; on public lobbying, 27; on submarines, 169; "The Navy and Public Indoctrination," 74; on value of publicity, 45–46; on Washington Conference, 46–48
Knox, Frank, 116, 224
Koch, Ralph A., 44–45, 57–58, 60, 76
Krause, Sidney M., 114

labor unions, 23, 35, 56
Ladies' Home Journal, 62
Laning, Harris, 129
Lansdowne, Zachary, 67, 171, 172
Larsen, Roy, 133
Lawyer's Secret, A (film), 95
League of Nations, 25–26, 144
Leahy, William, 124, 125, 126, 132, 187, 211, 216
Lee, Ivy, 8
Lee, Willis A., Jr., 138
Leigh, Richard H., 86, 94
Leighton, Frank, 130
Lejuene, John A., 50
Lemneck, Arthur, 117–18
Let's Join the Navy (film), 123
Lewis and Clark Exposition, 13
Lindbergh, Charles, 81, 199
Linton, James M., 84
Lippmann, Walter, 108
Literary Digest, The, 200
Littlehale, George Washington, 199
Lloyd, Harold, 38, 141
Lloyd George, David, 27, 98

lobbying activities, 9–10, 10, 27
Loew, Marcus, 83
London Naval Conference of 1935, 118–19, 201–2, 209
London Naval Treaty of 1930, 111, 113
Long, E. John, 220
Los Angeles Times, 31, 179, 194
Lovette, Leland P., *131*, 131–33, 219–20, *220*, 227
Luce, Stephen, 6, 9, 103

Macy, Nelson, 130, 209
Madame Butterfly (film), 15
Magruder, Thomas P., 71–72, 81, 175
Mahan, Alfred Thayer, 6, 9, 32, 50, 55, 103, 189, 194, 201, 211–12
Mahan: The Life and Work of Captain Alfred Thayer Mahan, U.S.N. (Puleston), 211–12
Manchuria, 208
Manning the New Navy (Harrod), 6
Mare Island explosion, 23
Mare Island Naval Yard, 136
Marine Corps, 59; interwar development of, 4; Motion Picture Board staffing and, 119–20; Publicity Bureau of, 13–14, 16, 68, 240n50
"Marines Are Here, The" (script), 126
Marshall Fields department stores, 69
Martinek, Frank, 115–16, 119, 153, 250n28
masculinity: depiction in films, 147–48; hegemonic, 136
mass communications, 79
Massie, Thalia, 102
Massie, Tommie, 102
mass information, 20–21
Mayer, Louis B., 111
Mayflower (presidential yacht), 24
Mayo, Henry T., 28
McCamy, James, 217–18
McCann Rescue Chamber, 186, 216
McCarthy, D. L., 85–86
McClure, S. S., 53

McClure's, 52–53
McCormick, Robert R., 200
McIntyre, Marvin Hunter, 21, 22, 24, 37
McKinley, William, 10
McNamee, Luke, 43, 48–49, 51–52, 190, 229
medals controversy, 28
Melhorn, Charles, 34
Mellon, Andrew, 36
"Men Must Live Straight If They Would Shoot Straight" (Daniels), 136
Men Without Women (film), 88, 105, 149–50, 183
Merchant Marine, 46, 57, 85, 196–97
Mercury Racer, 177
Metro Goldwyn Mayer, 83, 88, 89–94, 93, 110, 113, 119, 126, 128, 181, 184
Mexican-American War, 26
Mexico, 214
Meyer, George von Lengerke, 14
Midshipman, The (film), 84
Midshipman Jack (film), 152
Mississippi River recruiting trip, 37, 68
"Mistaken Publicity" (Blackburn), 42
Mitchell, William "Billy," 17; aerial bombing tests and, 32–34; as air power advocate, 4, 27–28, 32, 63; air racing and, 65; on aviation speed records, 166; court-martial of, 67–68, 173; criticism of army and navy air, 27–28; on defense budgeting, 31; early career, 27; "Has the Airplane Made the Battleship Obsolete?," 32; on navy innovation, 161; *Our Air Force*, 32–33; rivalry with William Moffett, 3; on *Shenandoah* crash, 172; on ship vulnerability, 31–33
Moffett, Jeanette, 62
Moffett, William Adger, 7, 17, 18, 41, *63*, 68, 93, 199, 204; air racing and, 65, 165–67, 176–77; airships and, 103, 167–68, 172–73, 180–81; death of, 184–85; distance flights and, 65–67; flight operations management and, 64–65;

as head of Bureau of Aeronautics, 62–68; as head of Great Lakes Training Center, 62; London Conference and, 202; public relations and, 3, 64, 162, 178, 181–82, 219; William Mitchell and, 34
Momsen, Charles "Swede," 182
Momsen lung, 182–83, 186
Monogram Pictures, 126
Monroe Doctrine, 25–26
"Monster Dry Docks Keep Our Navy in Lighting Shape" (Armagnac), 124
Monthly Information Bulletin, 48, 77–78
Morale Division, Bureau of Navigation, 44
Morrow Board, 68, 172–73
Motion Picture Board, 17, 18, 86–96, 149, 186, 207, 219; aviation projects and, 128–29; B-movies and, 125–26; changes in personnel on, 88; criteria for cooperation on films, 87–88; depictions of espionage in films and, 119–20; *Follow the Fleet* and, 120–22; *Hell Divers* and, 89–94; inconsistency of, 88; members of, 86; objections to cooperation with film industry, 94–95, 117–18; security concerns and, 105–6
Motion Picture Exchange, 38, 81, 87, 95
Motion Picture Herald, 111, 129
Motion Picture Patents Company, 13
Motion Picture Producers and Distributors Association, 56, 83, 121, 148
multimedia conglomerates, 110
munitions industry, 206
Munn, Orson, 60–61
Murder in the Fleet (film), 119, 121
museum exhibits, 120
Mussolini, Benito, 114
Mystery Ship (film), 94

Naquin, Oliver, 215
Nashville, Tenn., 53
National Air Races, 178

National Balloon Races, 163
National Broadcasting Company, 79–80, 81
National Film Publicity Campaign, 69
National Industrial Recovery Act, 109, 156, 204–5
National League of Women Voters, 35
National Recovery Administration, 204
National Student Committee, 36
National Women's Party, 35
nativism, 191
Naval Academy, 83–84, 85, 126, 132, 140, 146, 148
Naval Act of 1916, 16, 17, 23, 25, 39, 188–89
naval administration reform hearings, 28–29
Naval Aristocracy, The (Karsten), 6
naval arms limitation movement, 4, 17, 31, 34–37, 40–42, 47, 72, 97, 200
naval arms race, 10, 30
naval aviation, 34; air racing and, 65, 163, 166; carriers and, 179; criticism of, 114; depiction in films, 90; distance flights, 65–67, 163; exhibition flights, 178; film projects on, 128–29; financial economies in, 202; flight operations management and, 64–65; Moffett as public face of, 64; Navy Day and, 53; public exposure to, 164–65; public relations campaigns for, 63–68; public relations evolution in, 162; value of in naval warfare, 62–63; Washington Conference impact on, 164–65. *See also* aviation and air power
Naval Commission on Training Camp Activities, 137
Naval Communication Service, 79
naval construction program: battleships and, 162–63; "building holiday" and, 30–31; Congressional response to, 4; Geneva Conference and, 200; Great Depression and, 18, 204; impact of World War I on capital ship construction, 23–24, 25; Japanese, 30–31, 40, 118–19, 201; justification for, 200–201; Navy League and, 12; political support for, 106; 1916 program, 27, 30; 1919 program, 24–26; public objections to, 21, 34–37; public support for, 209; Washington Conference and, 40; WWI impact on, 16
Naval Customs, Traditions, and Usage (Lovette), 131
naval district liaisons, 58, 75–76
Naval Historical Foundation, 62
Naval Historical Society, 62
naval history, 61–62, 201
Naval Institute, 26, 49, 62, 74
Naval Institute Press, 131
Naval Instructions, 14
naval intelligence, director of, 58
navalist movement, 9, 188–89, 204, 206
Naval Observatory, 203
"Naval Officer and the Civilian, The" (Stevens), 42
naval officers: attitudes on publicity, 3, 47, 78–79; attitudes toward press, 75; on battleships, 164; civilian attitude toward, 42; Information Section and, 7–8; medal controversy and, 28; as naval district liaisons, 58; prior enlisted, 152–53; public relations policy and, 103; recruiting officers, 70–71; retired, in public relations work, 55; as technical advisors, 127–28. *See also* naval personnel
Naval Order of the United States, 9, 10, 100
naval personnel: African Americans, 155–57; personnel strength, 48, 189, 226, 255n29; physical and moral fitness of, 137–38; post-service employment and, 142–43; postwar demobilization of, 137; reforms aimed at, 136–37; retired, in public relations work, 55. *See also* enlisted personnel; naval officers

naval policy, books on, 211–12
Naval Power in the War (Gill), 76
naval recruiting. *See* recruitment
naval reservists, 75–76, 146
Naval War College, 37, 54–55, 191
Navarro, Ramon, 84
Navies and Nations (Bywater), 61
Navy, The: Defense or Portent? (Beard), 203–4
Navy, U.S.: administrative and financial efficiencies in, 194–95; administrative reform in, 28–29; battle "E" competitions, 149; budget, 226; in economic prosperity, 195–97, 202–6; "Gun Club" in, 164; history of, 61–62; interwar transition of, 3–4; manpower, 48, 143, 255n29; organizational culture in, 6; peacetime role debate, 189; silent service culture in, 5, 7, 14, 42, 46, 51, 59, 71, 79, 86, 94, 103, 115, 118, 128, 228
"Navy and Economy, The" (Magruder), 71–72, 175
"Navy and Public Indoctrination, The" (Knox), 74
Navy and the Near East, The (film), 197
navy bands, 62, 80–81, 109–10
Navy Blue and Gold (film), 157
Navy Boys behind the Big Guns; or, Sinking the German U-Boats (Davidson), 138
Navy Boys on Special Service; or, Guarding the Floating Treasury (Davidson), 139
Navy Boys series, 169
Navy Communication Service, 203
Navy Day, 7, 17, 64, 80, 192, *193*, 197, 215; as annual event, 57; creation of, 50–52; impact of, 54; impact of Great Depression on, 99; local celebrations, 56–57; media assistance in, 52–53; Midwest as target for, 53; navy in promotion of, 52; Navy League proposal of, 51; officers' promotion of, 53–54; second, 55–57; security concerns and, 122–23

Navy League Journal, 11
Navy League of Great Britain, 10
Navy League of the United States, 7, 10–12, 17, 18, 189; banning of from official ties with navy, 22–23, 38–39; "Conversations with the Country" meetings, 228; criticism of in Congress, 99–100; fund-raising efforts, 100–101, 130–31; impact of disarmament movement on, 39; internal conflicts, 100–101, 107; Mare Island explosion and, 23; on merchant marine, 197; Moffett and, 64; Navy Day and, 50, 51, 55; as navy partner, 49; preparedness message and, 223–24; radio industry and, 80; relief work, 39; support for naval personnel bill, 48; Washington treaties and, 190–91
Navy News Bureau, 5, 17, 224, 225; arms limitation movement and, 40; budget cutbacks' impact on, 37; creation of, 21–23; film industry and, 38; naval advisors to, 21–22; purpose of, 22; U.S. fleet review and, 24–25
Navy Press Room, 37–38, 44
navy public relations: as "closed system," 224–25; Congress ban of, 16; counterintelligence activities and, 7, 76; Daniels and, 14–16; film productions as sources for study of, 6–7; navy culture hindering, 41; political support for, 106–7; reservists in, 75–76; staffing for, 7–8; studies concerning, 5–6; in wartime, 109. *See also* public relations; *specific organizations*
Navy Recruiting Bureau, 38, 75
Navy War Plans Division, 43
navy yards, 72
networking, 109
New Deal agencies, 106, 204, 218
Newmeyer, Fred C., 38
"new navy," 9

Newport News Shipbuilding and Drydock, 206
Newport Training Station homosexuality investigation, 29–30, 137
News of the Day, 113
"Newspapers and the Navy" (Baldwin), 74–75
newsreels, 95–96, 113–14, 123, 184
New York American, 72
New York Daily Mirror, 112
New York Evening Mail, 188
New York Evening Post, 181
New York Herald, 61, 163
New York Herald Tribune, 124
New York Journal, 9
New York Navy Club, 50
New York Navy Yard, 136
New York Shipbuilding, 206
New York Times, 30, 34, 60, 74, 94, 101, 133, 160, 169, 178, 179, 180, 194, 208, 212, 217
New York Tribune, 32
New York World, 9, 31, 36, 111, 172
New York World's Fair, 214–15, 217
New Zealand, 65, 192
Nicaraguan earthquake of 1931, 203
Night Watch (film), 87
Noonan, Fred, 210
North American Review, 9
North Island Air Station, 89, 92
Nulton, L. M., 81
Nungesser, Charles, 210
Nye, Gerald, 117–18, 206, 223
Nye Committee, 206

Office of Information, 78
Office of Naval Intelligence (ONI), 41, 43; development of, 5; Information Section of, 5; *Intelligence Manual*, 77, 107–10, 122, 216; investigations of public relations threats by, 114–15; *Monthly Information Bulletin*, 48, 77; Physical, Chemical, and Photographic Laboratory, 115; Press Relations office, 43; *The United States Navy in Peacetime: The Navy in Relation to the Industrial, Scientific, Economic, and Political Developments of the Nation*, 202–3. See also Information Section of ONI
Office of Naval Records and Library, 7, 43
Office of Public Information, 49
Office of Public Relations, 224
Office of the Chief of Naval Operations, 6, 41, 64
Olympic Games of 1920, 138
One-Power Standard, 30
On the Bottom (Ellsberg), 174
Order No. 78, 14–15
organizational culture, 6
Orr, William A., 89, 91, 93
Ostfriesland (German battleship), 33–34
Our Air Force (Mitchell), 32–33
Our Navy in the Near East (film), 70, 144
"Our Post War Mission" (Knox), 26–27
"Our Vanishing History and Traditions" (Knox), 62

pacifism, 79, 97
Panama Canal, 101, 179
Panama Canal Commission, 15–16
Panic of 1893, 10
Pan-Pacific Union, 67
Paramount Pictures, 57, 83, 87, 95, 96, 102, 113, 123
Patchin, Frank Gee, 12
Pathé Gazette, 96
Pathé Journal, 96
Patrick, Mason, 167
"Patriotic Reasons for the Navy League of the United States," 12
peace movement, 35
Pearson, Drew, 98
Peary, Robert E., 198
"Pensacola" (script), 128–29
Peril, The (film), 13
Pershing, John J., 27

Philadelphia Inquirer, 188
Philadelphia Navy Yard, 72
Philbert, Helene, 44–45, 131, 214
Philco, 115
Philippines, 191
Photographic Section, Bureau of Aeronautics, 44
physical fitness standards, 137–38
Pigboats (Ellsberg), 184
Pigboats (film), 105, 184
Pilat, Oliver, 122–23
Pinchot, Gifford, 15–16
Pizzitola, Louis, 112
PN-9 flying boats, 66, 67, 171, 179
Poland, 219
polar exploration, 198–99
Popular Science, 123–24
Porter, David Dixon, 52
Portsmouth Navy Yard, 216
Powell, Eleanor, 126
Powell, Halsey, 45, 58, 60, 71
Pratt, William Veazie, 21–22, 50–51, 85, 90, 95, 99, 189, 262n3
preparedness message, 191, 200, 207–8, 210–13, 221, 223
"President and the Navy, The" (press release), 100
presidential yacht, 24
press and media: assistance with Navy Day, 52–53; content analysis of articles in, 217–18; Denby on cooperation with, 57–58; Fleet Problems and, 59–60; foreign influence on, 60–61; Knox on role of in arms limitation movement, 47; local papers, 76–77, 146–47; naval officers' attitudes toward, 75; navy policy on incorrect information, 77; public relations policy toward, 77–79; William Hearst and, 111–12; writing course for, 54–55
Press Branch, District, 109
press conferences, 59
press liaisons, 71
Press Relations office, 43
press releases, 16, 58–59
print media, 5
Proceedings, 26, 42, 62, 76, 78
Production Code, 149
profiteering, 117–18, 206
propaganda, 45; films as, 85–86, 94; Knox on foreign use of, 60–61; in naval expansion, 211; navy's avoidance of, 58–59, 118
Propaganda (Bernays), 108, 225
Providence Journal, 30
pubic relations strategy, 218–19
public affairs, defined, 8
public affairs officers, 5, 20
public events planning, 217
public health campaigns, 135–39
Public Health Service, 135
publicity: defined, 8; Knox on value of, 45–46; versus lobbying, 10; oversight policies and, 120; recruiting and, 11–12
Publicity Bureau, 13–14, 16, 68, 240n50
publicity of transformation, 18
public opinion: on arms limitation, 34–37; on enlisted personnel, 136; on naval officers, 42; on navy's purpose, 79; on submarine warfare, 168–69, 173, 186; on William Hearst, 114
Public Opinion (Lippmann), 108
public opinion polling, 226–27
public relations: versus advertising, 8; during Civil War, 8–9; data collection as modern element of, 225–26; defined, 8; naval history and, 61–62; naval officers' view of, 3. *See also* navy public relations
Public Relations Branch, 18, 104, 114; enlisted marine billet in, 119–20; Navy League and, 130; political support for, 106; *Squalus* incident and, 216–17; staffing of, 130–31, 219–20
public relations policy, 77–78
public speakers, 21

Public Works Administration, 204–5
Public Works of Art Project, 154
Puleston, William, 115, 123, 211–12
Pulitzer, Joseph, 9, 31, 111
Pulitzer Trophy, 165, 166, 167

Quakers, 36

race relations, 102
Radford, Arthur, 88
Radio Corporation of America, 79
radio industry, 5, 76; FDR's administration's support of, 106; Navy Day broadcasts, 57; navy policy and, 81; navy relationship with, 79–80, 129–30
radio ownership, 5, 80
Raleigh News and Observer, 14
Rappaport, Armin, 50
Rathom, John R., 29–30
Read, A. C., 64, 163
Reavis, L. U., 124–25
Recruiting Bureau, 44; experimentation with recruiting methods, 139–40; Information Section collaboration with, 68; press liaisons, 71; sales talks, 69; use of civilian advertising firms by, 68–69; use of films by, 84–85
recruiting films, 69–70, 144
recruiting officers, 70–71
recruiting posters, 140, *141*, *142*, 144, *145*, 155, *156*, *158*, 164, *165*, 204, 206, *207*, *221*, 221–22, *222*
Recruiting Service, 11–12, 15
recruiting stations, 11, 70–71, 84–85
recruitment: of African Americans, 155–56; comic strips in, 115–16; film industry impact on, 13, 90; foreign travel as inducement to, 138–39, 143, 155; funding of, 69; in inland states, 11; Marine Corps and, 14; post-service jobs and, 142–43; preparedness message in, 221–22; traveling recruiting parties in, 68

Reeves, Joseph Mason, 91, 98, 105–6, 127, 179
reference files, 59
Reinicke, Frederick G., 127, 131
religious groups, 36
Republic Steel, 123
Rise of American Naval Power, The (Sprout and Sprout), 212
Rittenhouse, David, 166, 177
RKO Pictures, 95, 120, 121
Roberts, Helen, 25
Rock, George H., 175
Rodgers, John, 67, 171
Rodgers, William L., 210
Rodman, Hugh, 24, 54, 154
Rogers, Ginger, 120, 121
Rogers, Ledyard, 53–54
Roosevelt, Franklin D., 24–25, 29–30, 37, 106, 111, 204, 209, 211, 215, 224
Roosevelt, Henry L., 154, 205–6
Roosevelt, Nicholas, 194
Roosevelt, Theodore, 9, 10, 11, 50, 51
Roosevelt, Theodore, Jr., 35, 43, 49; air races and, 167; on Americanism, 143–44; "Intelligent Publicity," 37, 54–55; Navy Day and, 50–51, 56
"Roosevelt and the Navy: Recollections, Reminiscences, and Reflections" (Sims), 53
Rosalie (film), 126
Royal Air Force, 27
Royal Navy, 23
Russell, John H., 119
Russia, 97, 191

Sailing on the Silver Screen (Suid), 6
Sailor Be Good (film), 95
Sailor-Made Man, A (film), 38, 141–43
sales talks, 69
Salute (film), 85, 148
San Diego Naval Air Station, 81
San Diego Union-Tribune, 124
San Francisco Examiner, 111

Saturday Evening Post, 34, 71, 142, 175
Schneider, Jacques, 163
Schneider Cup, 65, 88, 165, 166, 167, 177
Schofield, Frank, 94–95, 98, 117
Scientific American, 60–61
scientific missions, 197–99
Scott, Bryon, 211
Scouting Fleet, 59–60, 81, 140, 215
Scovel, F. Donald, 5, 13, 20, 118
"Sea Eagles" (screenplay), 89–91
seaplane races, 88
seaplanes, 53, 88, 163, 166, 197
sea power, 9, 189, 210, 211–12
Sea Power, 32, 39, 130, 223
Sea Power in the Pacific (Bywater), 48, 61
sea power triad, 196
search operations, 210–11
Seas Beneath, The (film), 87, 94
secretary of the navy, 49, 59, 224
security concerns, 59–60, 91; floating dry docks and, 123–24; heightened emphasis on, 122–23; submarine films and, 127–28; technical advisors and, 127–28. *See also* intelligence work
self-transformation narrative, 150–51
Selig, William, 113
Semmes, Raphael, 52
Senn, Thomas J., 93
Sergeant York (film), 223
Shearer, William, 96–99, 104, 201
shipbuilding companies, 98, 206
ship commissioning ceremony, 24–25
Shipmates (film), 88, 94
Shipmates Forever (film), 113, 152, 157
Shore Leave (film), 84
Shore Leave (play), 120
Shriner's Convention (1924), 64
Shulman, Mark Russell, 9
Sims, William S., 26, 34, 37, 43, 52–53; administrative reforms and, 28–29; "Certain Naval Lessons of the Great War," 28; civilian writers' course

and, 55; medals controversy and, 28; "Roosevelt and the Navy: Recollections, Reminiscences, and Reflections," 53
Sinclair, Harry F., 195
Smith, Alfred, 99
Smith, Norman M., 124
Soldier Field, 146
Son of a Sailor (film), 208
Sousa, John Philip, 62
Southwick, E. P., *92*
Spanish-American War, 9, 35, 112
Special Committee on Investigation of the Munitions Industry, 206
Special Service Squadron, 81, 140
Sprout, Harold, 212
Sprout, Margaret, 212
SS *Lusitania*, 168
Standard Oil, 196
standing military, 26
Standley, William H., 105, 118, 122–23, 125
Stapler, John T. G., 71
state fairs, 67
Steinbeck, John, 151
Stevens, William O., 42
Stimson, Henry L., 201, 208
Stirling, Yates, 12, 102
St Louis Post-Dispatch, 144–45
St. Louis recruiting station, 69
St. Louis World's Fair, 13
Stockton, Robert F., 232n13
Stockwell, Maud C., 94
strategic communications, 8
Stratemeyer, Edward, 12
Stratemeyer Syndicate, 12
student groups, 36
Submarine (film), 88, 105, 125, 156–57, 182, 186, 207–8
submarine accidents, 170–76, 182, 184–85, 215–17
Submarine D-1 (film), 105, 113, 127–28, 186
Submarine Patrol (film), 157
submarine safety, 174–76, 182–83, 186, 187

submarines and submarine force, 4; midget, 97; proposed ban on, 169, 173; public relations evolution in, 162, 168–70; roles and mission, 183–84; security issues and, 124–25, 127–28; as threat to surface fleet, 33; unrestricted submarine warfare, 168–70; Washington Conference impact on, 164–65; in World War I, 23
"Submarine Story" (script), 127
Suid, Lawrence, 6, 88, 183
"Summerville Number Four" (screenplay), 95
Supply Corps, 195
"Supply of Naval Information to the Public–Discussion of Press Relations" (memo), 78
surface fleet: aerial bombing tests and, 32–34, 163–64; Mitchell on vulnerability of, 31–33; Washington Conference and, 40; in World War I, 23
Sutherland, George, 36
Swanson, Claude, 110, 117, 120, 132, 154
Sydney Morning Herald, 192

Tail Spin (film), 178
Taussig, J. K., 119–20
Taylor, Courtney E., 124–25, 126, 129
Teapot Dome Scandal, 195
technical advisors, 88–89, 127–28
technology: air racing program impact on, 166–67; mistrust of, 161
Thach, John S., *92*
Thomas, Elbert, 117
Thompson, Robert, 23, 39
three planes of warfare, 4, 162, 187
Three Sea Hawks, 177–78
Thurber, Harry, 220–21
Time magazine, 133
Top Gun (film), 228
Top Hat (film), 120
Towers, John, 163

Train, Charles, 209
training exercises, 42, 101. *See also fleet problem* entries
"Training Men for the Navy and the Nation" (Daniels), 142–43
Trammell, Park, 106
transatlantic flight, 64, 163
treaty cruiser, 60
Treaty of Versailles, 191
Trimble, William F., 6, 62, 165
True to the Navy (film), 149
Turkey, 70, 144, 209

U-boats, 23, 33, 87, 168
United States Merchant Marine, 46, 57, 85
United States Midshipman Afloat, A (Stirling), 12
United States Military Academy, 83, 126, 146, 148
United States Navy Band, 80–81, 109–10
United States Navy in Peacetime, The: The Navy in Relation to the Industrial, Scientific, Economic, and Political Developments of the Nation (ONI), 202–3
United States Steel, 35
Universal Newsreel, 184
Universal Studio, 96, 113
University of Wisconsin, 5
Upton, Emory, 32
U.S. Congress: administrative reforms hearings, 28–29; air racing and, 177; ban of government public relations activities by, 16; investigation of navy cooperation with film industry, 117–18, 223; naval aviation and, 27–28, 63; naval construction bills and, 12, 25, 200–201; naval personnel bill and, 48, 189–90; navy budget and, 226; Navy League and, 99–100; navy's direct lobbying of, 9–10; Newport homosexuality investigation and, 30; profiteering investigations, 206;

reduction of post-revolution military by, 26; response to naval construction program, 4; Shearer investigation and, 98–99
USS *Akron*, 90, 103, 180–81, 184–85, 199
USS *Arkansas*, 84, 154–55
USS *Aroostook*, 101
USS *Chauncey*, 145
USS *Colorado*, 210
USS *Constitution*, 81, 199–200
USS *Cuttlefish*, 124
USS *Delphy*, 145, 160
USS *Enterprise*, 185, 205
USS *Frederick*, 38
USS *Indiana*, 32
USS *Iowa*, 33
USS *Jupiter*, 64
USS *Langley*, 64–65, 178
USS *Lexington*, 89, 101, 172, 178, 179, 202, 203, 210
USS *Los Angeles*, 185
USS *Macon*, 185
USS *New Mexico*, 24
USS *New York*, 14
USS *Nicholas*, 161
USS *Panay*, 211
USS *Paulding* (CG-17), 174
USS *Princeton*, 232n13
USS *Ranger*, 185
USS *Rochester*, 263n15
USS *S-4*, 174–75, *176*, 182, 216
USS *S-5*, 170
USS *S-48*, 170–71
USS *S-51*, 171–76, 216
USS *Saratoga*, 89–90, 91, 93, 101, 177–78, 179, *182*, 202, 204, *205*
USS *Shenandoah*, 56, 65, *66*, 167–68, 198; crash of, 67, 171–73, 180–81
USS *S.P. Lee*, 161
USS *Squalus*, 215–17
USS *Tennessee*, 24–25, 68, 215
USS *Tuscaloosa*, 123
USS *West Virginia*, 215

USS *Wyoming*, 133, 154–55
USS *Yorktown*, 185, 205
USS *Young*, 145, 160

Vandenberg, Arthur, 206
venereal disease campaign, 135–36
Via Wireless (film), 14
Vidor, King, 83
Vinson, Carl, 106
Vinson-Trammell Act, 109, 130, 156, 205–6
Virginia Capes bombing tests, 32–34, 140, 163–64
Vosseller, Aurelius, 128

Wadsworth, James W., 100
Wagner, Frank D., 91
Walker, Bernard, 60–61
Wallis, Hal, 127
Walt Disney, 223
Ward, Henry M., 12
War Department, 68
warfare, "three planes" of, 4, 162, 187
Warner Brothers, 87, 89, 105, 113, 127, 128, 151, 186, 223
Warner-Pathé, 96
War of 1812, 26
War Plan Orange, 183, 194
Warren, Lee P., 32
Washington Evening Star, 154
Washington Herald, 117
Washington Naval Conference of 1921–22, 4, 17, 61, 72, 74, 118; disarmament movement in facilitating, 36–37; farewell address, 188; Hearst's opposition to, 111–12; impact on aviation and submarines, 164–65; impact on Navy League, 39; Knox on, 46–48; submarines and, 169; treaties arising from, 39–40
Washington Navy Yard Band, 80–81
Washington Post, 22, 103, 154–55
Washington Star, 102
Washington Treaty system, 18

Watson, Edward, 145, 160–61
Wead, Frank "Spig," 88–89, 116–17, 127, 166, 178, 179, 181, 186, 208, 223, 228
We Build a Navy series, 201
Welles, Gideon, 8–9
West Point, 83, 126, 146, 148
What Happened at Jutland (Gill), 76
What Price Glory (film), 83
Whig Party, 26
Whiting, F. E. M., 78–79, 123
Whitten-Brown, Arthur, 163
Wilbur, Curtis D., 57, 71, 72, 86, 101, 171, 172, 175, 199
Williams, Alford, 65, 166, 177
Williams, Clarence, 43–44
Williams, James T., 112
Wilson, Eugene E., 64
Wilson, Woodrow, 4, 16, 21, 24, 26, 135, 143
Winchell, Walter, 112, 115
Wings (film), 83
Wings of the Navy (film), 113, 129
Wings over Honolulu (film), 126
Wiseman, William, 98
WNYC radio, 129–30
Wold, Emma, 35
Women's Christian Temperance Union, 36
Women's Committee on World Disarmament, 35
Women's International League for Peace and Freedom, 35, 206
women's movement, 35
Women's Non-Partisan League, 35
Women's Peace Party, 35
Women's Republican Club of Massachusetts, 190
Woodward, Clark, 214, 215
Worden, John L., 114–15
World's Fair of 1904, 13
World's Fair of 1939, 214–15, 217
World's Work, 32, 34
World War I: fleet engagements in, 23; fleet review following, 24–25; Germany air raids in, 27; impact on naval construction, 16; mass information and, 20–21; medals controversy following, 28; "merchants of death" and, 117–18; newsreels and, 96; postwar demobilization, 137; submarines in, 23
World War II, 219
Wright Brothers, 64
Wrigley, William, 62

Yardley, Herbert, 102
Yarnell, Harry, 93–94, 100
yellow journalism, 9
Youth Companion, 12
youth-oriented literature, 12, 138–40, 153

Zukor, Adolph, 57, 83